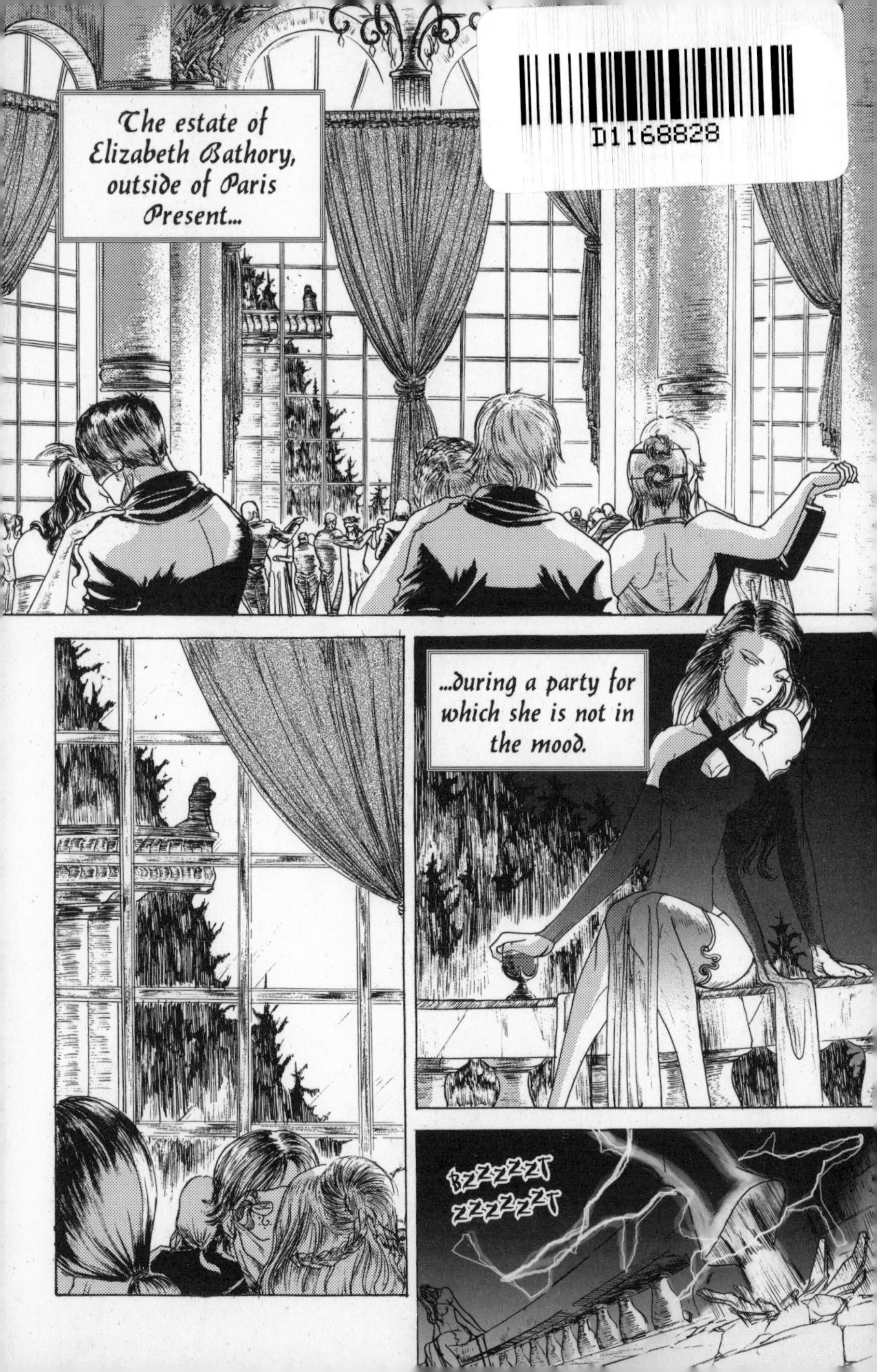
The estate of Elizabeth Bathory, outside of Paris Present...
...during a party for which she is not in the mood.
BZZZZZT
ZZZZZZT

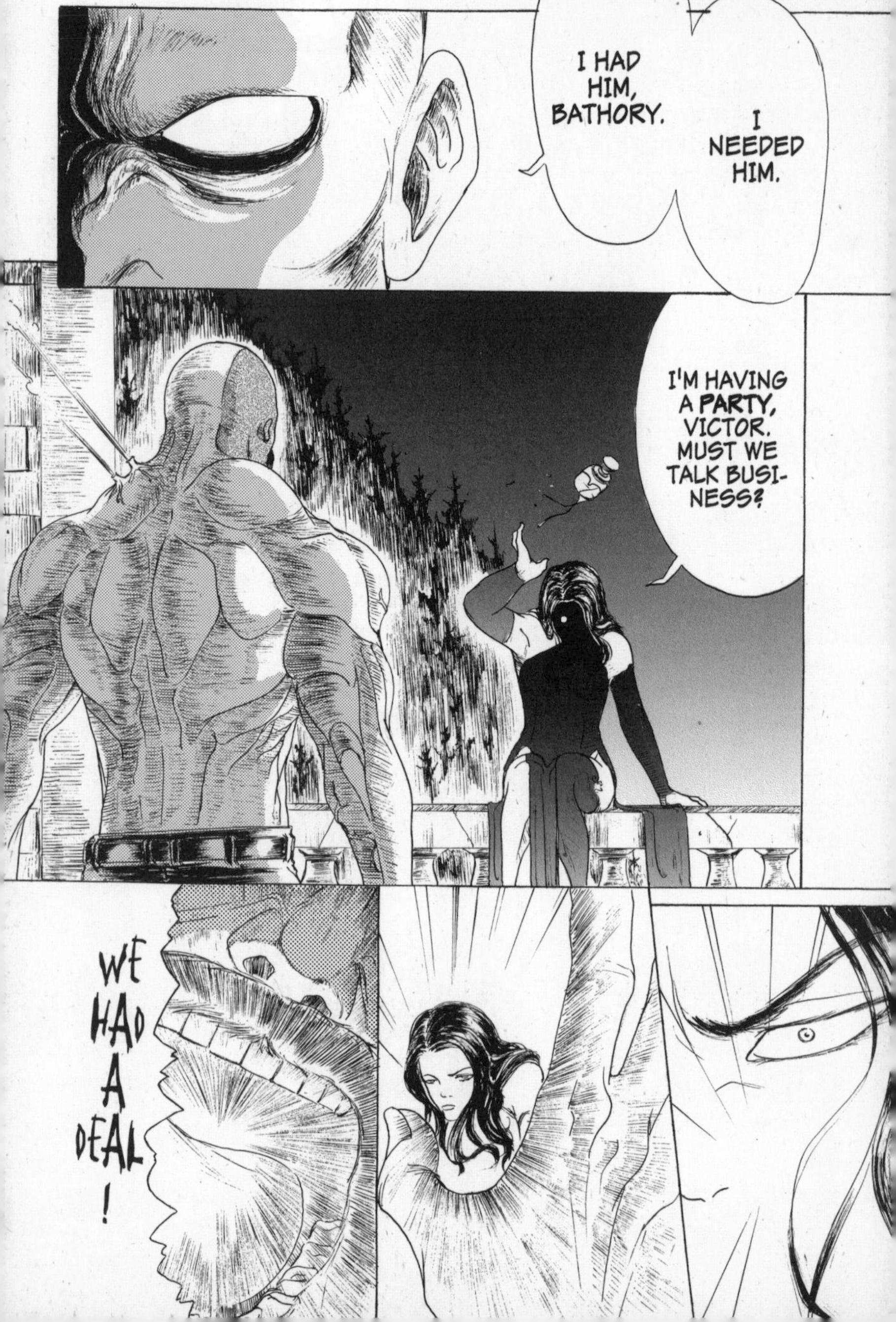
I HAD HIM, BATHORY.
I NEEDED HIM.
I'M HAVING A **PARTY**, VICTOR. MUST WE TALK BUSI-NESS?
WE HAD A DEAL!

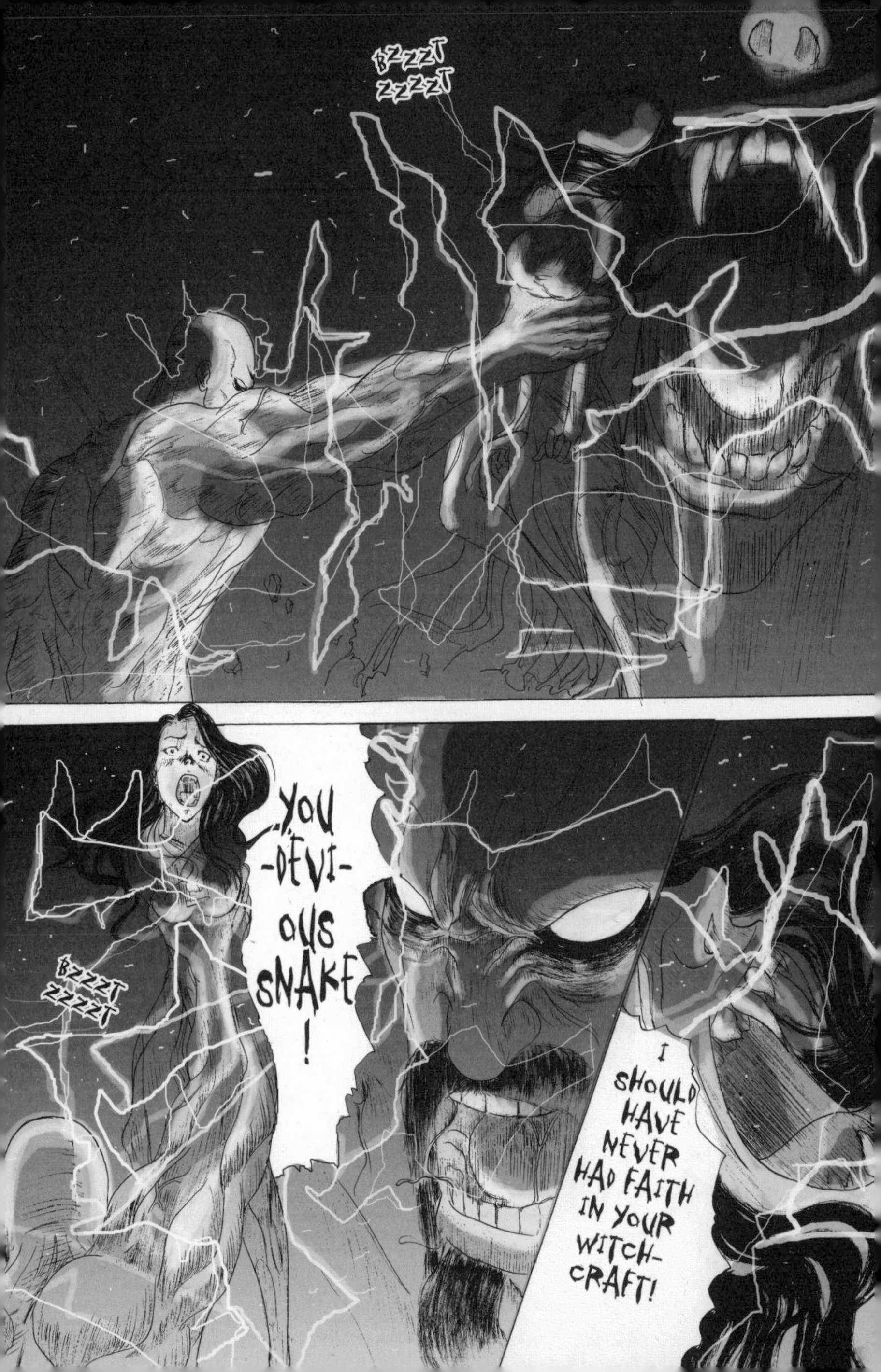
BZZZT
ZZZZT
BZZZT
ZZZZT
YOU DEVI-OUS SNAKE!
I SHOULD HAVE NEVER HAD FAITH IN YOUR WITCH-CRAFT!

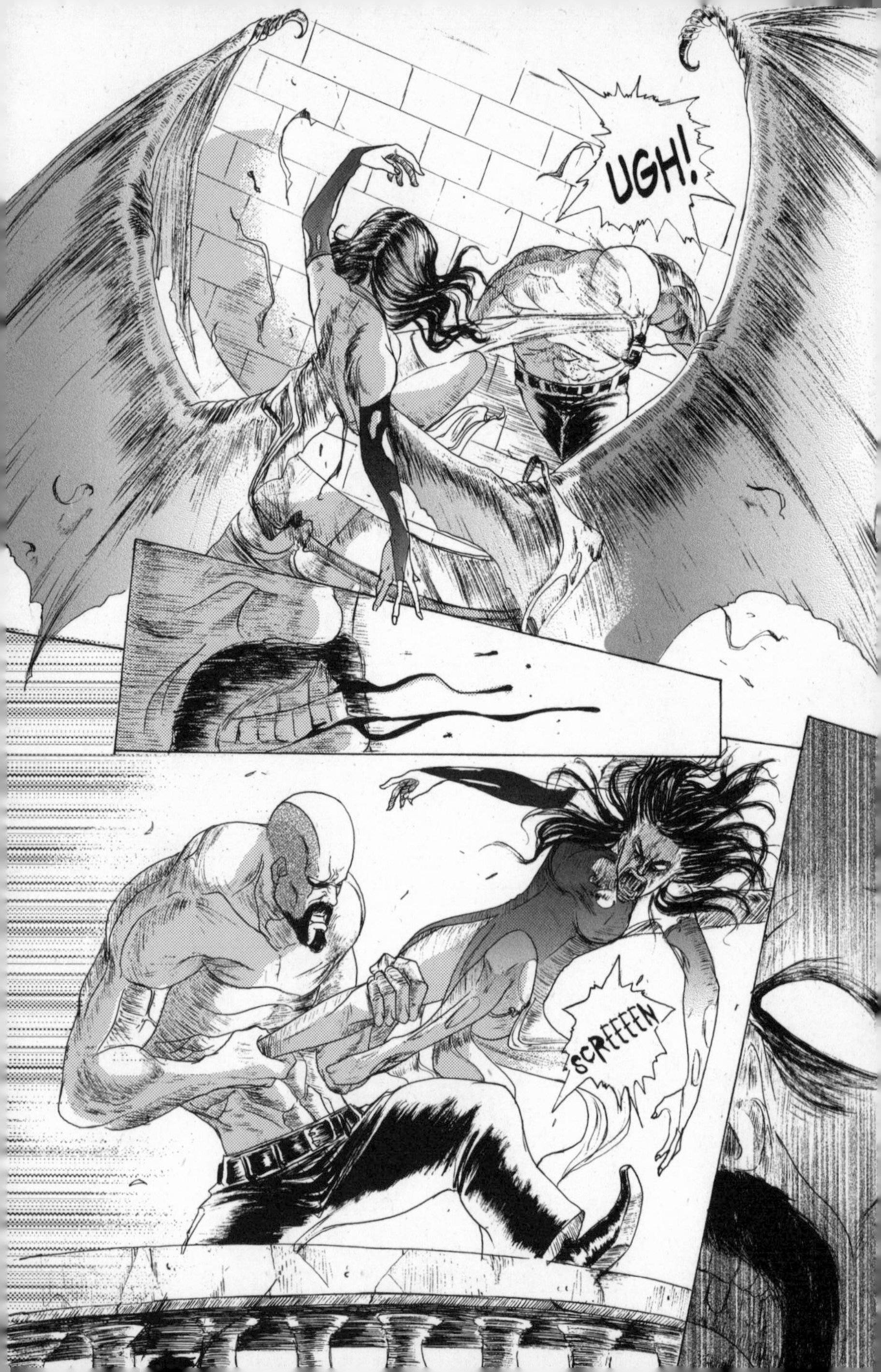

UGH!
SCREEEEN

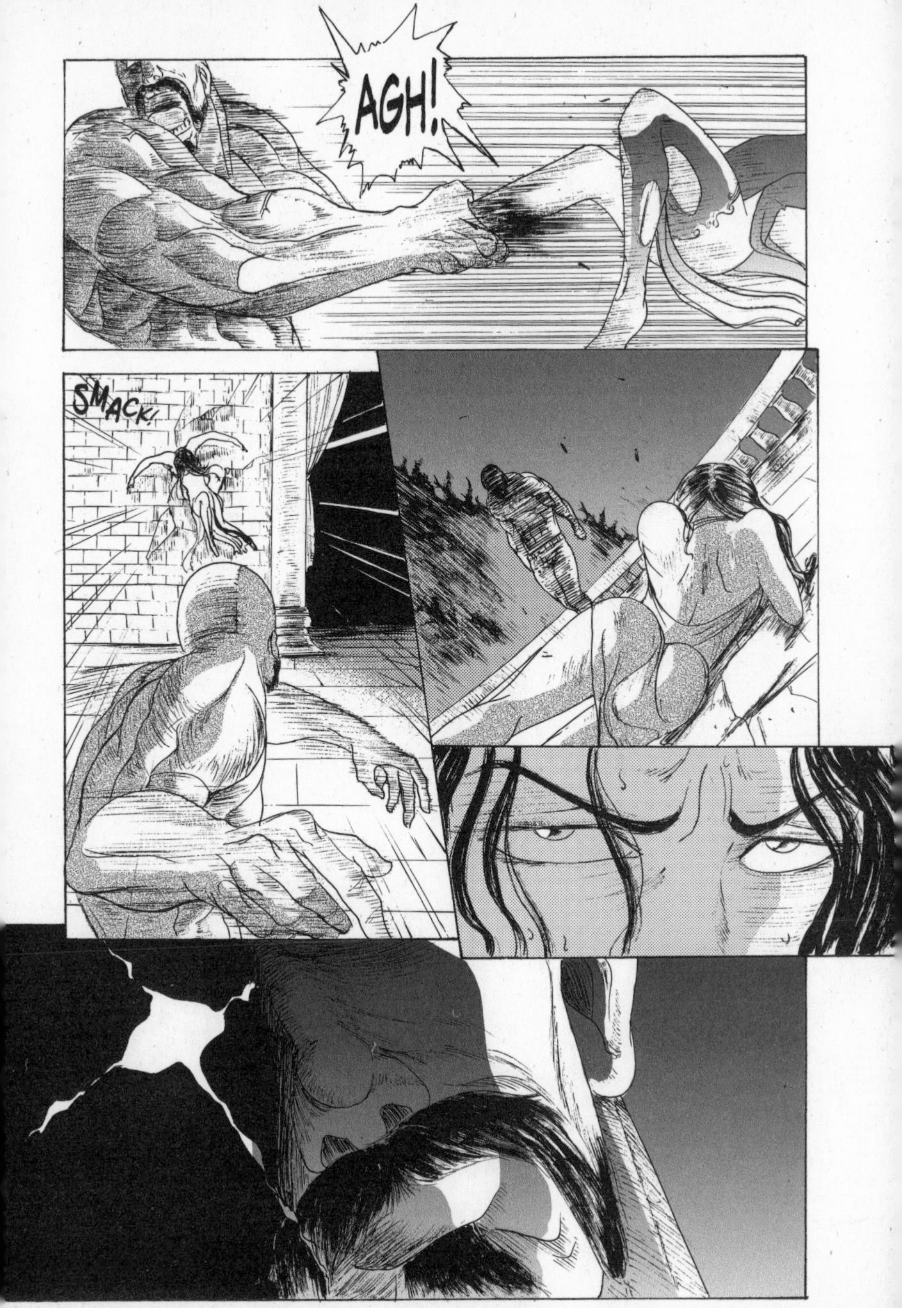
AGH!
SMACK!

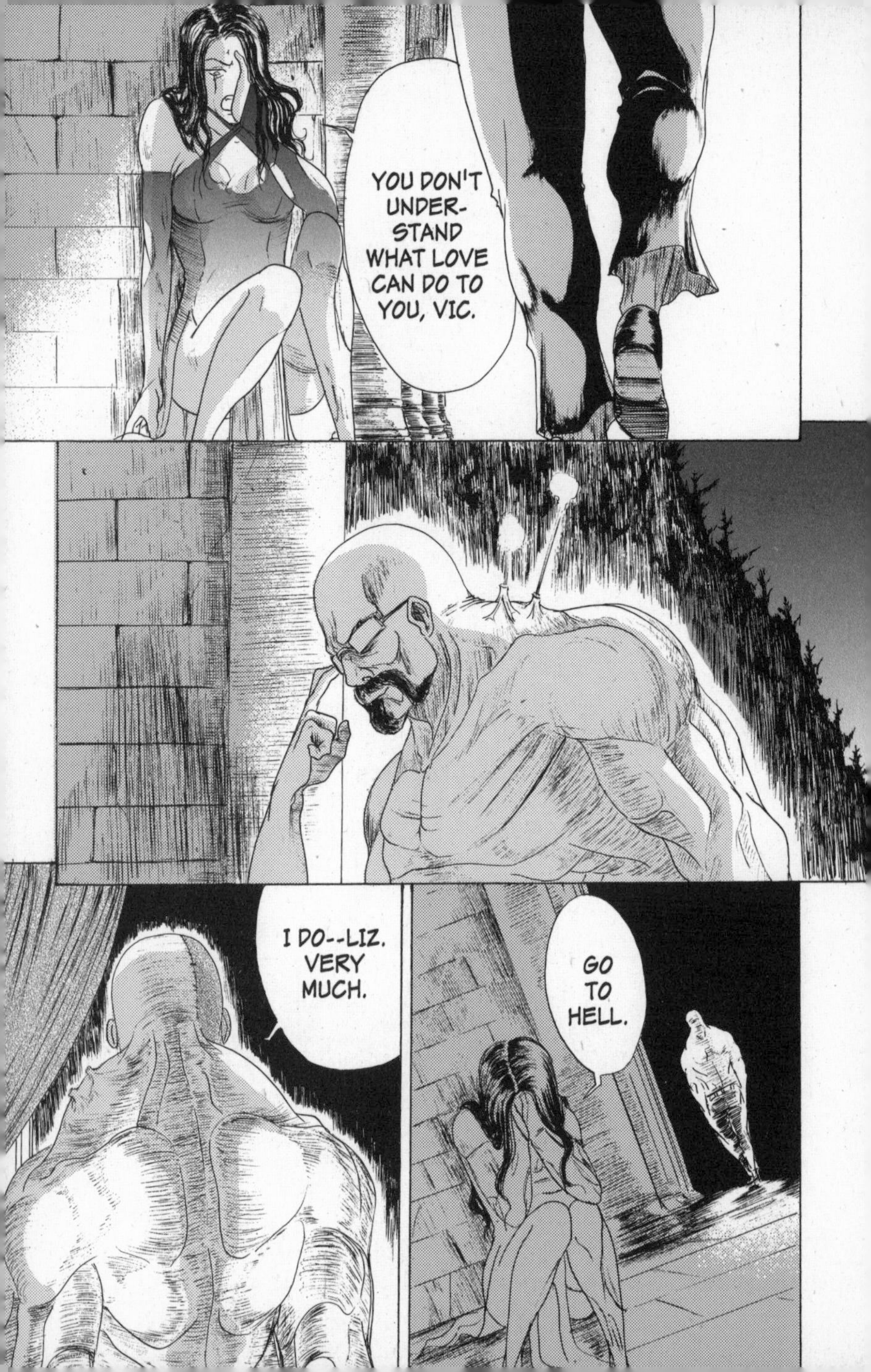
YOU DON'T UNDER-STAND WHAT LOVE CAN DO TO YOU, VIC.
I DO--LIZ. VERY MUCH.
GO TO HELL.

A MIDNIGHT OPERA

ACT III

CREATED BY
HANS "HANZO" STEINBACH

HAMBURG // LONDON // LOS ANGELES // TOKYO

A Midnight Opera Act III
created by Hans "Hanzo" Steinbach

Associate Editor - Lillian Diaz-Przybyl
Language Consultant - Madeleine Ange Blanche
Story Consultant - Christine Boylan

Lettering & Layout - Alyson Stetz & Bowen Park
Cover Design - Hans Steinbach

Editor - Luis Reyes
Digital Imaging Manager - Chris Buford
Pre-Production Supervisor - Erika Terriquez
Art Director - Anne Marie Horne
Managing Editor - Vy Nguyen
Production Manager - Elisabeth Brizzi
VP of Production - Ron Klamert
Editor-in-Chief - Rob Tokar
Publisher - Mike Kiley
President and C.O.O. - John Parker
C.E.O. and Chief Creative Officer - Stuart Levy

A  Manga

TOKYOPOP Inc.
5900 Wilshire Blvd. Suite 2000
Los Angeles, CA 90036

E-mail: info@TOKYOPOP.com
Come visit us online at www.TOKYOPOP.com

ISBN: 1-4278-0007-3

First TOKYOPOP printing: November 2006
10 9 8 7 6 5 4 3 2 1
Printed in the USA

Einblick and Leroux DeLaLune, two undead brothers, achieved what most of their kind would have thought impossible; they integrated the undead population seamlessly and secretly into human society. In their long, hard struggle, they allied themselves with the Calvinists of Western Europe and stood against the tyranny of the Catholic authority, specifically The Order under the leadership of Cardinal LaCroix, a secret group of holy warriors whose sole mission was to hunt down the undead and exterminate them.

1610-1850

The witch Elizabeth Bathory was targeted by The Order, her family killed and her life ruined, until she joined with Einblick and Leroux. However, her thirst for the blood of young virgins came into direct conflict with the undead community the brothers DeLaLune hoped to create. Leroux himself took particular interest in the salvation of Elizabeth, and for that she grew to love him. However, Leroux never learned how to return it.

1850

As centuries passed and complacency set in, Einblick chose to retire his leadership of the undead and pursue a career in music. His exceptional talent found him highly regarded in the most elite circles of Paris, where he met and fell in love with Christine Beaumont, a celebrated soprano virtuoso. A new life opened up for Einblick. Feeling abandoned, Leroux worked to protect his brother from the dangers that love poses to the undead, much less love for a human woman. For this he turned to Elizabeth Bathory, whose cure for Einblick's affliction was the death of Christine. Einblick, heartbroken, vanished, leaving only a grief-stricken Leroux and an increasingly devilish Elizabeth to lead the undead.

A hundred fifty years later

Einblick re-emerges as an underground goth metal sensation. He has fallen in love with yet another human woman, Dahlia Whyte, with whom he would have run away from Europe forever if it were not for the confluence of his past's myriad strains on his immediate present. The Order has regrouped and resumed its crusade against the undead. The peace Ein fought so hard to establish has frayed. Once again, his brother looks to him to save it all; a brother who Einblick now knows had something to do with the horrible death of his once-beloved Christine.

Now

Leroux and Einblick return to Paris from Prague, where they would have fallen to the multitudes of Elizabeth's undead hordes if it wasn't for the witch's monumental change of heart after a conversation with one Dahlia Whyte in a Parisian bar. This change of heart infuriated Victor Frankenstein who had teamed up with Elizabeth to capture the brothers DeLaLune. And Cardinal Clement LaCroix, aware now that both the brothers DeLaLune and Elizabeth Bathory are once again together and in Paris, organizes a final assault on the undead, turning to a spectre from his past for help.

FOREWORD

Hans Steinbach is about to start drawing my manga series *Poison Candy* for TOKYOPOP. So I have taken a great interest in *A Midnight Opera*. I wanted to be sure that this is the right guy to be interpreting my script. Now that the series is done, I'm reassured.

Hanzo couldn't have a more different background from my own. Until I was nineteen, I had barely set foot outside the county where I was born. I was twenty-five the first time I flew in a plane. Hanzo grew up travelling constantly, soaking up the cultures of a dozen different countries, the religions, the languages, the art and the music. His world spanned continents. I rarely met anyone who didn't have the same accent as me. But when I read *A Midnight Opera*, I recognise Hanzo's hero. Einblick DeLaLune is my fantasy alter ego. This is a character who speaks to every self-obsessed introverted fantasist who ever dreamed of getting up on a stage and blowing an audience away with ear-splitting guitar licks. Ein has it all-- the moody, pale degenerate beauty, the doomed love affairs, the dark longings and virtuoso skills with guitar and handguns. *A Midnight Opera* stirs a lot of memories of the stuff I was into as a teen-ager: horror movies like *Nosferatu* and *Night of the Living Dead*. The Gothic fantasy Gormenghast and the poisonous Maldoror by the Comte de Lautreamont. Alice Cooper's classic album *Killer*. Underground comics and the degenerate art of David Edward Britton. Still, when I tried to put my finger on why this character is the perfect synthesis of everything that made my teen years bearable, I couldn't quite figure it out.

Einblick DeLaLune is a beautiful loser in the style of Arthur Rimbaud and Jim Morrison. His lover is called Dahlia Whyte – an inversion of the Black Dahlia – the most famous, haunting victim of psychopathic murder of the 20th Century. It is the inversions and contradictions that make Ein so fascinating. He is a Pacifist and a Zombie Killer. He is Degenerate, Christian, Undead. When shadows fall across his face, his eye is transformed into the white orb of the full moon. All this is good. But there's one more element that made the connection, that reached out across the years. I spotted it in my third reading. It's the cigarettes, dummy! Einblick DeLaLune is a Smoker. In this brave new 21st Century world I had almost forgotten why smoking is cool. It's right there on the pack in black and white. "Smoking is bad for you." It gives you cancer and messes your heart and lungs and ultimately it will kill you. Every drag you take brings you a step closer to a miserable death. That's why smoking is cool. And Einblick smokes so very well, he uses a Zippo lighter. The cigarette hangs from his lips at precisely the right angle. He exhales through the nose. He flicks his cigarette butt in a perfect arc across the face of the moon.

There are all kinds of reasons for digging this series: the languorous beauty of the art, the expert pacing and page design, the delicate line work, the narcotic sexuality and poetic blood-spilling, but in the end it's the ciggies that did it for me. This book should carry a government health warning: *A MIDNIGHT OPERA* IS BAD FOR YOU.   **--David Hine** (*Strange Embrace, Spawn, District X*)

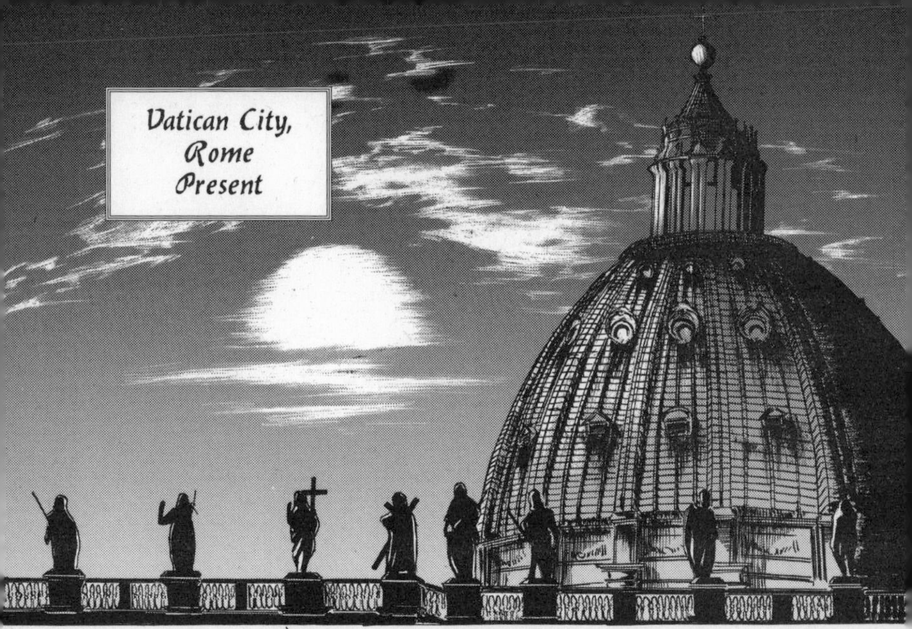
Vatican City,
Rome
Present
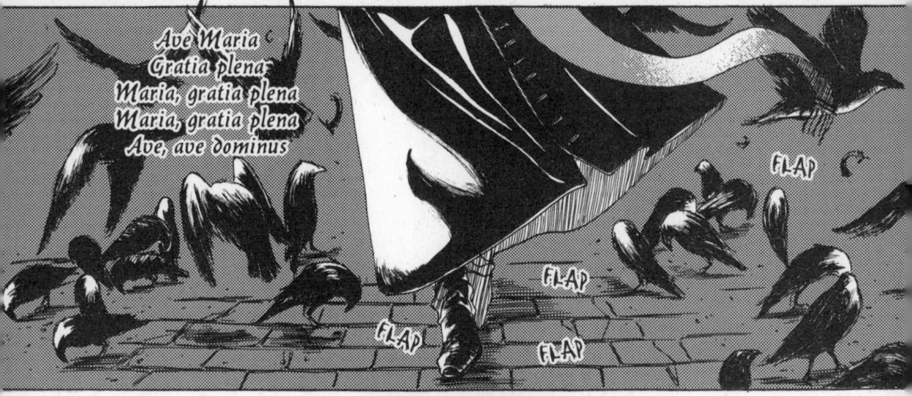
Ave Maria
Gratia plena
Maria, gratia plena
Maria, gratia plena
Ave, ave dominus
FLAP
FLAP
FLAP
FLAP
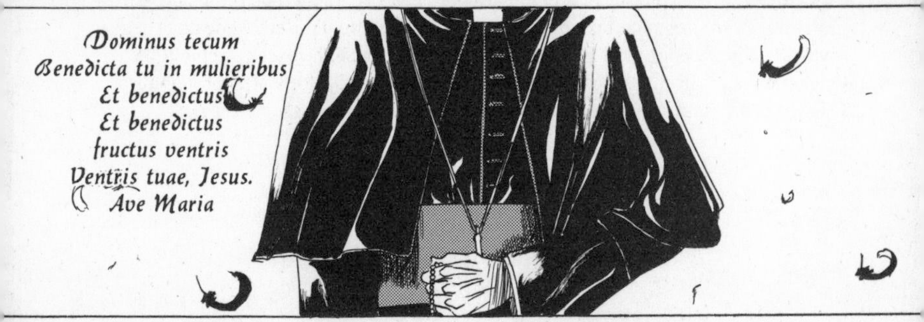
Dominus tecum
Benedicta tu in mulieribus
Et benedictus
Et benedictus
fructus ventris
Ventris tuae, Jesus.
Ave Maria

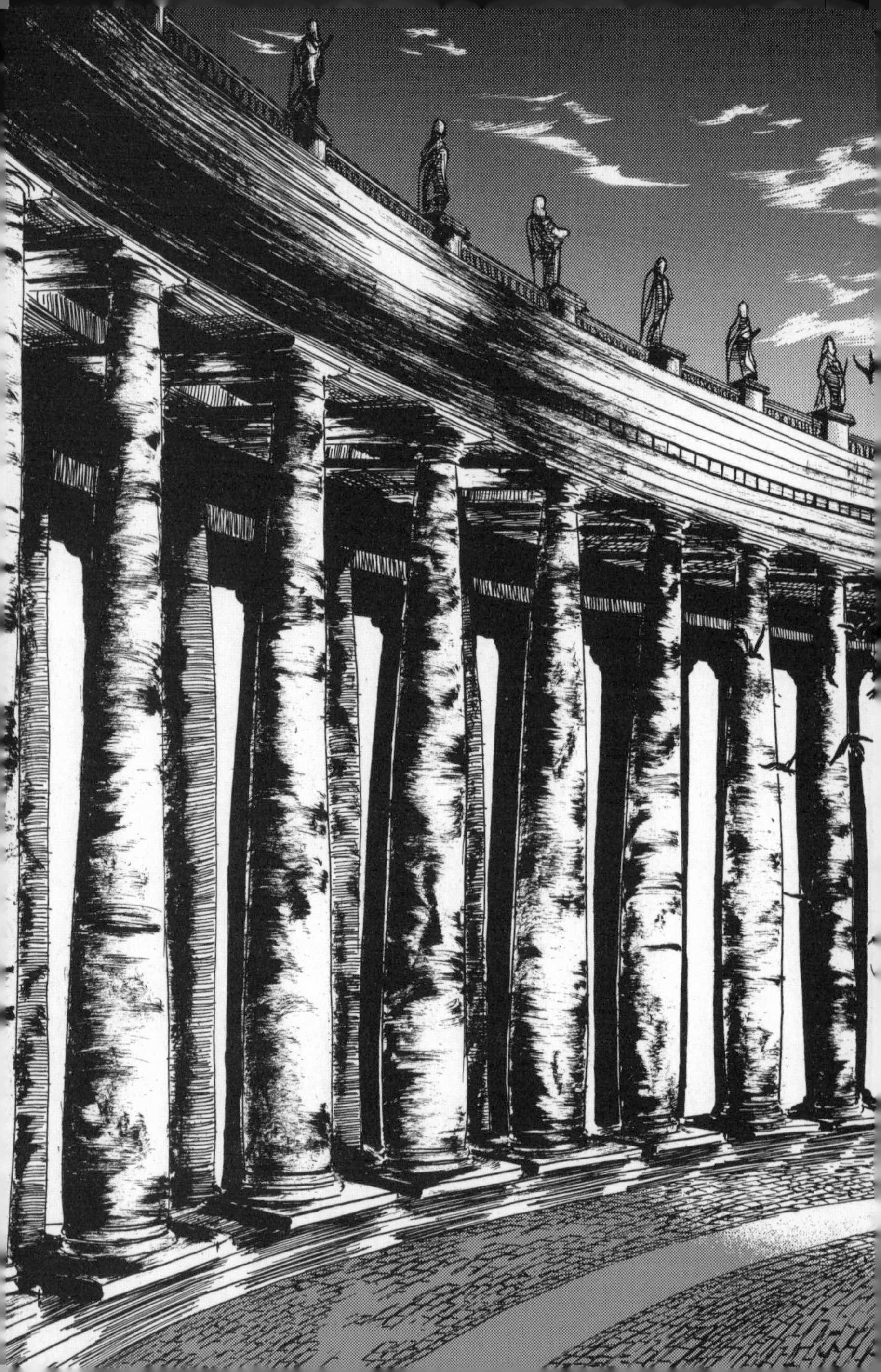

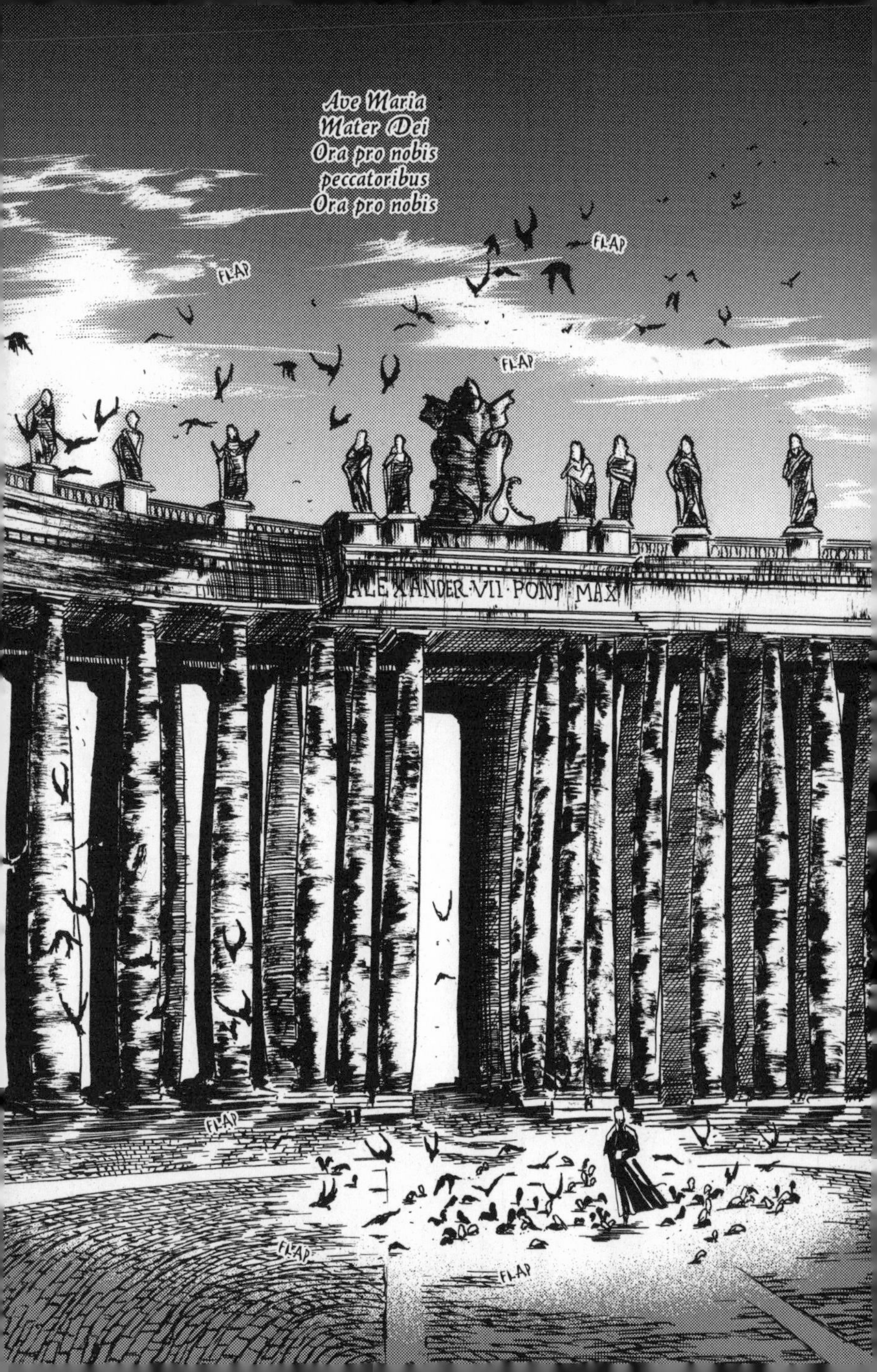
Ave Maria
Mater Dei
Ora pro nobis
peccatoribus
Ora pro nobis
FLAP
FLAP
FLAP
ALEXANDER·VII·PONT·MAX
FLAP
FLAP
FLAP

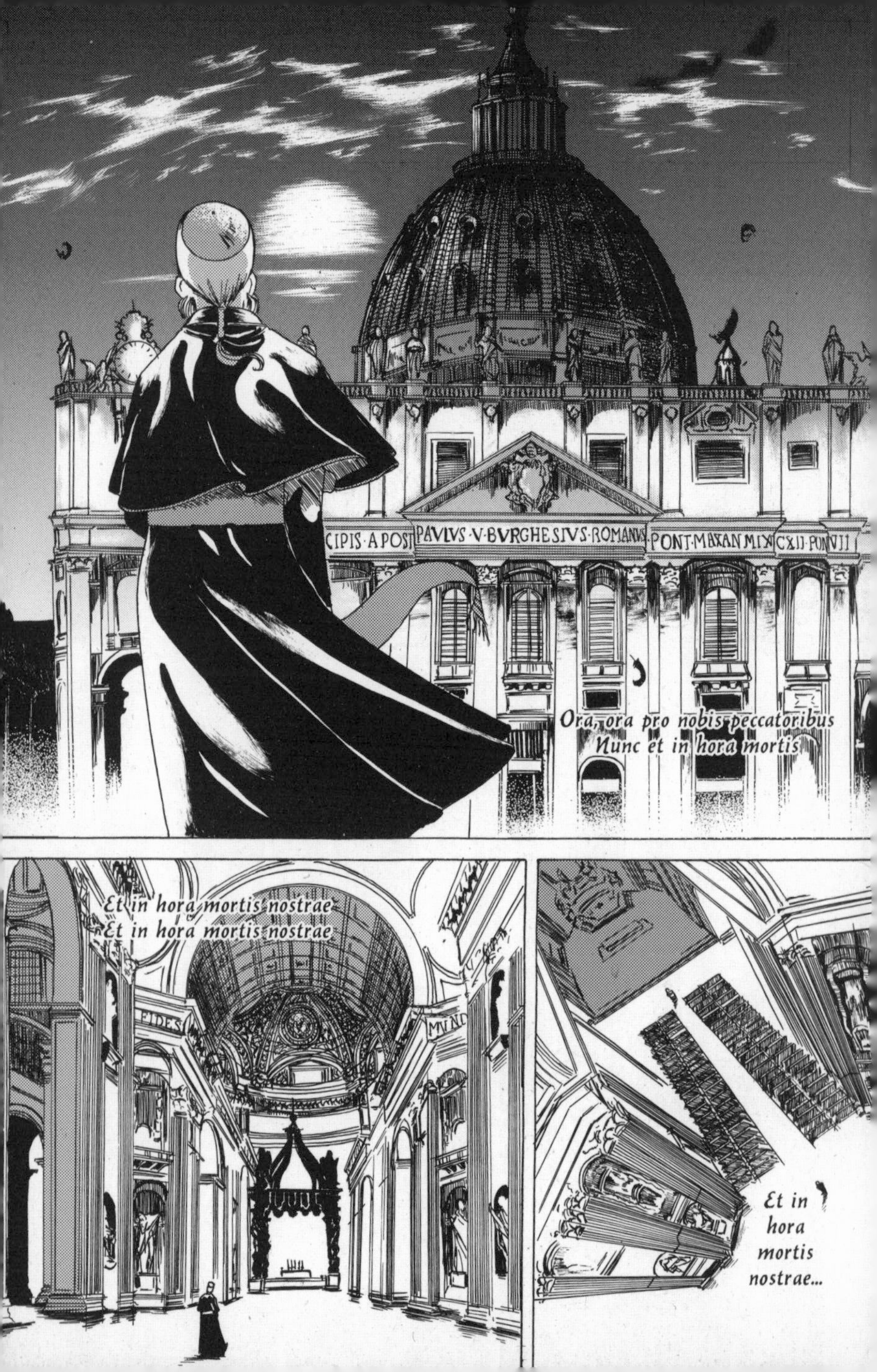
PAVLVS·V·BVRGHESIVS·ROMANVS
Ora, ora pro nobis peccatoribus
Nunc et in hora mortis
Et in hora mortis nostrae
Et in hora mortis nostrae
FIDES
Et in hora mortis nostrae...

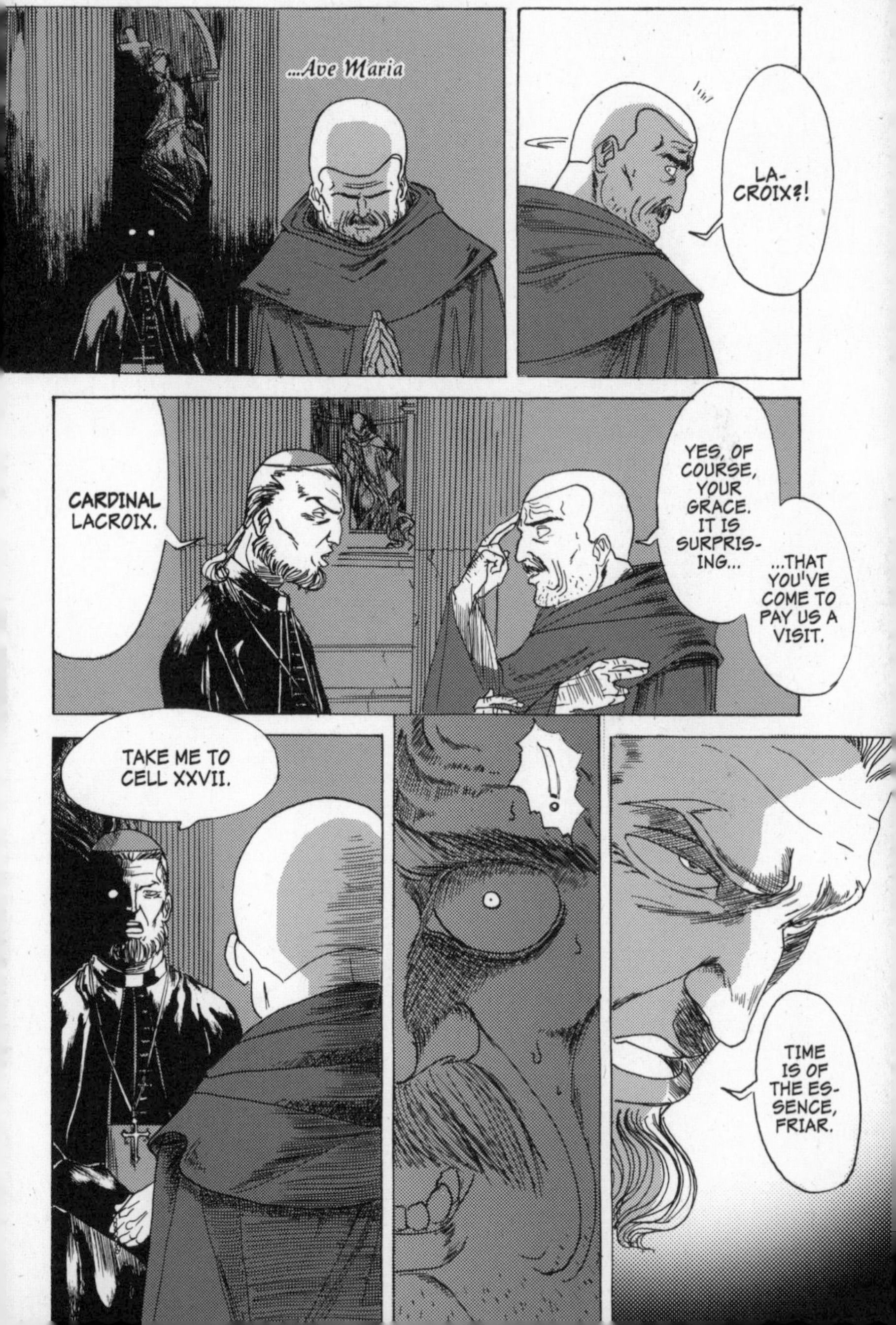
...Ave Maria
LA-CROIX?!
CARDINAL LACROIX.
YES, OF COURSE, YOUR GRACE. IT IS SURPRIS-ING...
...THAT YOU'VE COME TO PAY US A VISIT.
TAKE ME TO CELL XXVII.
!
TIME IS OF THE ES-SENCE, FRIAR.

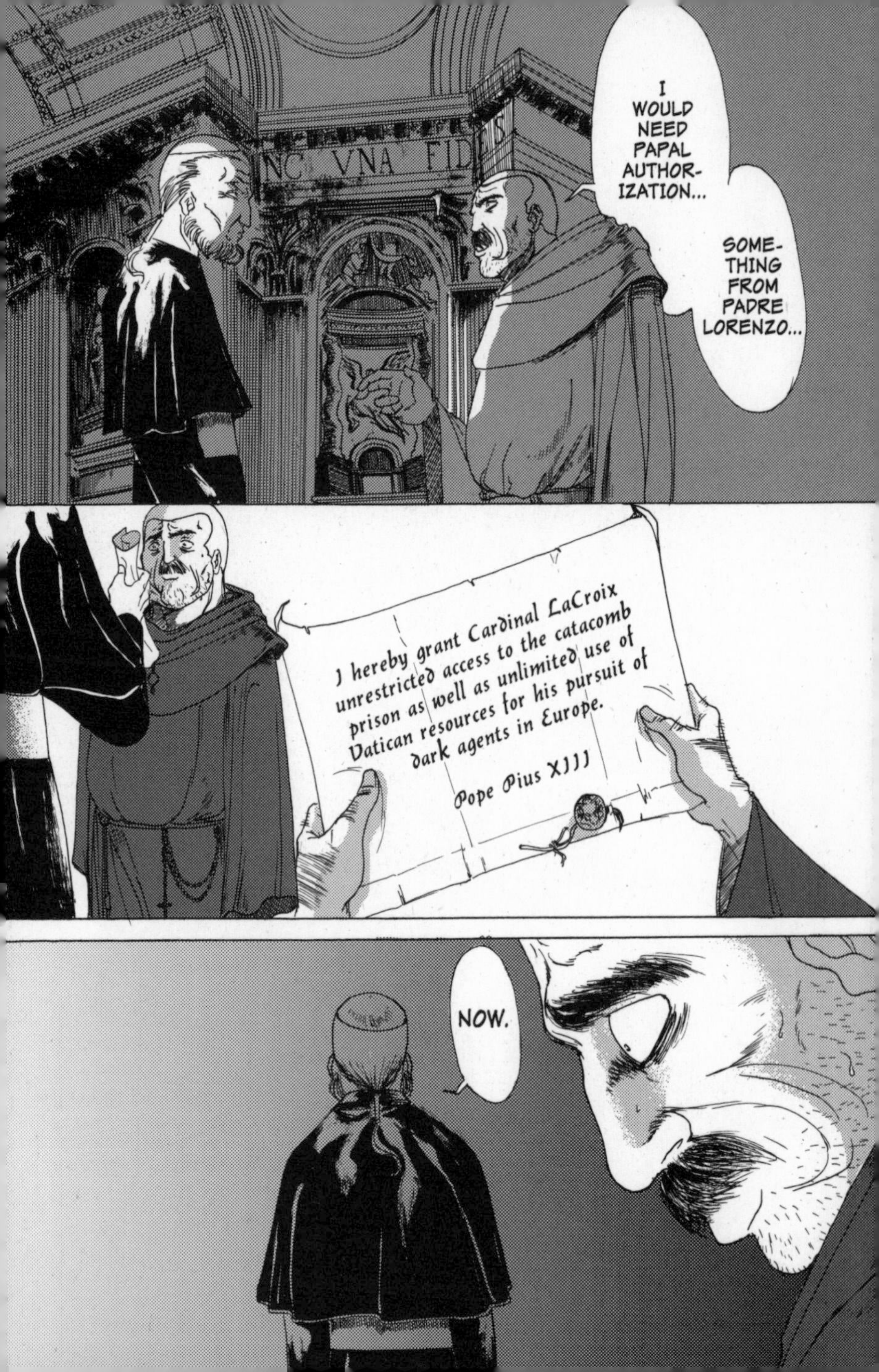
I WOULD NEED PAPAL AUTHOR-IZATION...
SOME-THING FROM PADRE LORENZO...
NCI VNA FIDES
I hereby grant Cardinal LaCroix unrestricted access to the catacomb prison as well as unlimited use of Vatican resources for his pursuit of dark agents in Europe.
Pope Pius XIII
NOW.

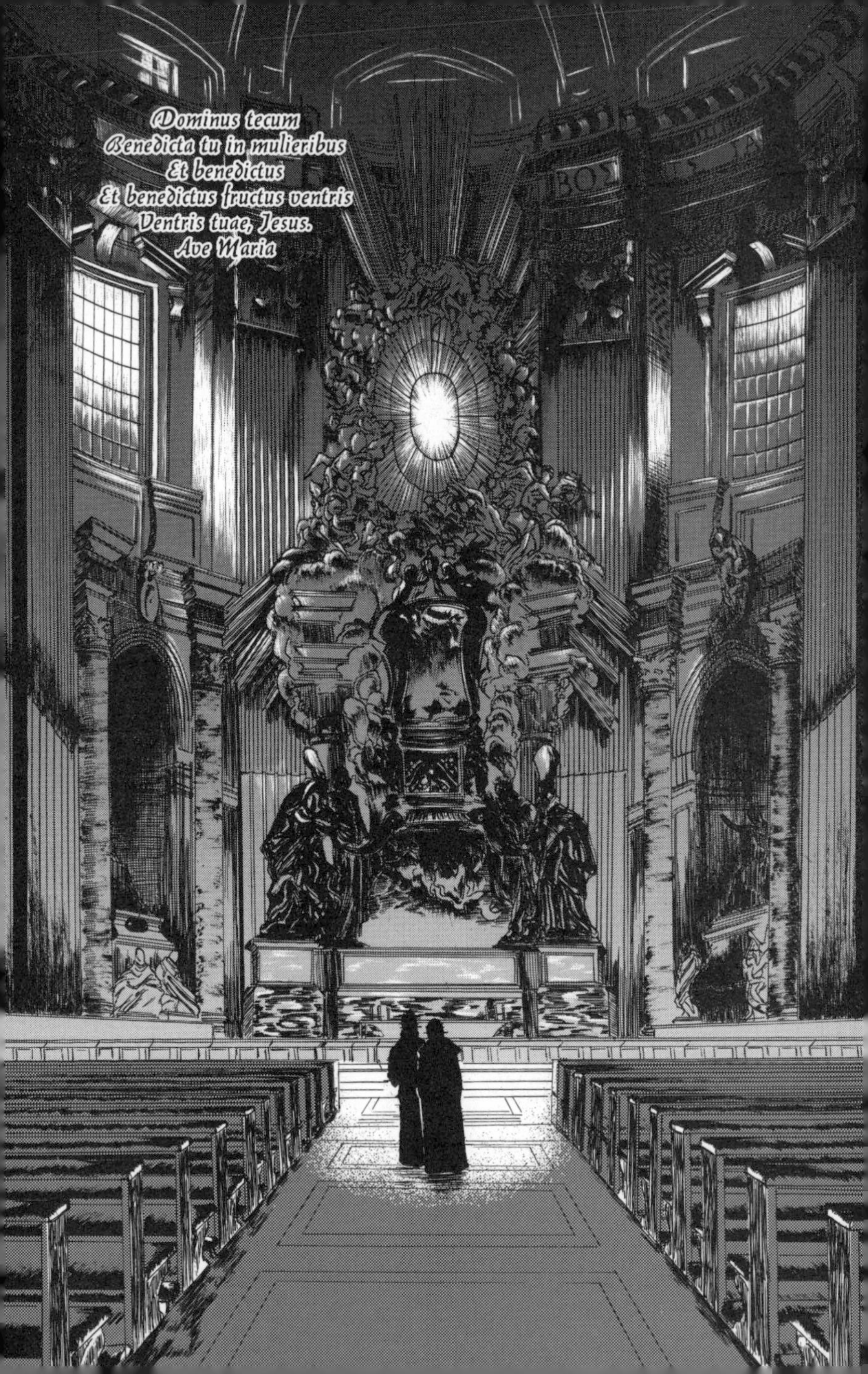
Dominus tecum
Benedicta tu in mulieribus
Et benedictus
Et benedictus fructus ventris
Ventris tuae, Jesus.
Ave Maria

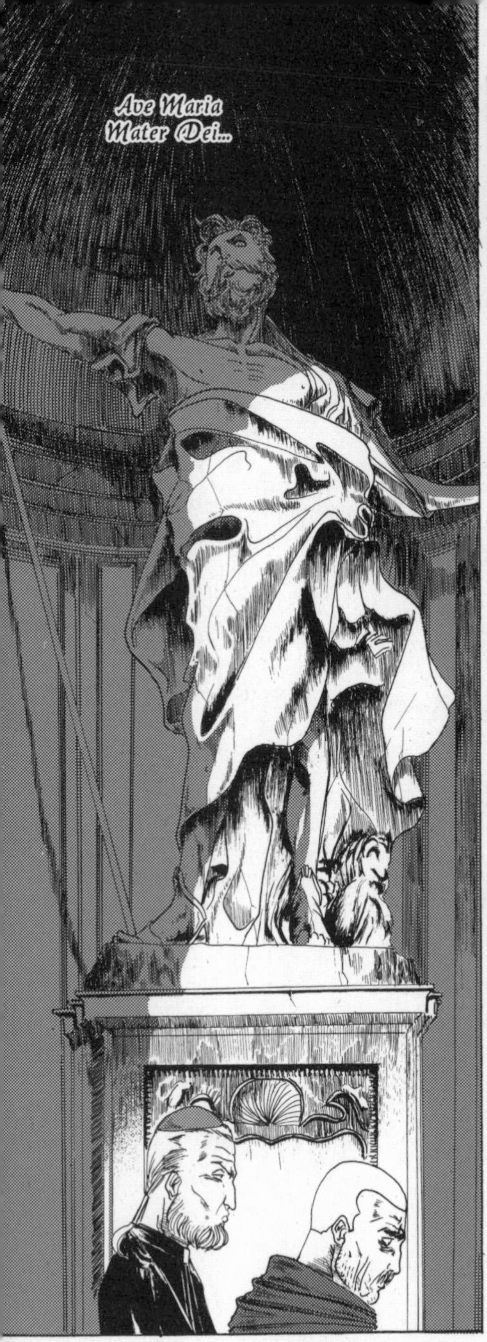
Ave Maria
Mater Dei...

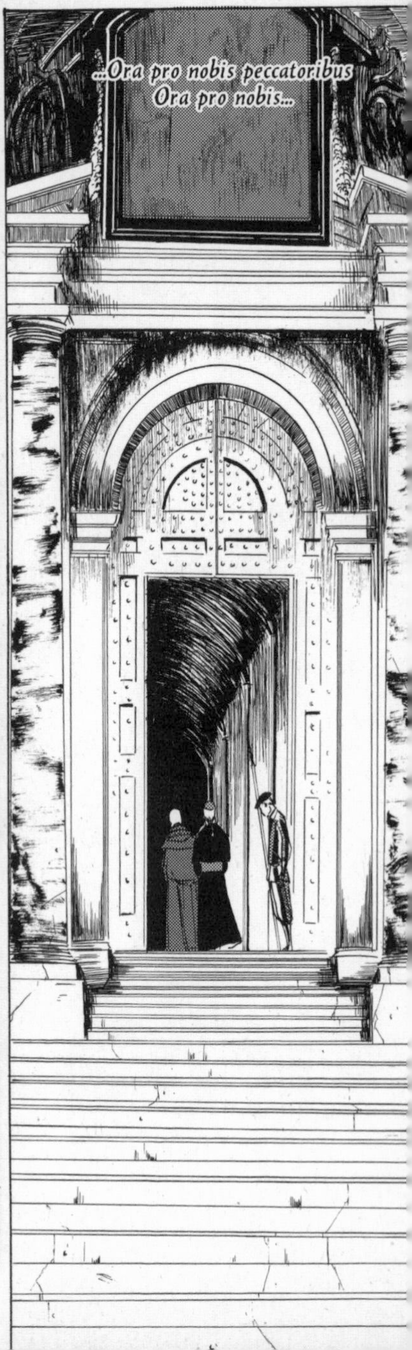
...Ora pro nobis peccatoribus
Ora pro nobis...

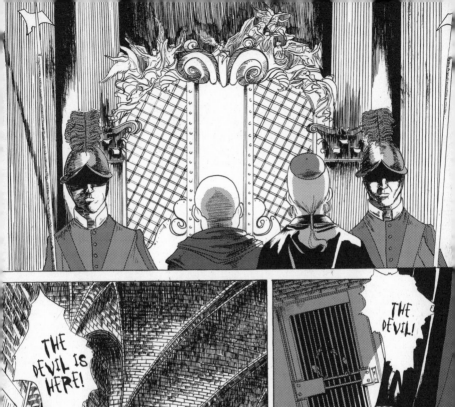

THE DEVIL IS HERE!

THE DEVIL!

THE DEVIL

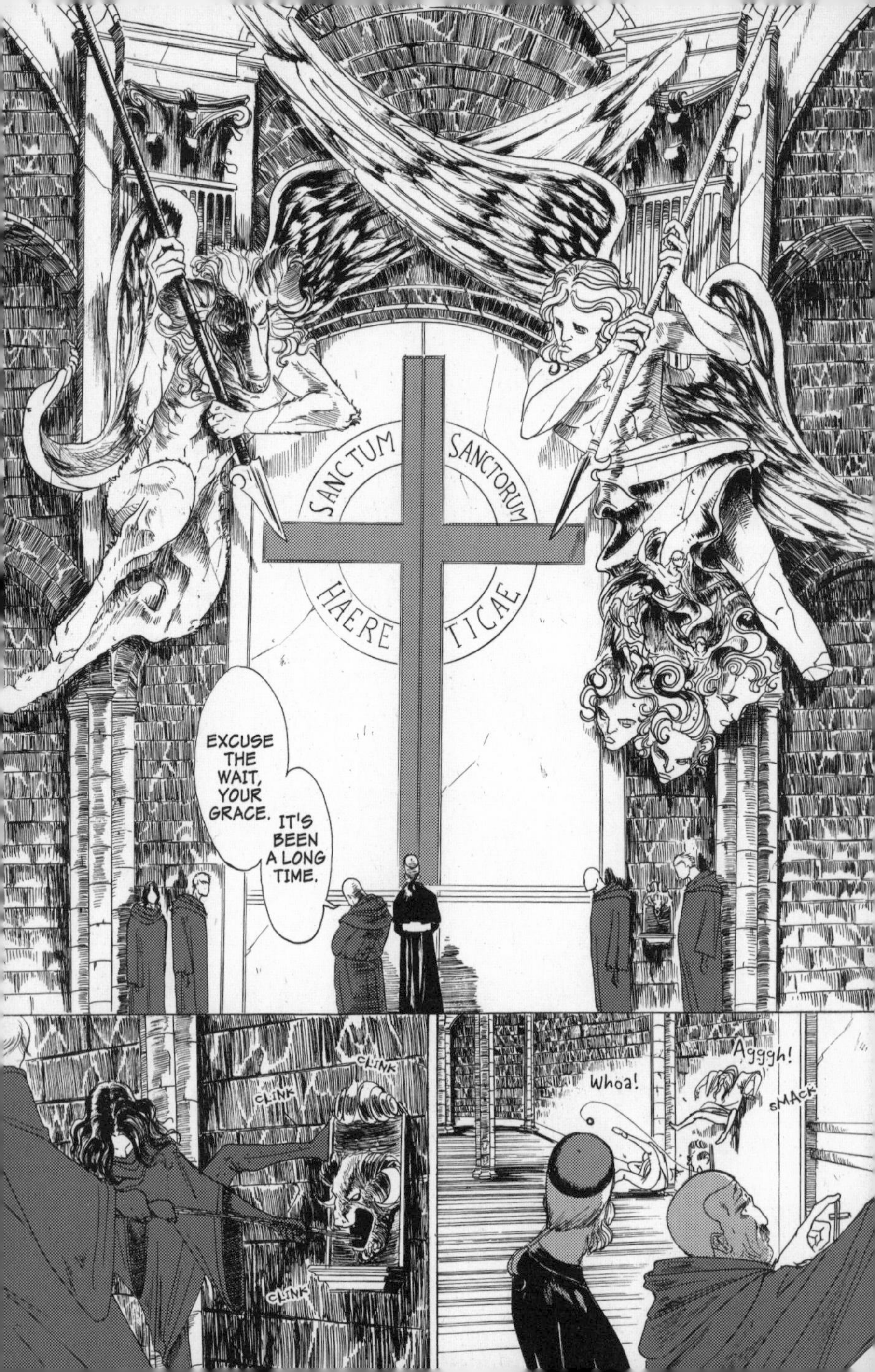
SANCTUM SANCTORUM HAERETICAE
EXCUSE THE WAIT, YOUR GRACE. IT'S BEEN A LONG TIME.
Agggh!
SMACK
Whoa!
CLINK
CLINK
CLINK

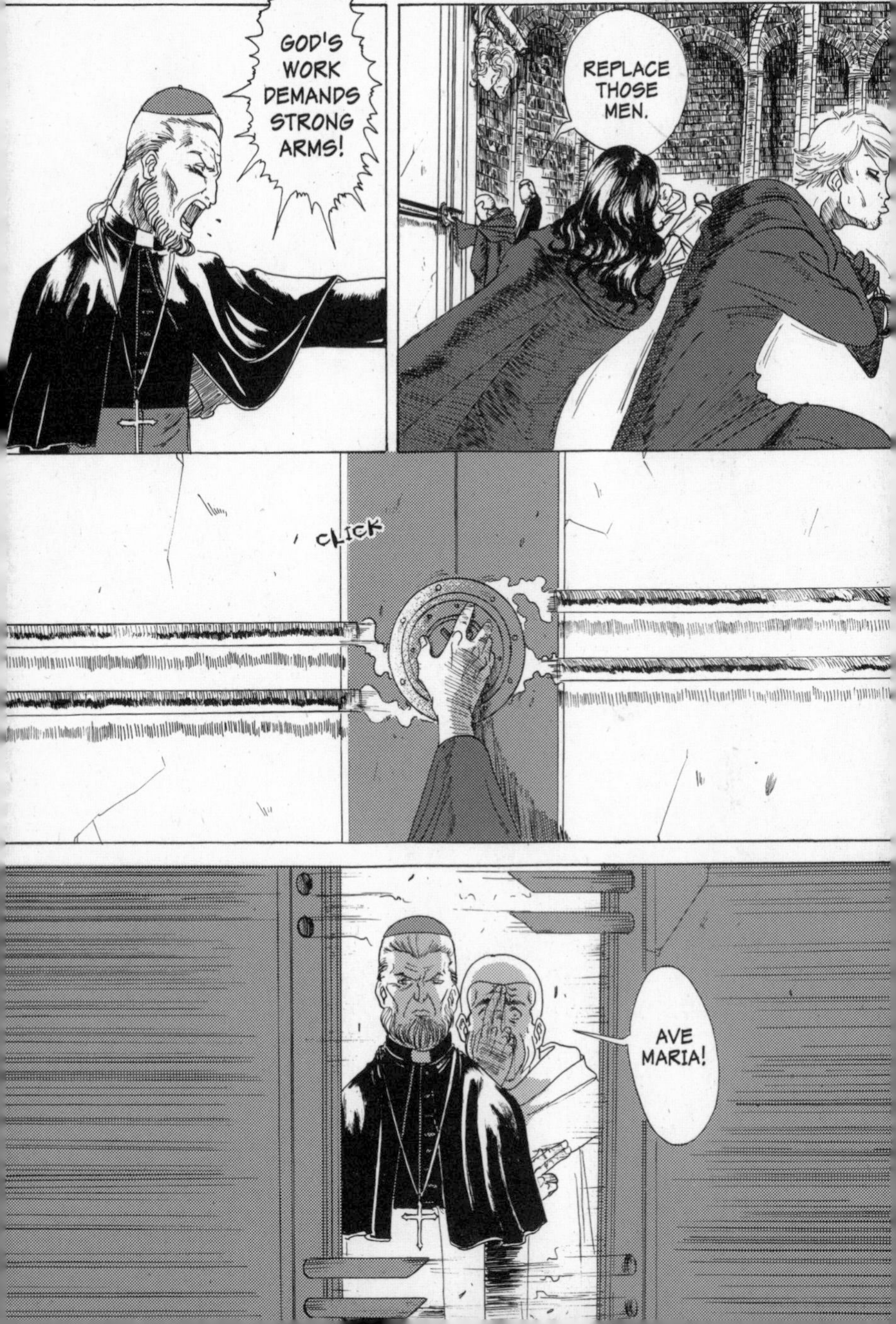
REPLACE THOSE MEN.
GOD'S WORK DEMANDS STRONG ARMS!
CLICK
AVE MARIA!

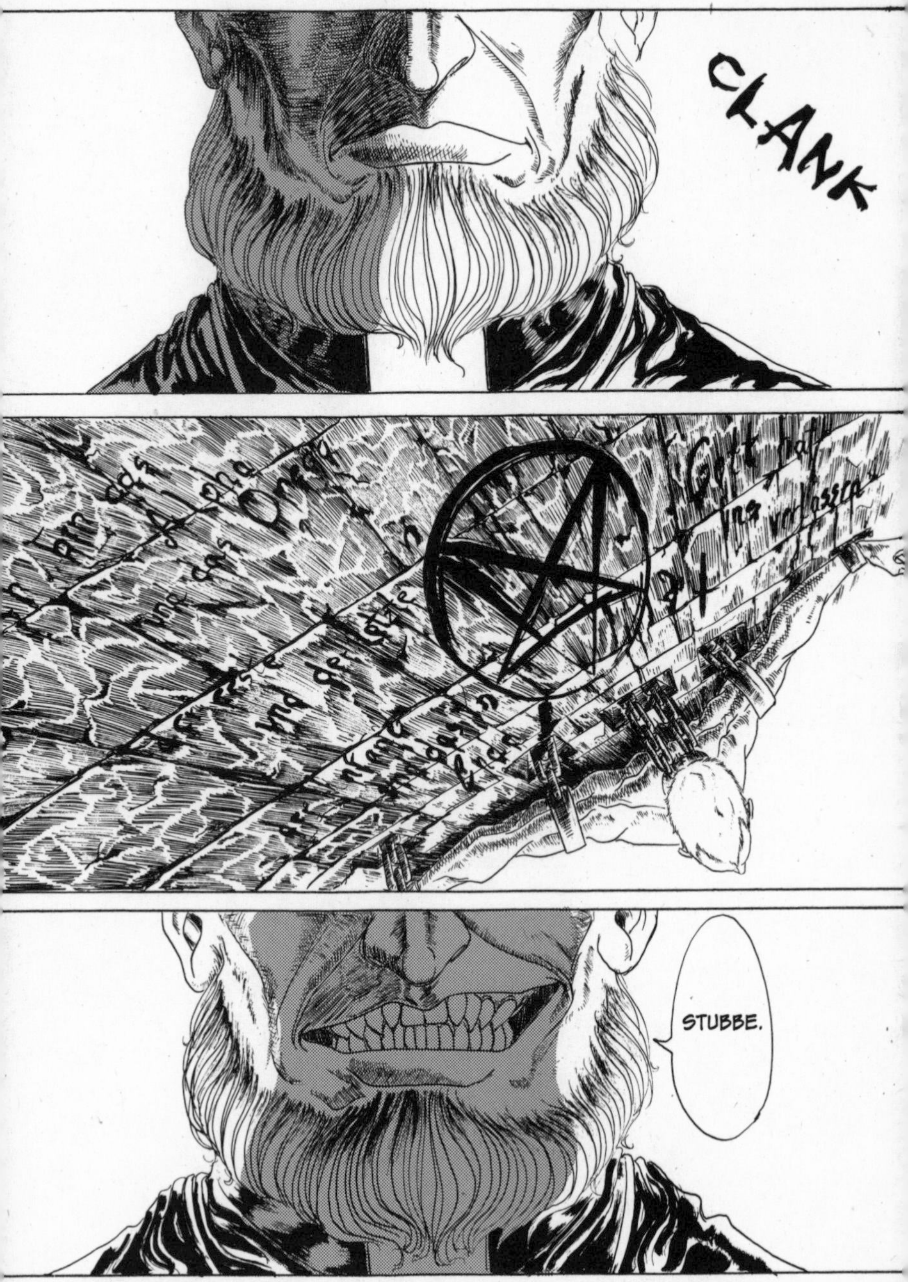
CLANK
STUBBE.

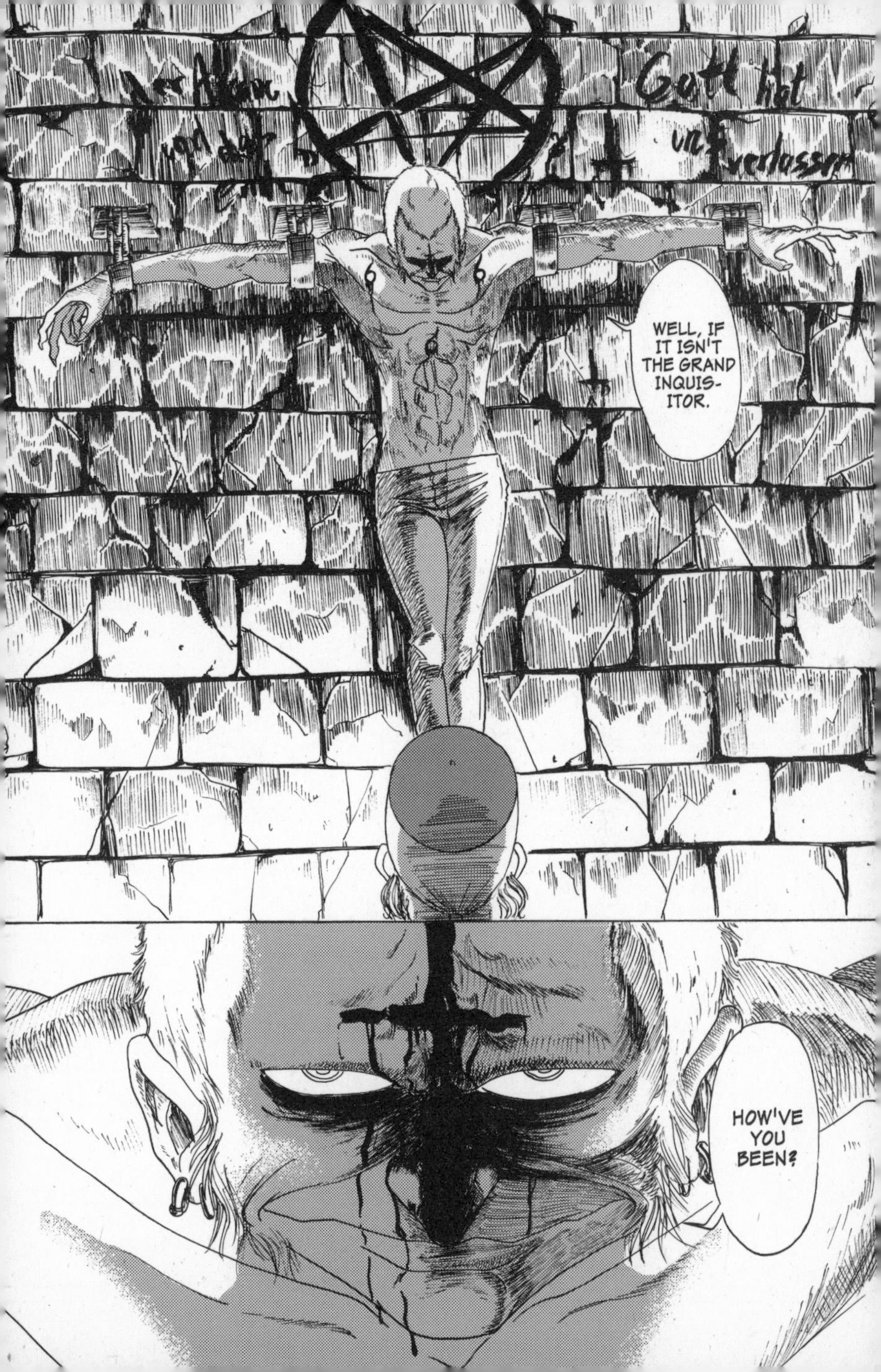
WELL, IF IT ISN'T THE GRAND INQUIS-ITOR.
HOW'VE YOU BEEN?

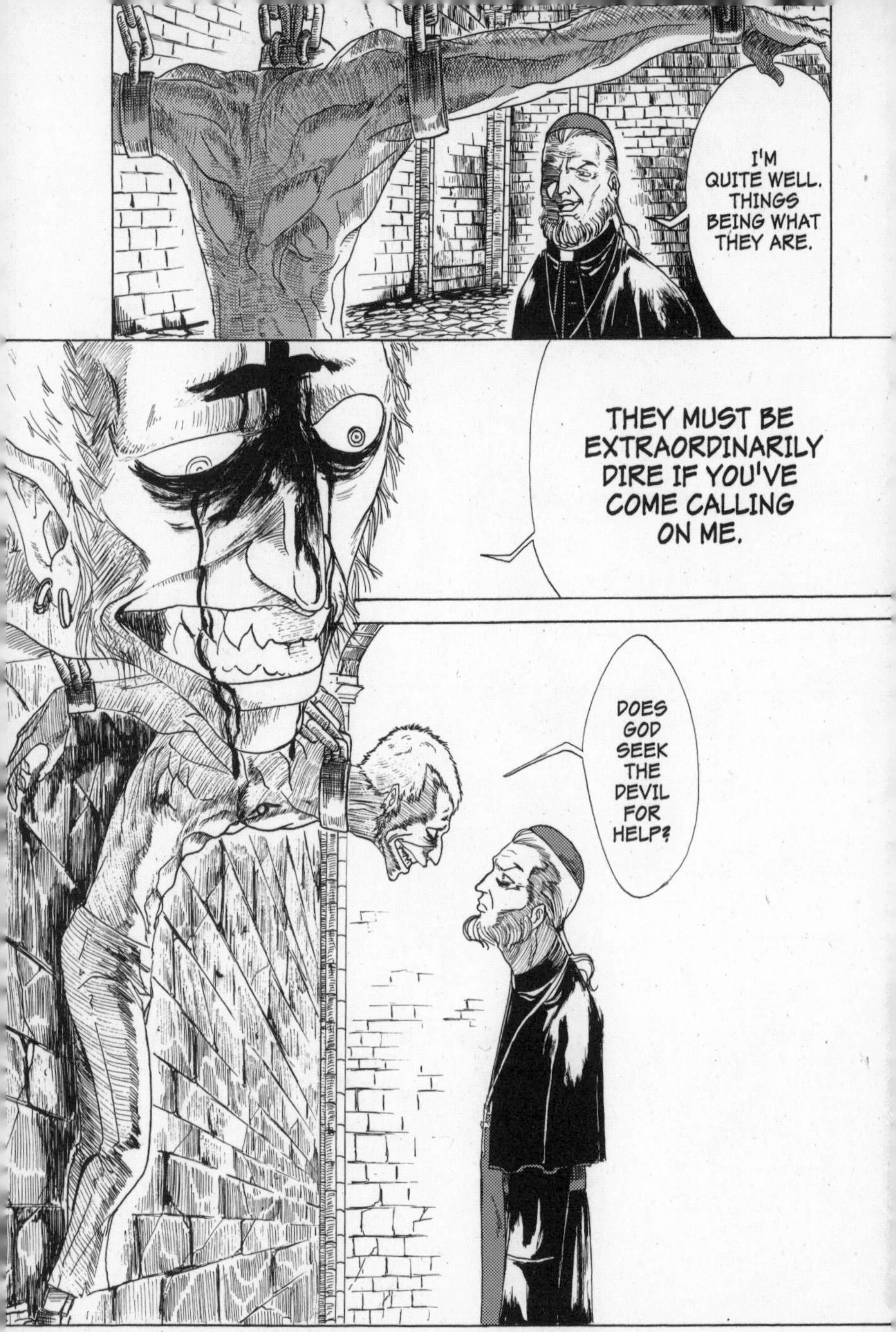
I'M QUITE WELL. THINGS BEING WHAT THEY ARE.
THEY MUST BE EXTRAORDINARILY DIRE IF YOU'VE COME CALLING ON ME.
DOES GOD SEEK THE DEVIL FOR HELP?

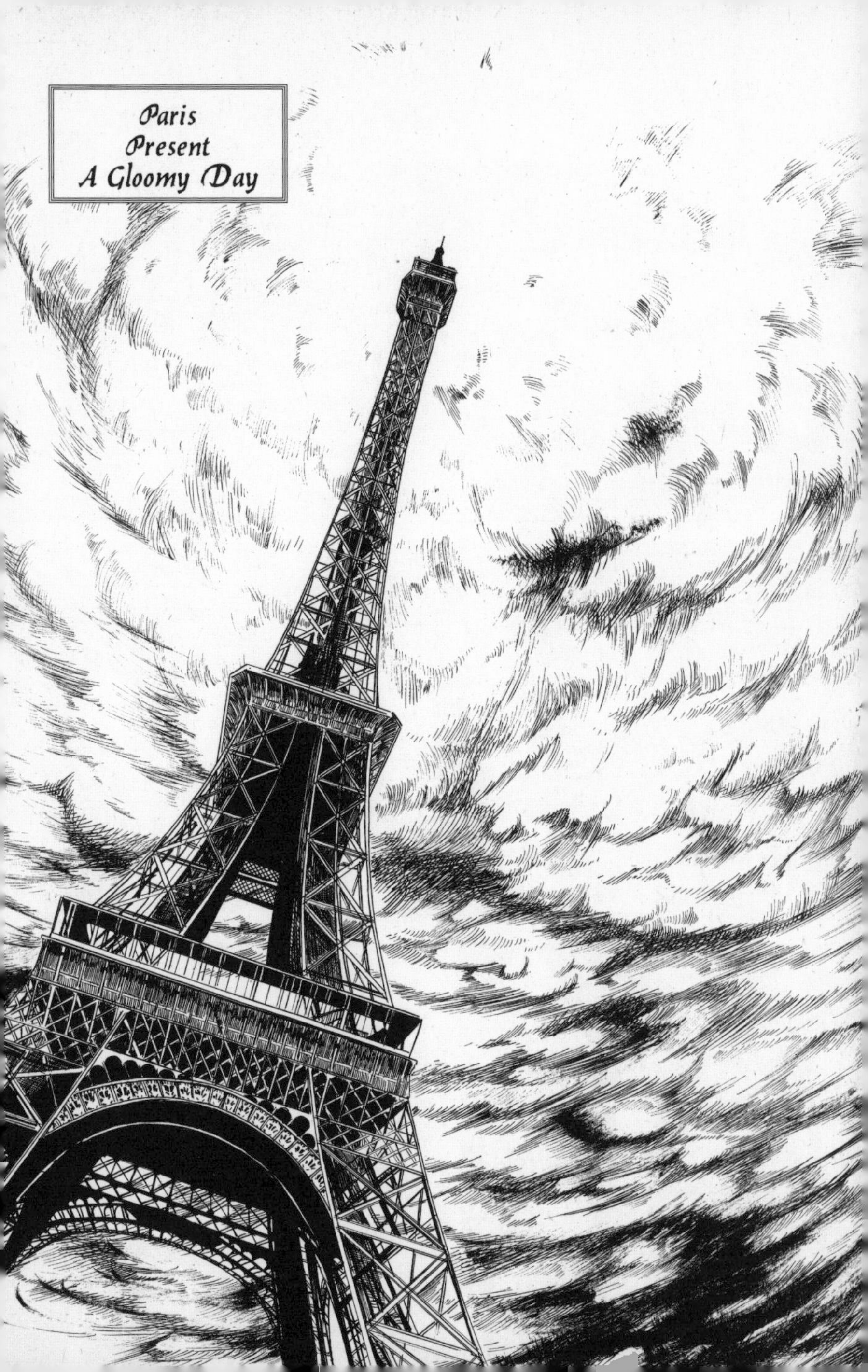
Paris
Present
A Gloomy Day

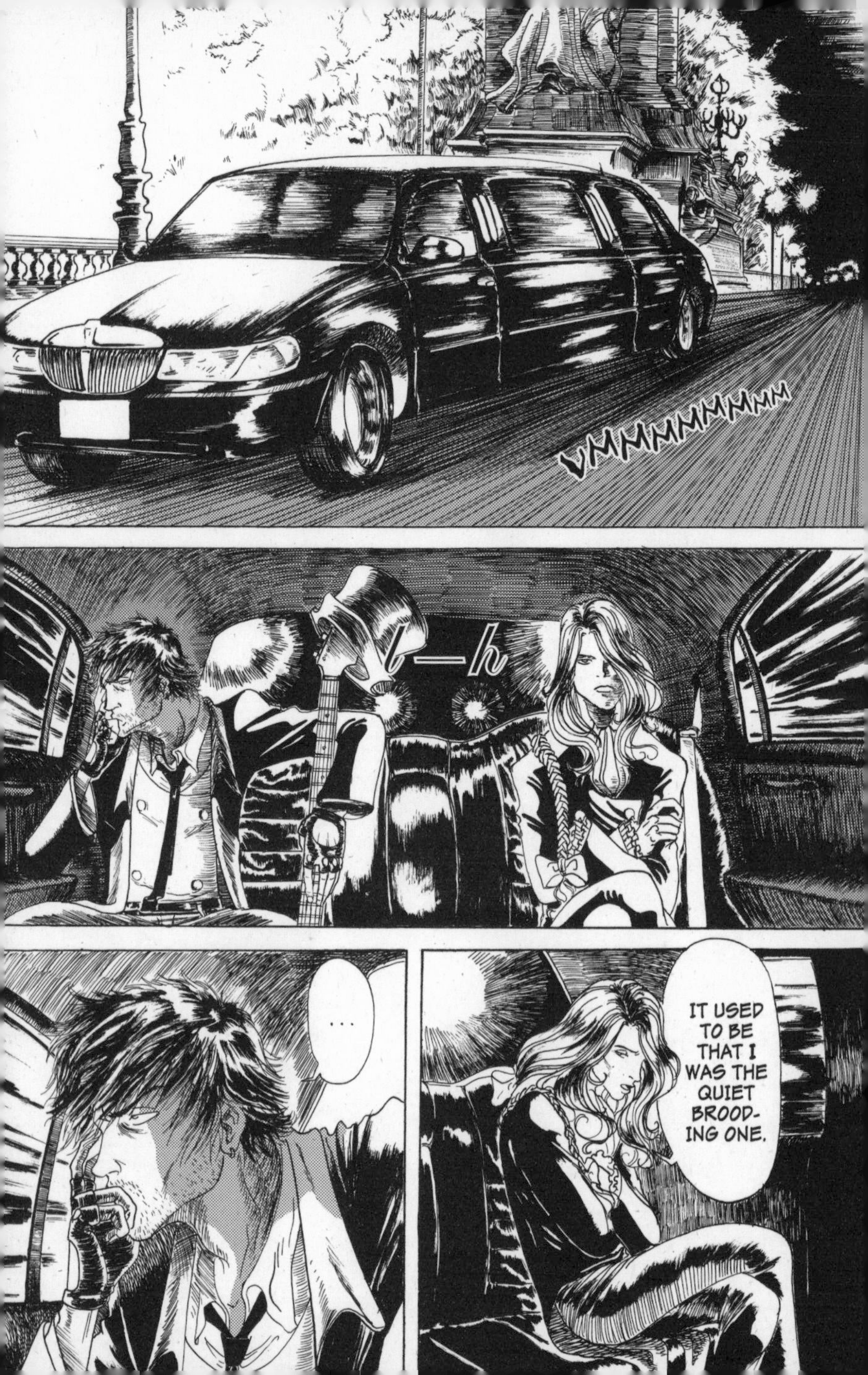
VMMMMMMMMM
b—h
IT USED TO BE THAT I WAS THE QUIET BROOD-ING ONE.
. . .

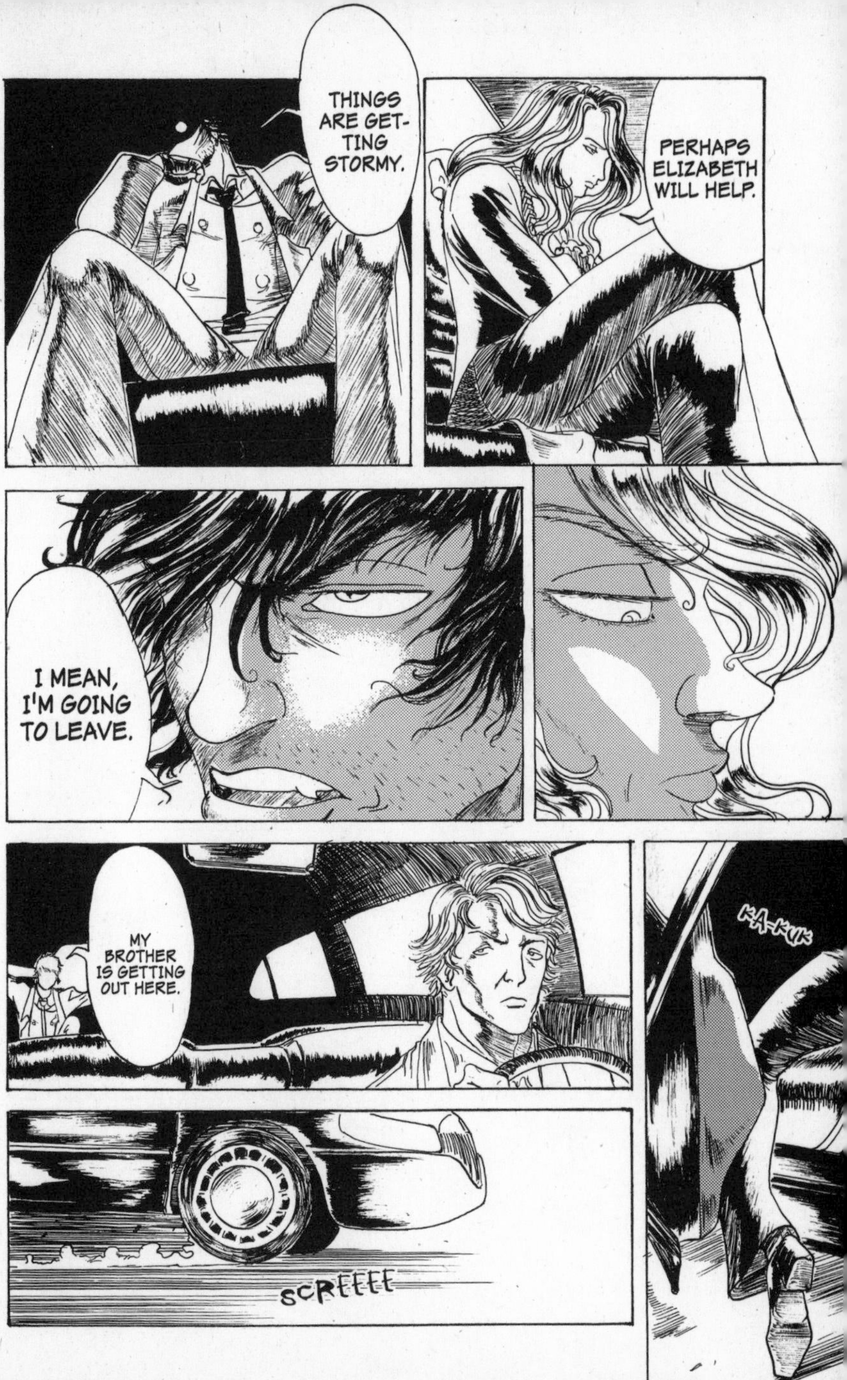
PERHAPS ELIZABETH WILL HELP.
THINGS ARE GET- TING STORMY.
I MEAN, I'M GOING TO LEAVE.
KA-KUK
MY BROTHER IS GETTING OUT HERE.
SCREEEE

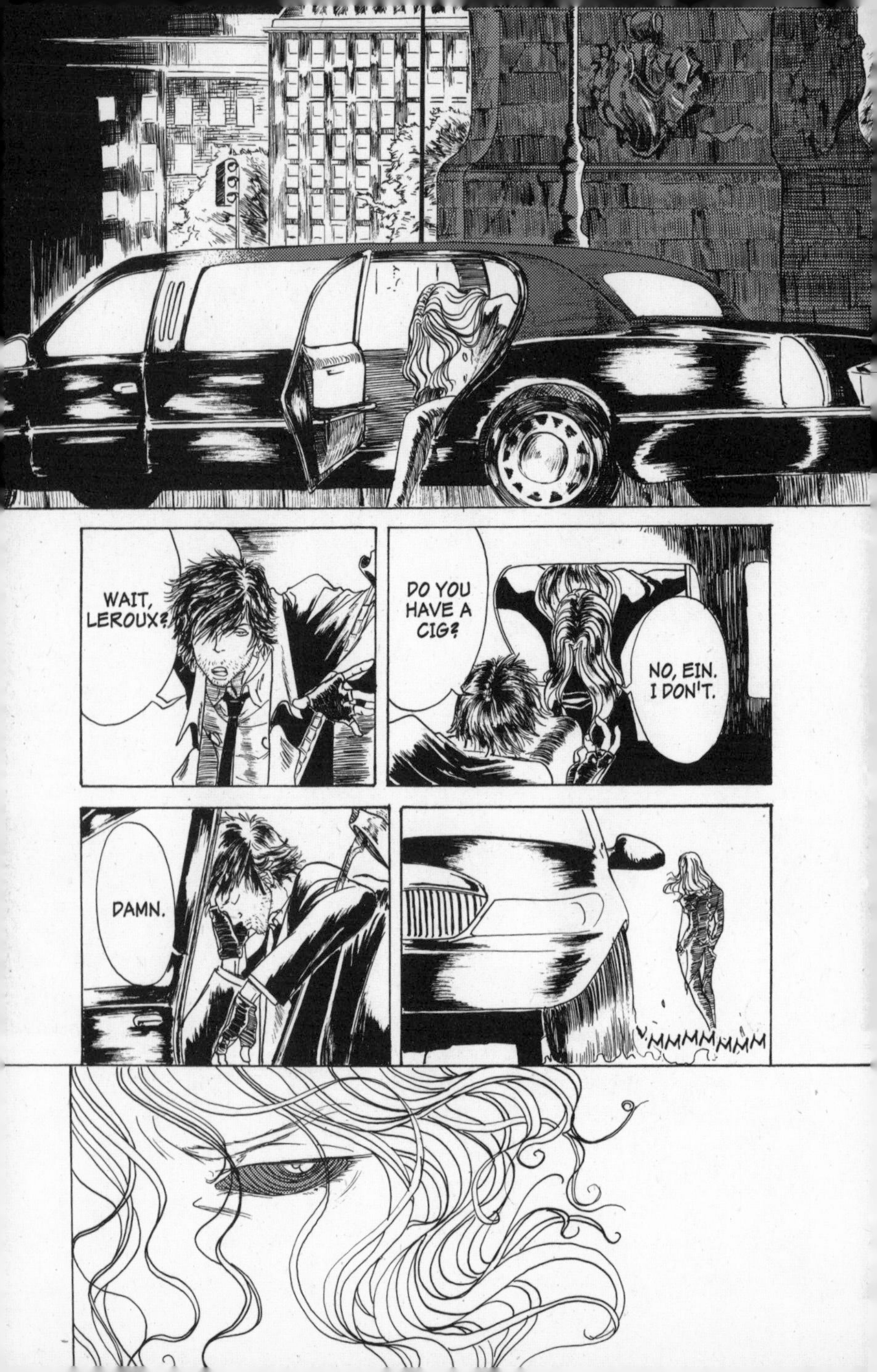
WAIT, LEROUX?
DO YOU HAVE A CIG?
NO, EIN. I DON'T.
DAMN.
VMMMMMMM

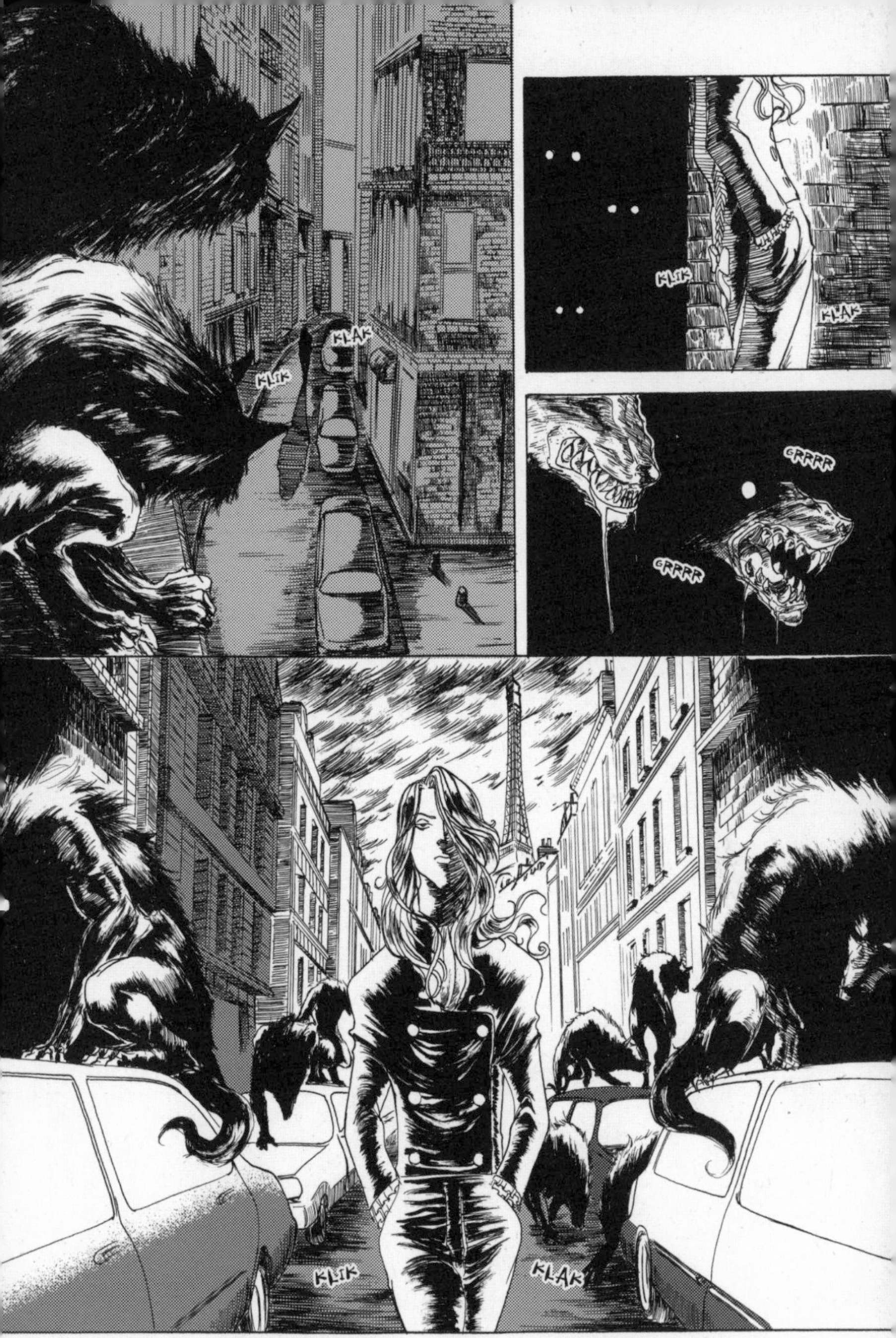
KLAK
KLIK
GRRRR
GRRRR
KLAK
KLIK
KLAK
KLIK

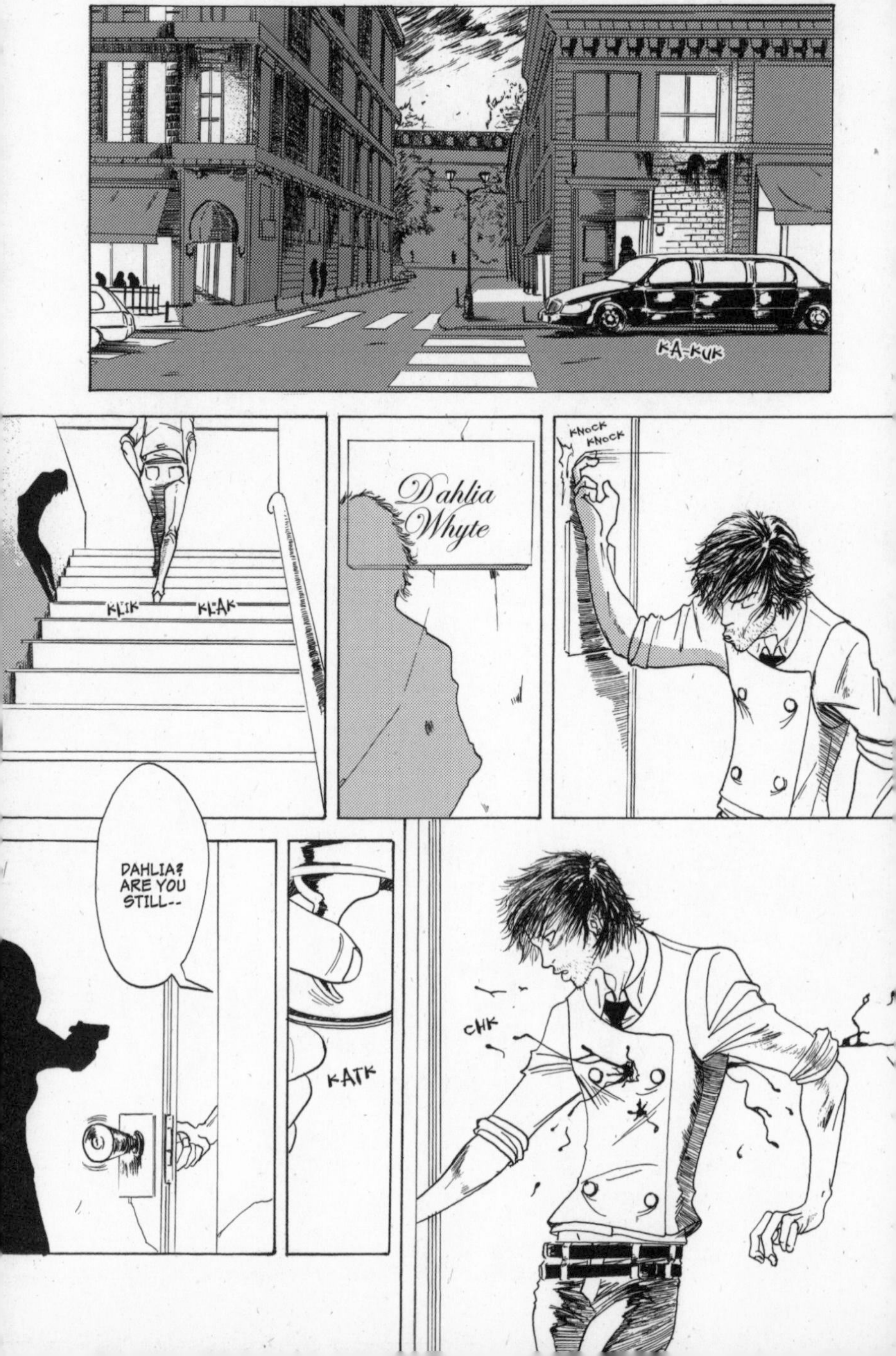
KA-KUK
KLIK
KLAK
Dahlia Whyte
KNOCK KNOCK
DAHLIA? ARE YOU STILL--
KATK
CHK

AGH!

THMP

HEY, BABY.

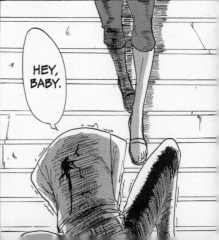

THNK

THNK

THNK

THNK

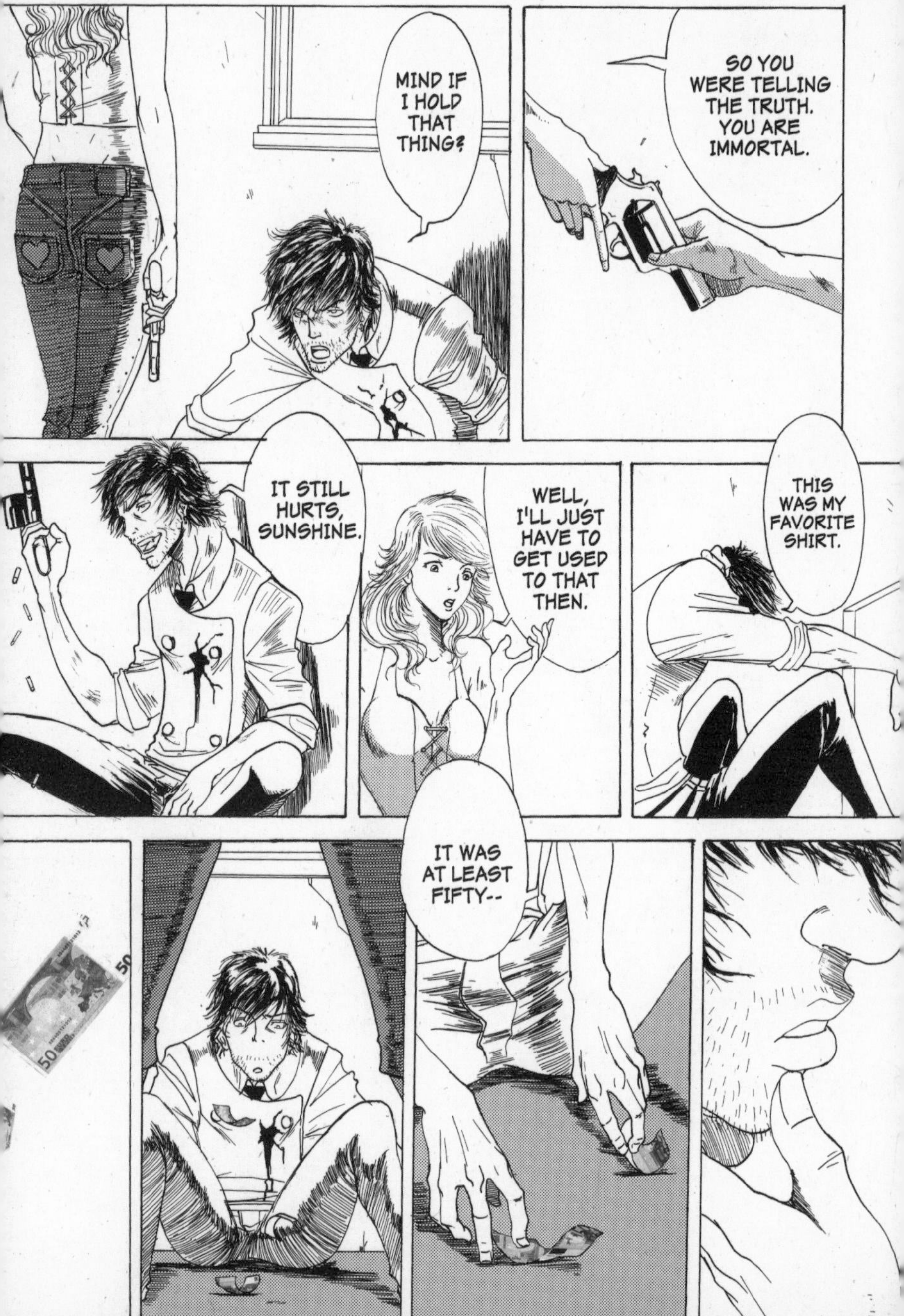
MIND IF I HOLD THAT THING?
SO YOU WERE TELLING THE TRUTH. YOU ARE IMMORTAL.
IT STILL HURTS, SUNSHINE.
WELL, I'LL JUST HAVE TO GET USED TO THAT THEN.
THIS WAS MY FAVORITE SHIRT.
IT WAS AT LEAST FIFTY--

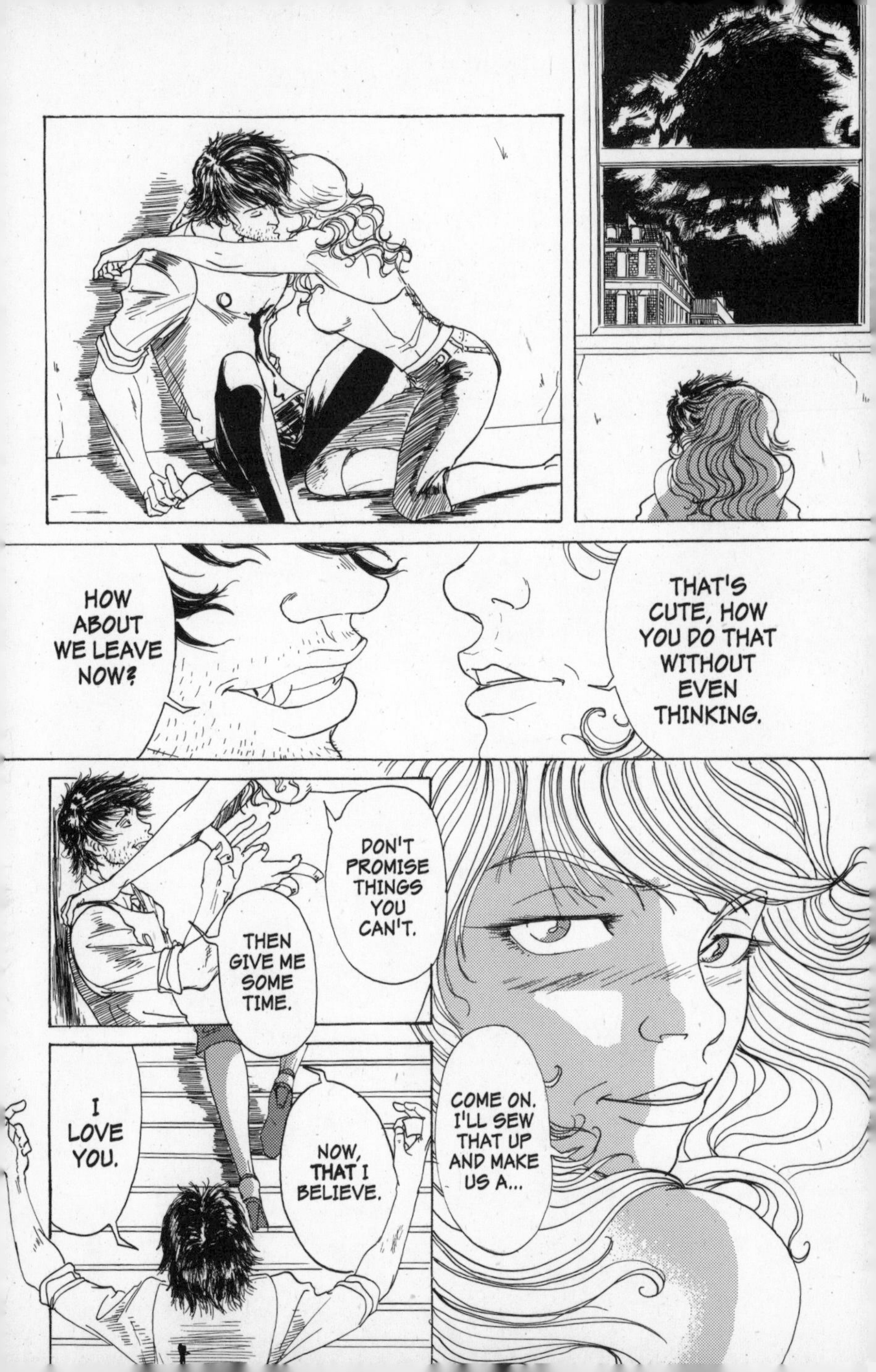
HOW ABOUT WE LEAVE NOW?
THAT'S CUTE, HOW YOU DO THAT WITHOUT EVEN THINKING.
DON'T PROMISE THINGS YOU CAN'T.
THEN GIVE ME SOME TIME.
I LOVE YOU.
NOW, THAT I BELIEVE.
COME ON. I'LL SEW THAT UP AND MAKE US A...

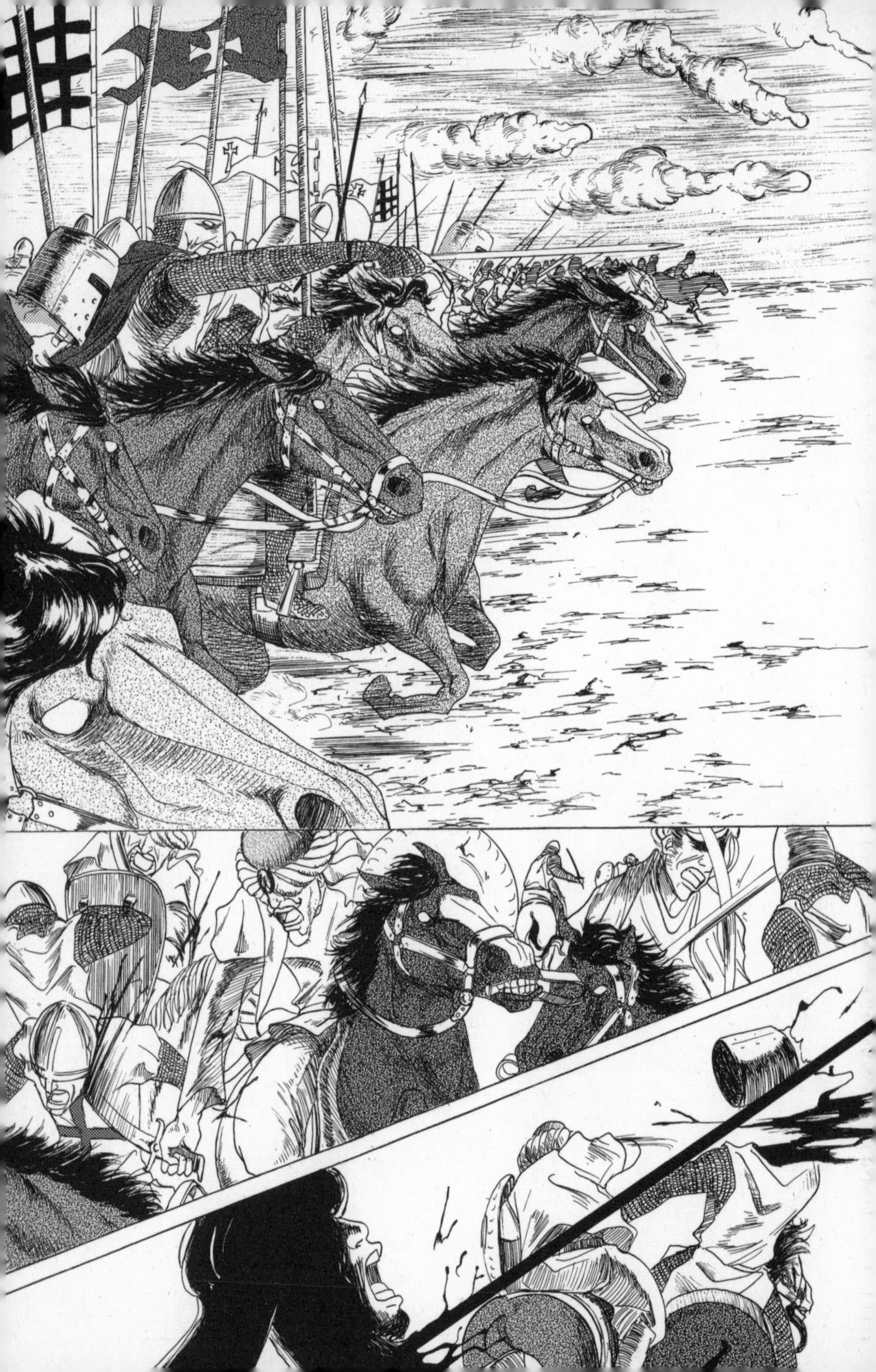

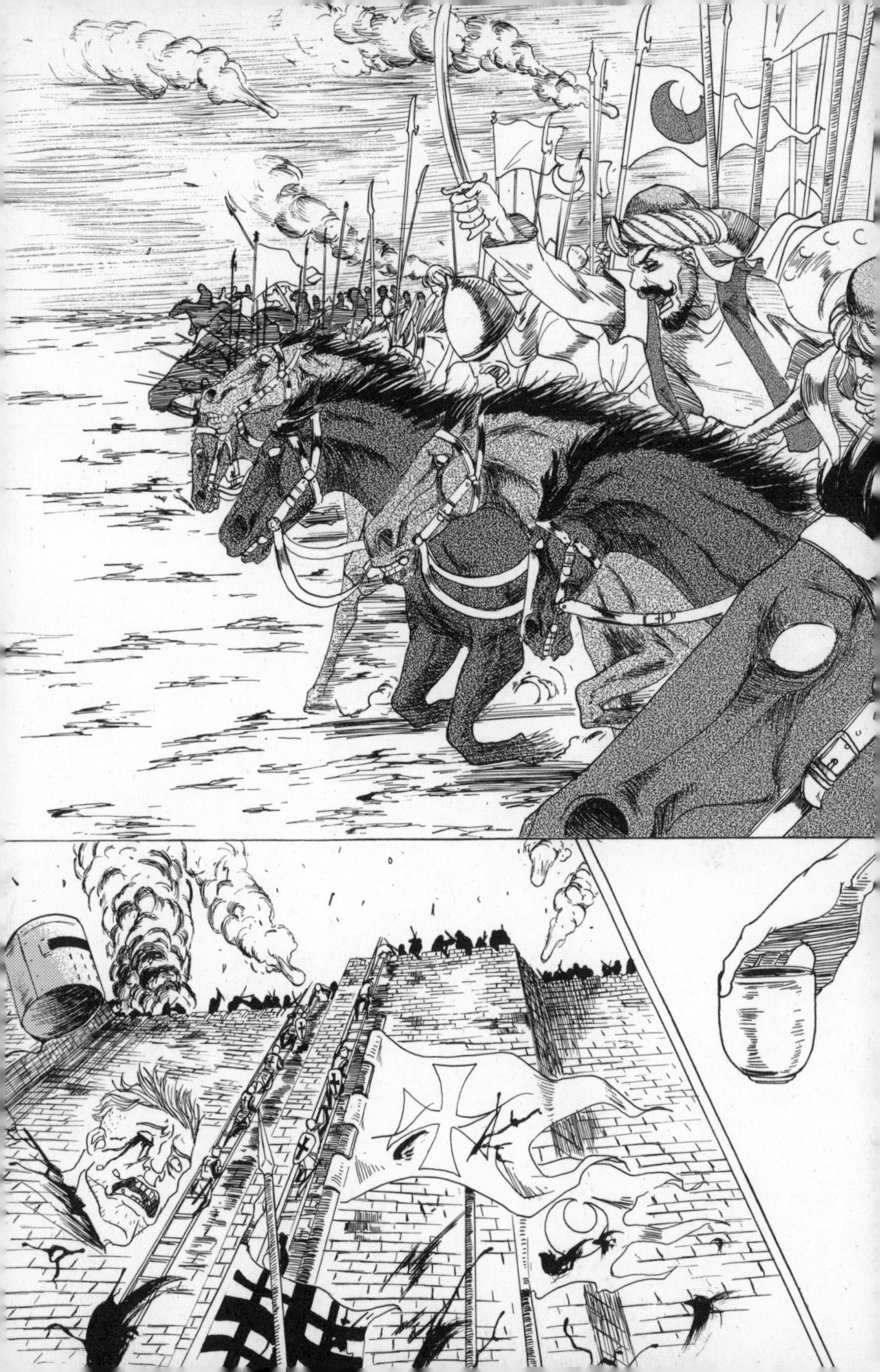

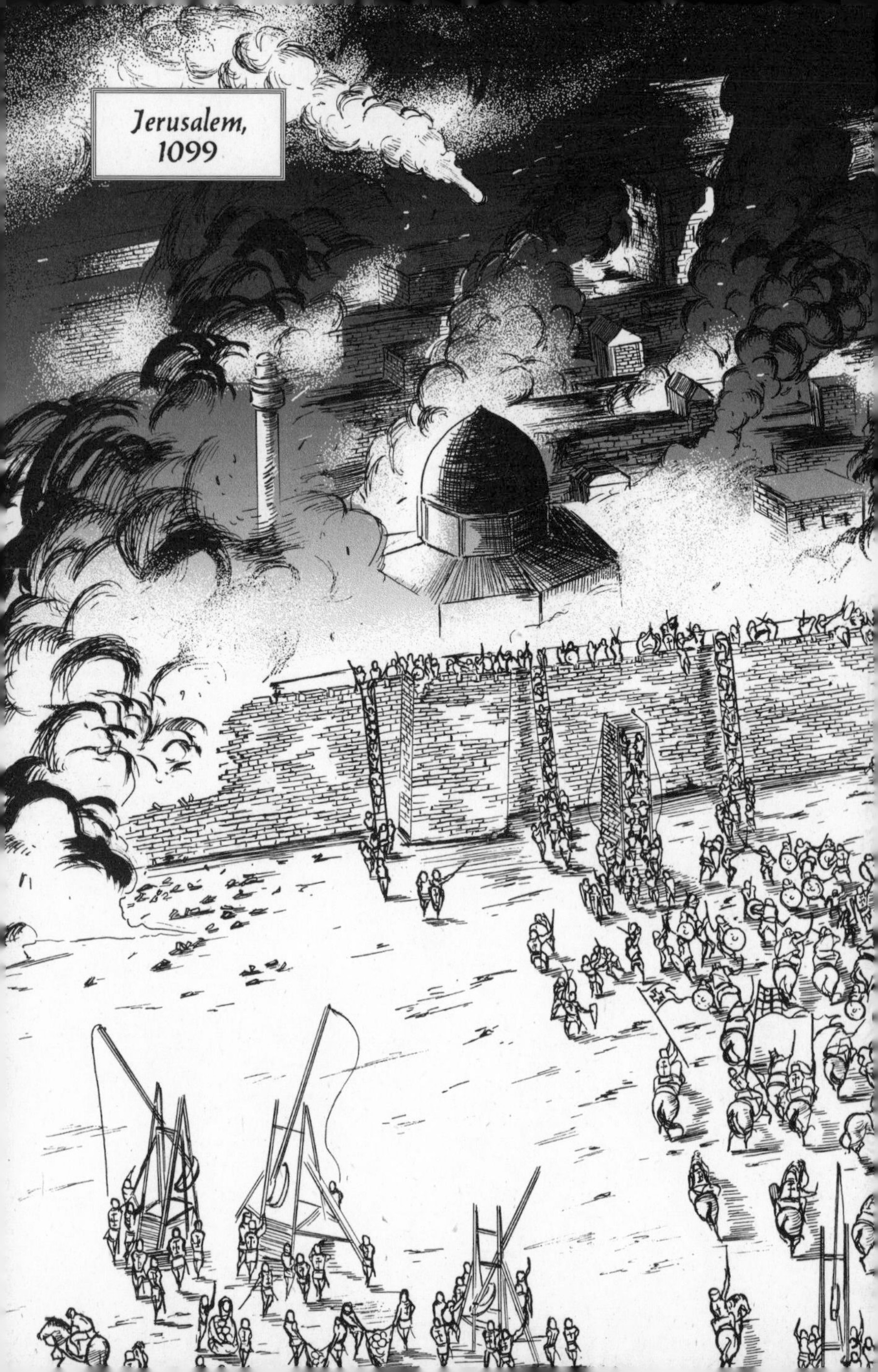
Jerusalem, 1099

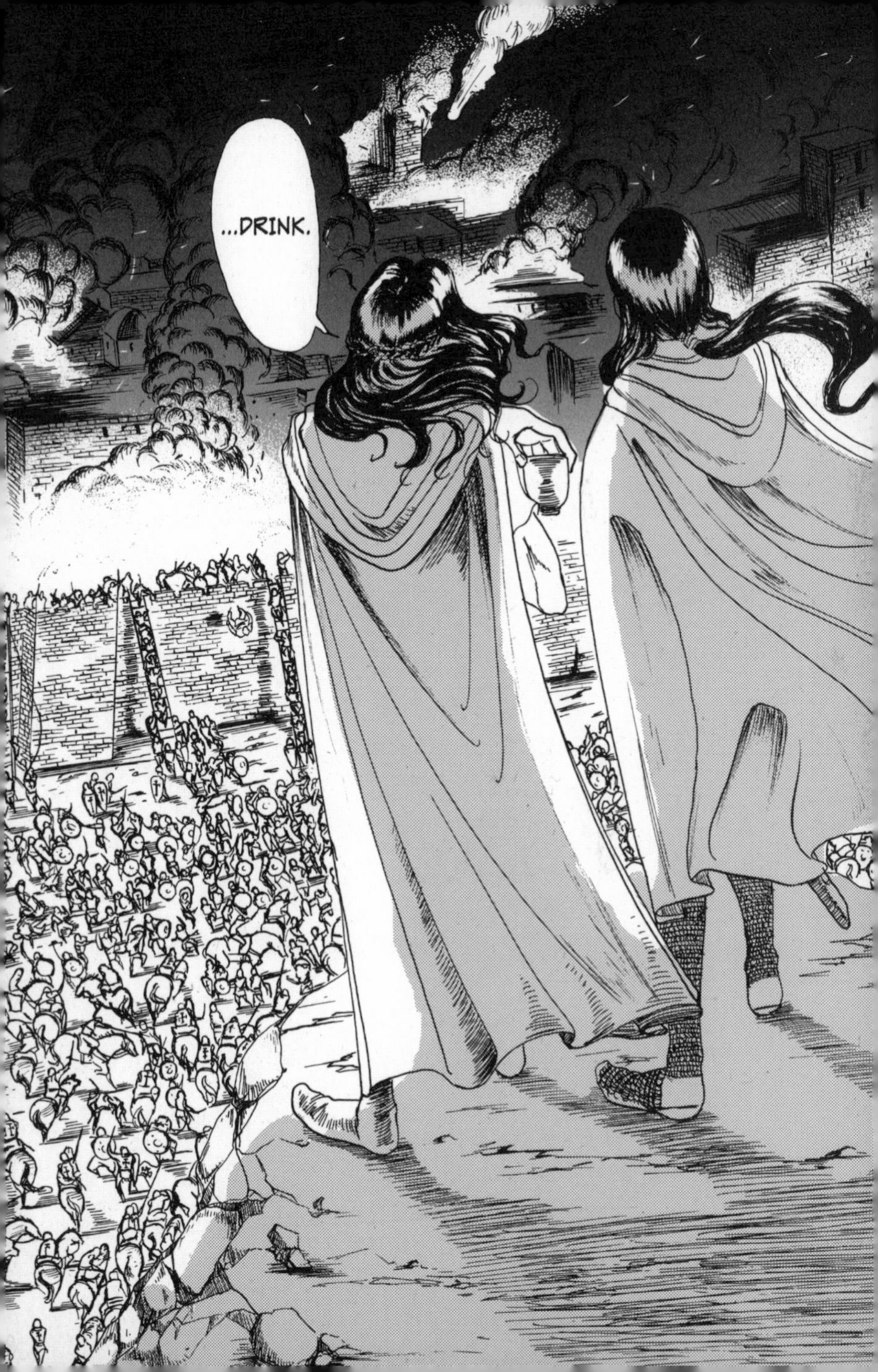
...DRINK.

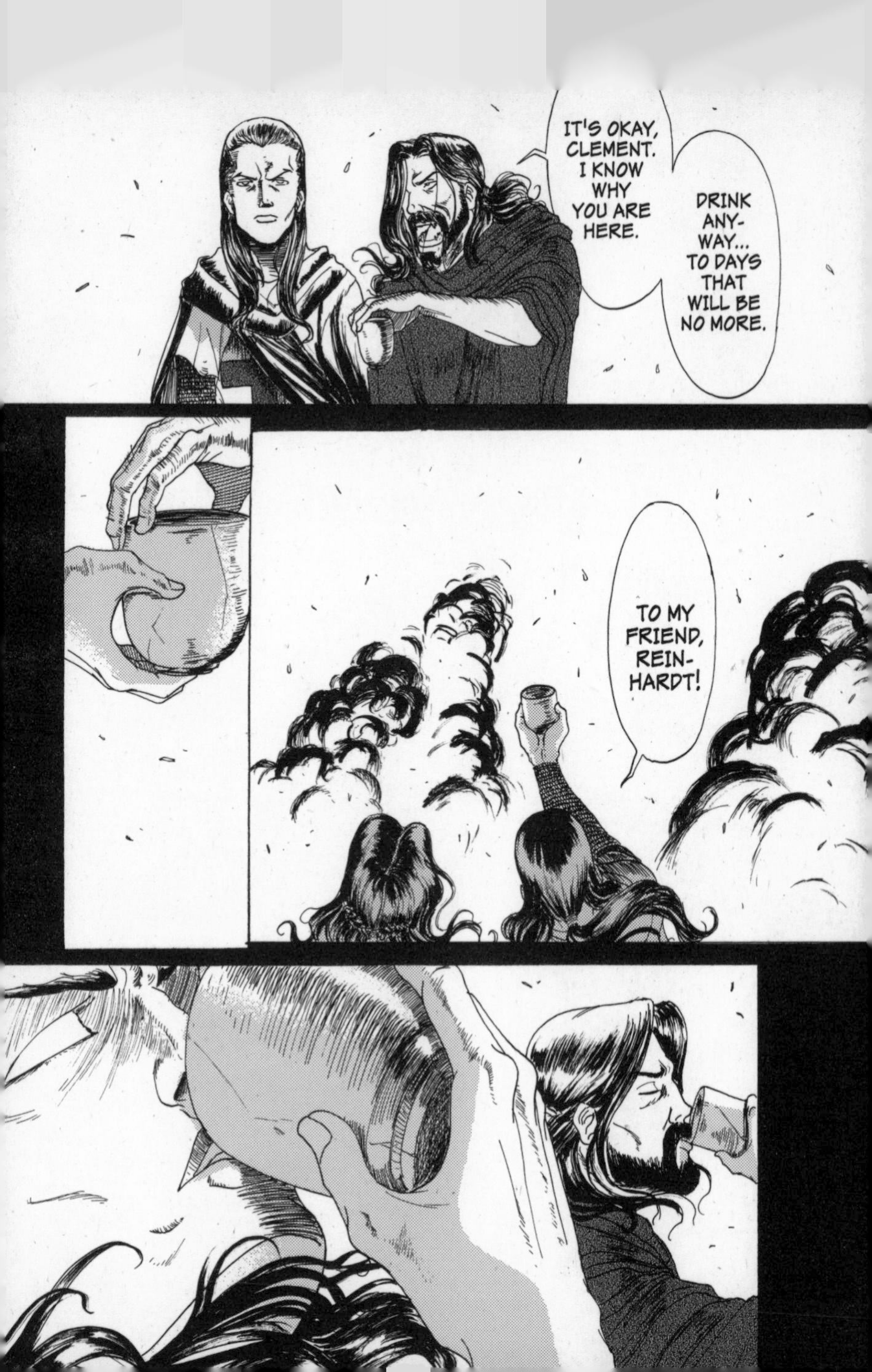
IT'S OKAY, CLEMENT. I KNOW WHY YOU ARE HERE.
DRINK ANY-WAY... TO DAYS THAT WILL BE NO MORE.
TO MY FRIEND, REIN-HARDT!

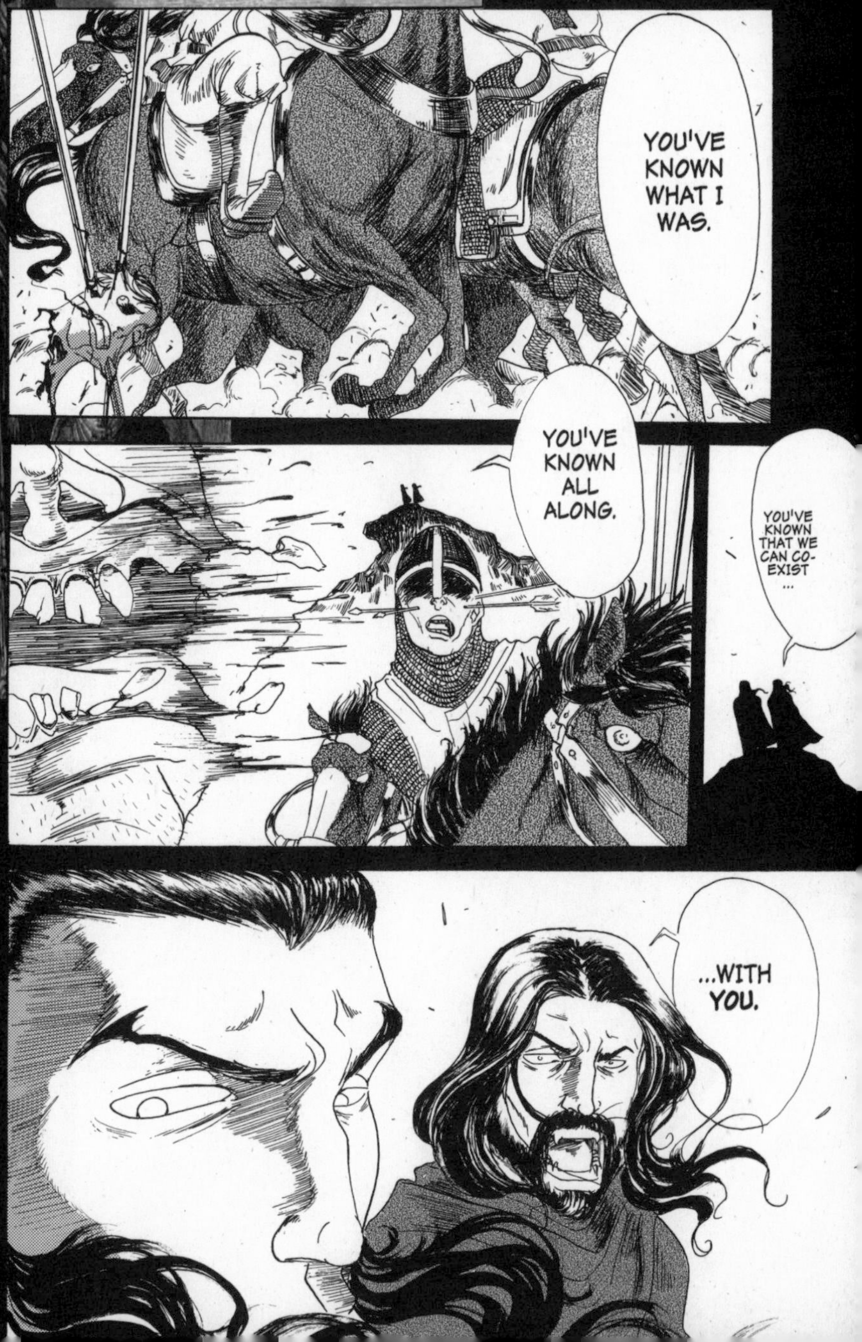
YOU'VE KNOWN WHAT I WAS.
YOU'VE KNOWN ALL ALONG.
YOU'VE KNOWN THAT WE CAN CO-EXIST ...
...WITH YOU.

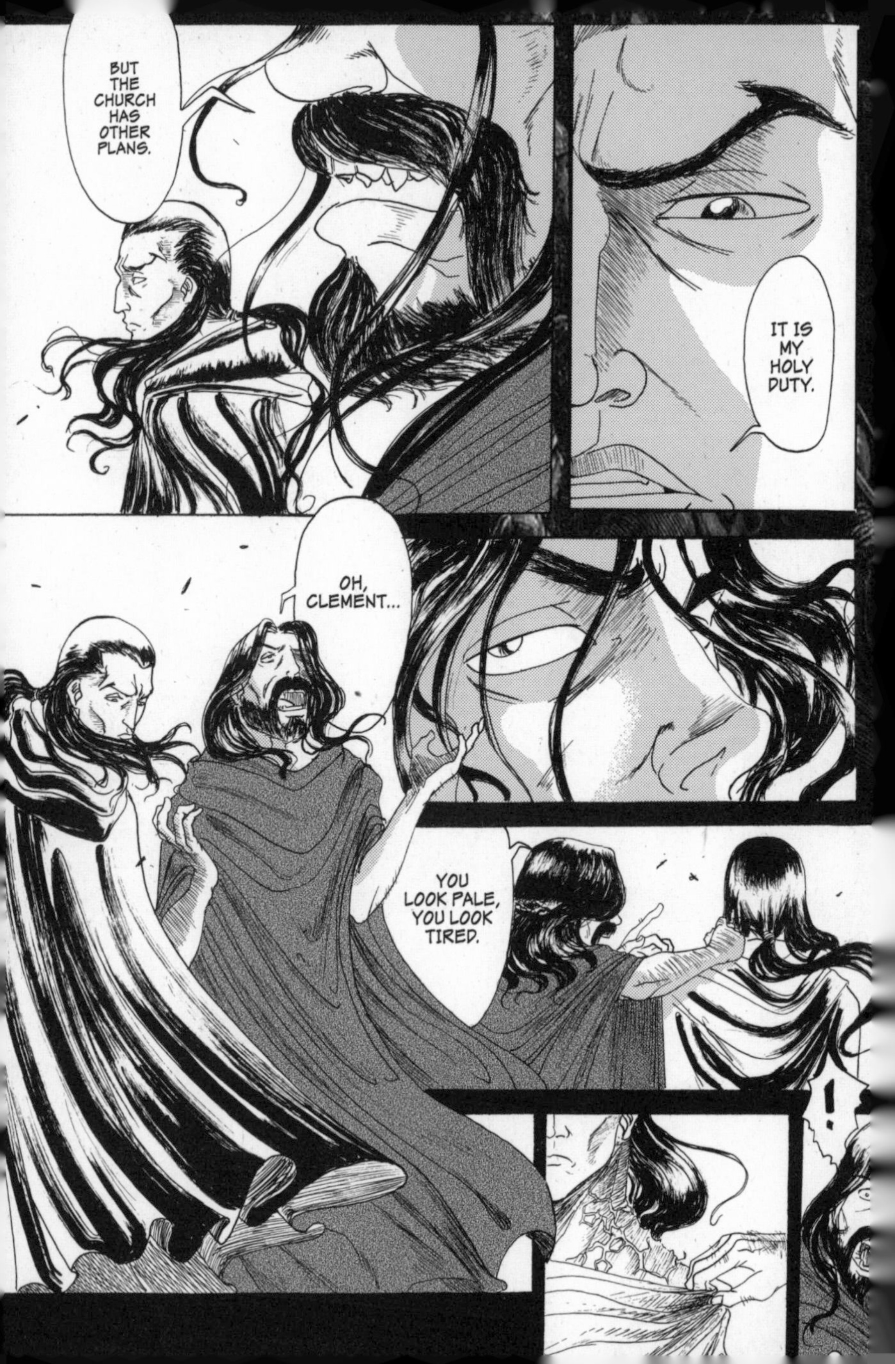
IT IS MY HOLY DUTY.
BUT THE CHURCH HAS OTHER PLANS.
OH, CLEMENT...
YOU LOOK PALE, YOU LOOK TIRED.
!

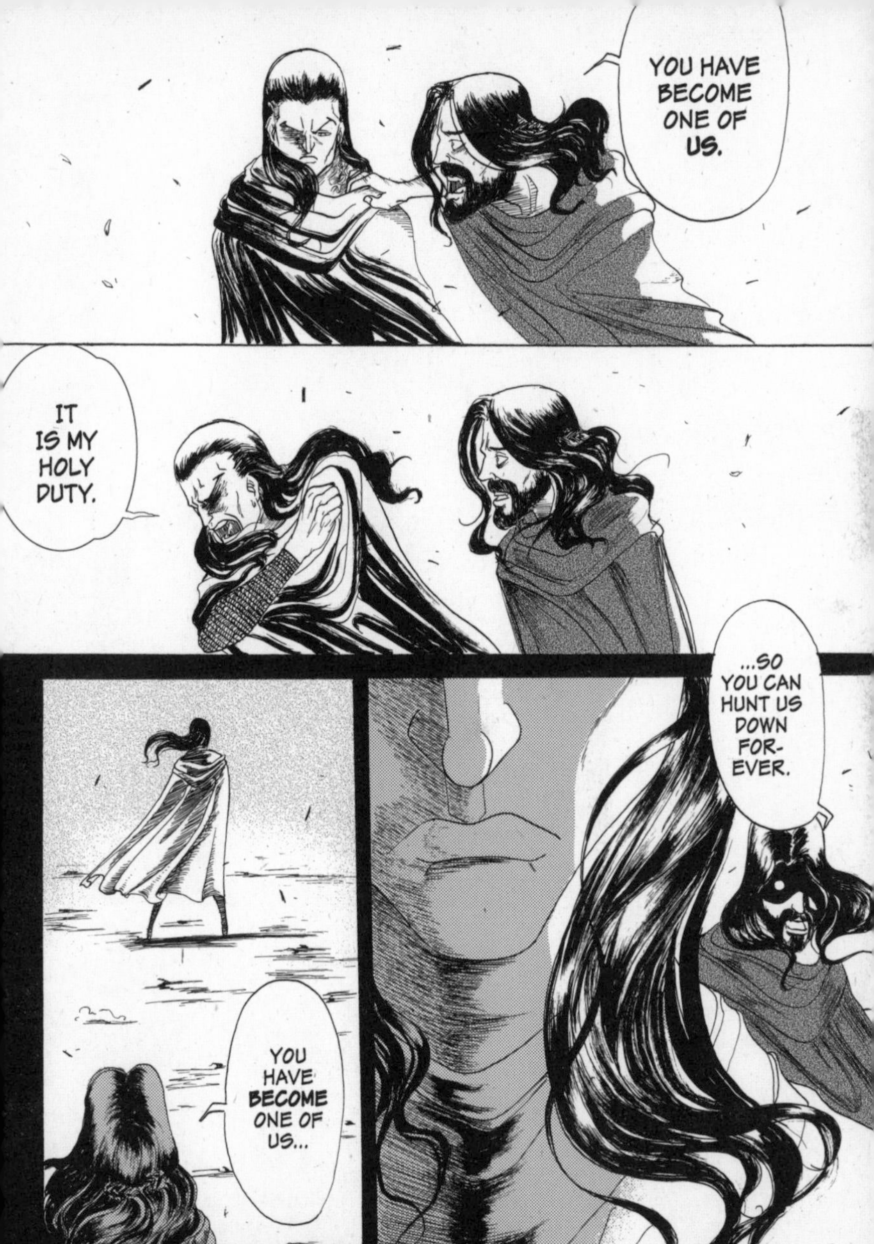
YOU HAVE BECOME ONE OF US.
IT IS MY HOLY DUTY.
...SO YOU CAN HUNT US DOWN FOR-EVER.
YOU HAVE BECOME ONE OF US...

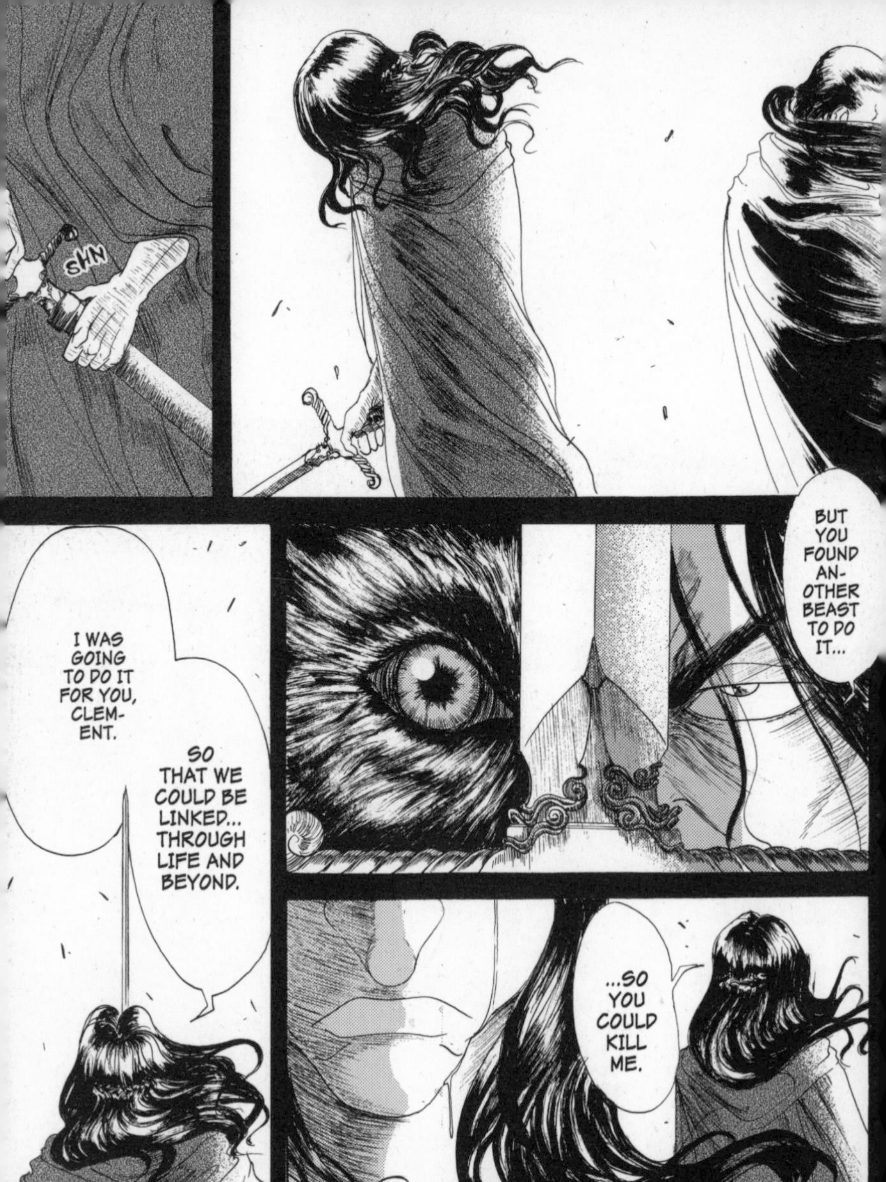
SHN
BUT YOU FOUND AN-OTHER BEAST TO DO IT...
...SO YOU COULD KILL ME.
I WAS GOING TO DO IT FOR YOU, CLEM-ENT.
SO THAT WE COULD BE LINKED... THROUGH LIFE AND BEYOND.

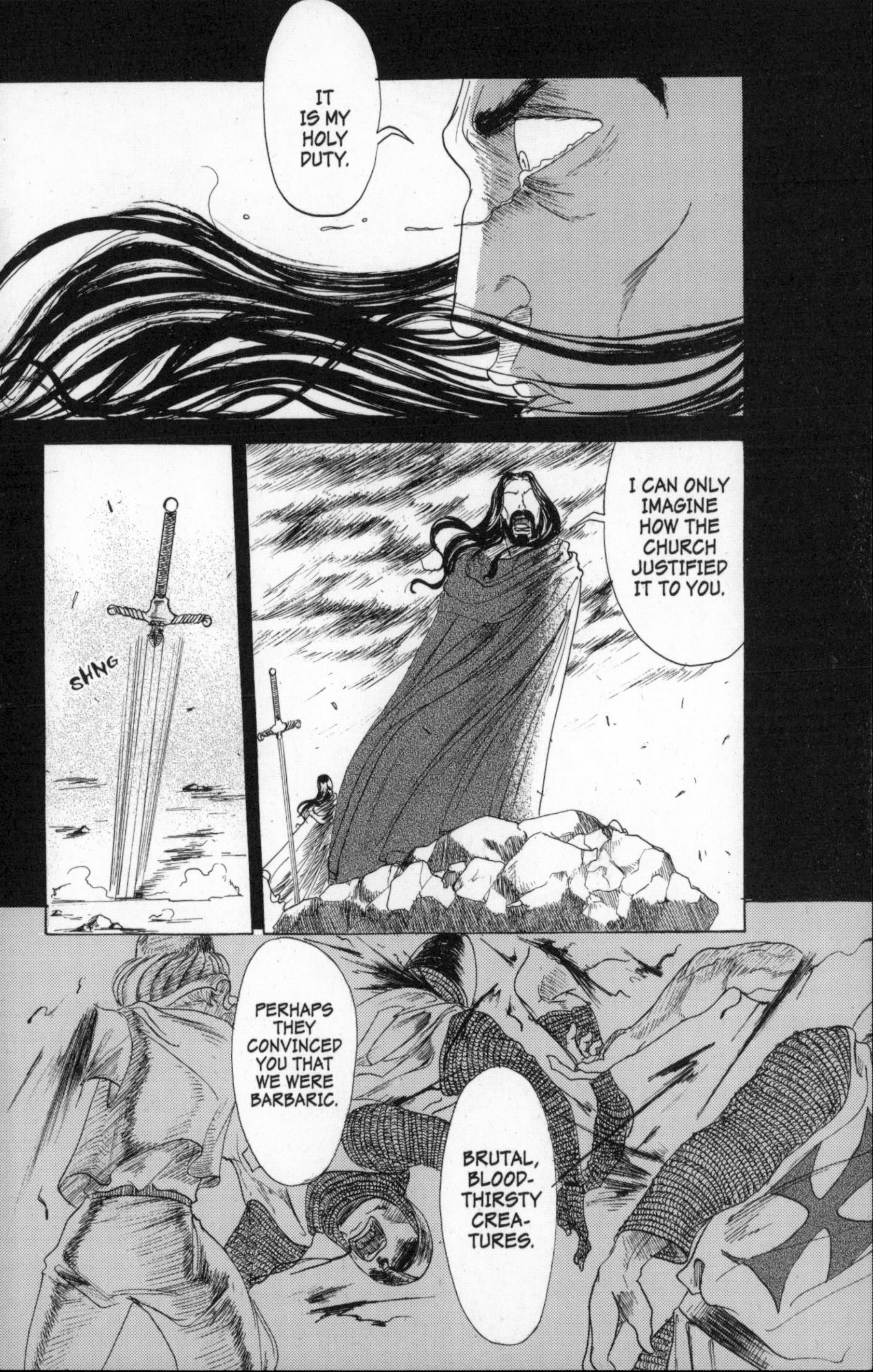
IT IS MY HOLY DUTY.
I CAN ONLY IMAGINE HOW THE CHURCH JUSTIFIED IT TO YOU.
SHNG
PERHAPS THEY CONVINCED YOU THAT WE WERE BARBARIC.
BRUTAL, BLOOD-THIRSTY CREA-TURES.

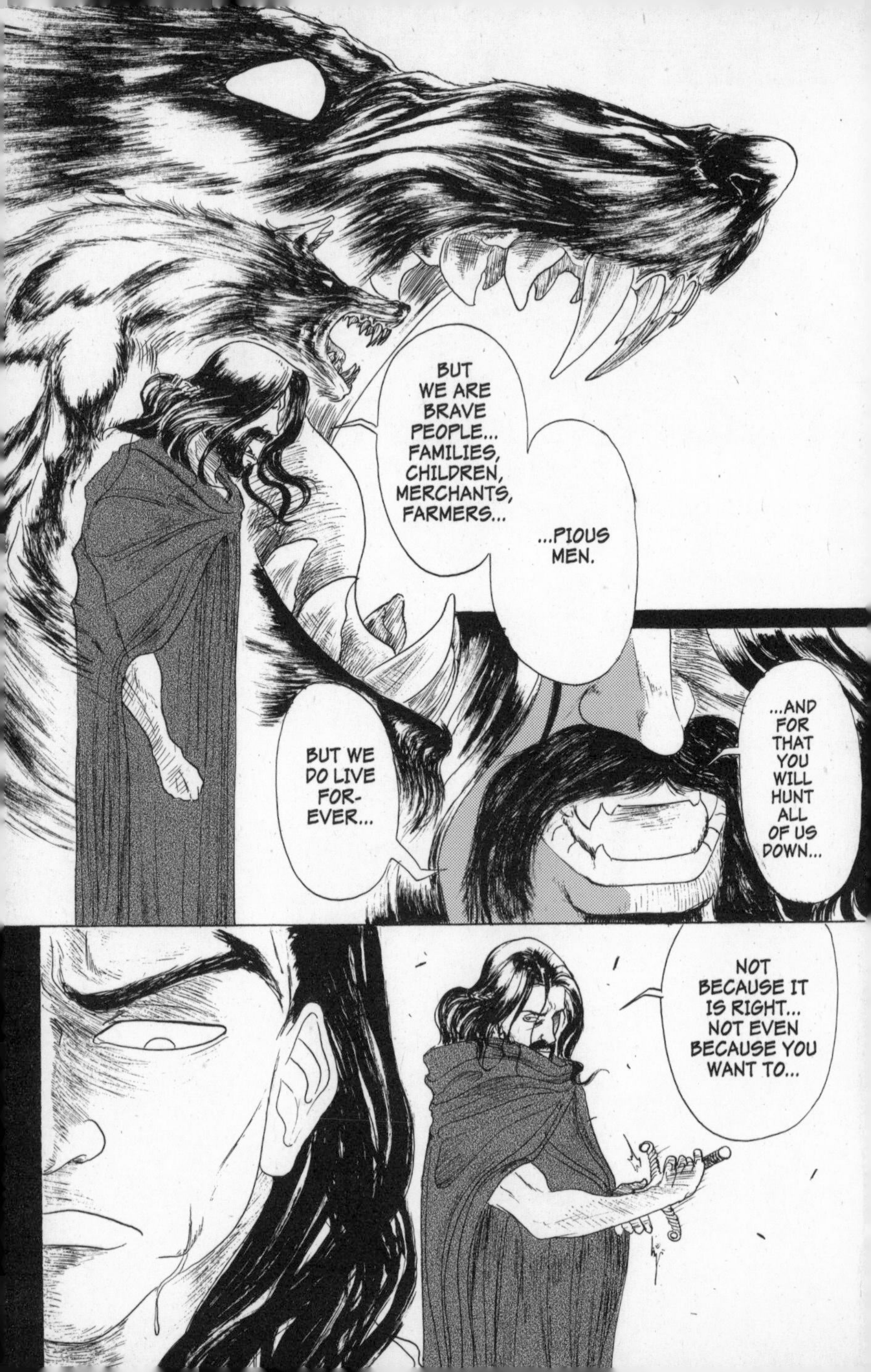
BUT WE ARE BRAVE PEOPLE... FAMILIES, CHILDREN, MERCHANTS, FARMERS...
...PIOUS MEN.
BUT WE DO LIVE FOR-EVER...
...AND FOR THAT YOU WILL HUNT ALL OF US DOWN...
NOT BECAUSE IT IS RIGHT... NOT EVEN BECAUSE YOU WANT TO...

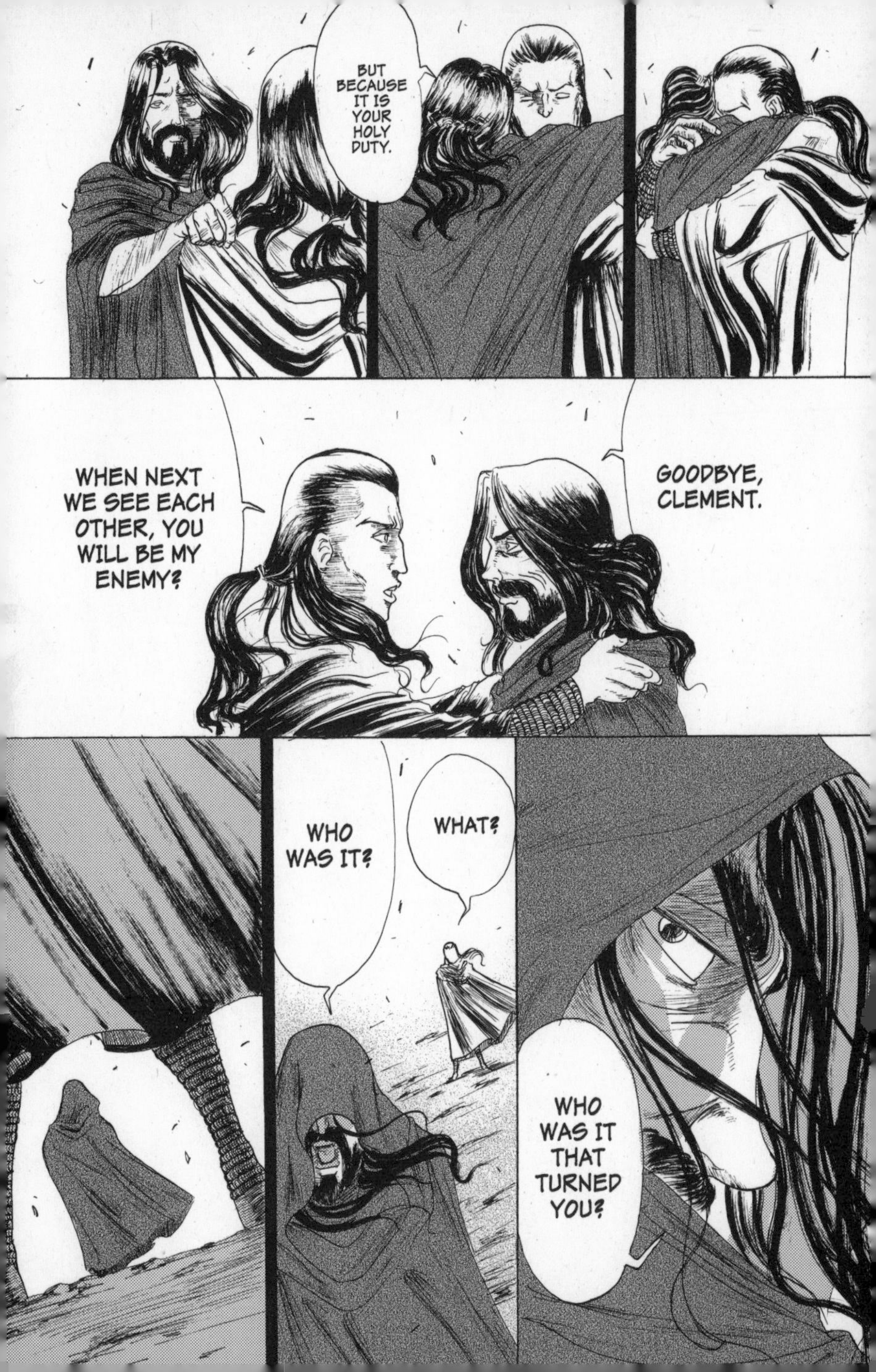
BUT BECAUSE IT IS YOUR HOLY DUTY.
WHEN NEXT WE SEE EACH OTHER, YOU WILL BE MY ENEMY?
GOODBYE, CLEMENT.
WHO WAS IT?
WHAT?
WHO WAS IT THAT TURNED YOU?

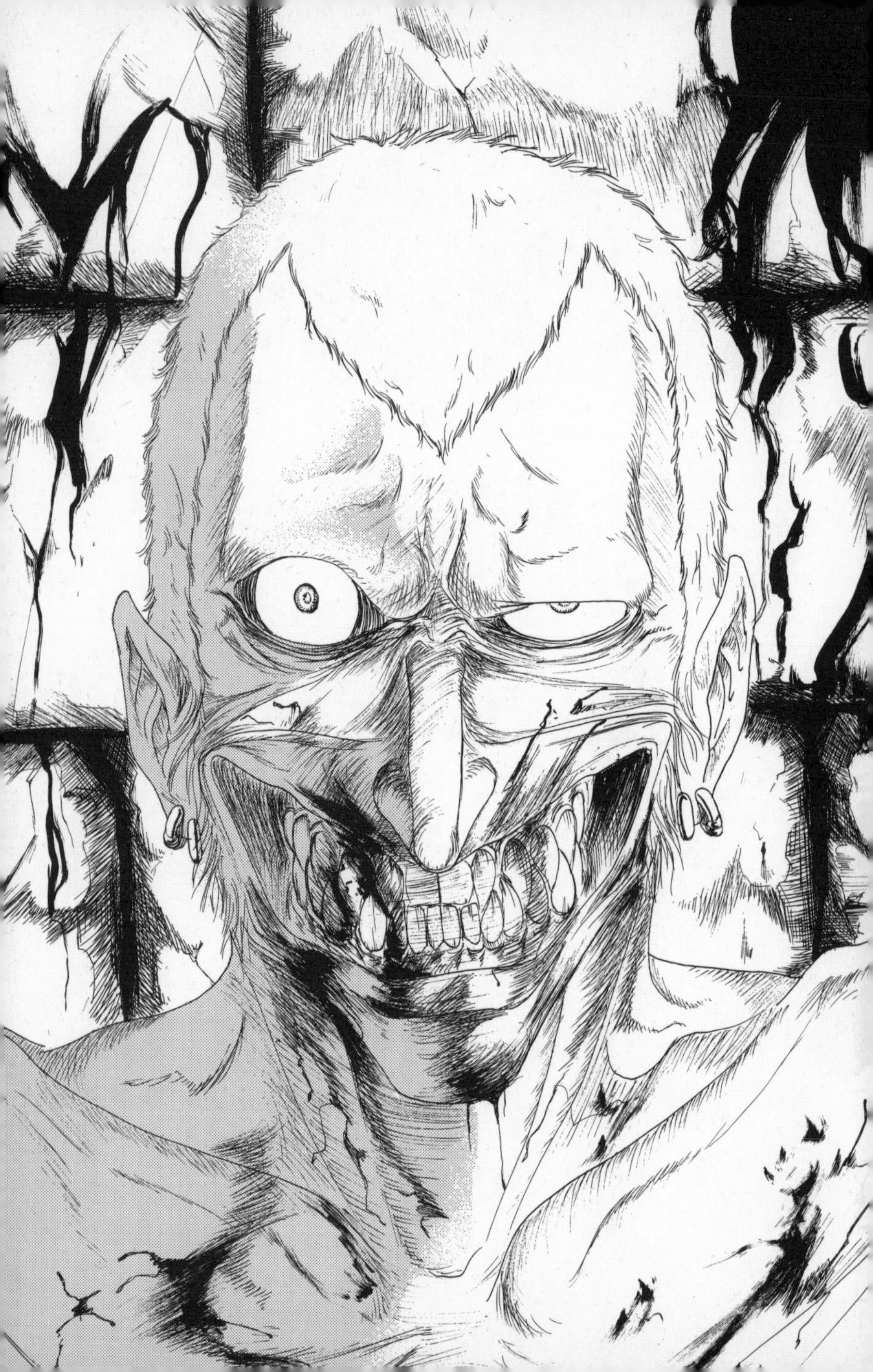

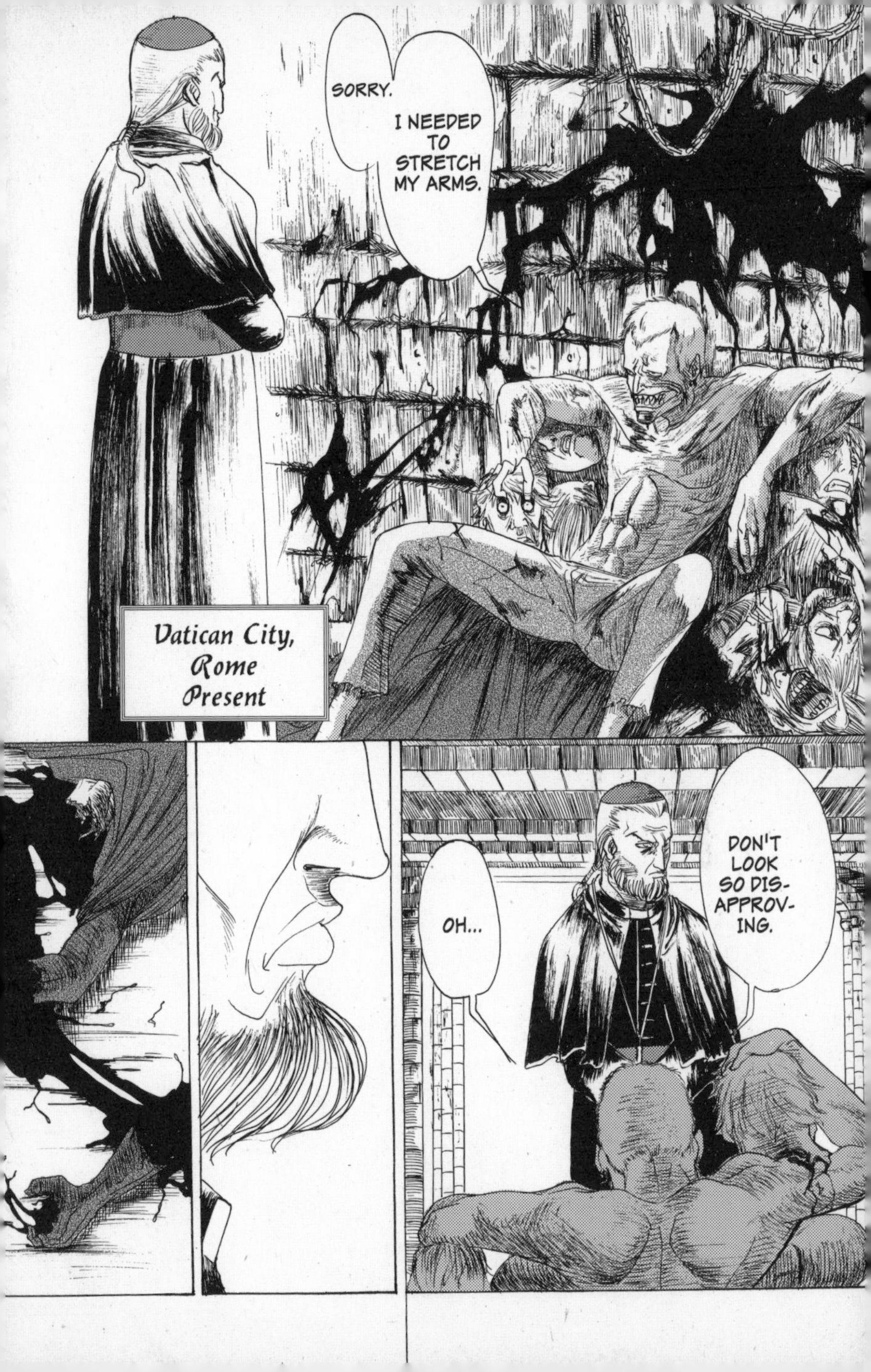
SORRY. I NEEDED TO STRETCH MY ARMS.
Vatican City, Rome Present
DON'T LOOK SO DIS-APPROV-ING.
OH...

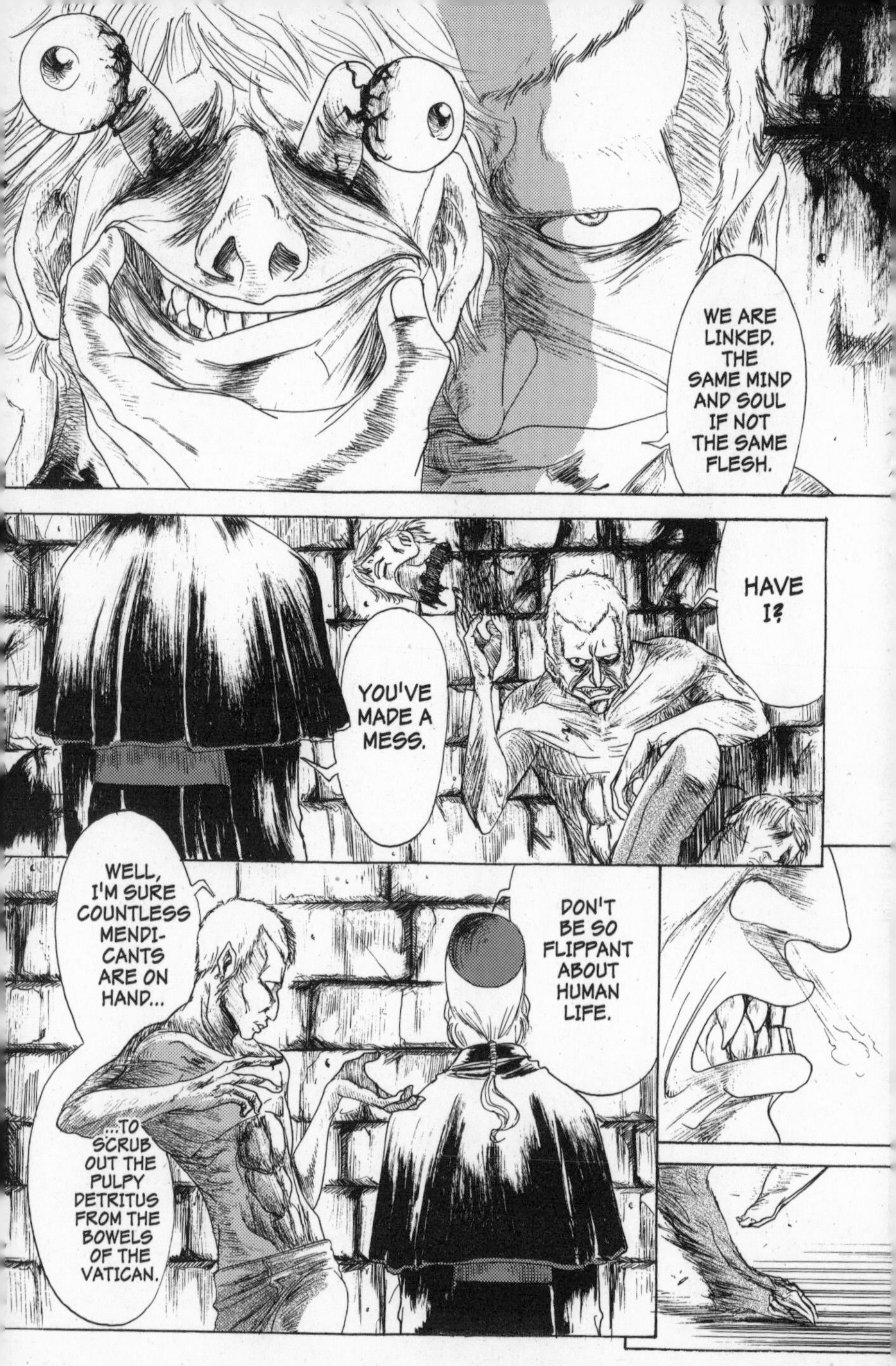
WE ARE LINKED. THE SAME MIND AND SOUL IF NOT THE SAME FLESH.
YOU'VE MADE A MESS.
HAVE I?
WELL, I'M SURE COUNTLESS MENDI-CANTS ARE ON HAND...
...TO SCRUB OUT THE PULPY DETRITUS FROM THE BOWELS OF THE VATICAN.
DON'T BE SO FLIPPANT ABOUT HUMAN LIFE.

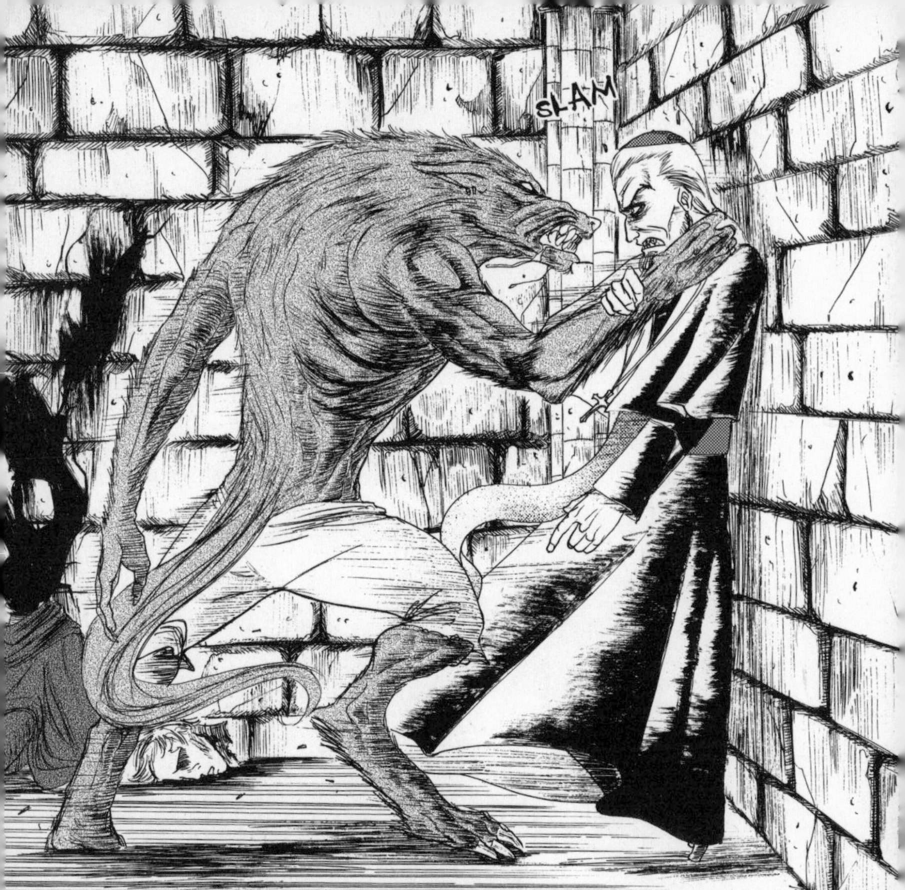
SLAM
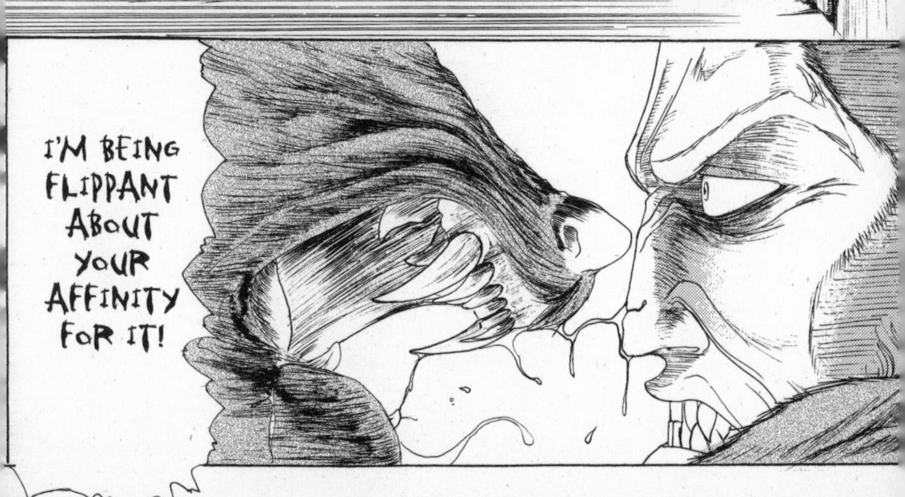
I'M BEING FLIPPANT ABOUT YOUR AFFINITY FOR IT!

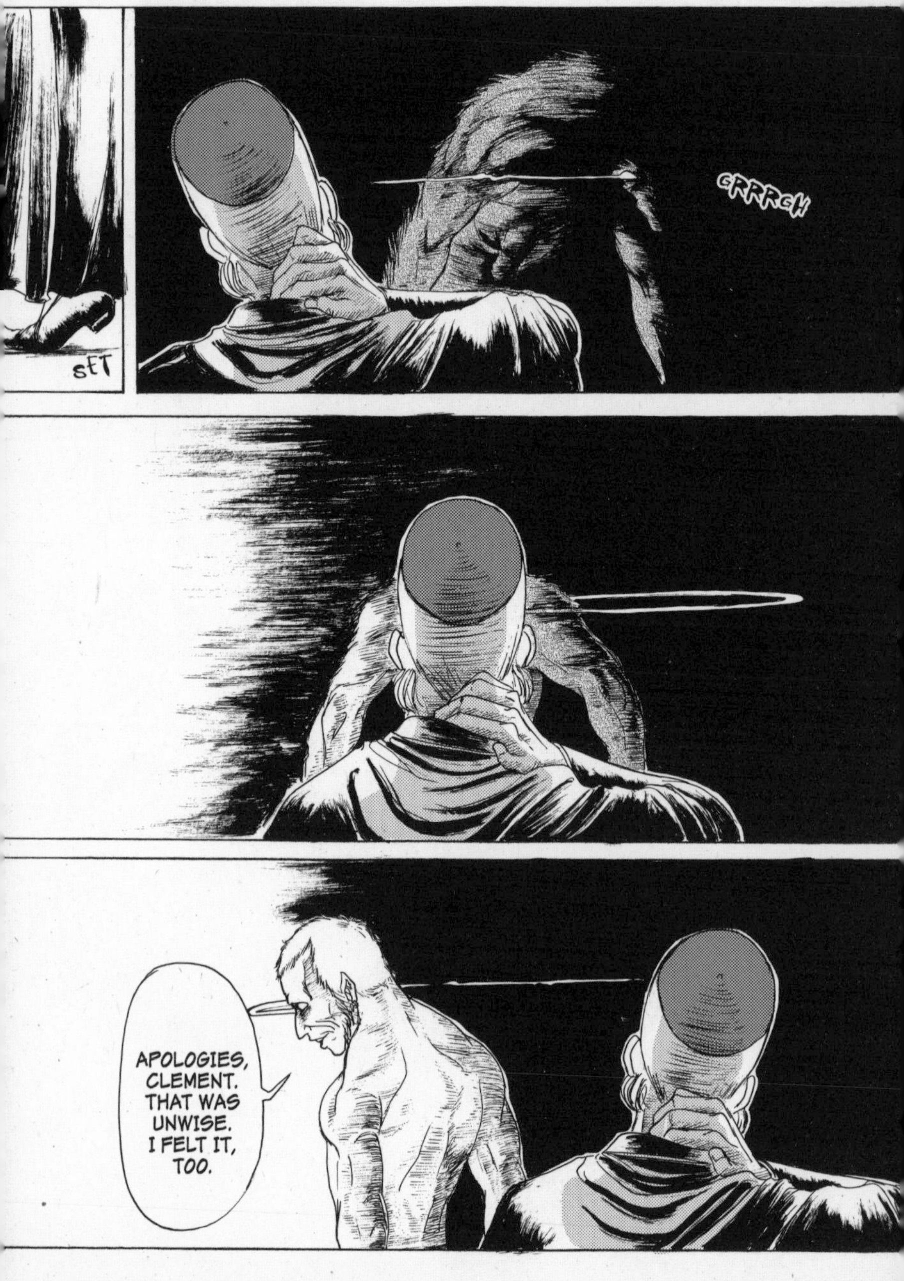
CRRRCH
sET
APOLOGIES, CLEMENT. THAT WAS UNWISE. I FELT IT, TOO.

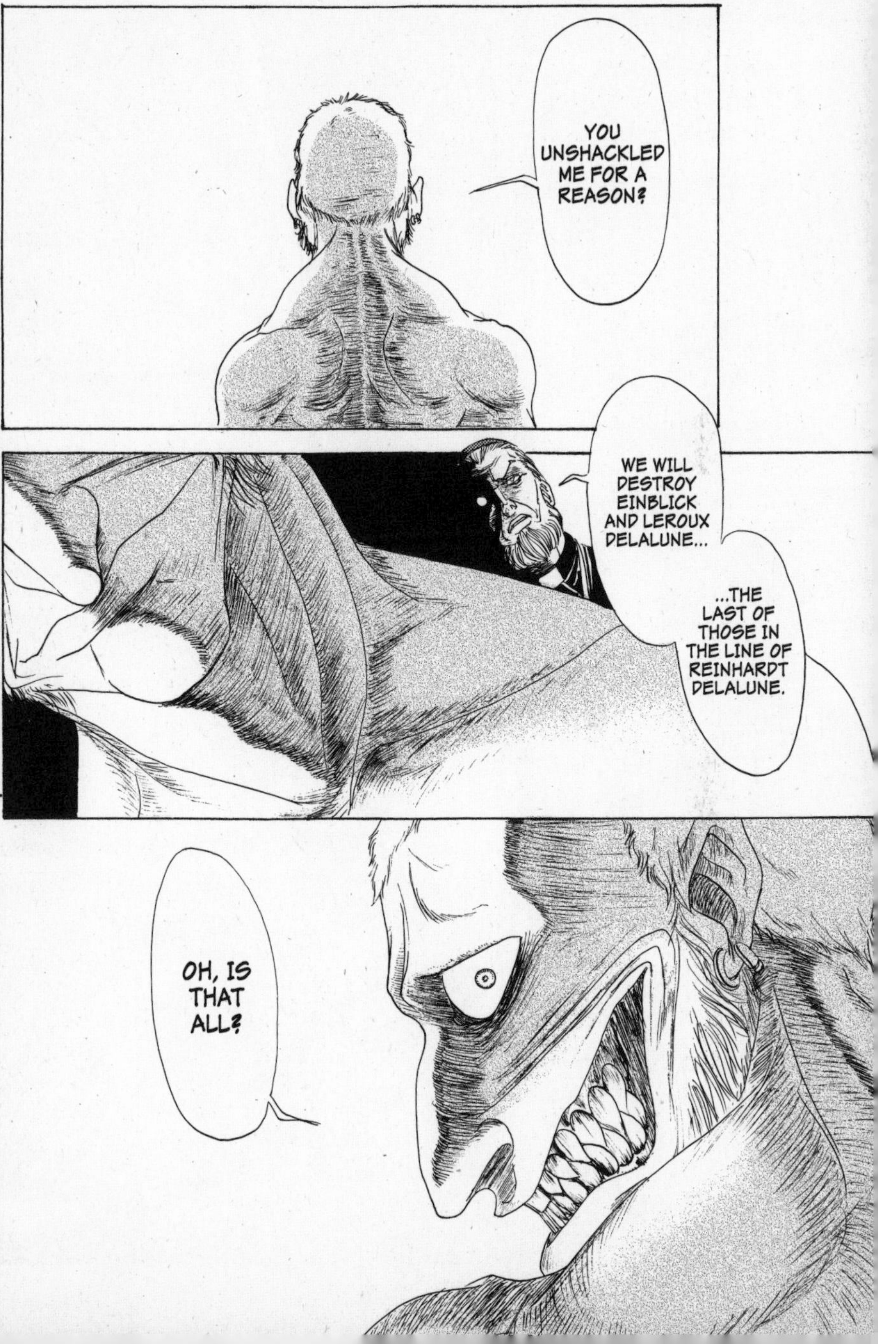
YOU UNSHACKLED ME FOR A REASON?
WE WILL DESTROY EINBLICK AND LEROUX DELALUNE...
...THE LAST OF THOSE IN THE LINE OF REINHARDT DELALUNE.
OH, IS THAT ALL?

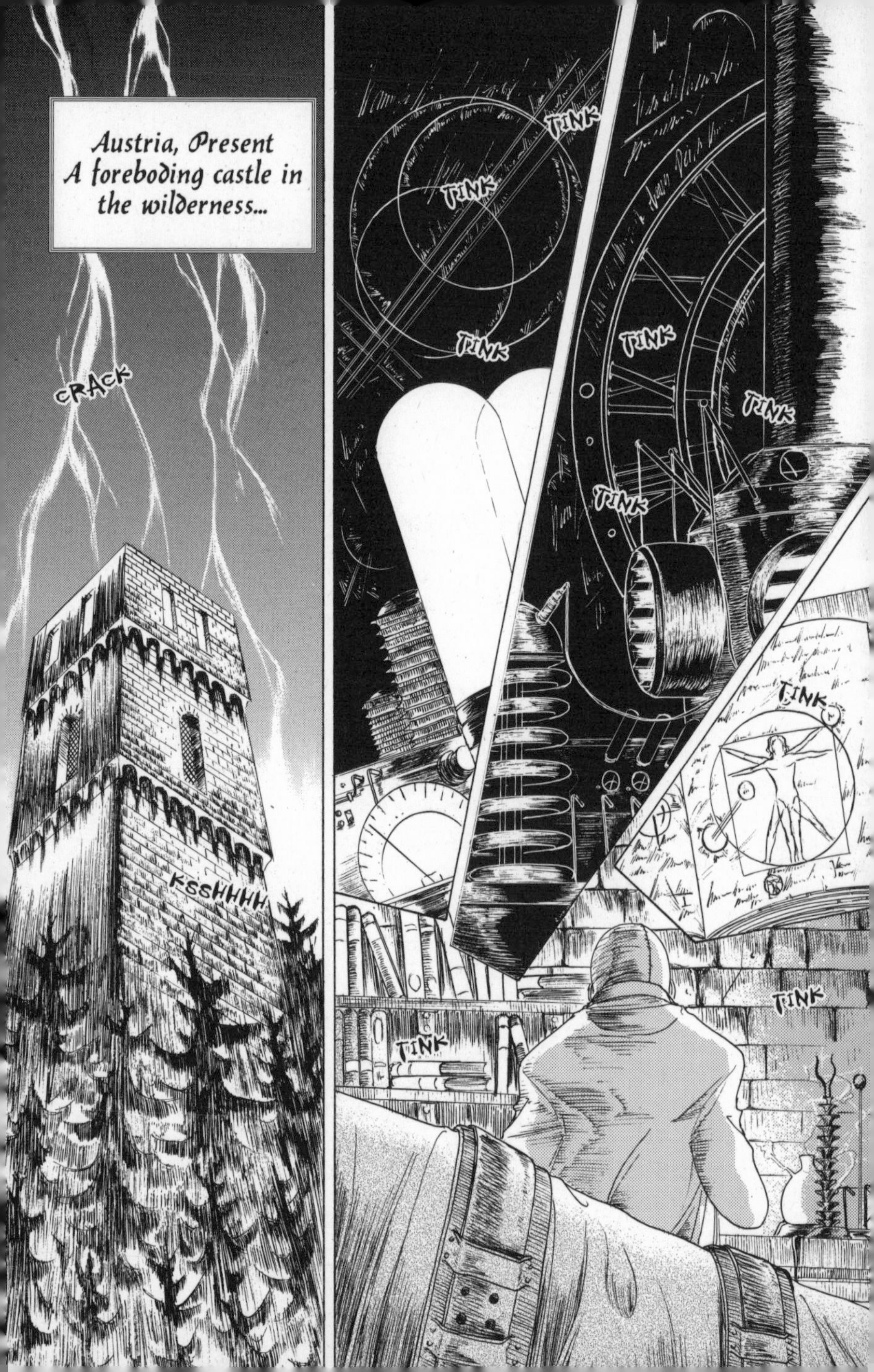
Austria, Present
A foreboding castle in the wilderness...
CRACK
KSSHHHH
TINK
TINK
TINK
TINK
TINK
TINK
TINK
TINK
TINK

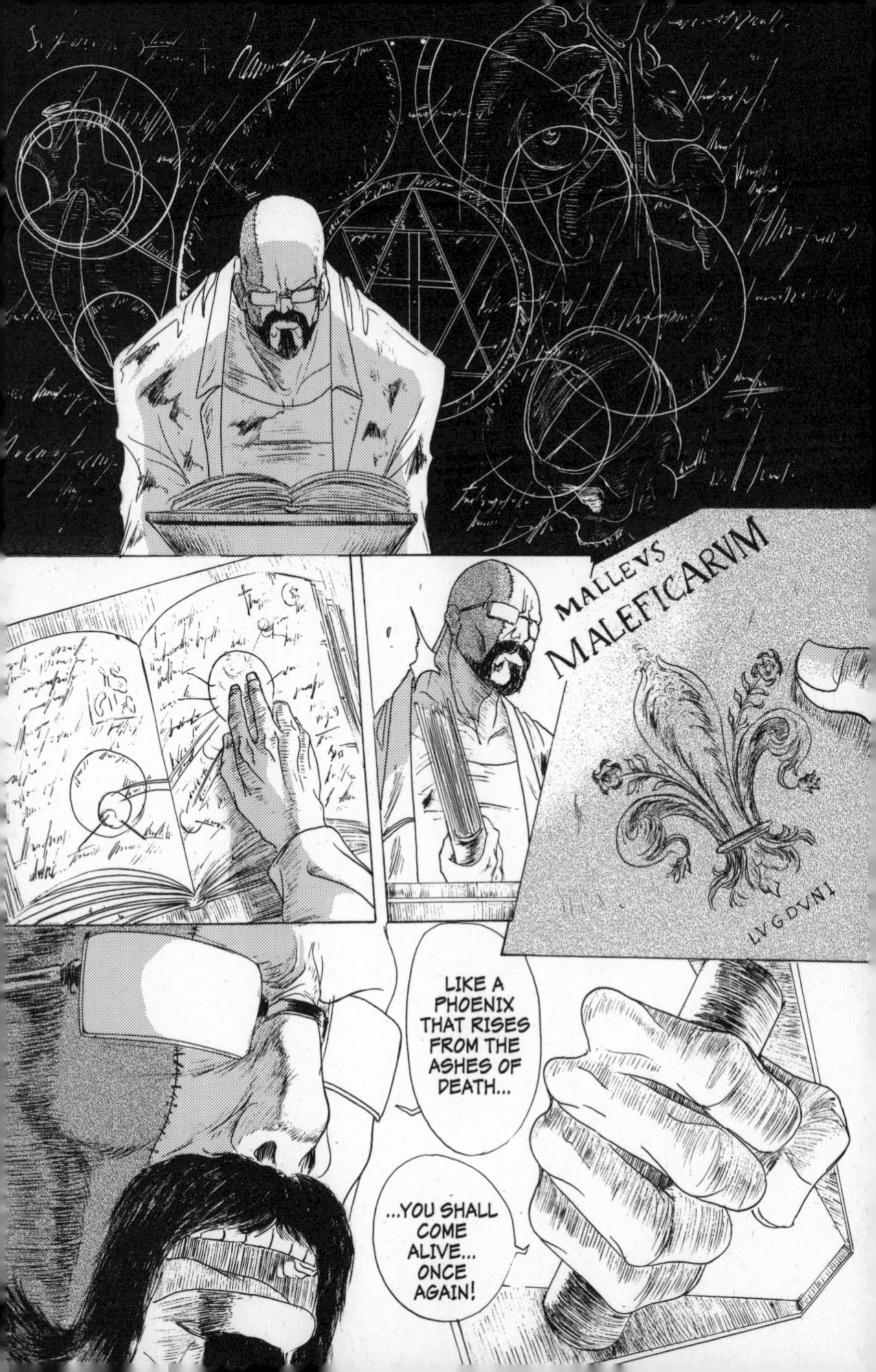
MALLEVS
MALEFICARVM
LVGDVNI
LIKE A PHOENIX THAT RISES FROM THE ASHES OF DEATH...
...YOU SHALL COME ALIVE... ONCE AGAIN!

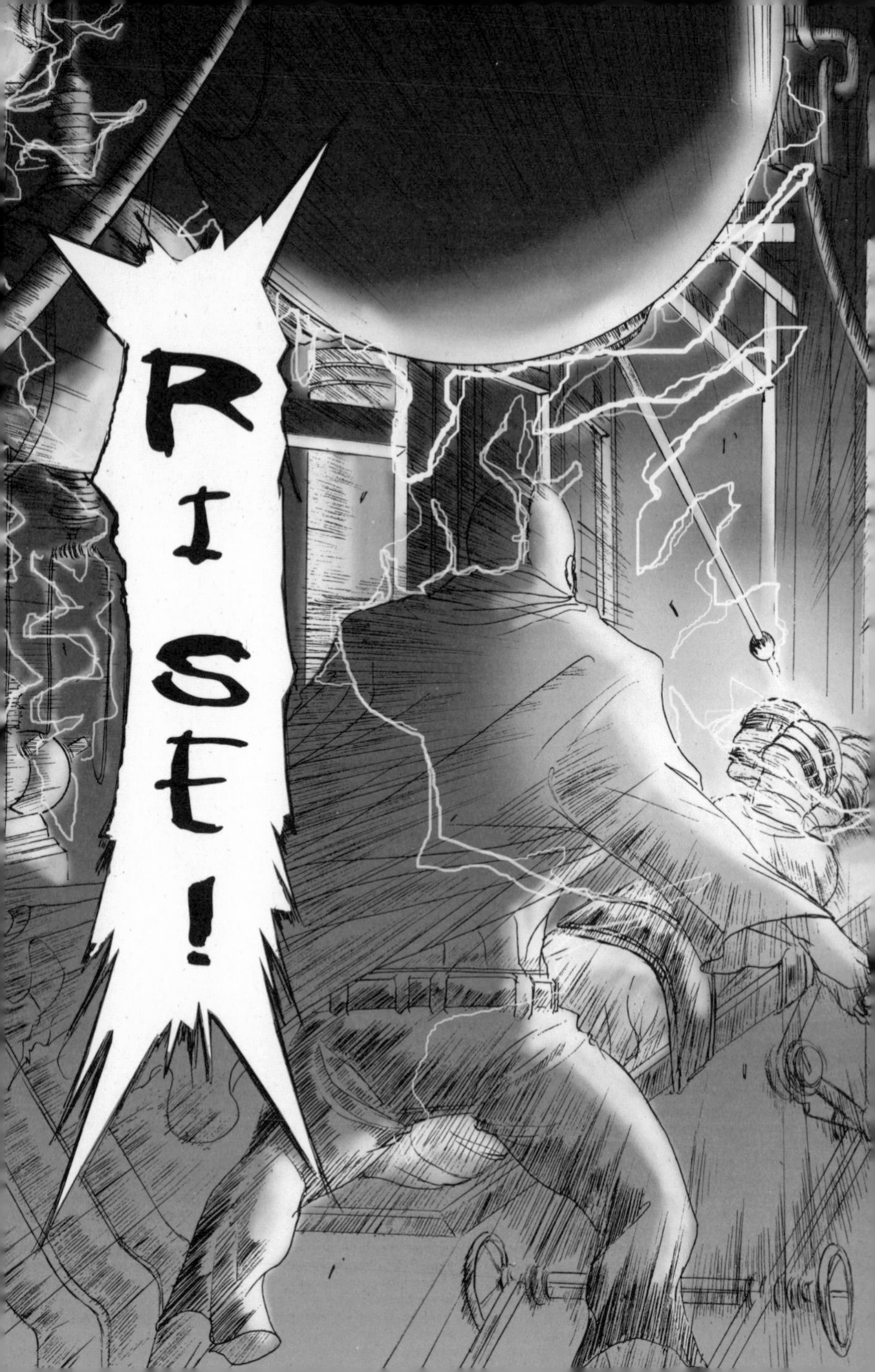
RISE!

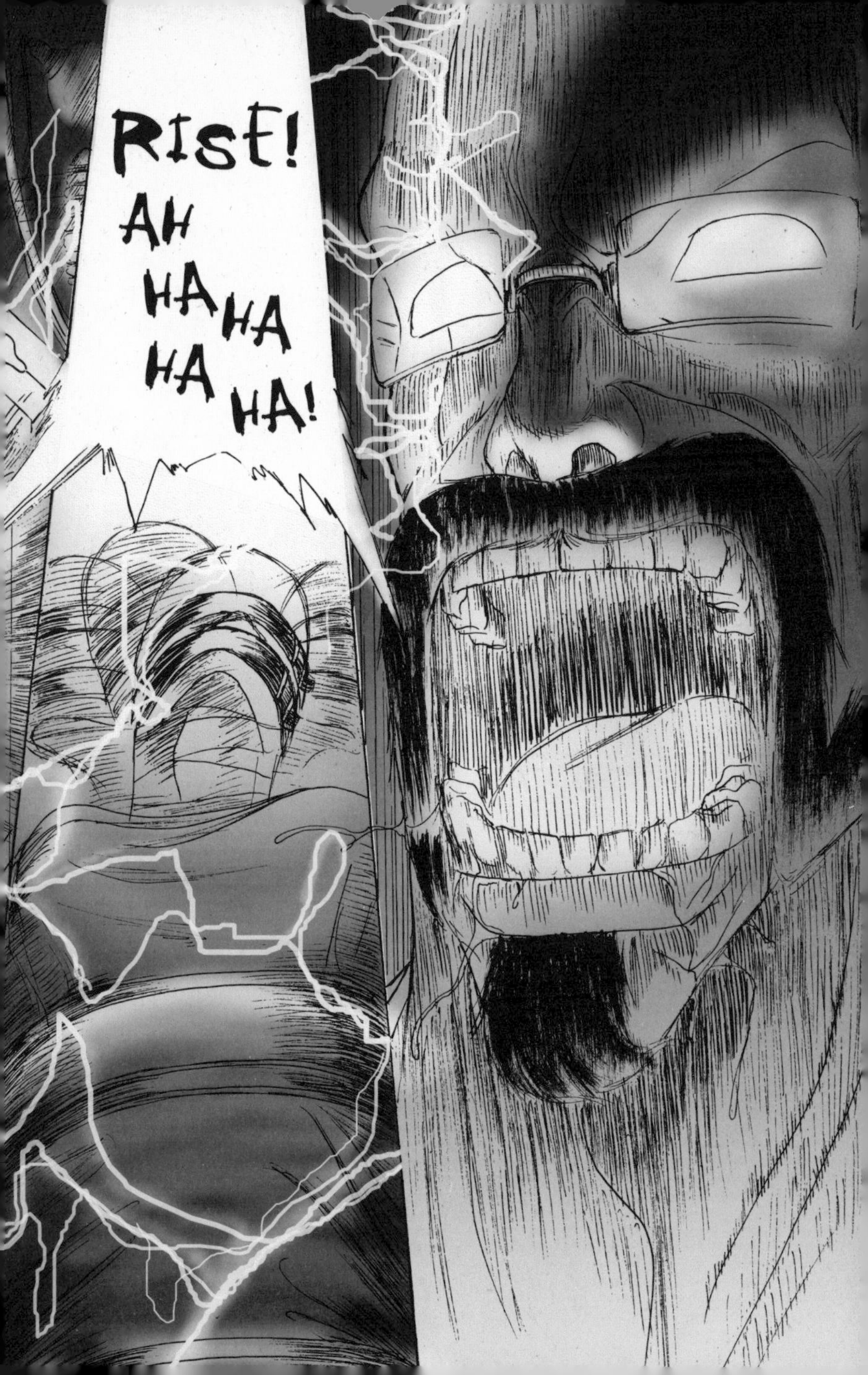
RISE!
AH HA HA HA HA HA!

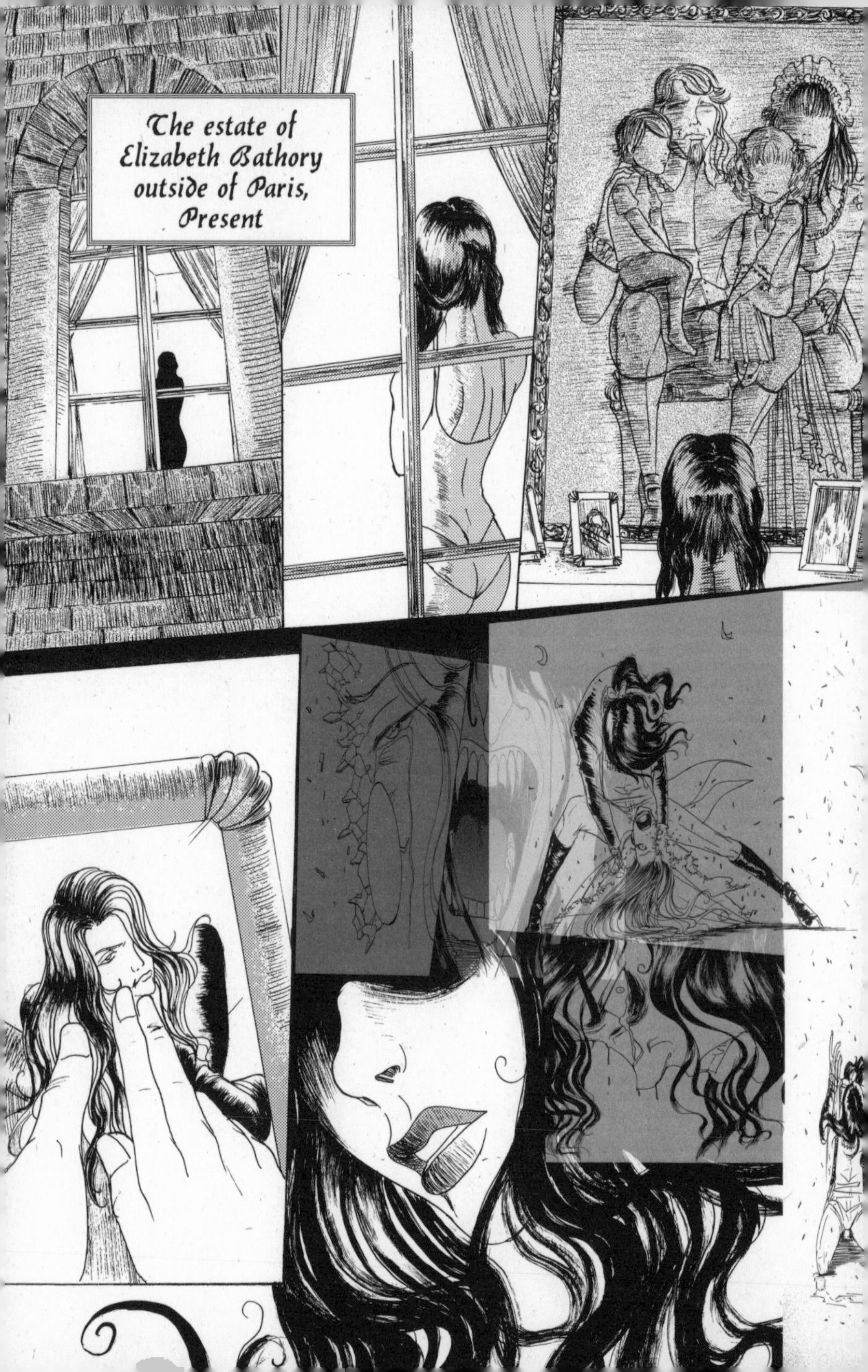
The estate of Elizabeth Bathory outside of Paris, Present

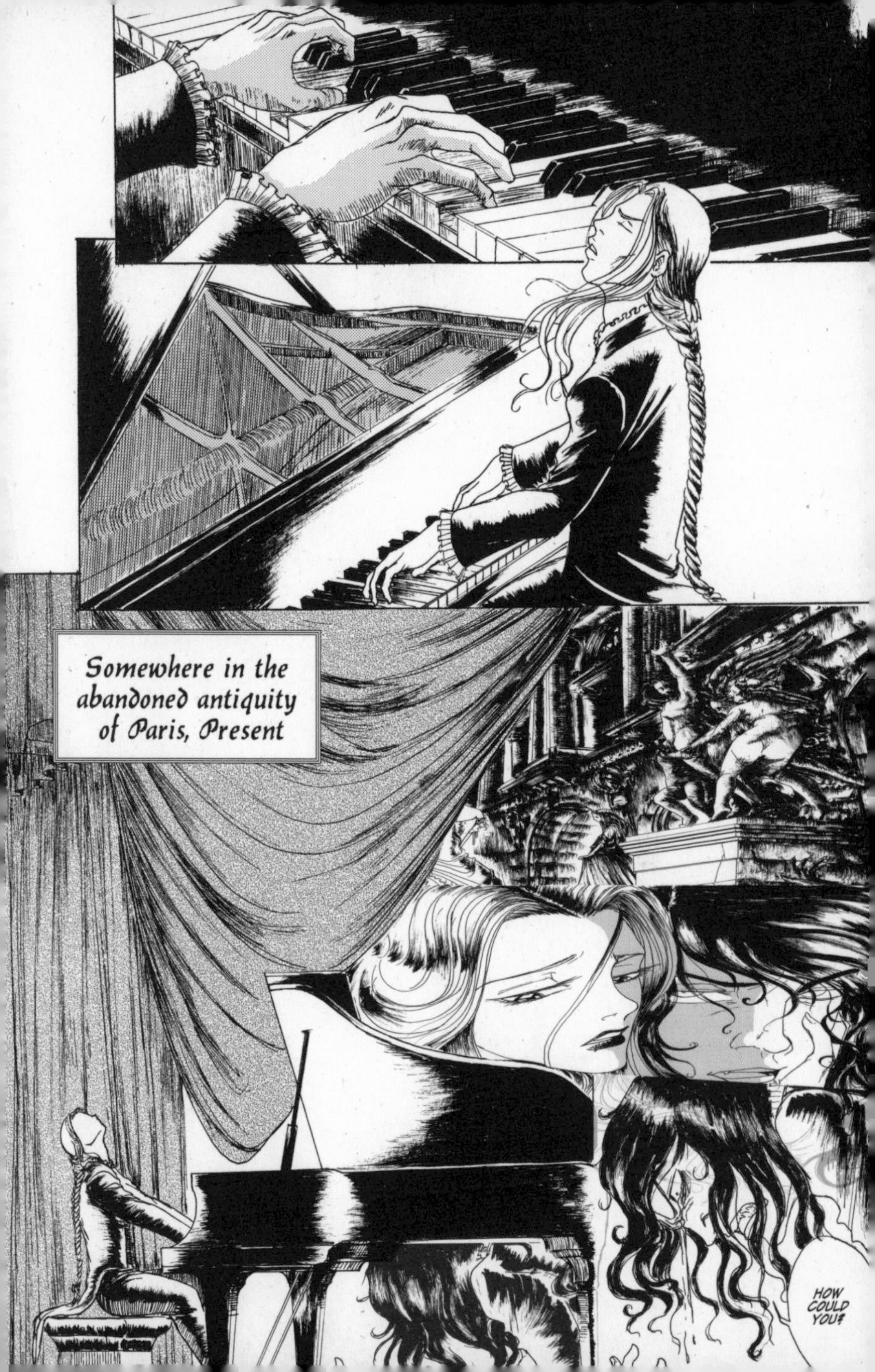
Somewhere in the abandoned antiquity of Paris, Present
HOW COULD YOU?

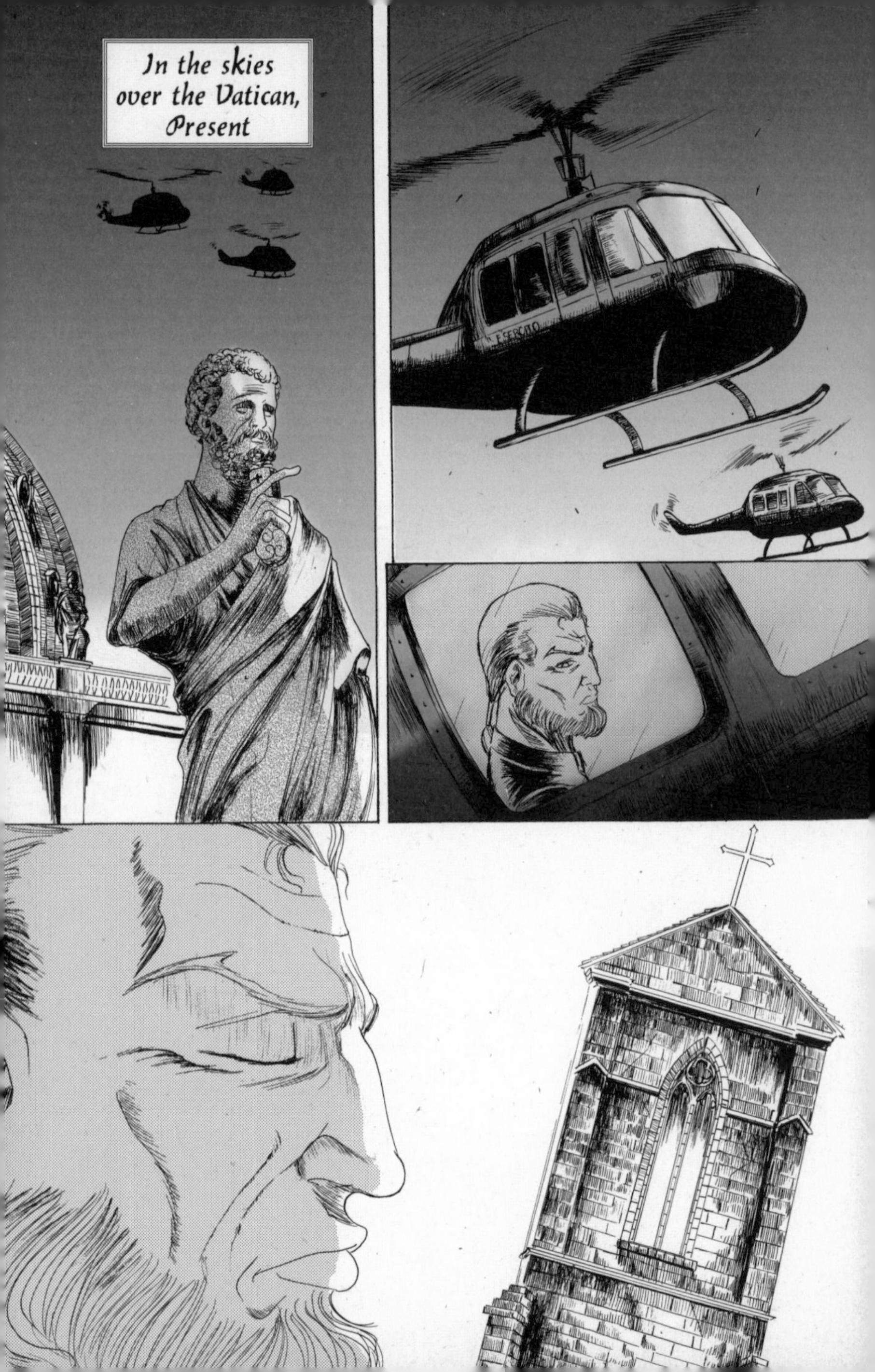
In the skies over the Vatican, Present

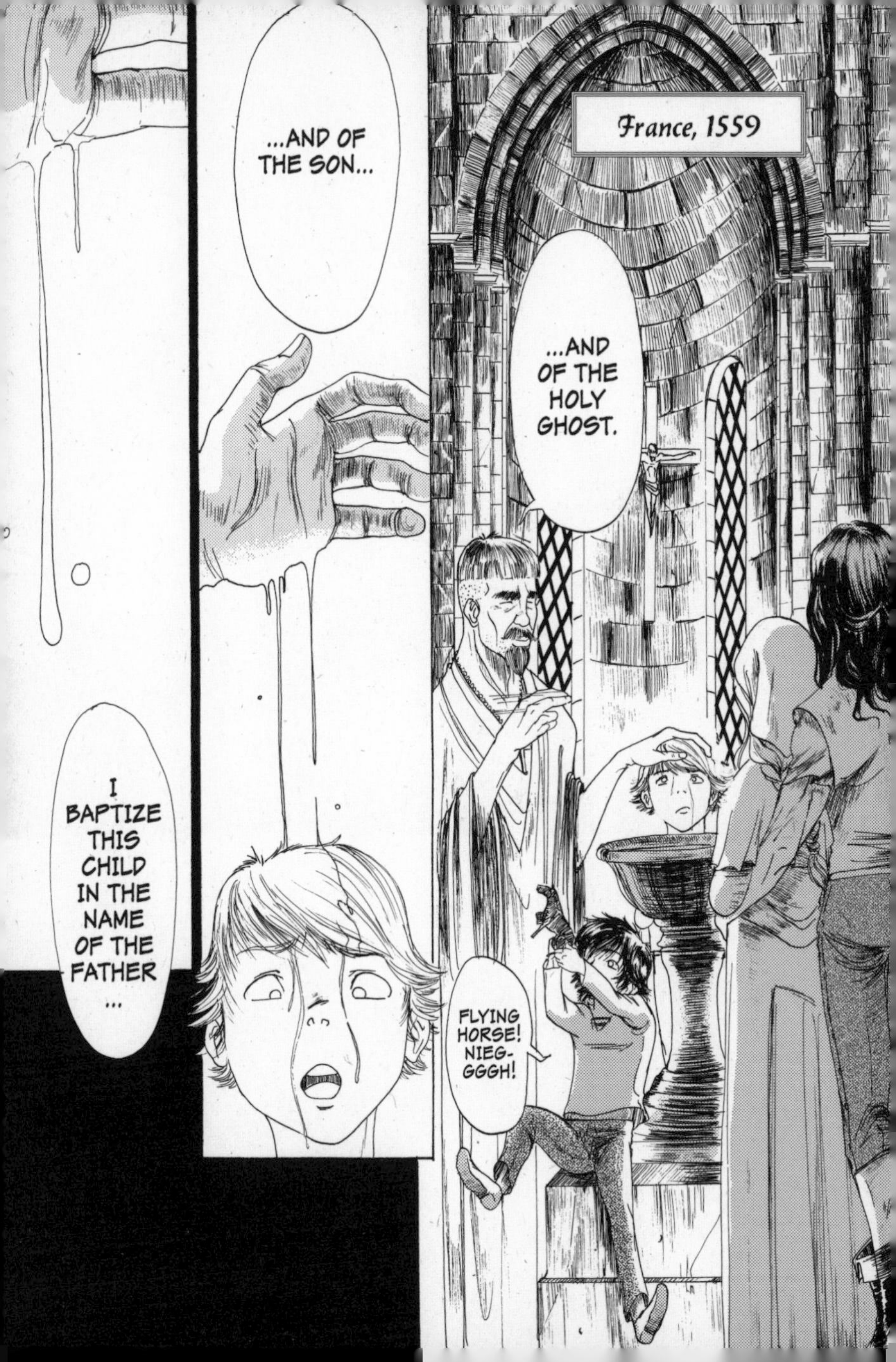
I BAPTIZE THIS CHILD IN THE NAME OF THE FATHER ...
...AND OF THE SON...
France, 1559
...AND OF THE HOLY GHOST.
FLYING HORSE! NIEG-GGGH!

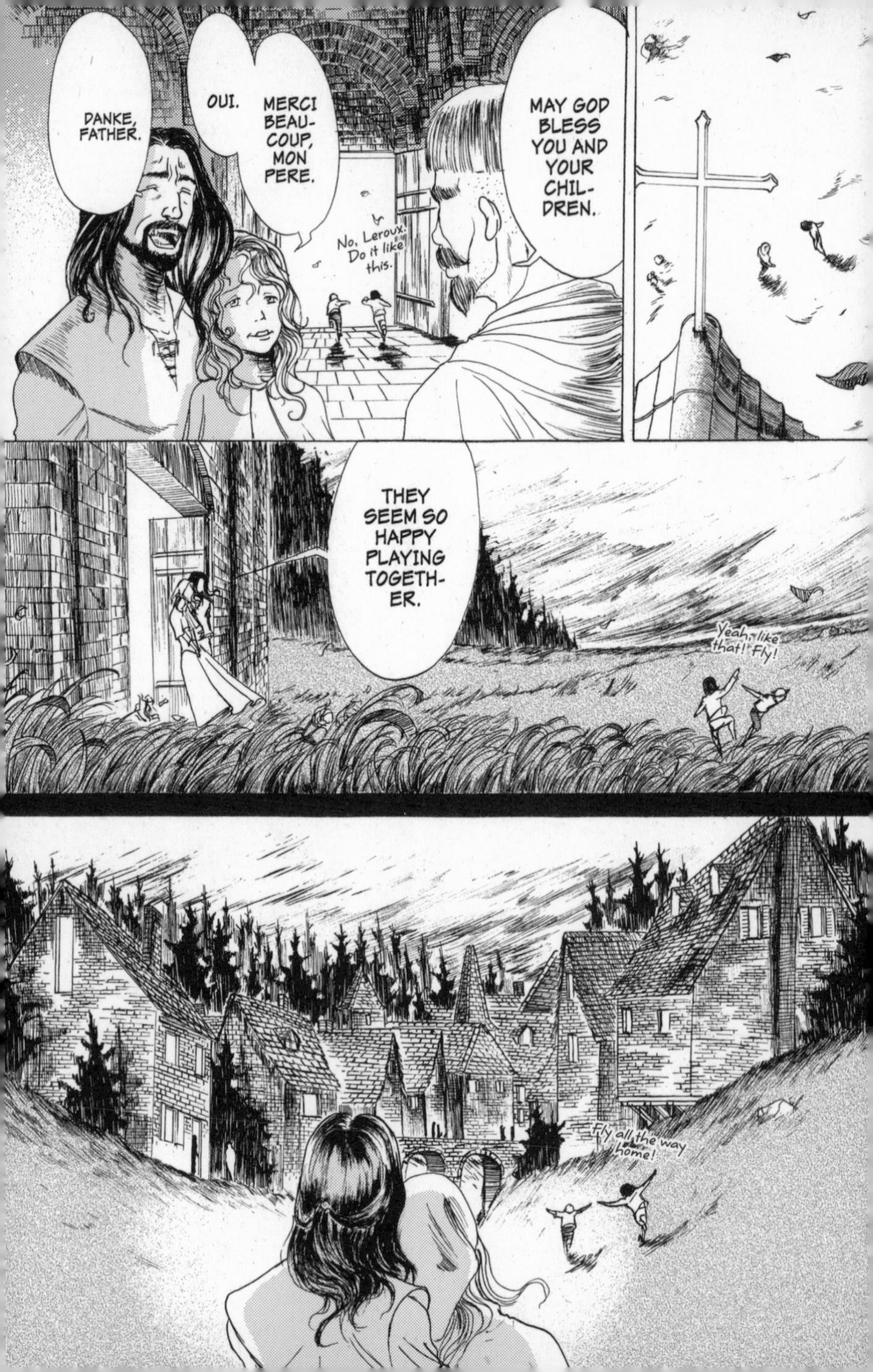
MAY GOD BLESS YOU AND YOUR CHILDREN.
MERCI BEAUCOUP, MON PERE.
OUI.
DANKE, FATHER.
No, Leroux. Do it like this.
Yeah, like that! Fly!
THEY SEEM SO HAPPY PLAYING TOGETHER.
Fly all the way home!

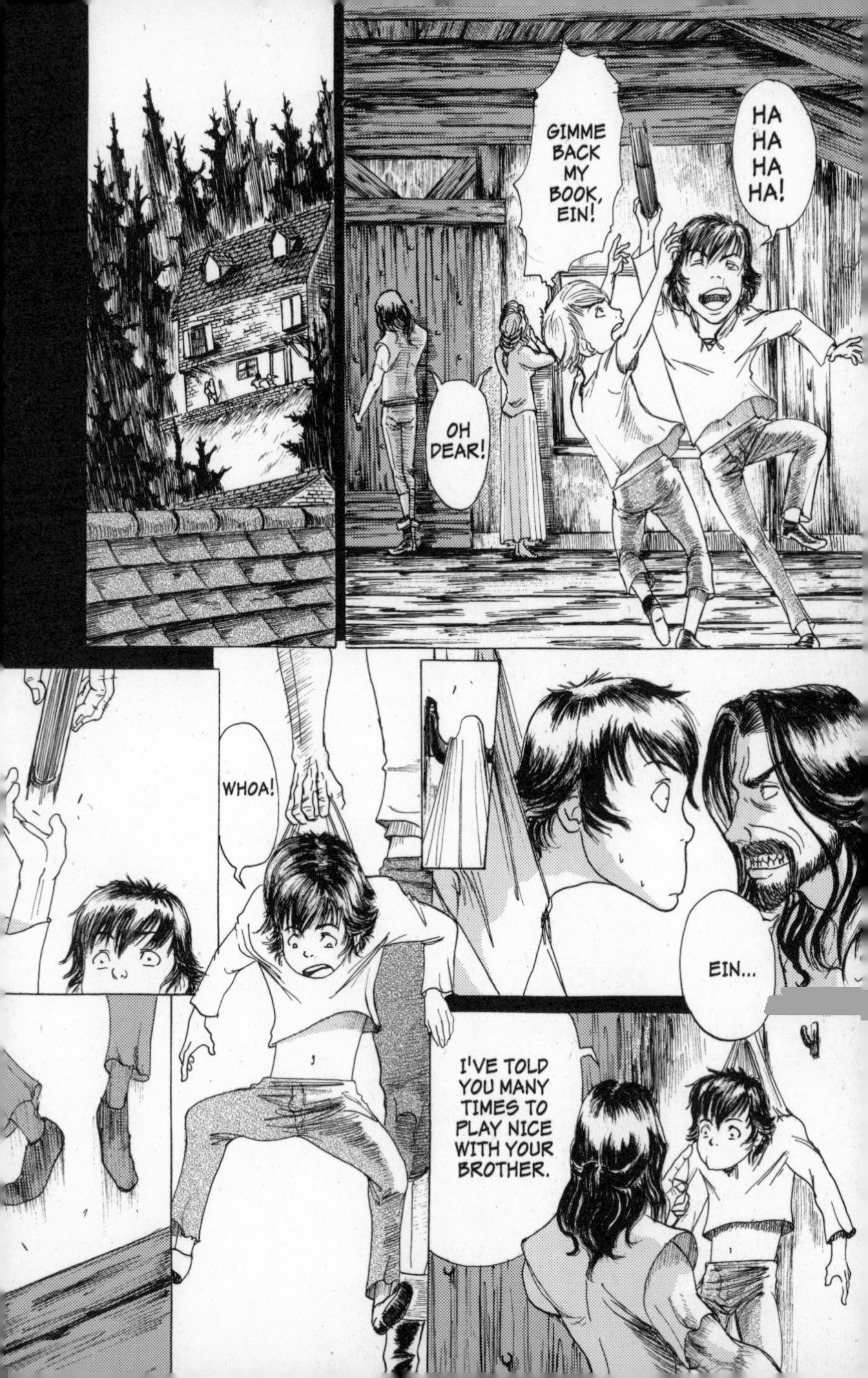
GIMME BACK MY BOOK, EIN!
HA HA HA HA!
OH DEAR!
WHOA!
EIN...
I'VE TOLD YOU MANY TIMES TO PLAY NICE WITH YOUR BROTHER.

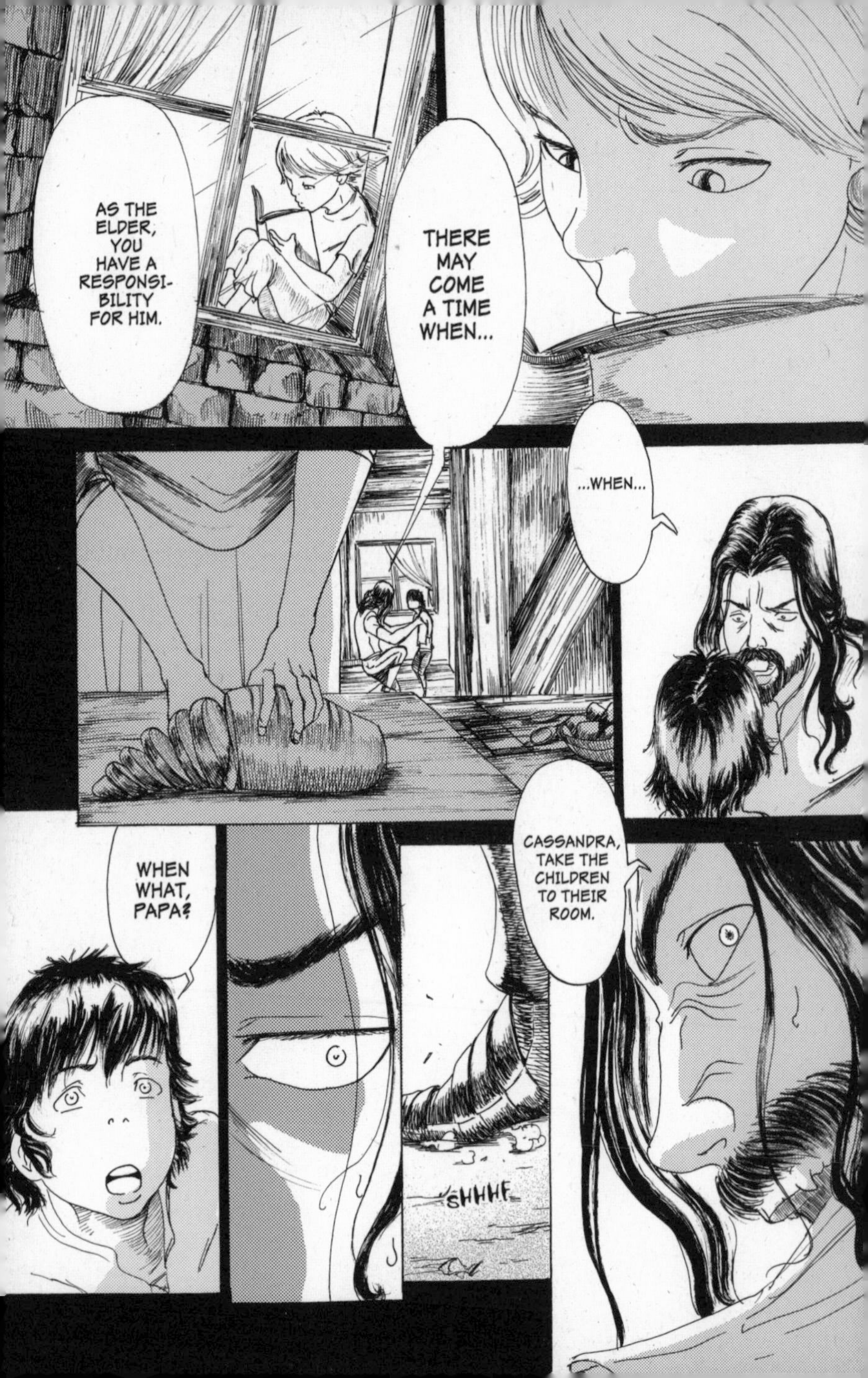
AS THE ELDER, YOU HAVE A RESPONSI-BILITY FOR HIM.
THERE MAY COME A TIME WHEN...
...WHEN...
WHEN WHAT, PAPA?
SHHHF
CASSANDRA, TAKE THE CHILDREN TO THEIR ROOM.

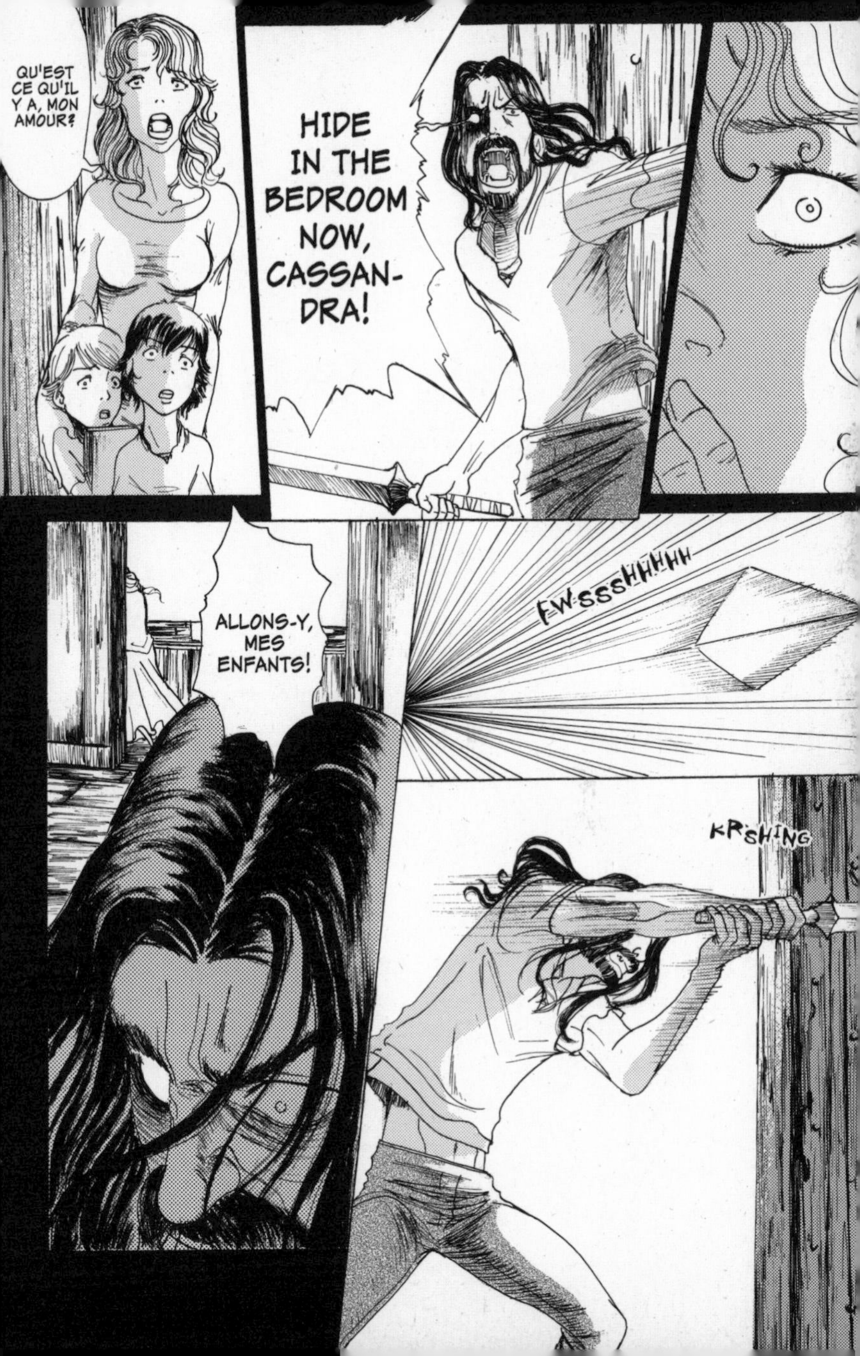
QU'EST CE QU'IL Y A, MON AMOUR?
HIDE IN THE BEDROOM NOW, CASSAN-DRA!
ALLONS-Y, MES ENFANTS!
FWSSSHHHHH
KRSHING

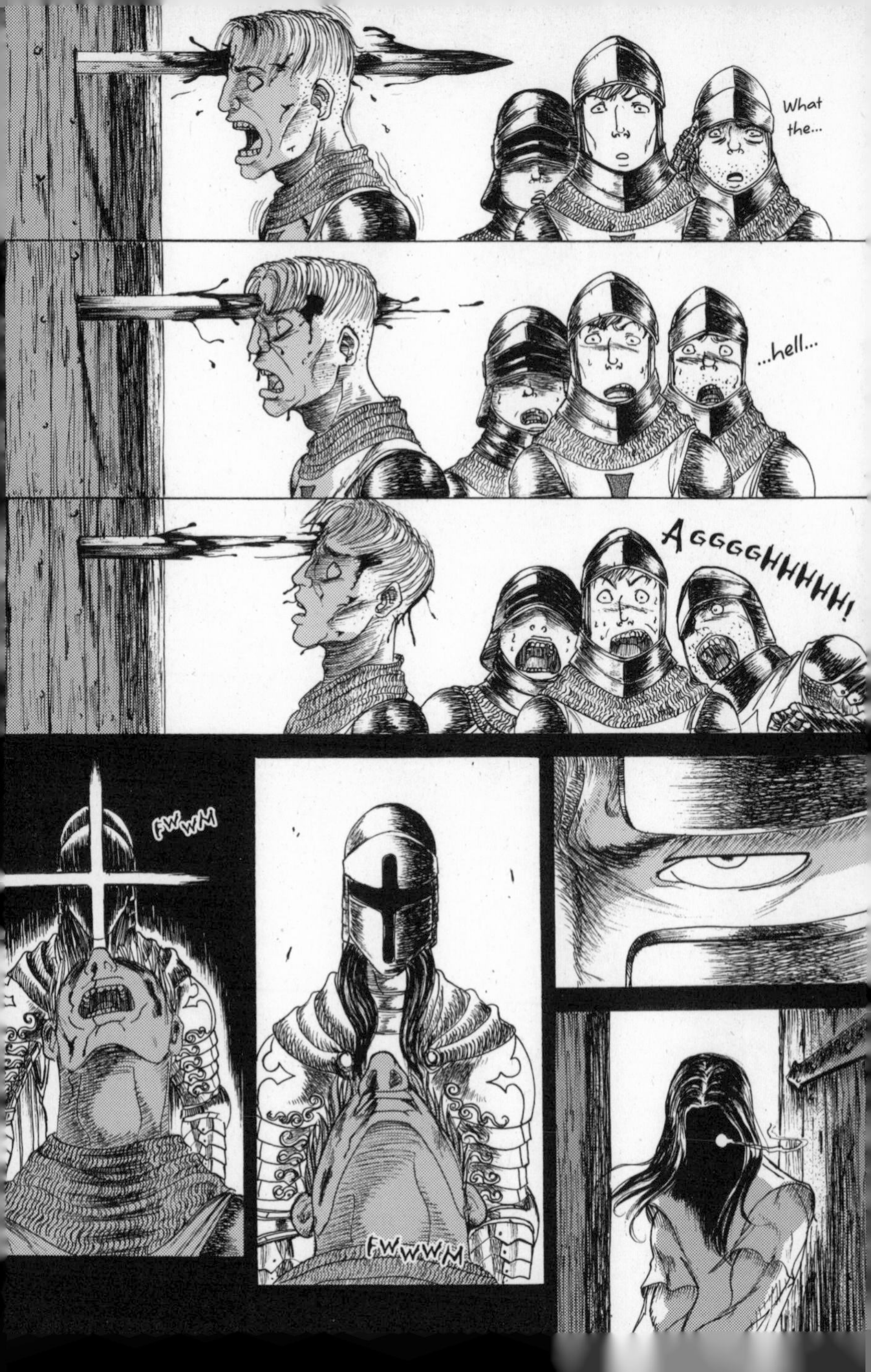
What the...
...hell...
AGGGGHHHHHH!
FWWM
FWWWM

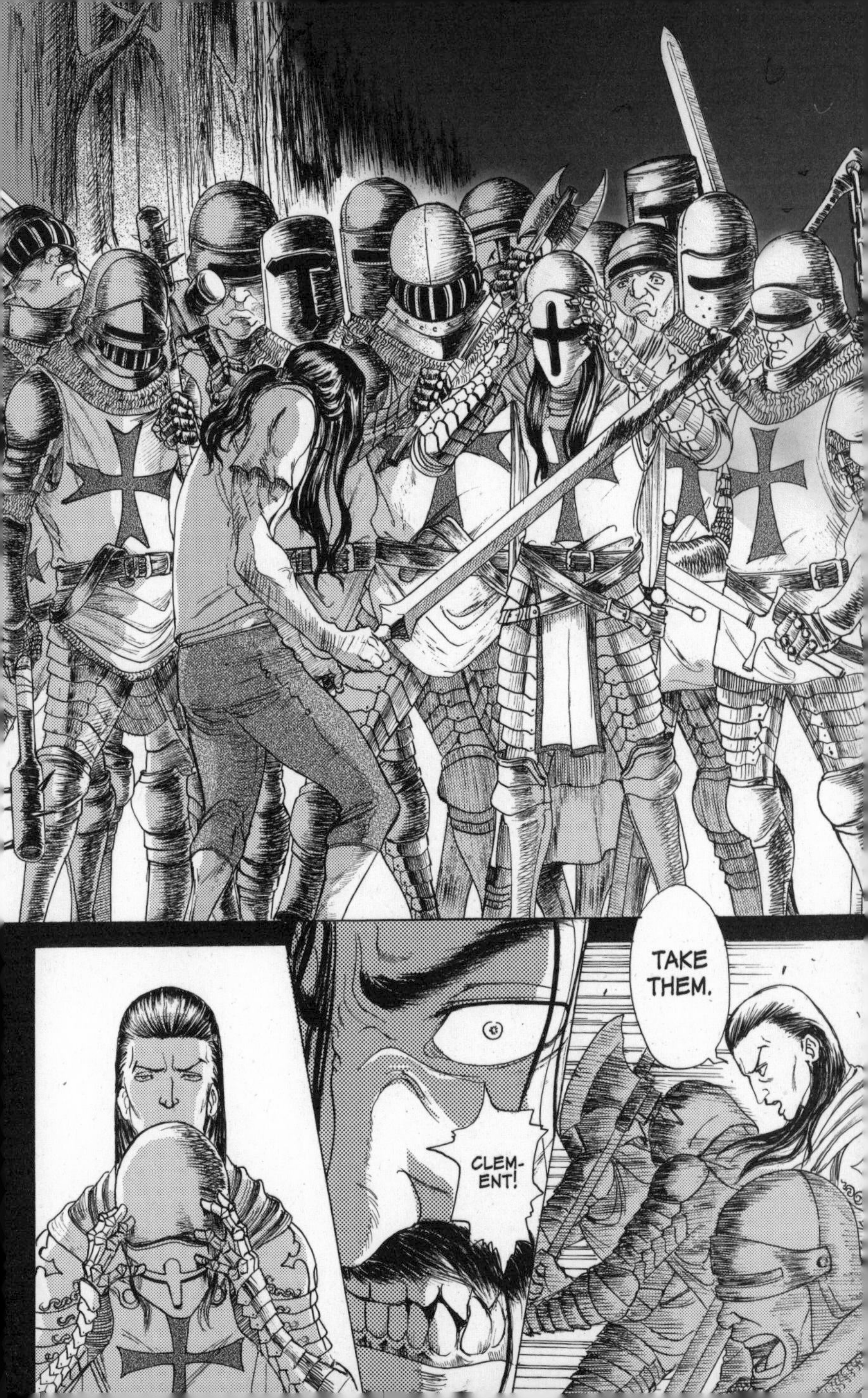
TAKE THEM.
CLEM- ENT!

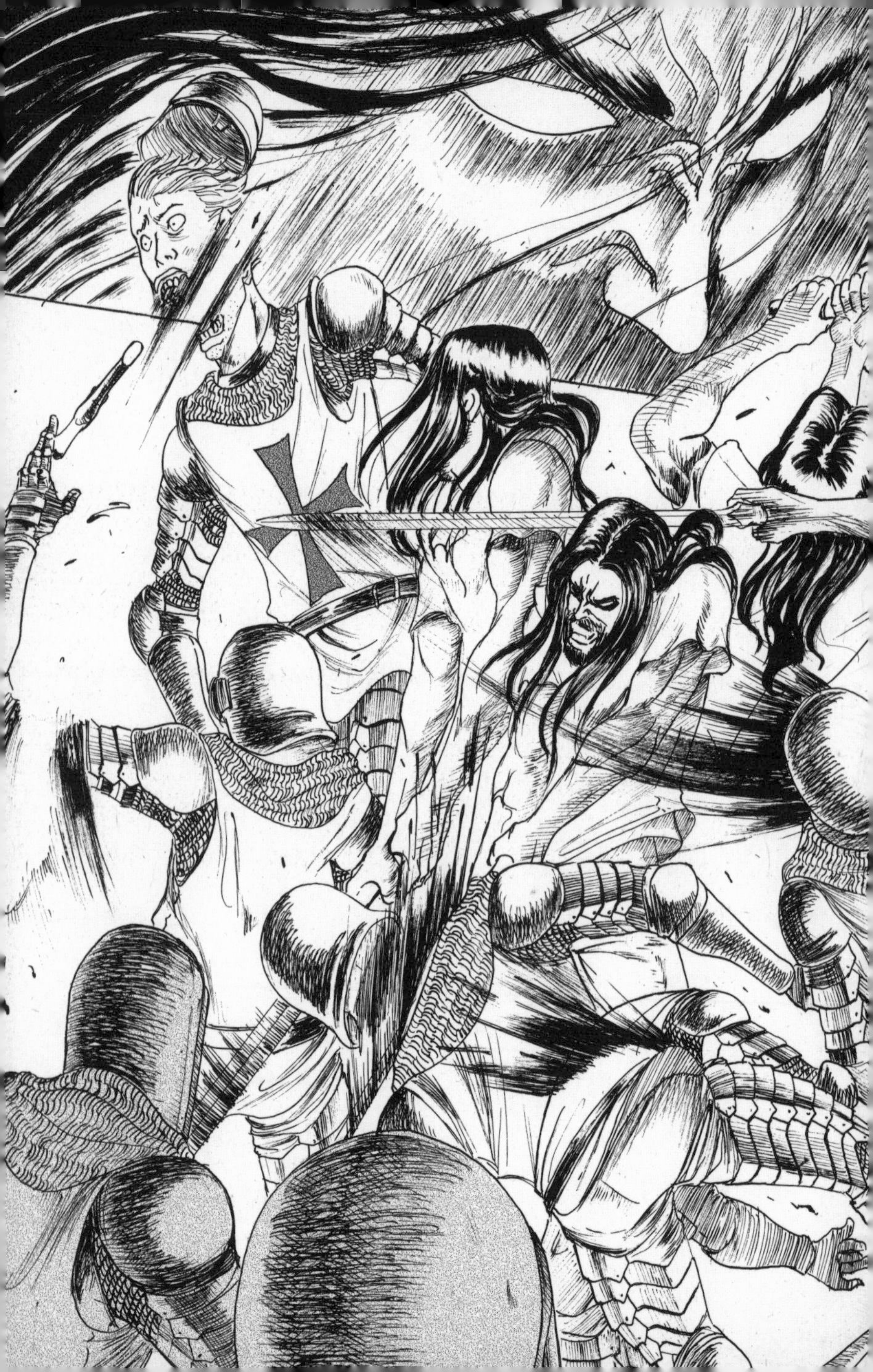

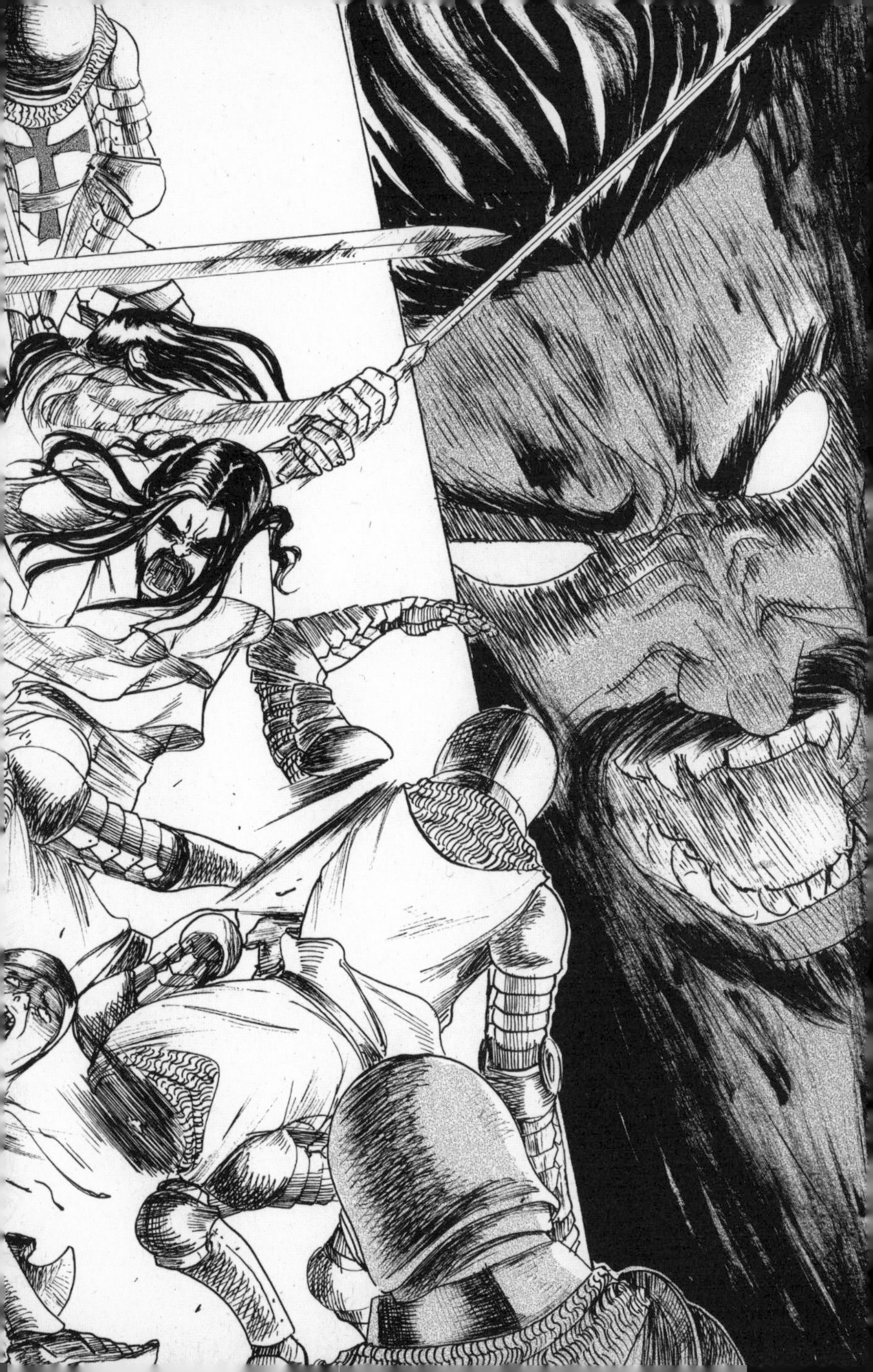

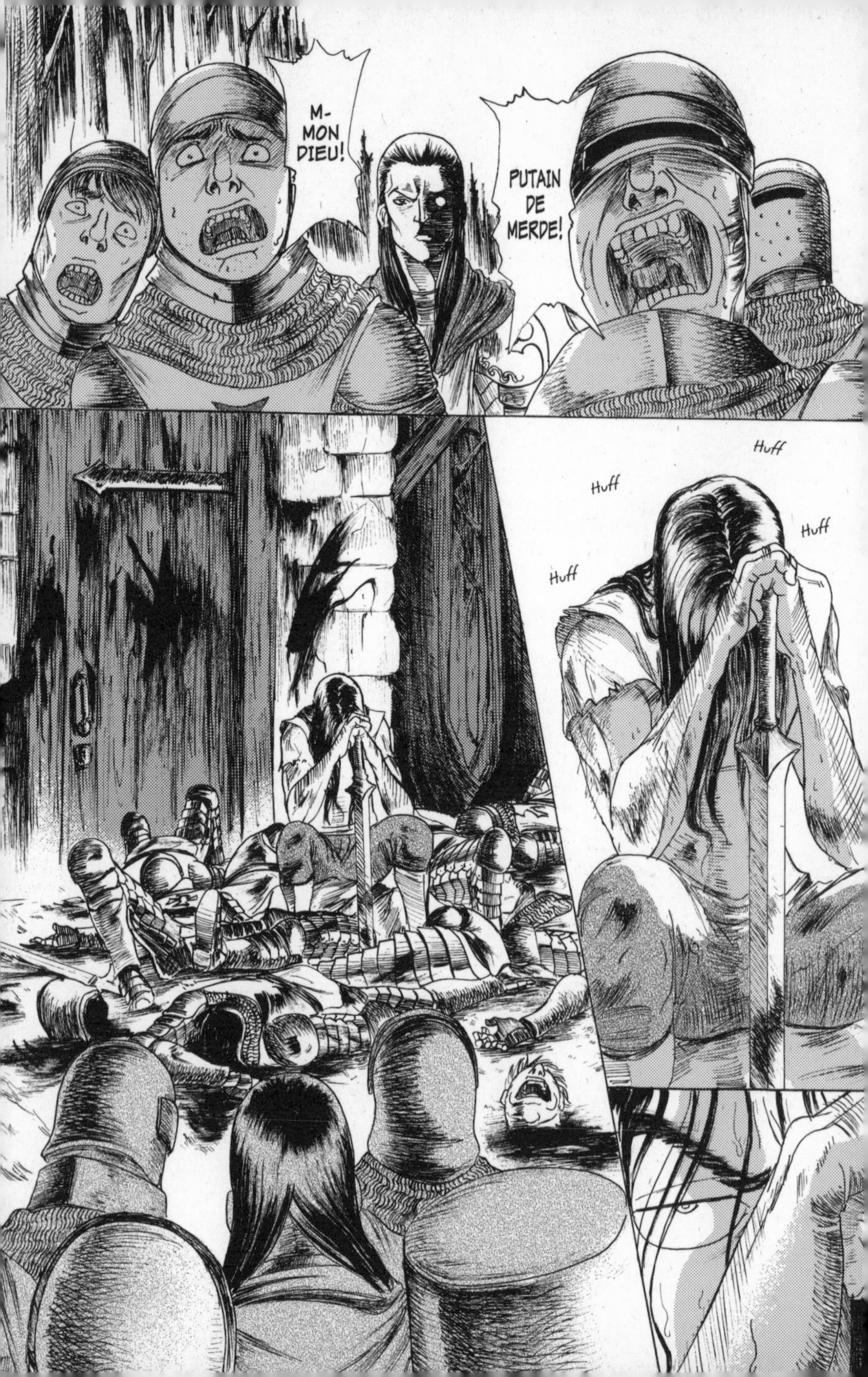
PUTAIN DE MERDE!
M-MON DIEU!
Huff
Huff
Huff
Huff

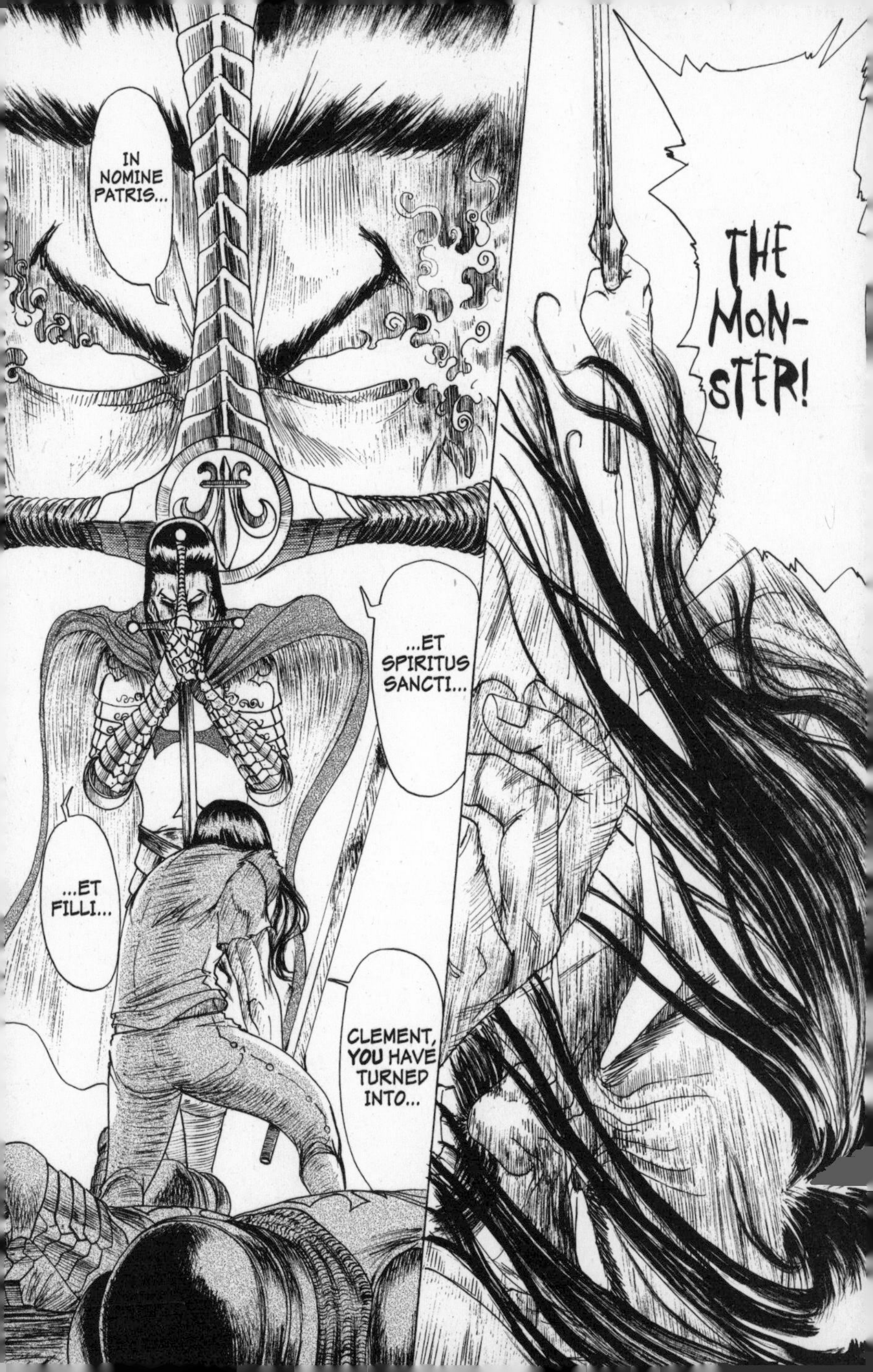

IN NOMINE PATRIS...
...ET FILLI...
...ET SPIRITUS SANCTI...
CLEMENT, YOU HAVE TURNED INTO...
THE MONSTER!

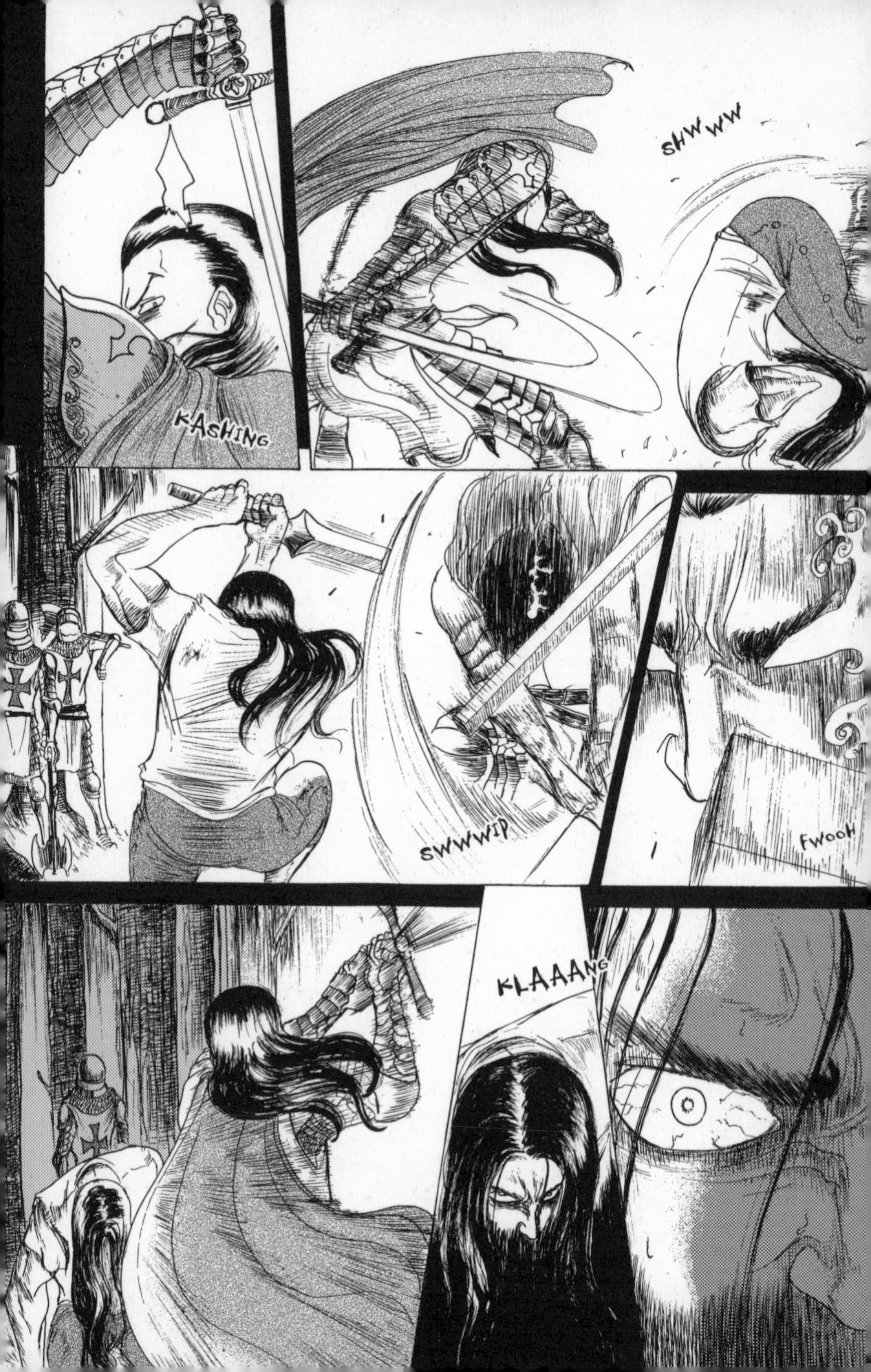
SHWWW
KASHING
FWOOH
SWWWIP
KLAAANG

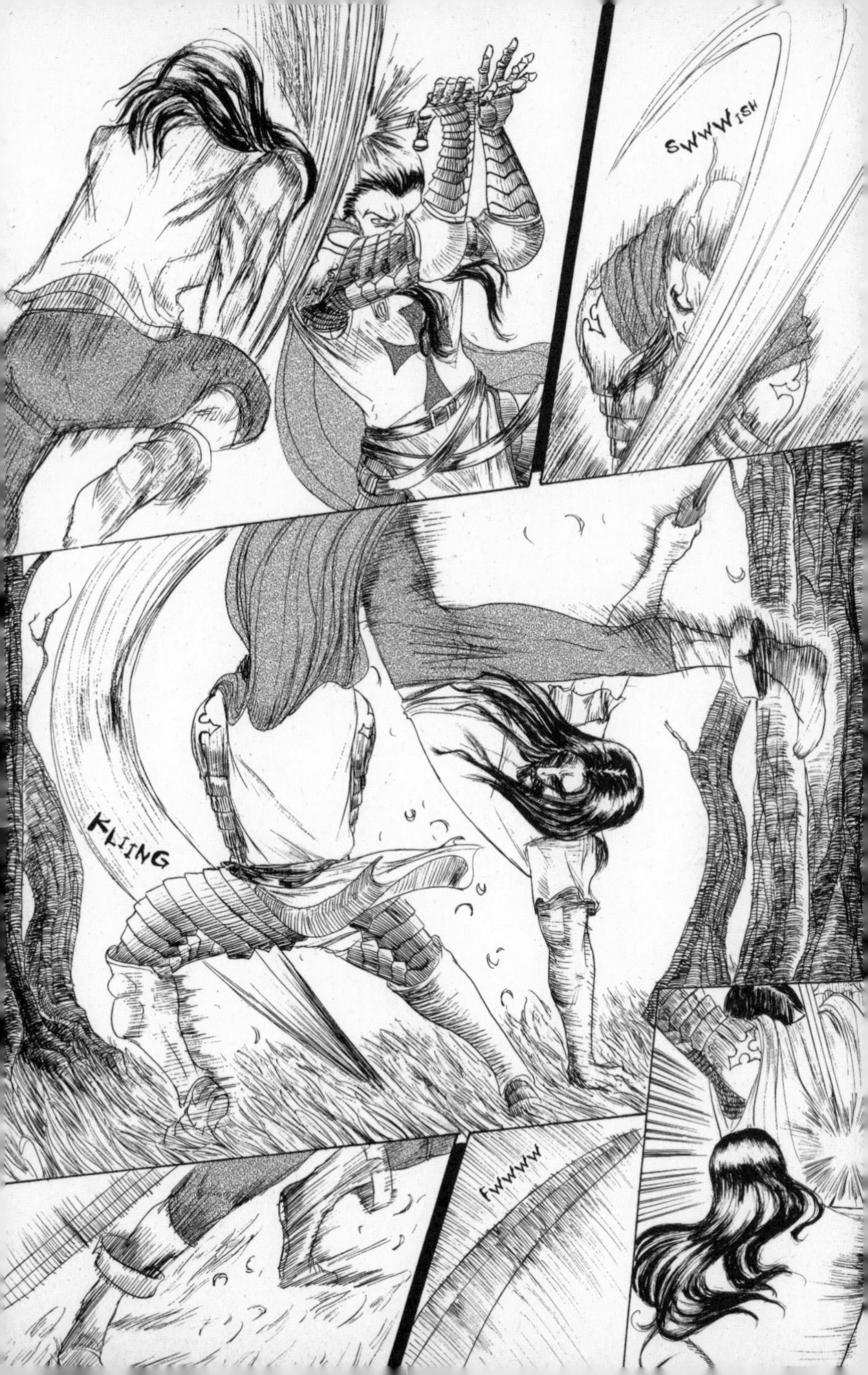
SWWWISH
KLIING
FWWWW

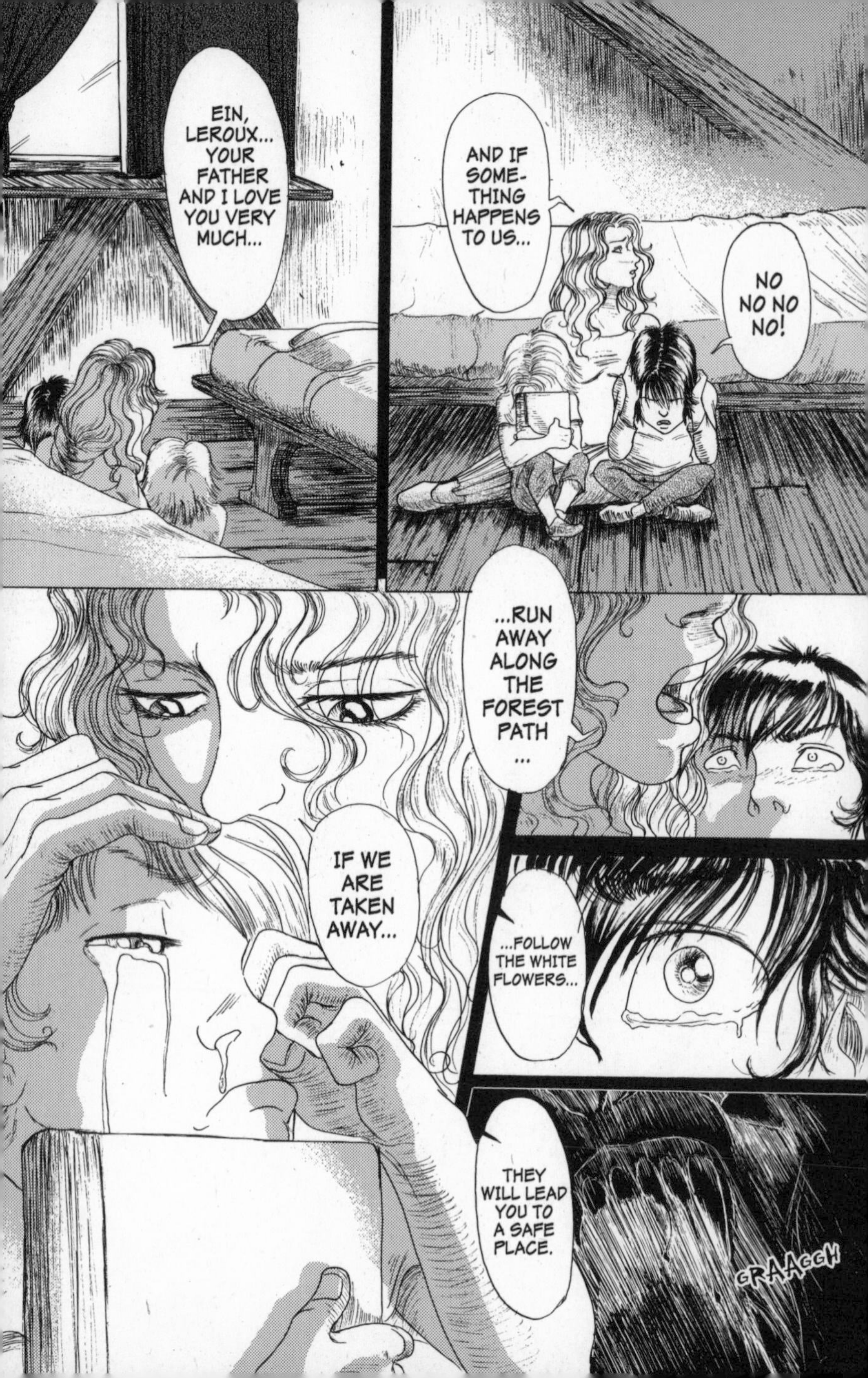
EIN, LEROUX... YOUR FATHER AND I LOVE YOU VERY MUCH...
AND IF SOME-THING HAPPENS TO US...
NO NO NO NO!
IF WE ARE TAKEN AWAY...
...RUN AWAY ALONG THE FOREST PATH ...
...FOLLOW THE WHITE FLOWERS...
THEY WILL LEAD YOU TO A SAFE PLACE.
GRAAAGGH

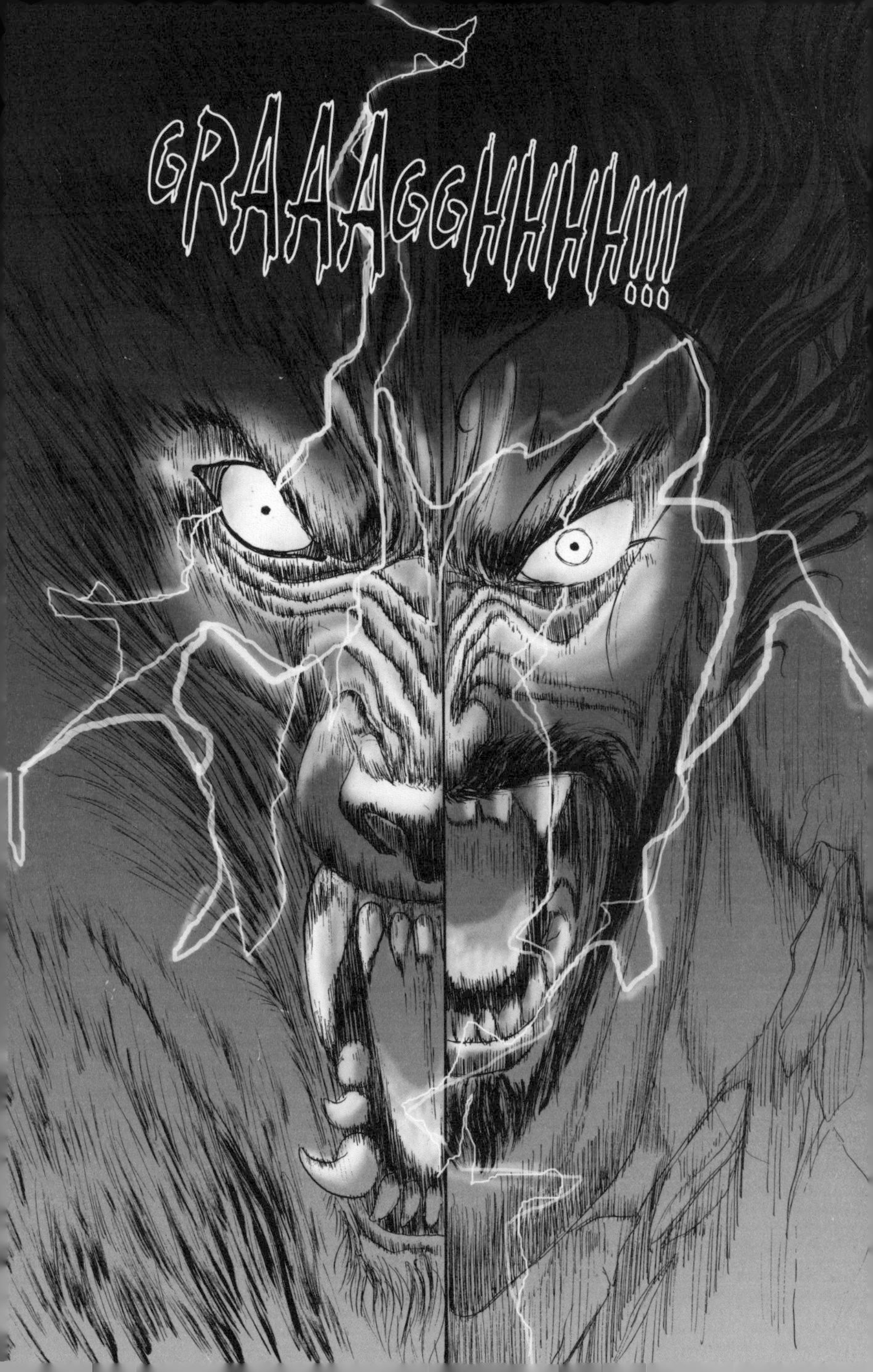
GRAAAGGHHHH!!!

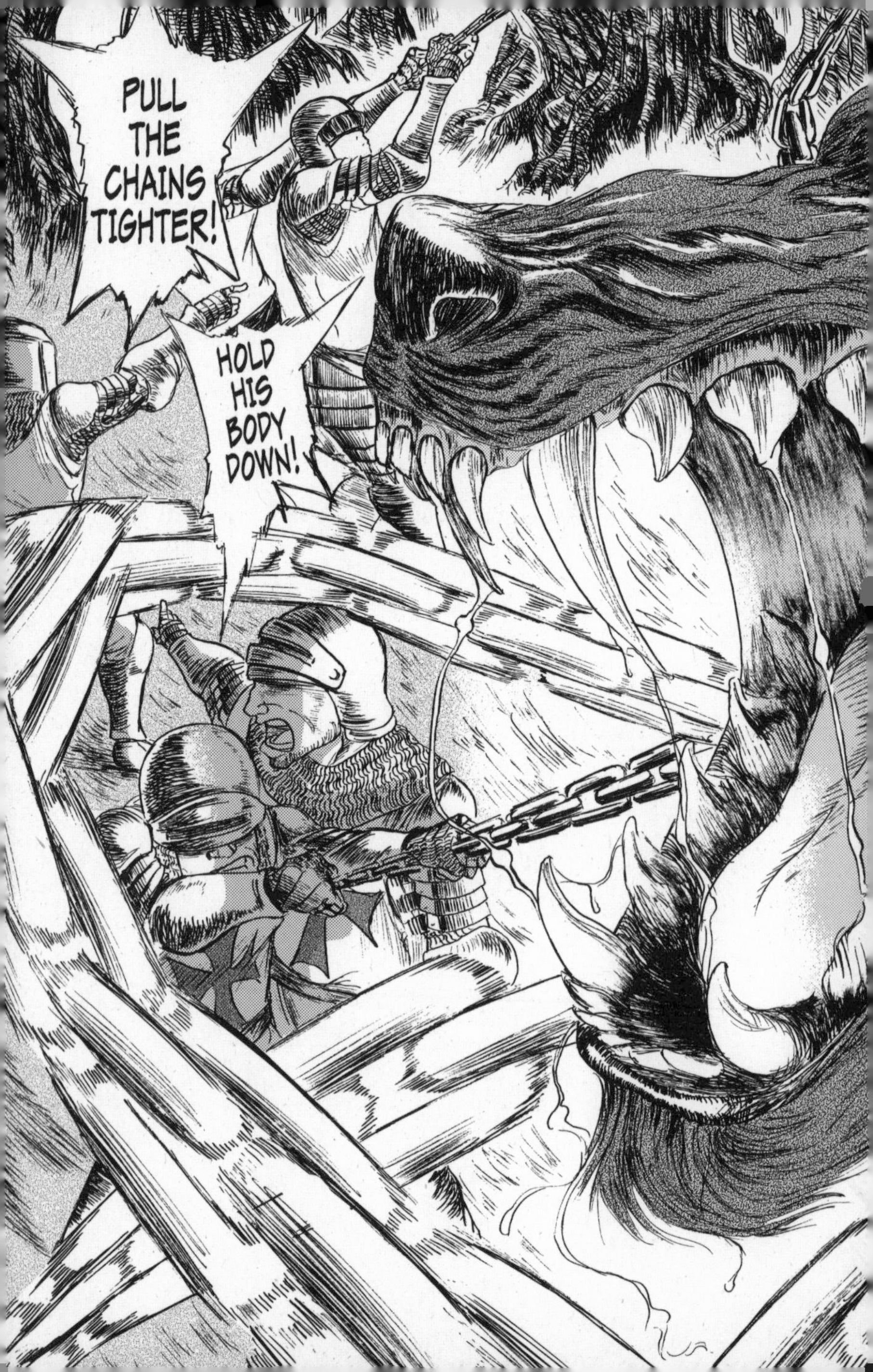
PULL THE CHAINS TIGHTER!
HOLD HIS BODY DOWN!

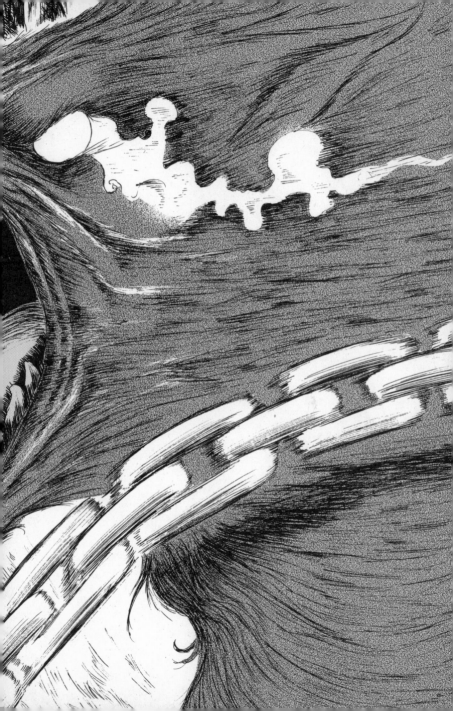

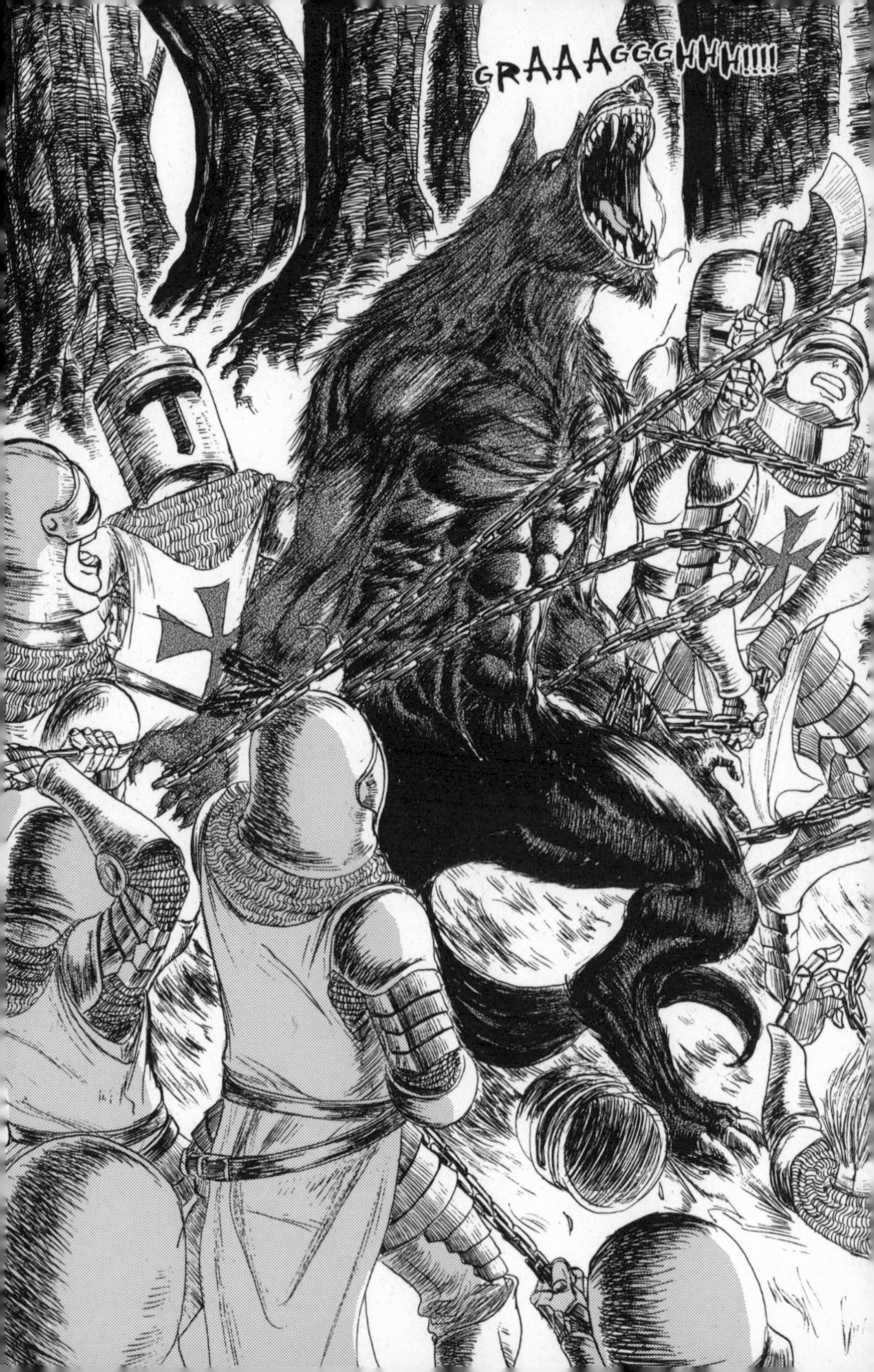
GRAAAGGGHHH!!!!!

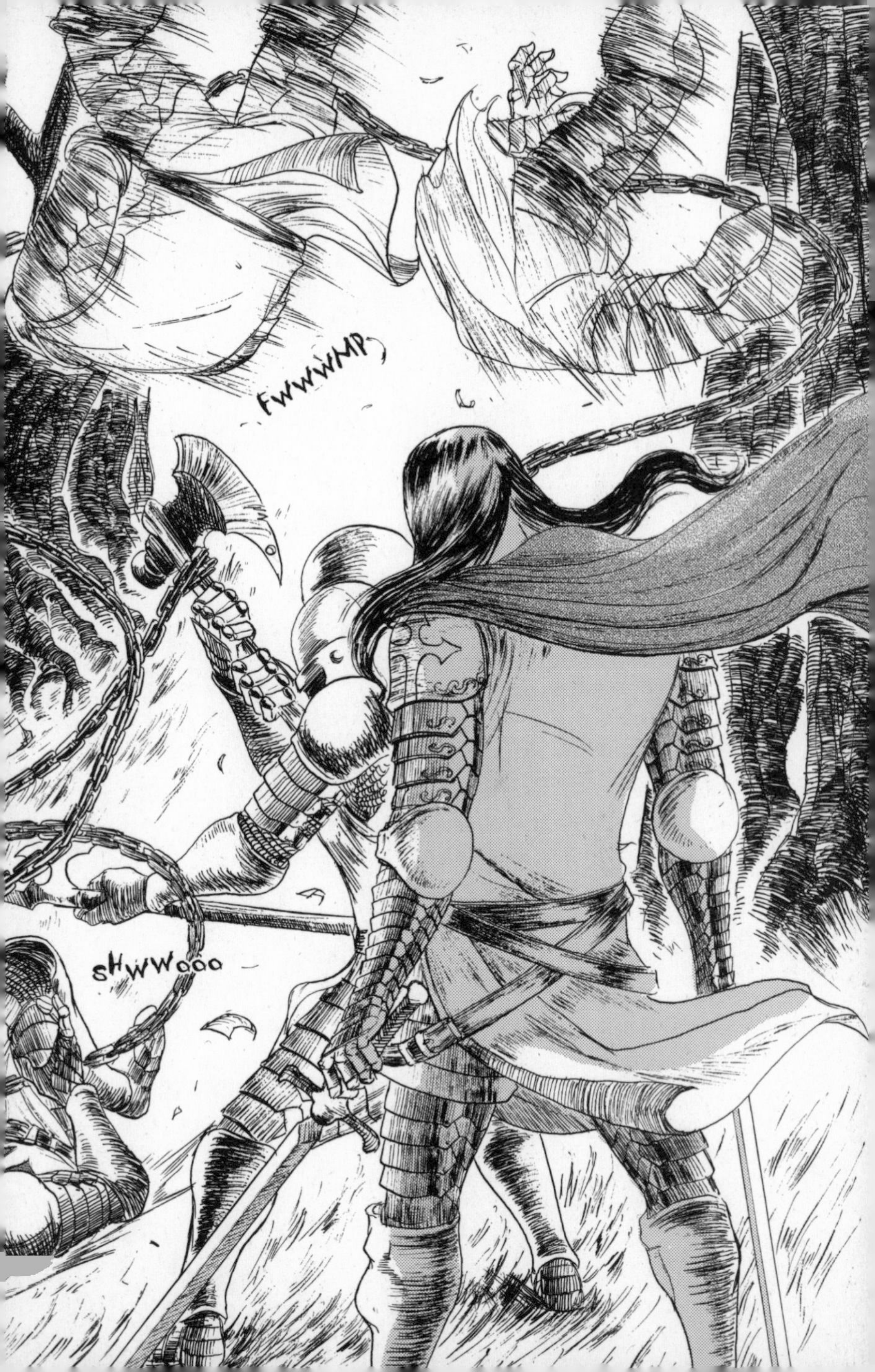
FWWWMP
SHWWOOO

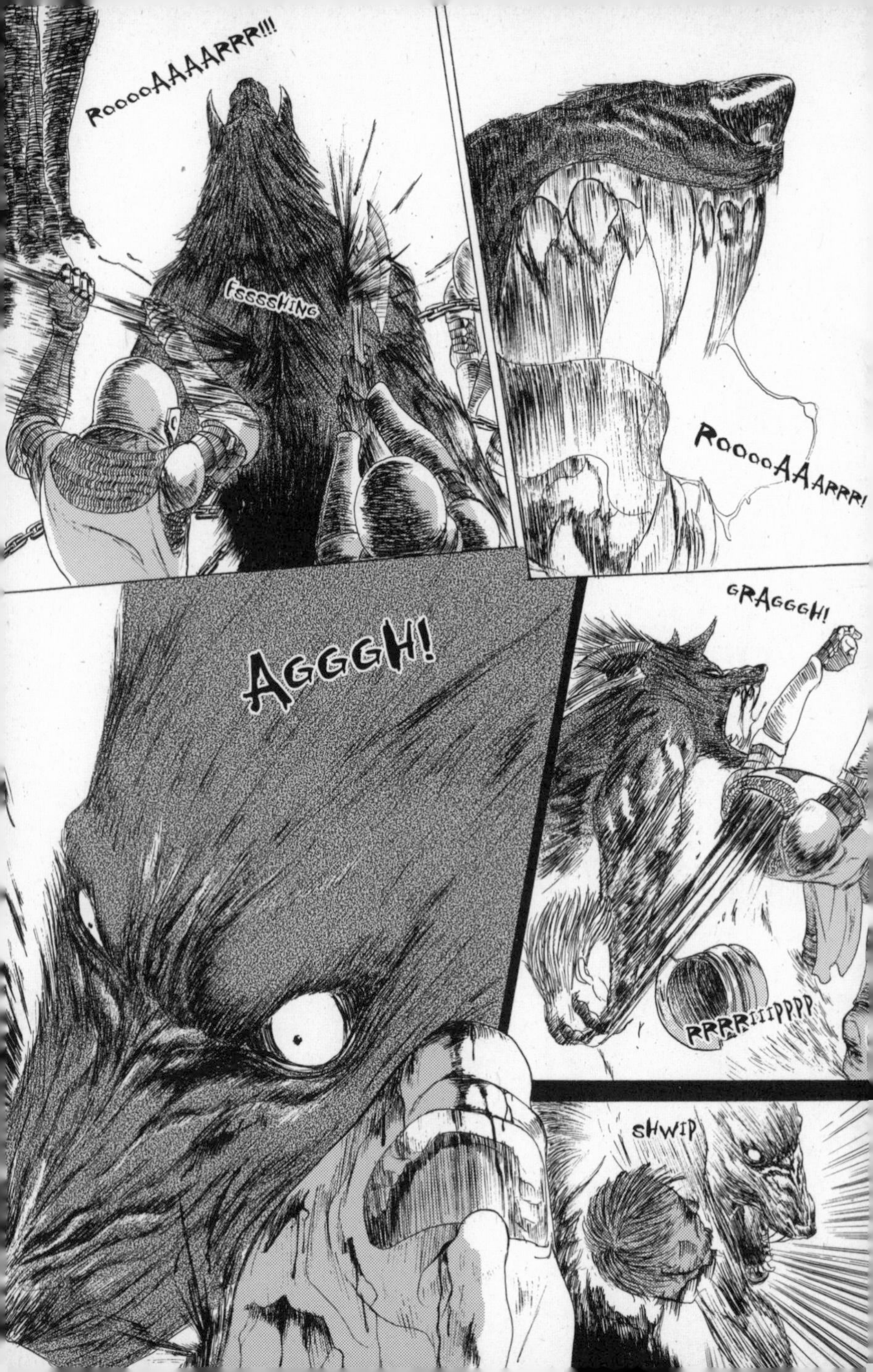
RooooAAARRR!
RooooAAAARRR!!!
FSSSSHING
GRAGGGH!
RRRRIIIPPPP
SHWIP
AGGGH!

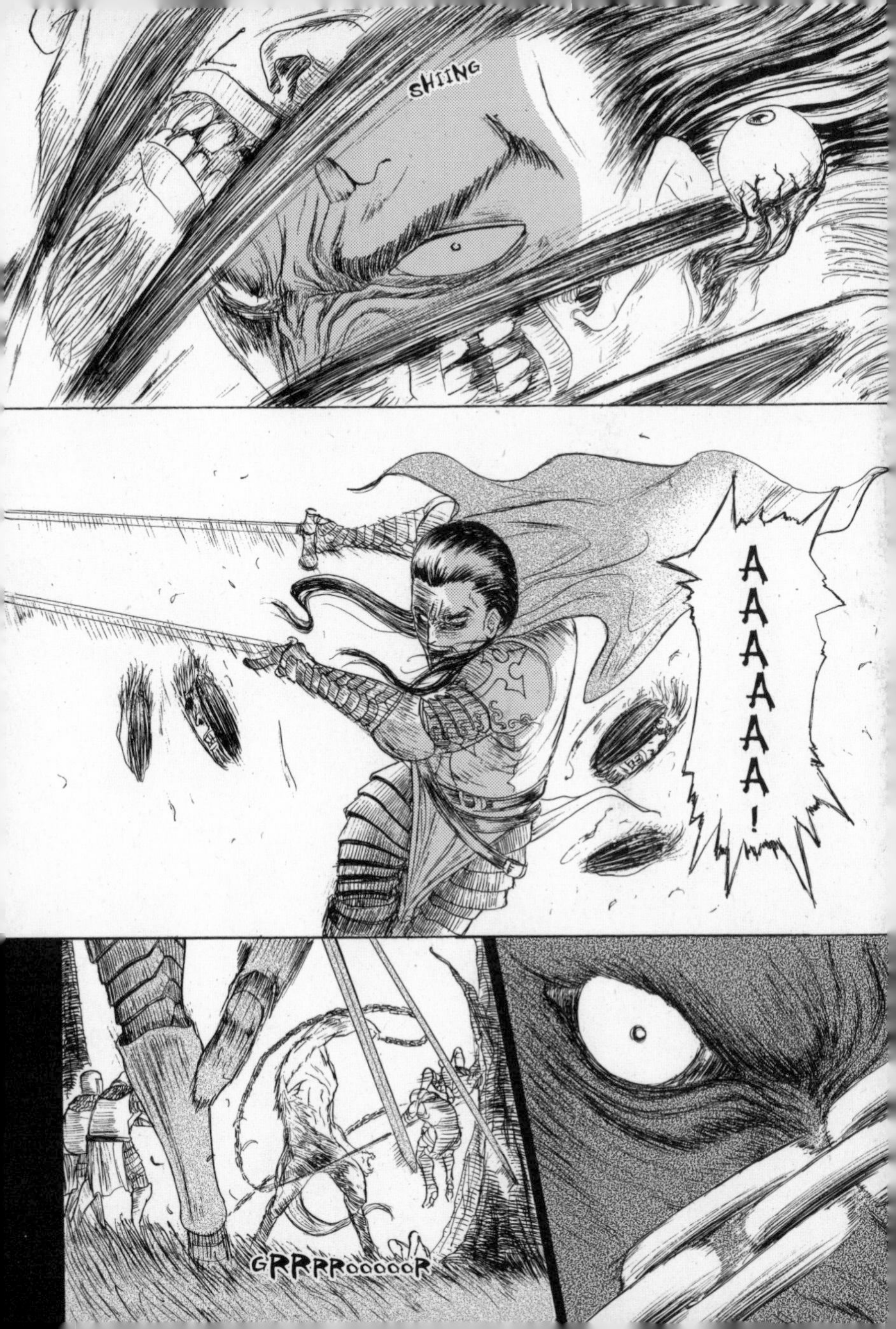
SHIING
AAAAAA!
GRRRRooooooR

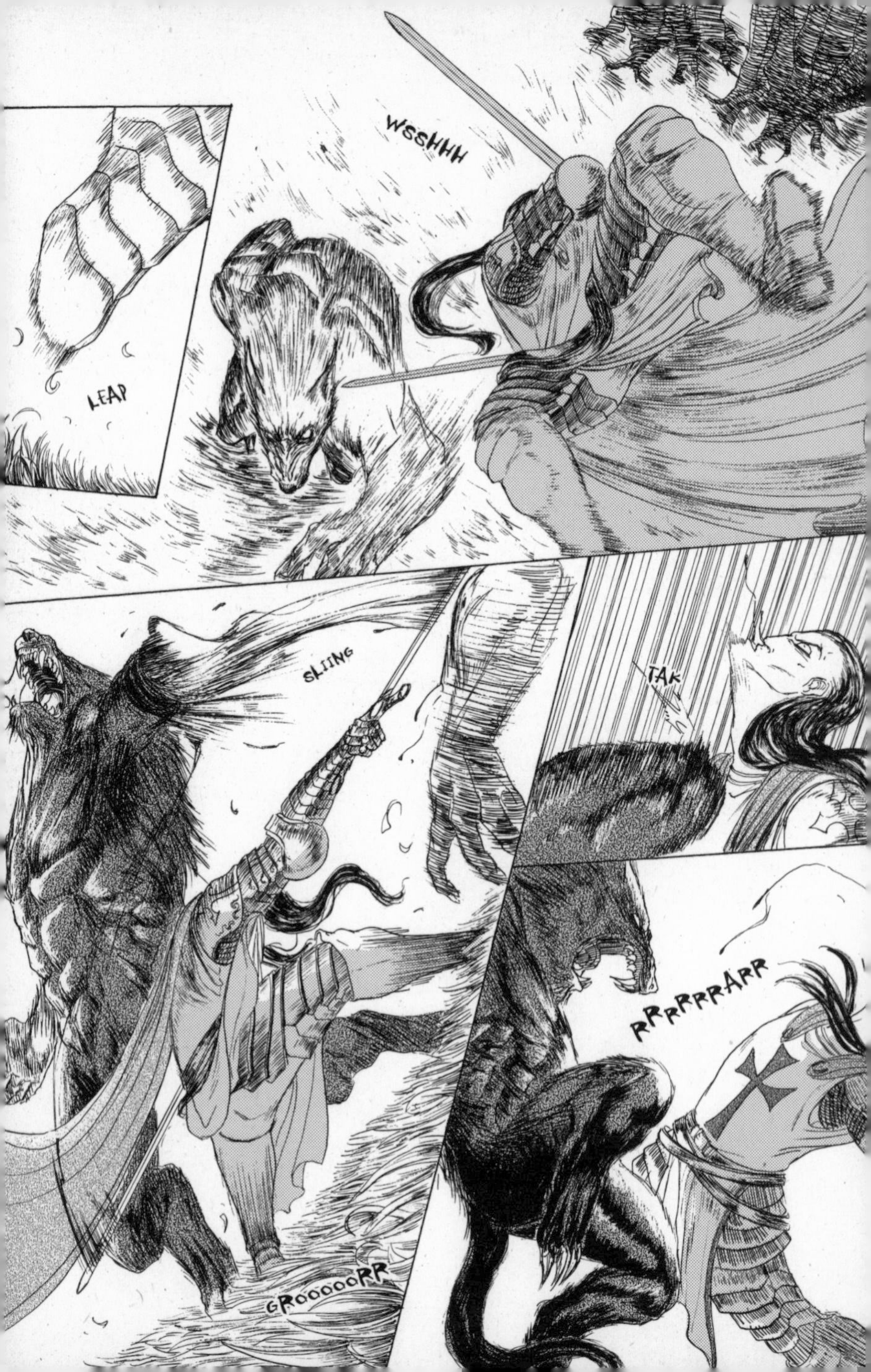
WSSHHH
LEAP
TAK
RRRRRRARR
SLIING
GROOOOORR

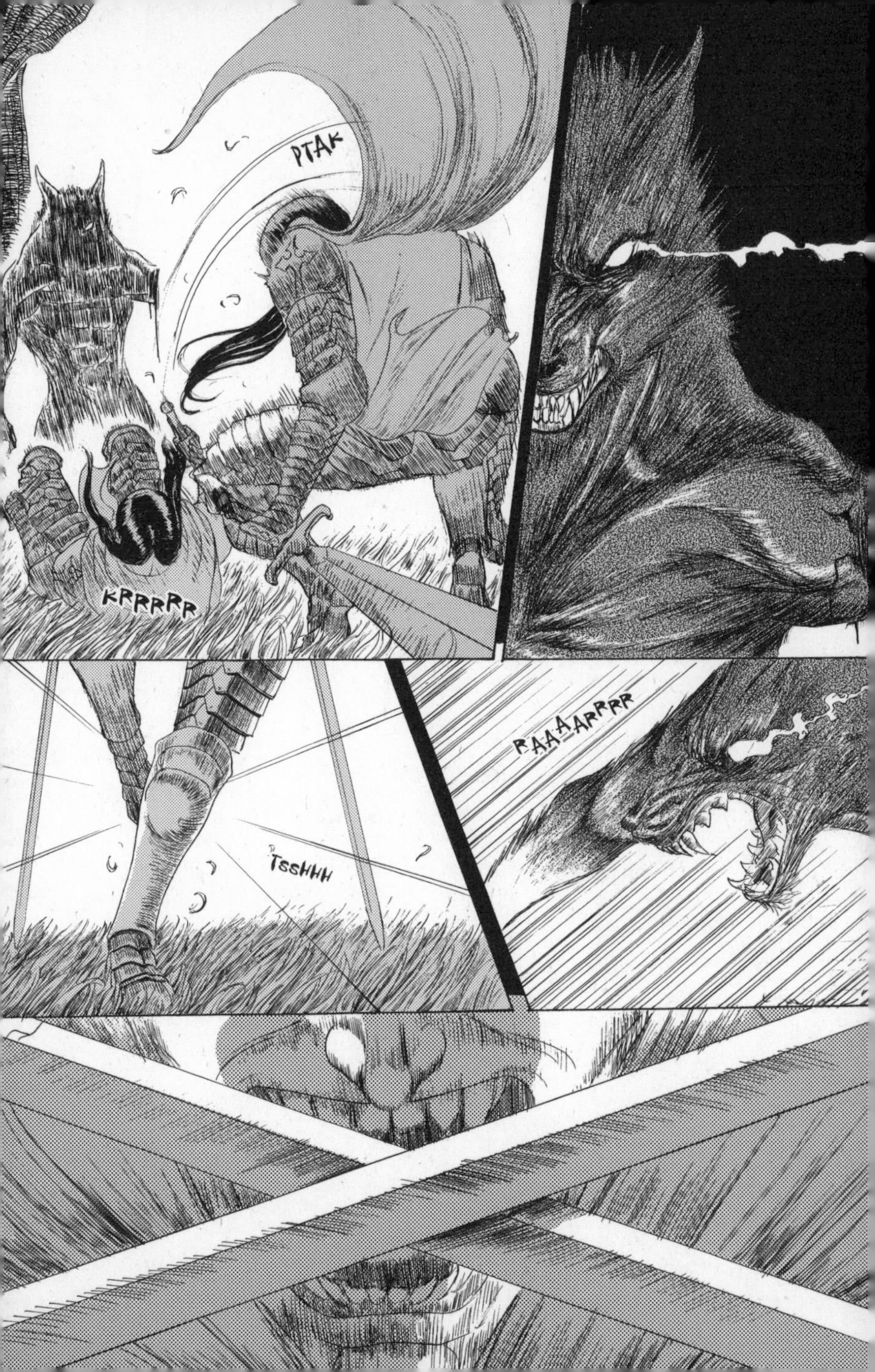
PTAK
KRRRRR
RAAAARRRR
TSSHHH

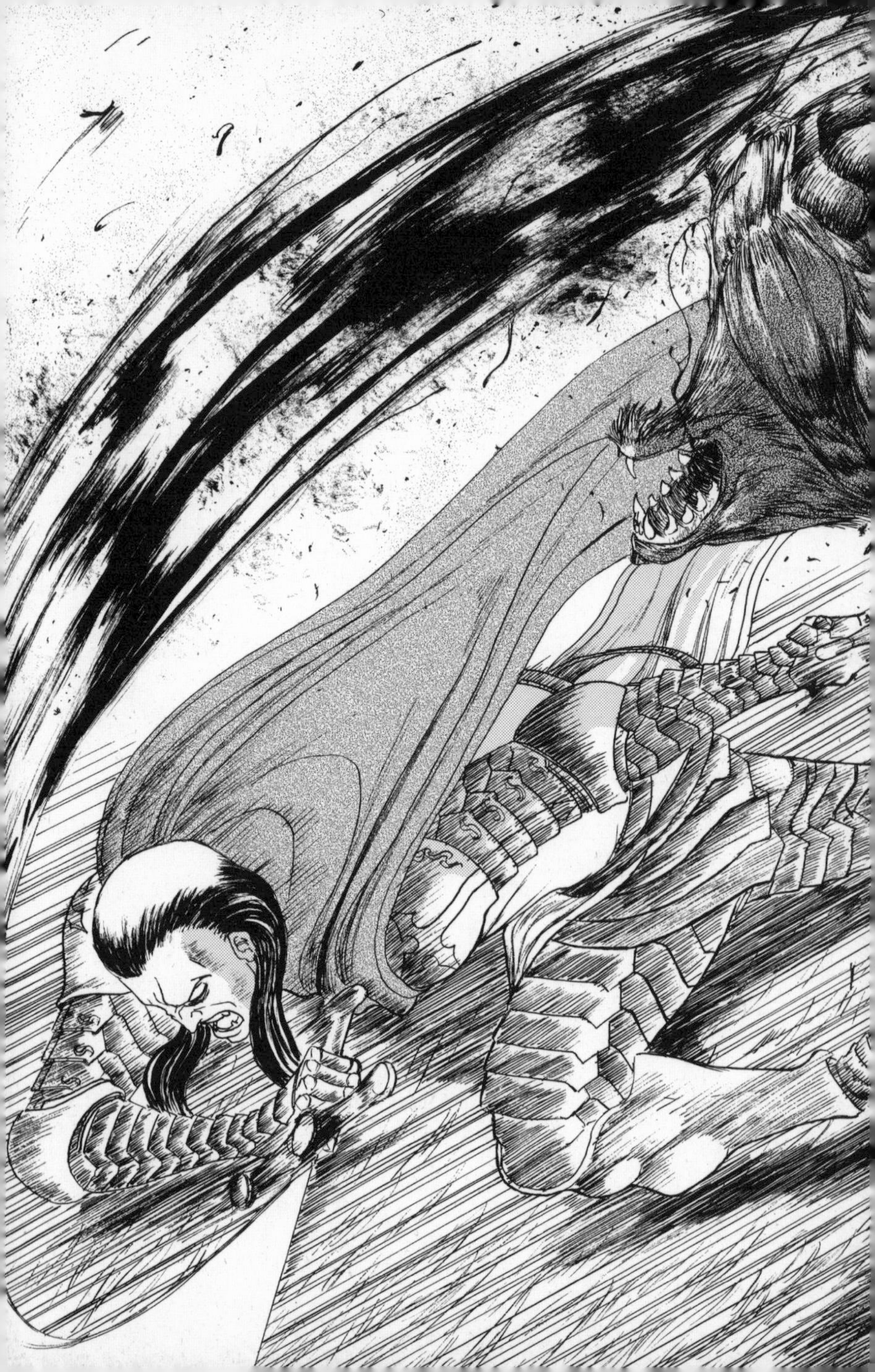

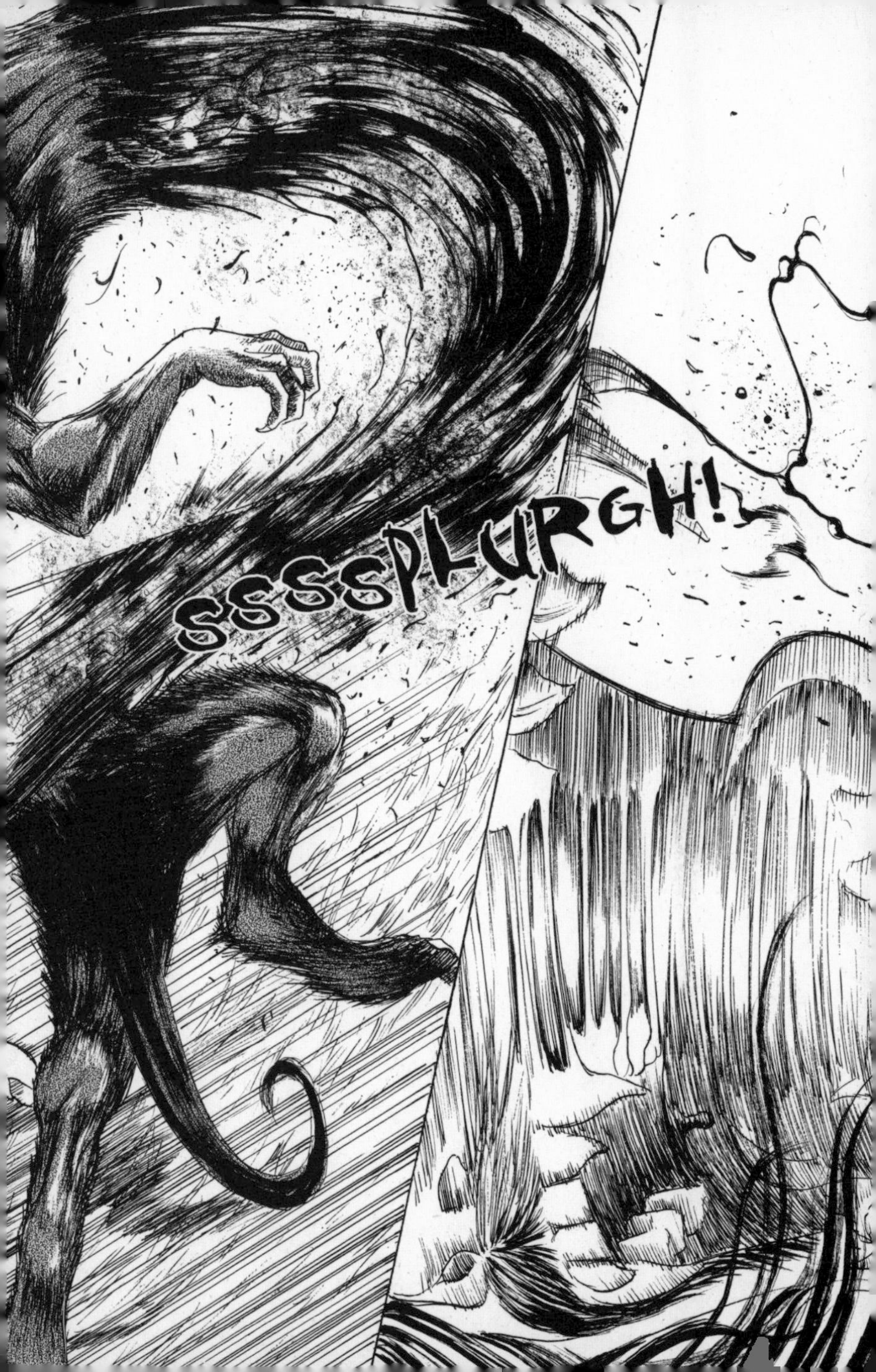
SSSSPLURGH!

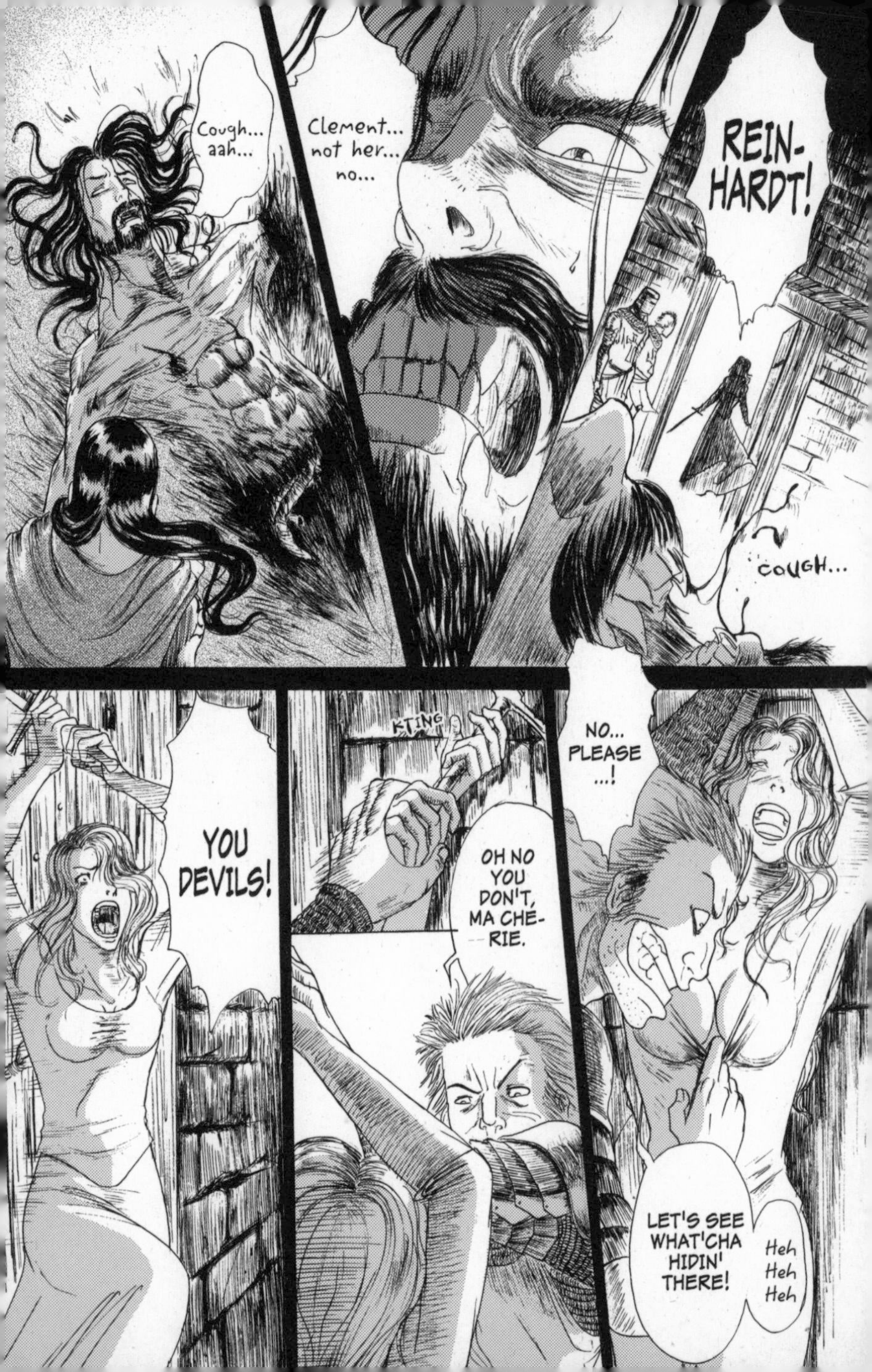
Cough... aah...
Clement... not her... no...
REIN-HARDT!
COUGH...
YOU DEVILS!
KTING
OH NO YOU DON'T, MA CHÉ-RIE.
NO... PLEASE ...!
LET'S SEE WHAT'CHA HIDIN' THERE!
Heh Heh Heh

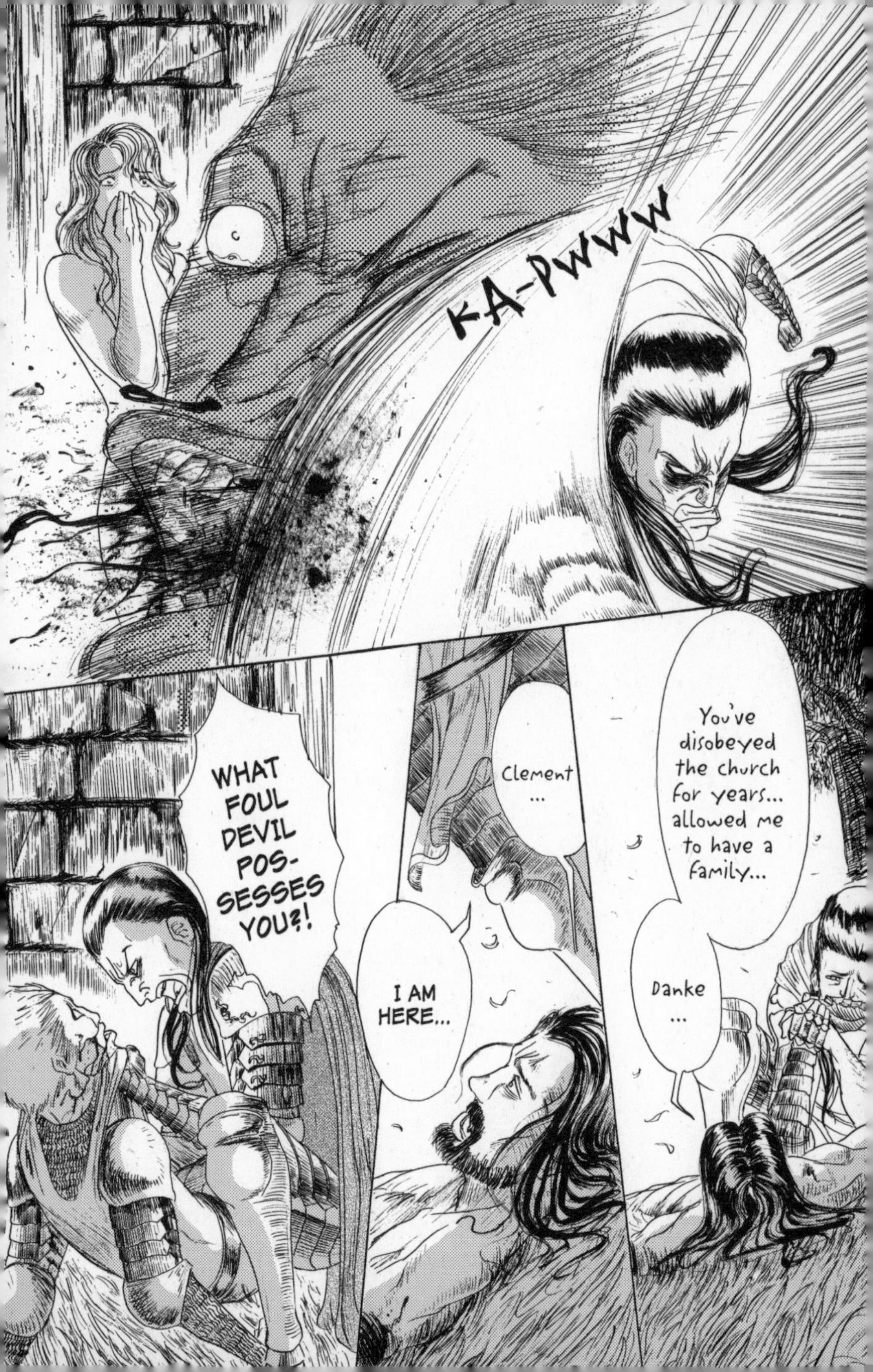
KA-PWWW
WHAT FOUL DEVIL POS-SESSES YOU?!
Clement ...
I AM HERE...
You've disobeyed the church for years... allowed me to have a family...
Danke ...

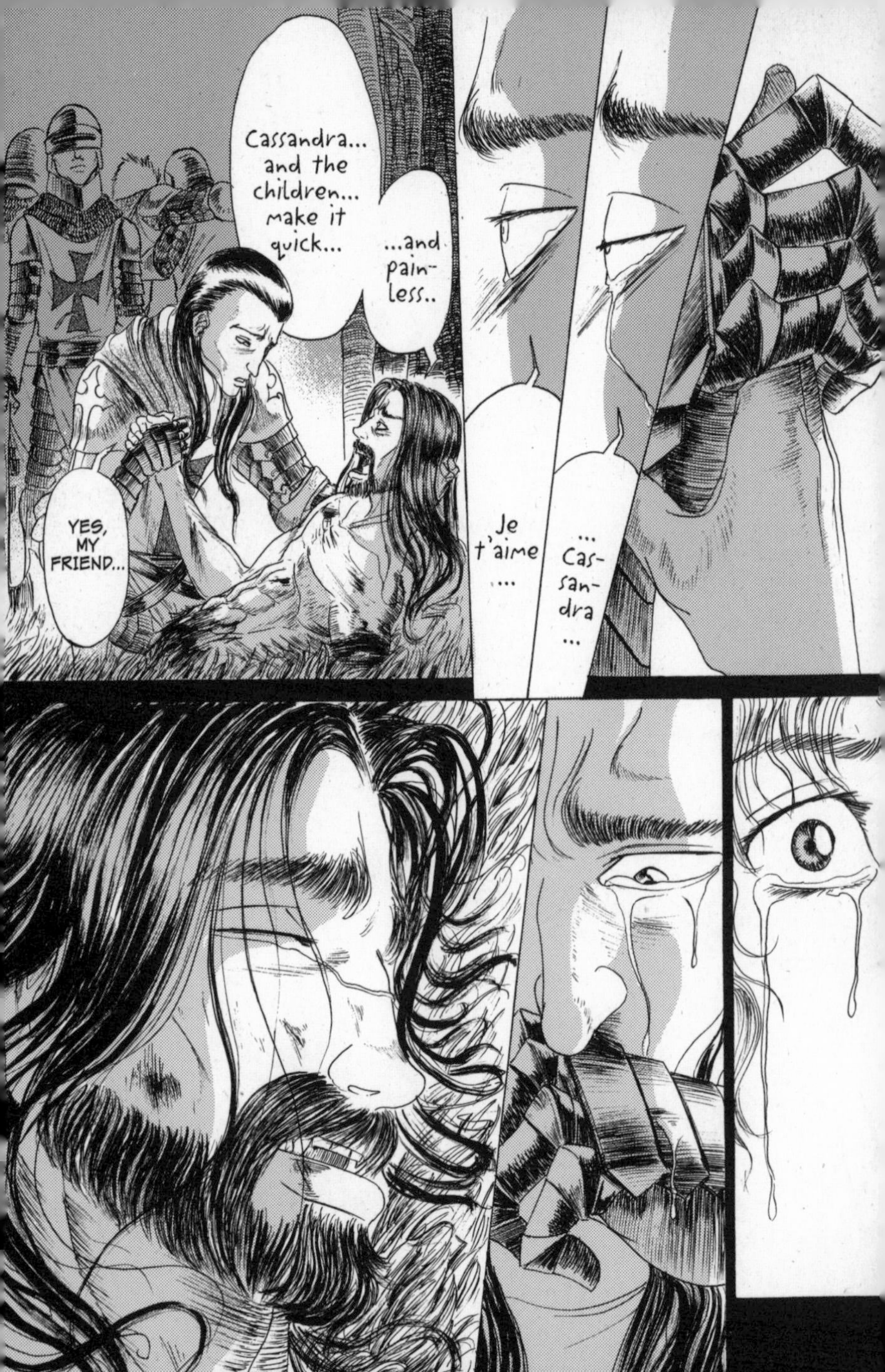
Cassandra... and the children... make it quick...
...and pain-less..
YES, MY FRIEND...
Je t'aime ...
... Cas-san-dra ...

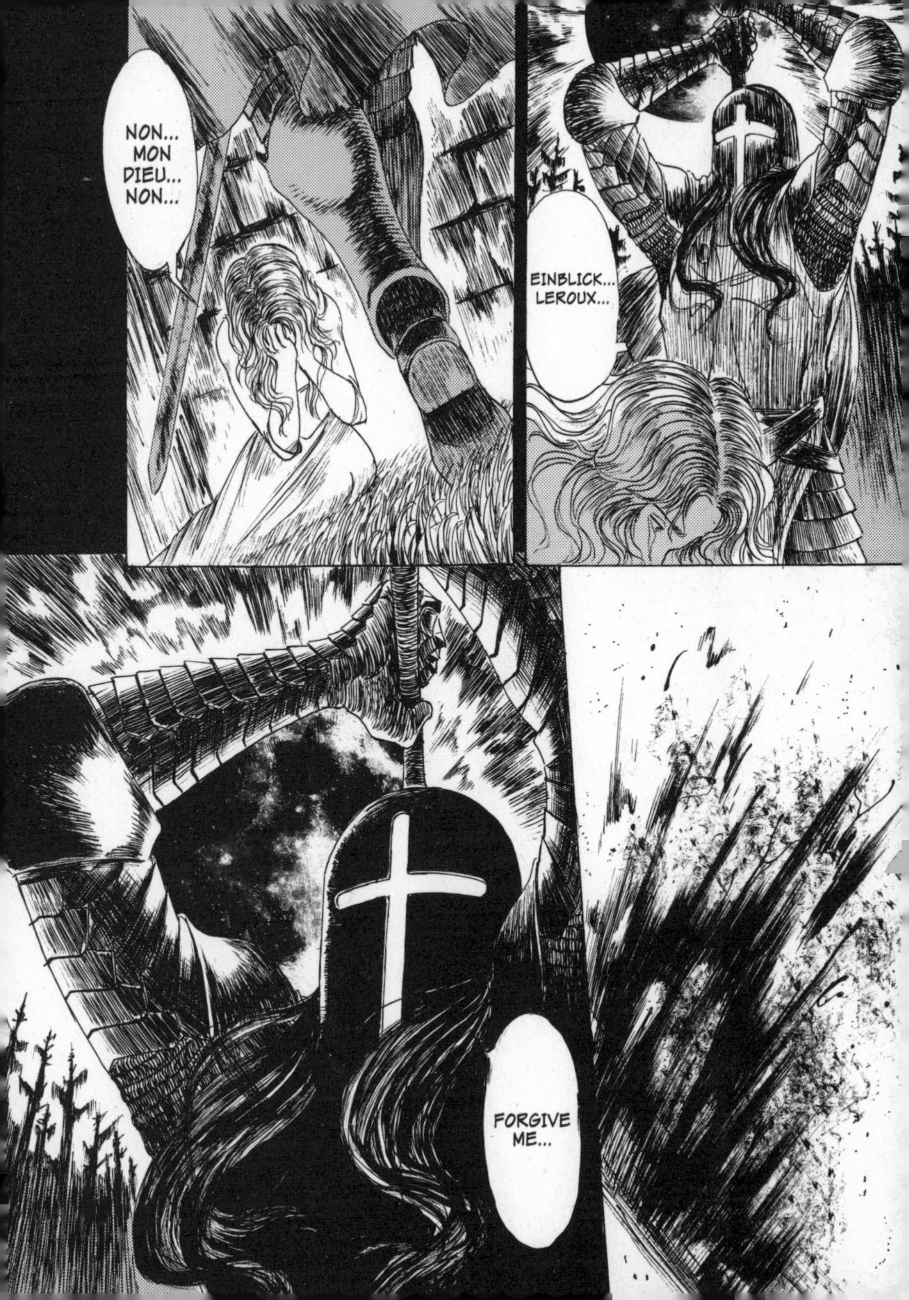
EINBLICK... LEROUX...
NON... MON DIEU... NON...
FORGIVE ME...

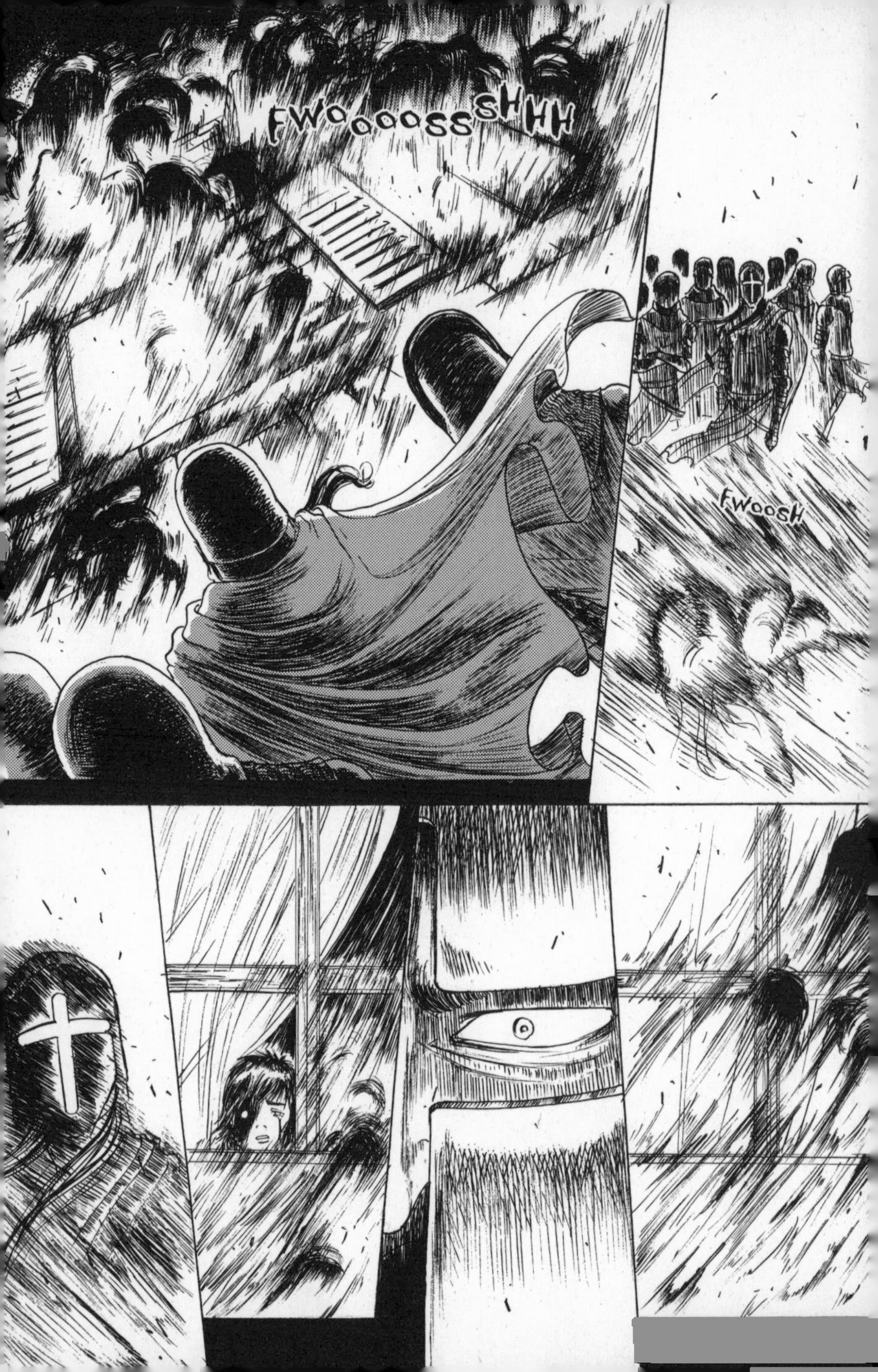
FWOOOOSSSHHH
FWOOSH

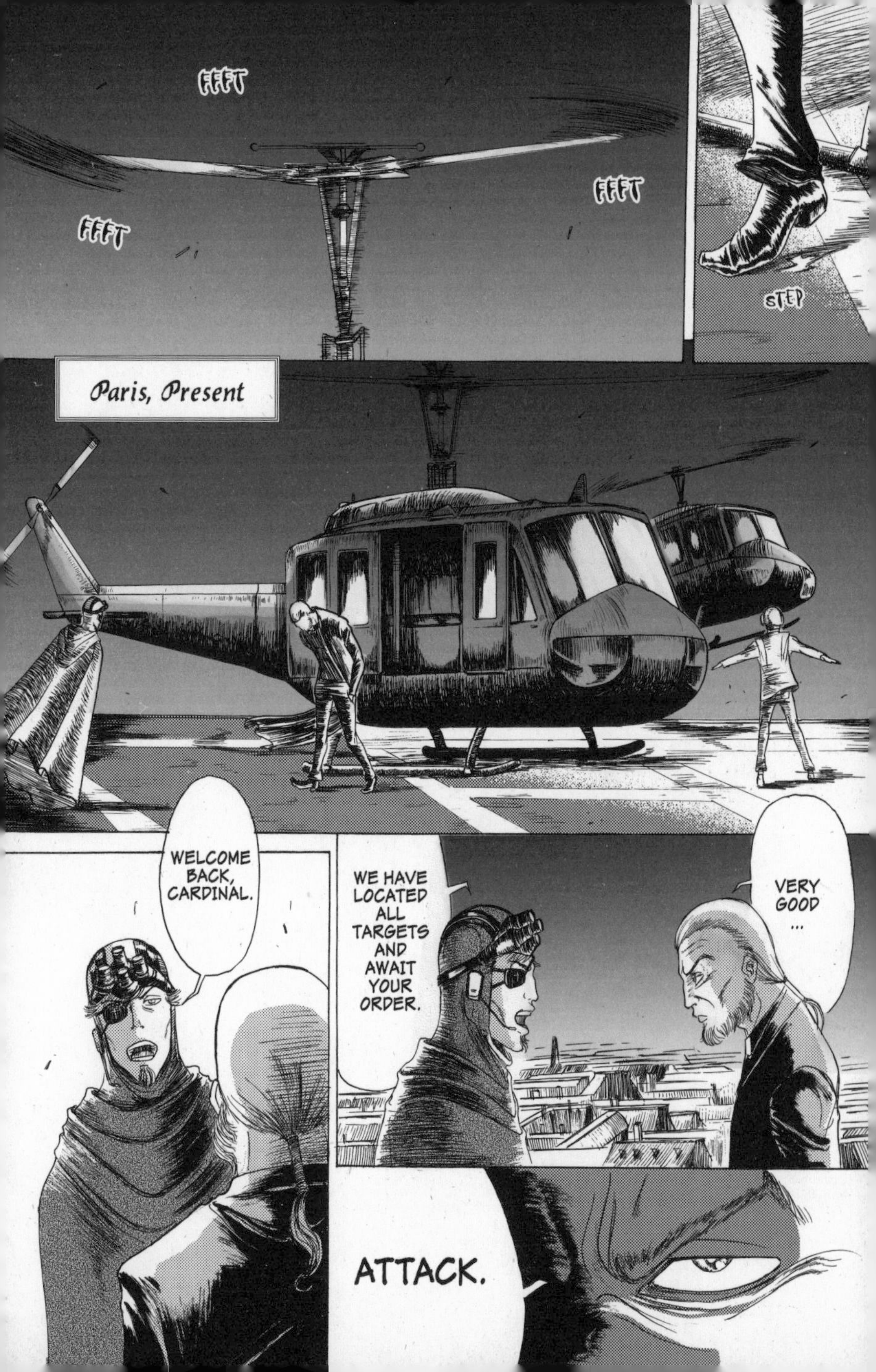
FFFT
FFFT
FFFT
STEP
Paris, Present
WELCOME BACK, CARDINAL.
WE HAVE LOCATED ALL TARGETS AND AWAIT YOUR ORDER.
VERY GOOD ...
ATTACK.

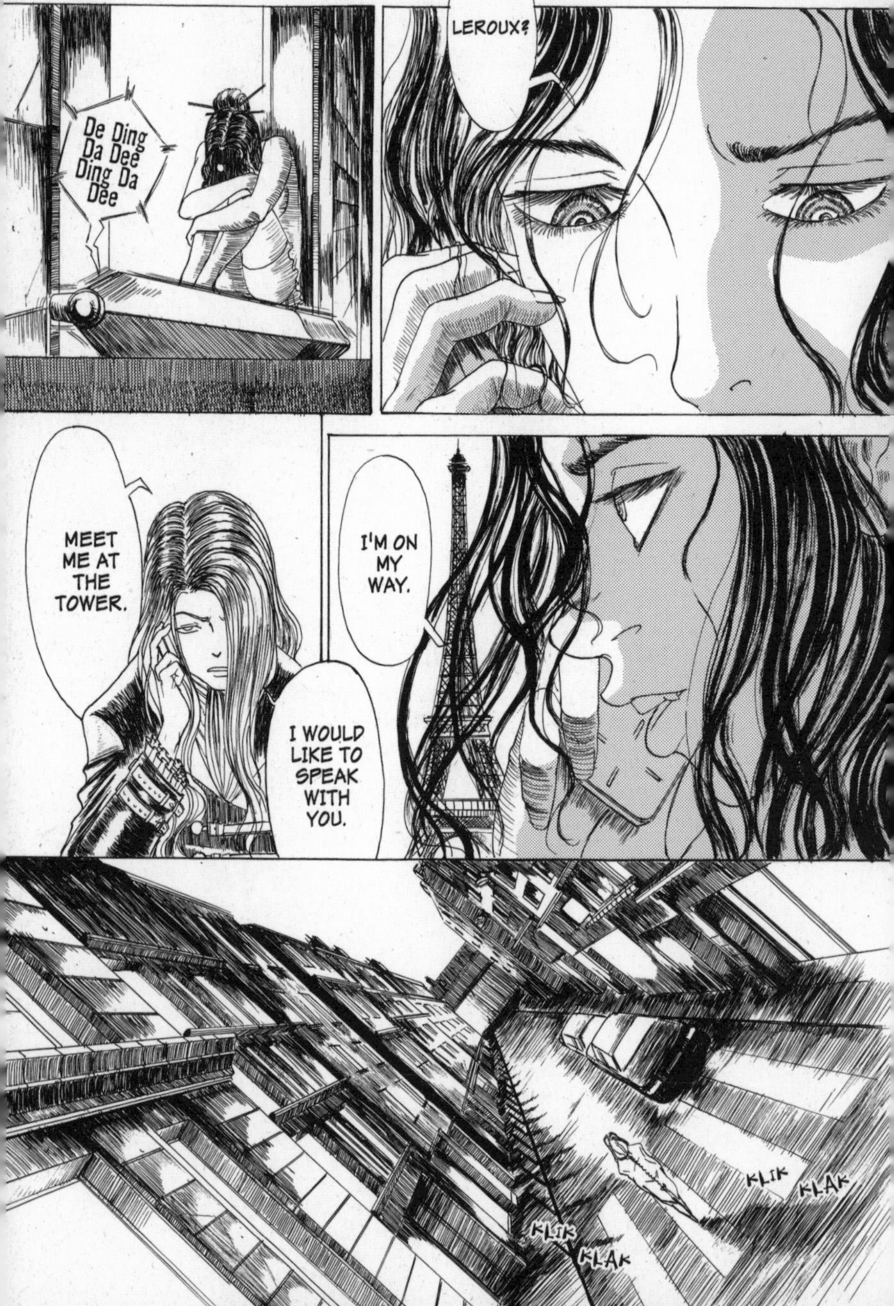
De Ding Da Dee Ding Da Dee
LEROUX?
MEET ME AT THE TOWER.
I WOULD LIKE TO SPEAK WITH YOU.
I'M ON MY WAY.
KLIK KLAK
KLIK KLAK

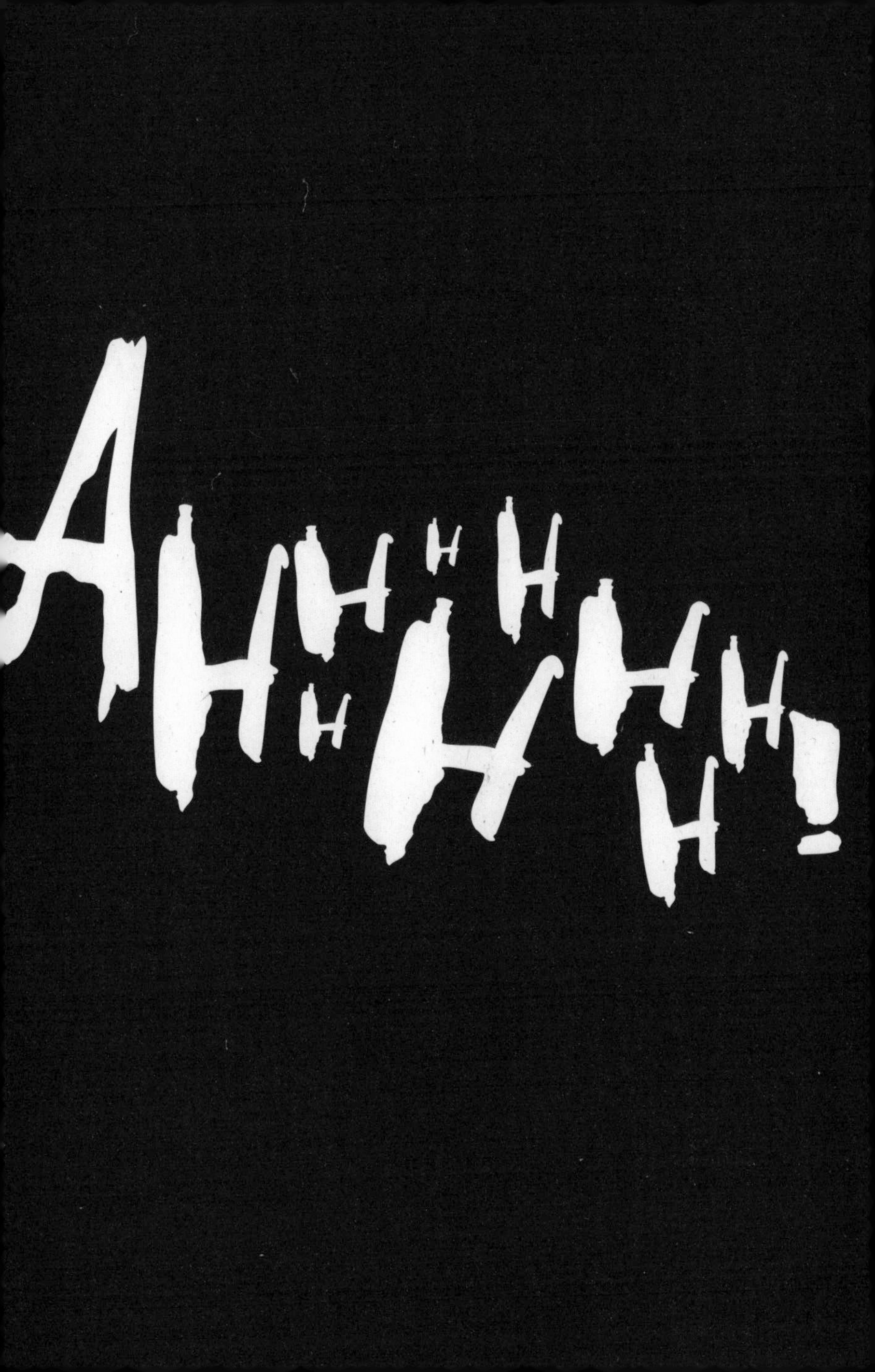
AHHHHHHHHH!

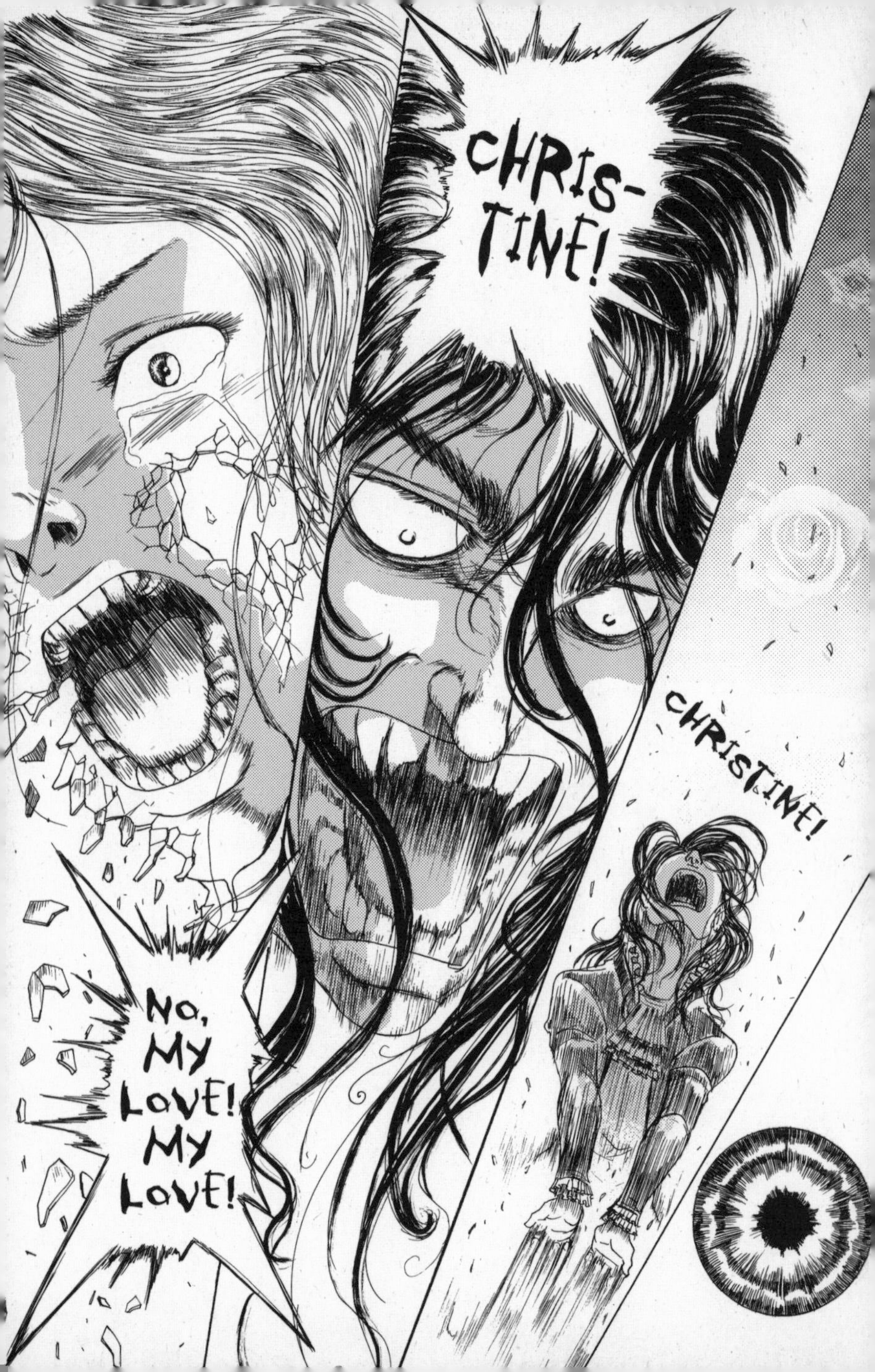
CHRISTINE!
CHRIS-TINE!
No, MY LOVE! MY LOVE!

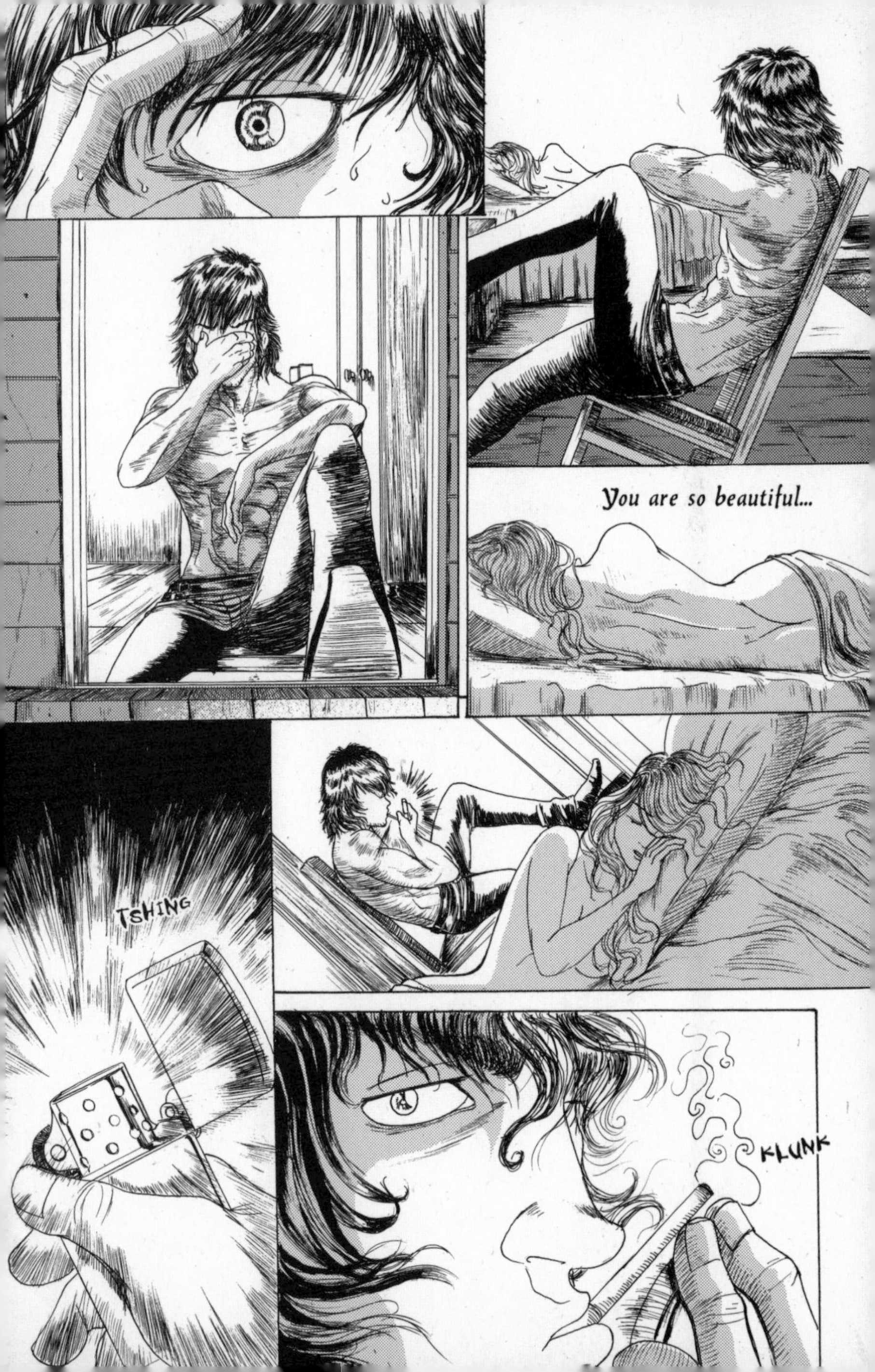
You are so beautiful...
TSHING
KLUNK

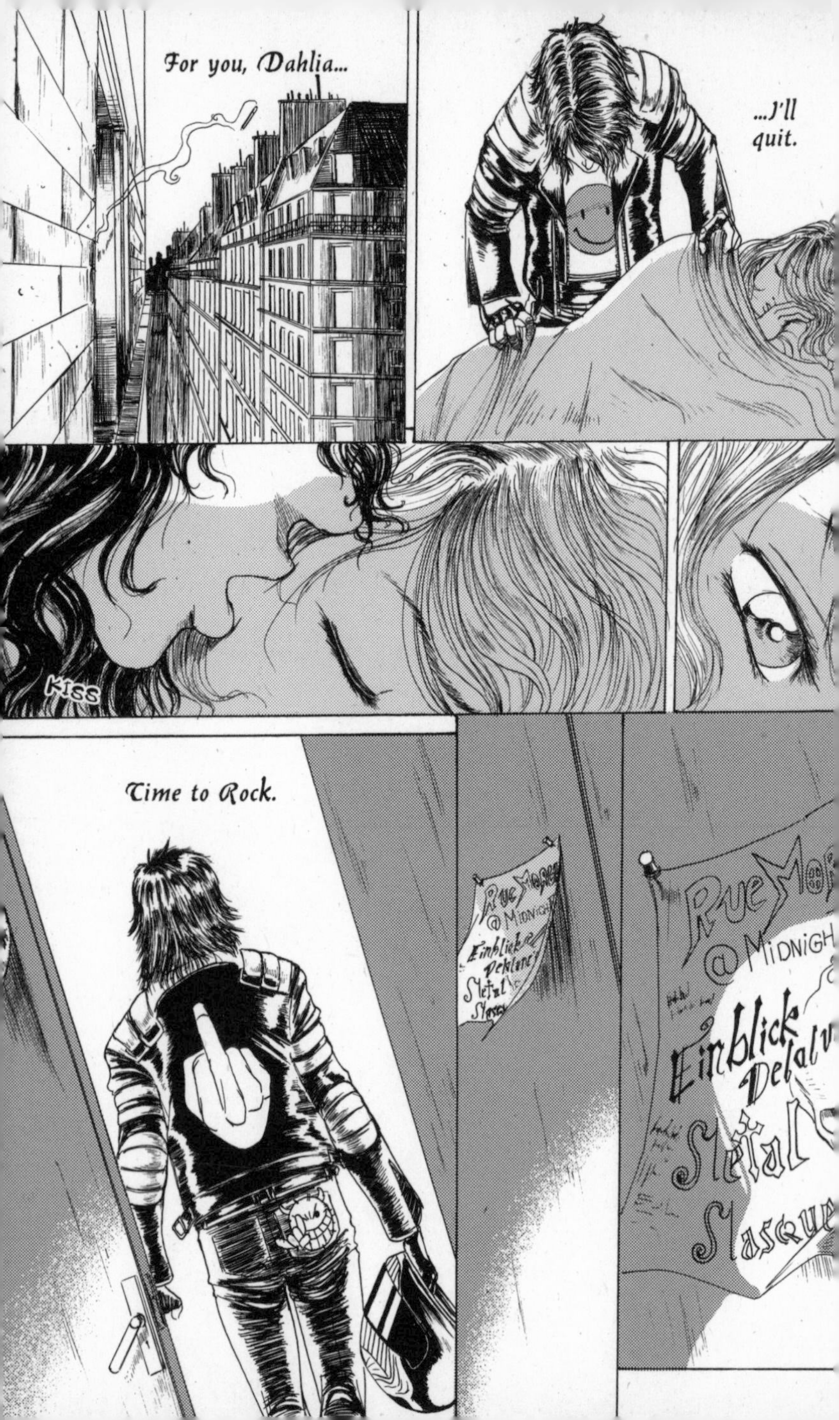
For you, Dahlia...
...I'll quit.
KISS
Time to Rock.
Einblick

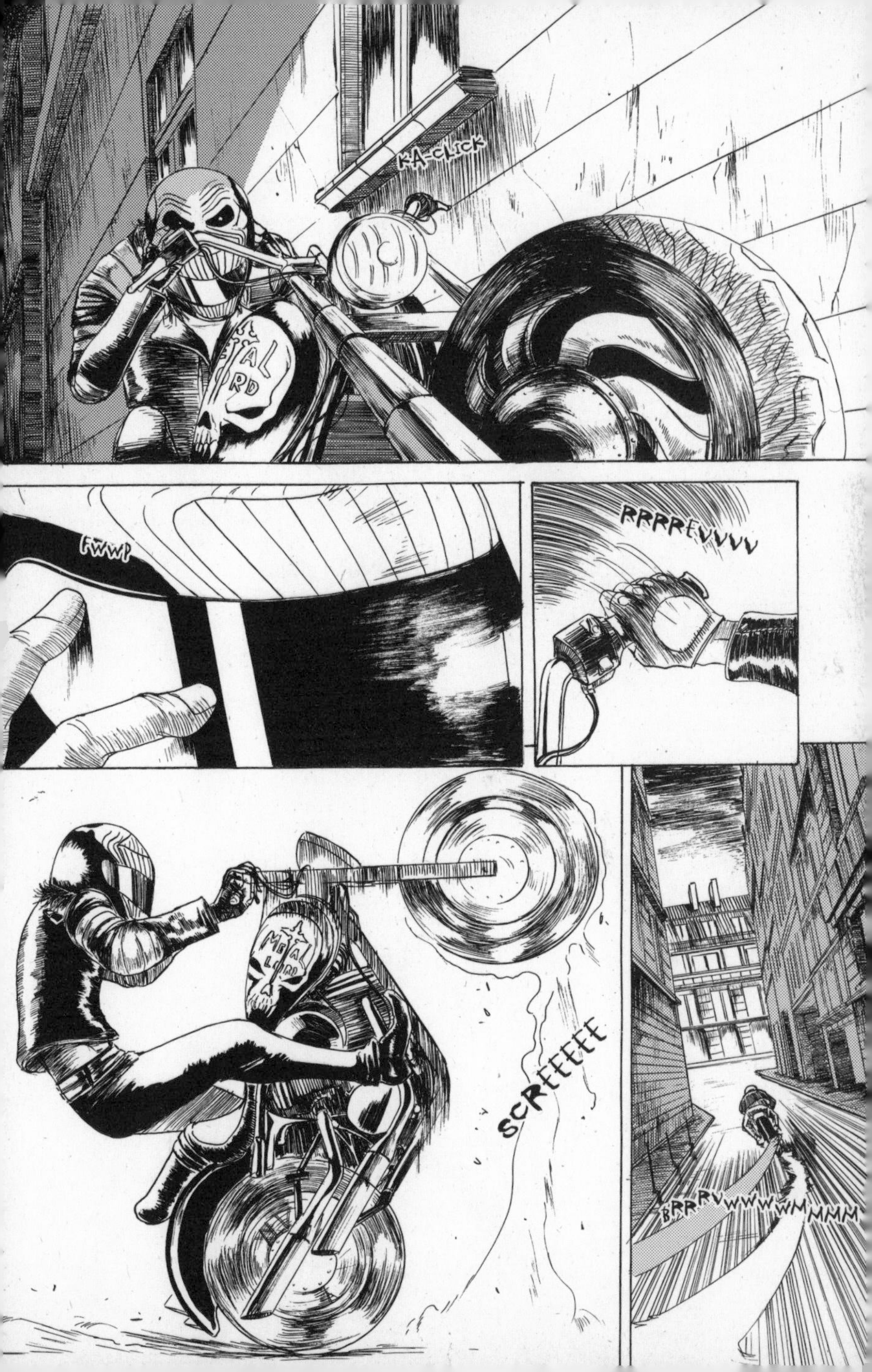
KA-CLICK
RRRREVVVV
FWWP
BRRRVWWWWMMMM
SCREEEEEE

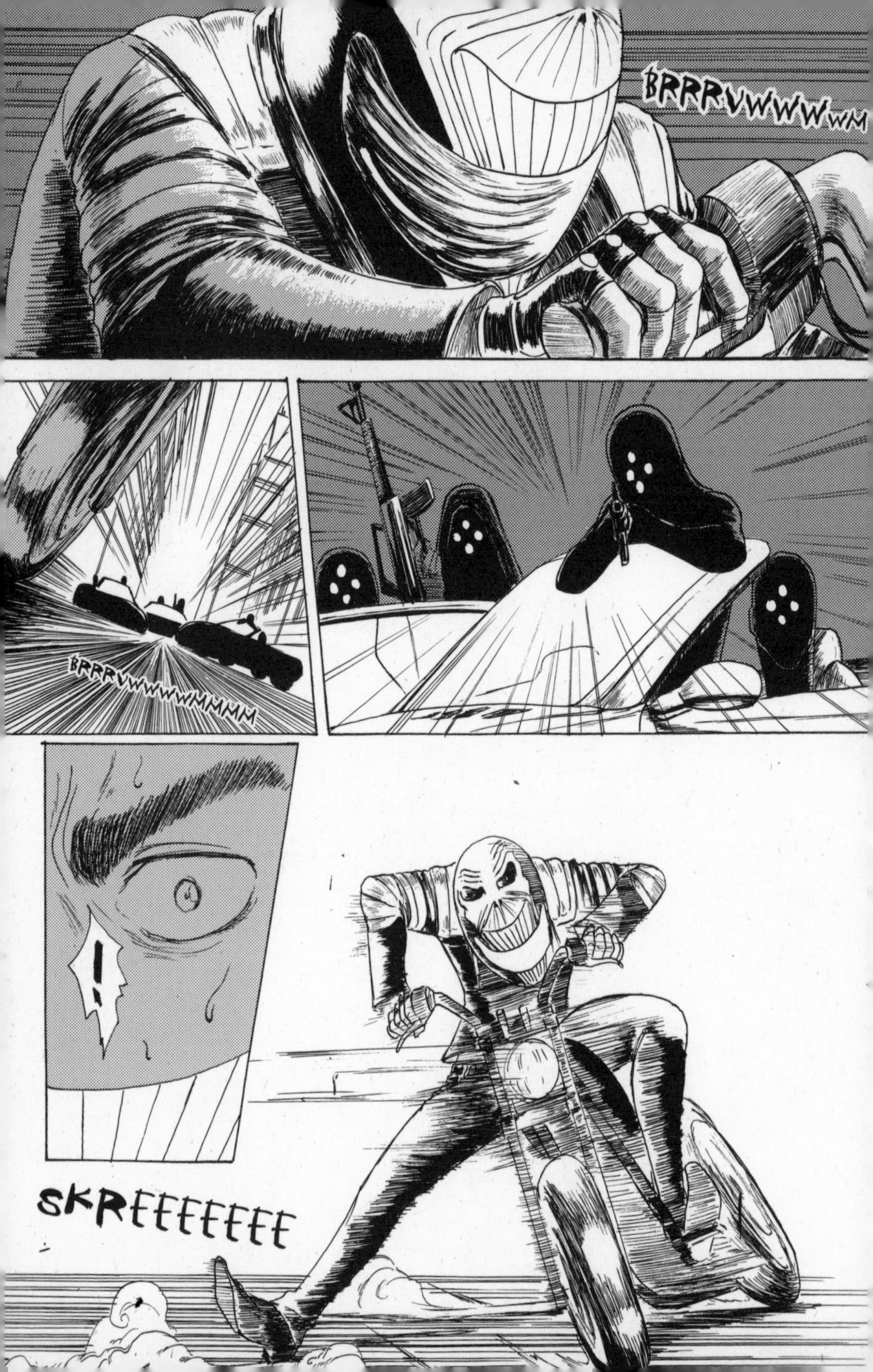
BRRRVWWWWwM
BRRRVWWWWWMMMM
!
SKREEEEEEE

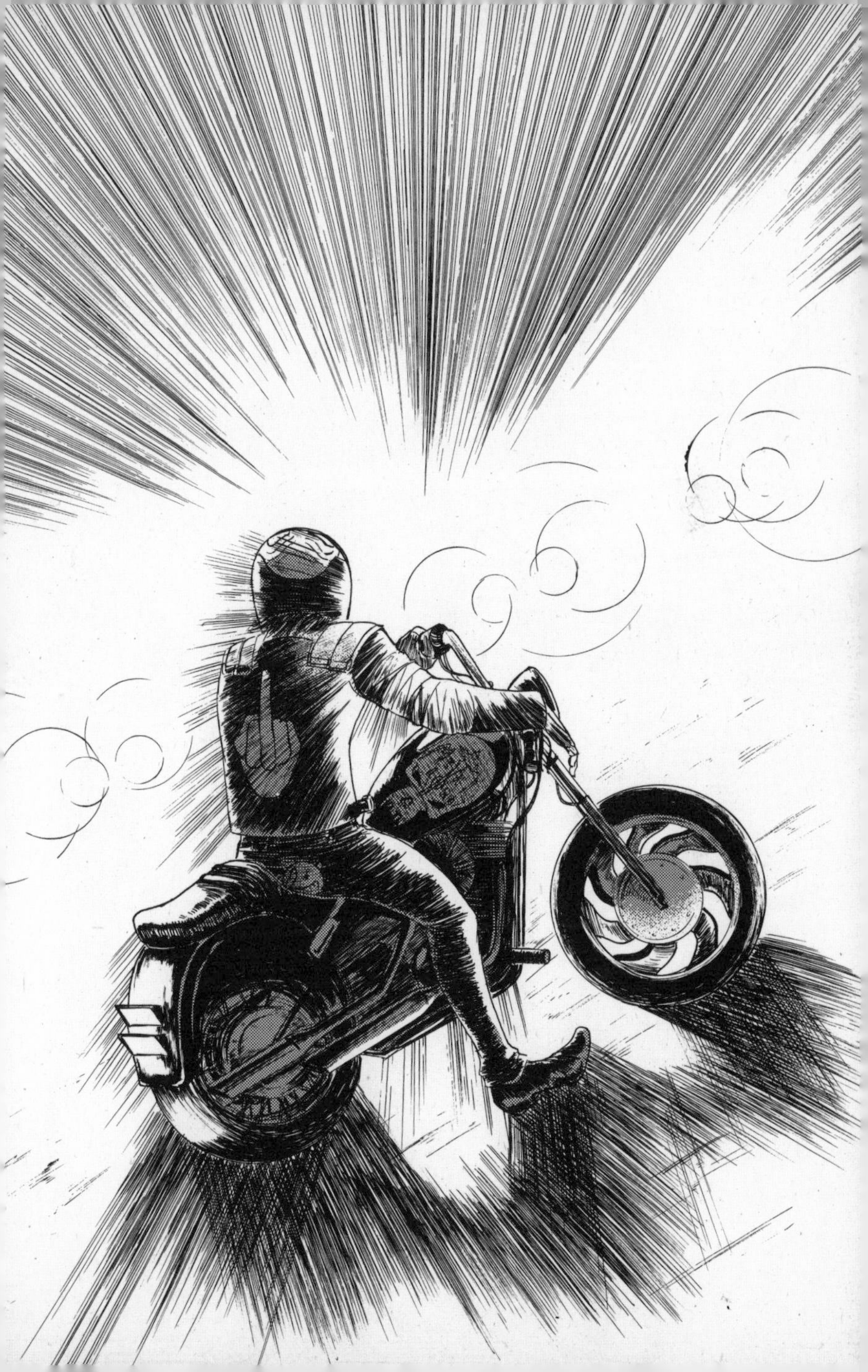

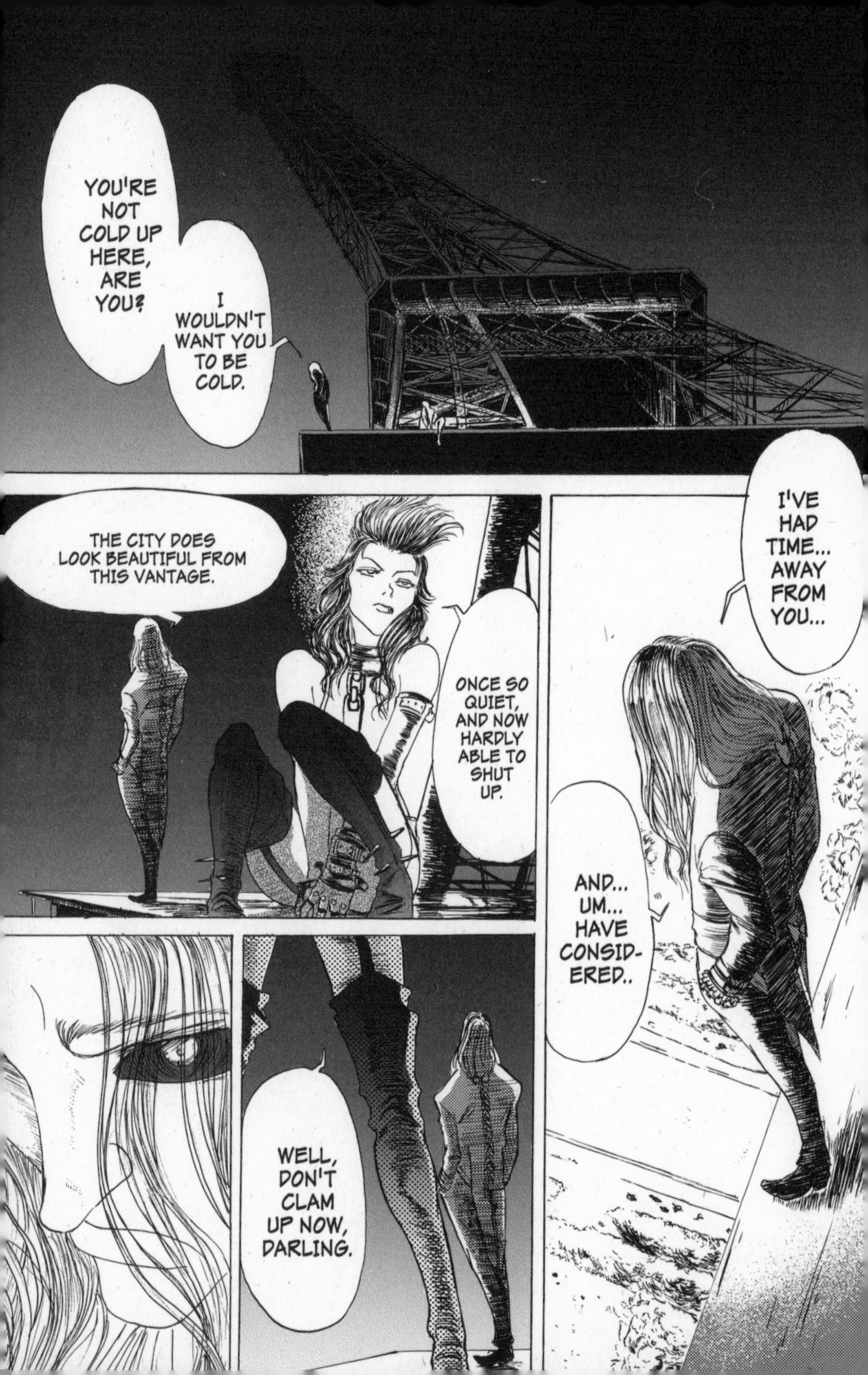
YOU'RE NOT COLD UP HERE, ARE YOU?
I WOULDN'T WANT YOU TO BE COLD.
THE CITY DOES LOOK BEAUTIFUL FROM THIS VANTAGE.
ONCE SO QUIET, AND NOW HARDLY ABLE TO SHUT UP.
I'VE HAD TIME... AWAY FROM YOU...
AND... UM... HAVE CONSIDERED..
WELL, DON'T CLAM UP NOW, DARLING.

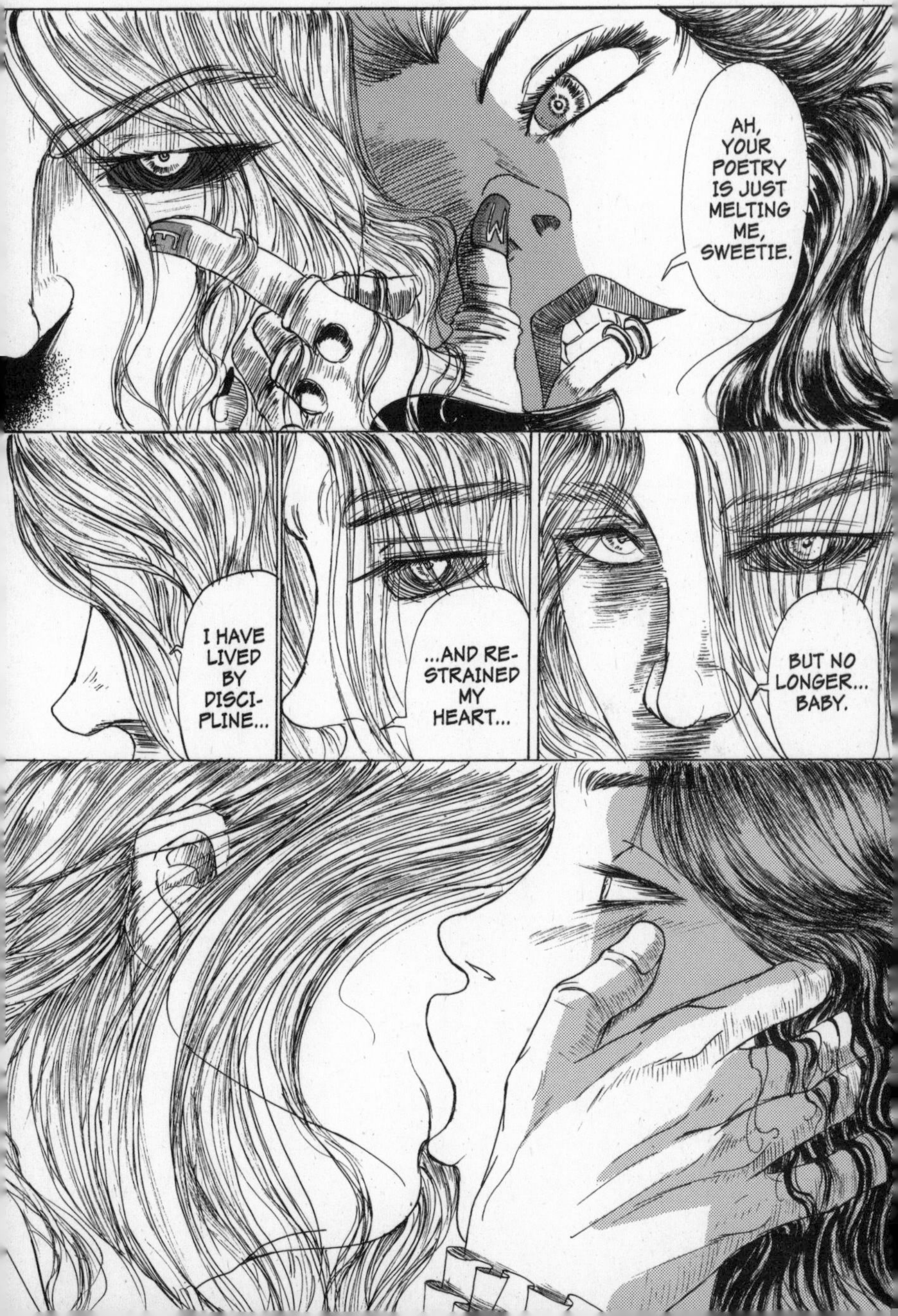
AH, YOUR POETRY IS JUST MELTING ME, SWEETIE.
I HAVE LIVED BY DISCI-PLINE...
...AND RE-STRAINED MY HEART...
BUT NO LONGER... BABY.

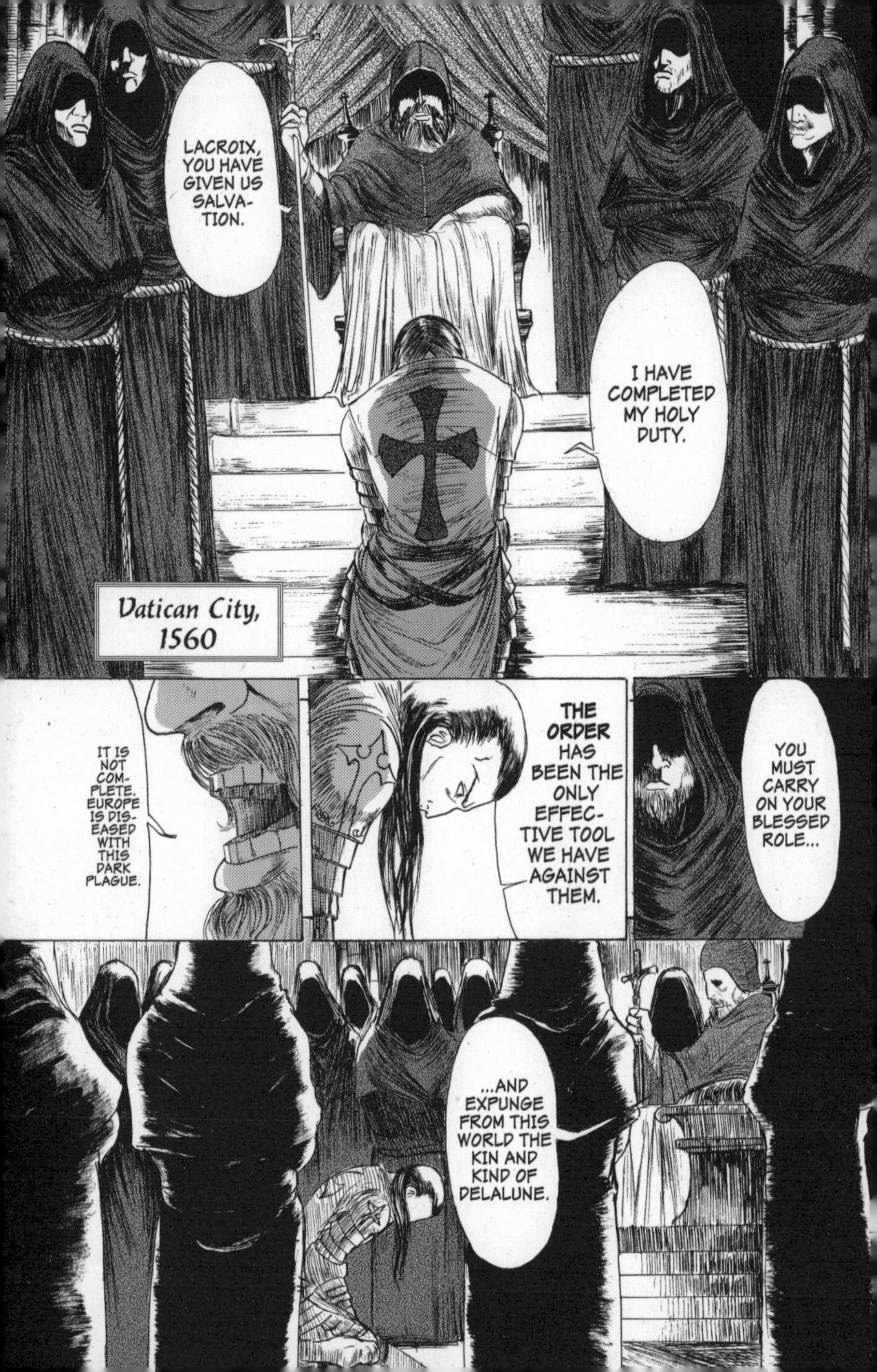
LACROIX, YOU HAVE GIVEN US SALVATION.
I HAVE COMPLETED MY HOLY DUTY.
Vatican City, 1560
IT IS NOT COMPLETE. EUROPE IS DISEASED WITH THIS DARK PLAGUE.
THE ORDER HAS BEEN THE ONLY EFFECTIVE TOOL WE HAVE AGAINST THEM.
YOU MUST CARRY ON YOUR BLESSED ROLE...
...AND EXPUNGE FROM THIS WORLD THE KIN AND KIND OF DELALUNE.

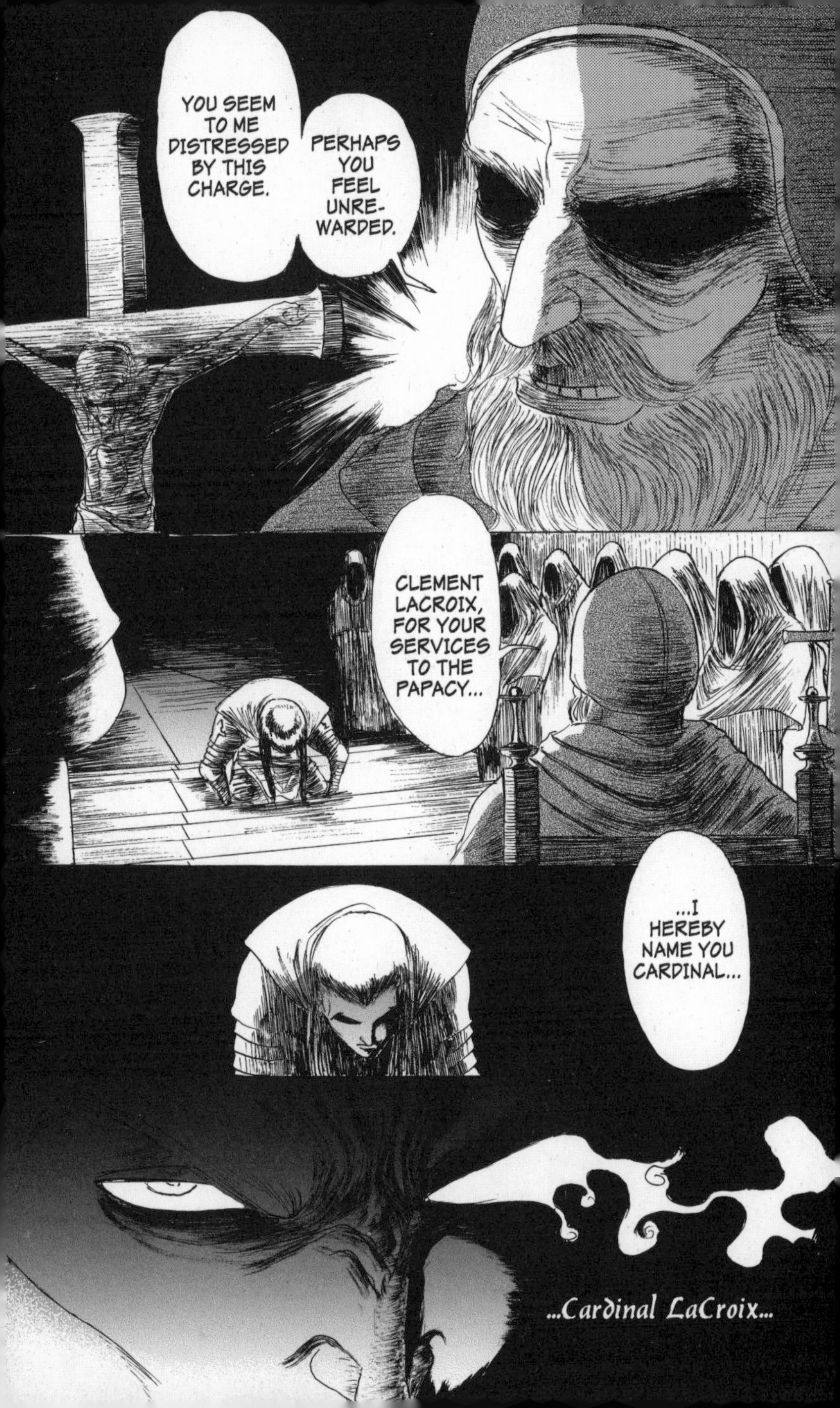
YOU SEEM TO ME DISTRESSED BY THIS CHARGE.
PERHAPS YOU FEEL UNRE-WARDED.
CLEMENT LACROIX, FOR YOUR SERVICES TO THE PAPACY...
...I HEREBY NAME YOU CARDINAL...
...Cardinal LaCroix...

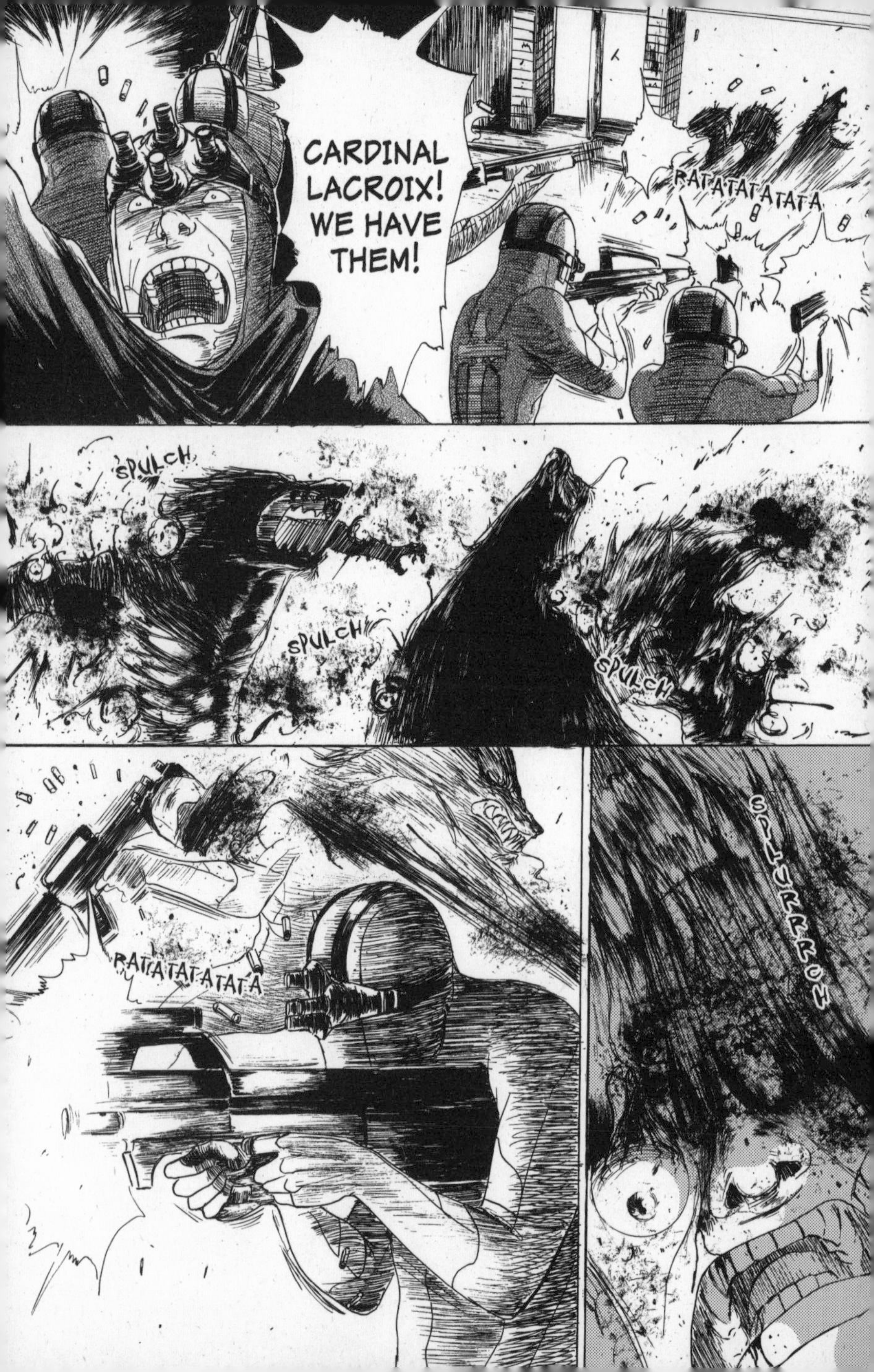
RATATATATATATA
CARDINAL LACROIX! WE HAVE THEM!
SPULCH
SPULCH
SPULCH
SPLURRRCH
RATATATATATA

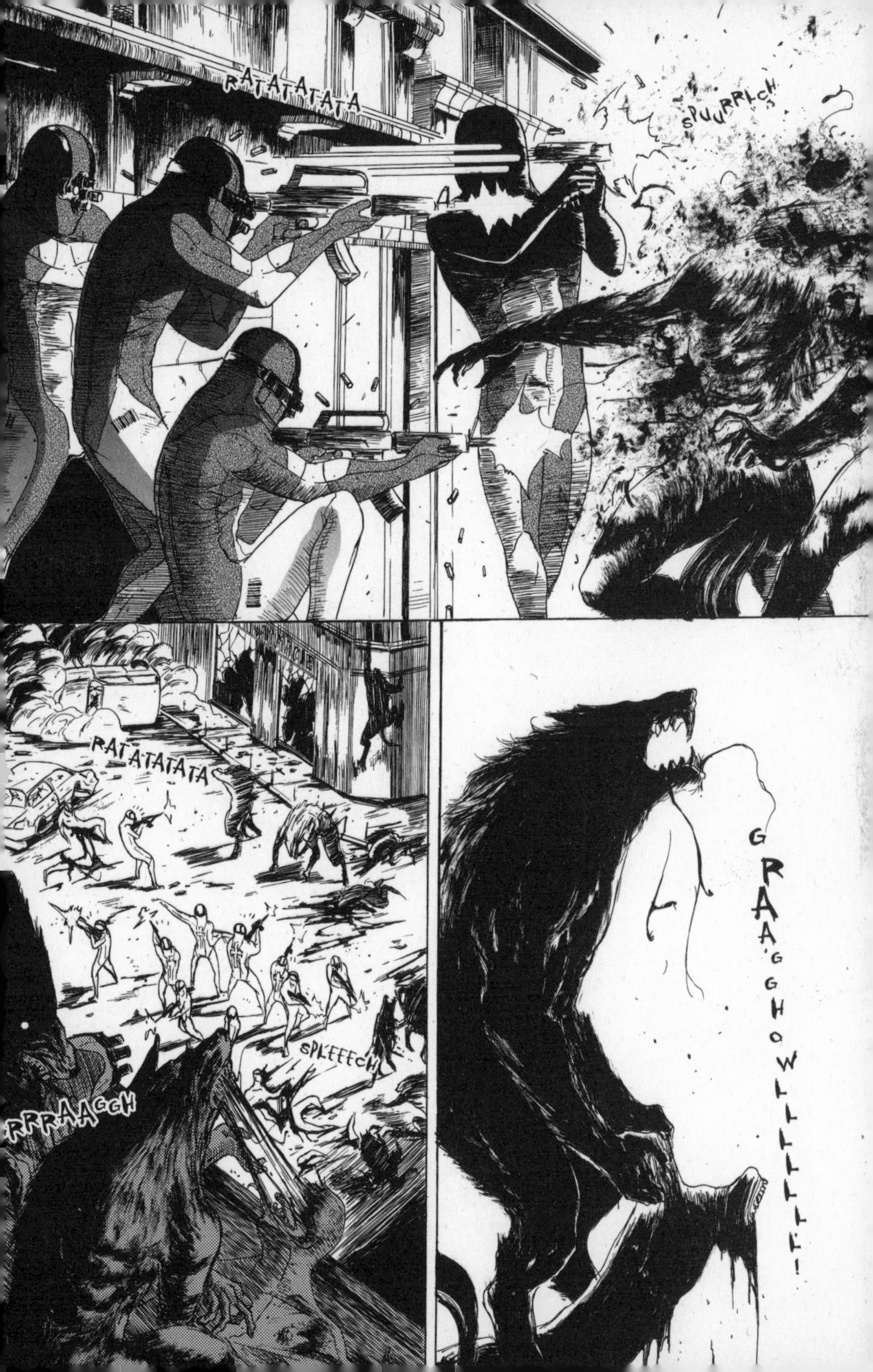
SPUURRLCH
RATATATATA
GRAAGGHOWLLLLLLL!
RATATATATA
SPLEEECH
RRRAAGGH

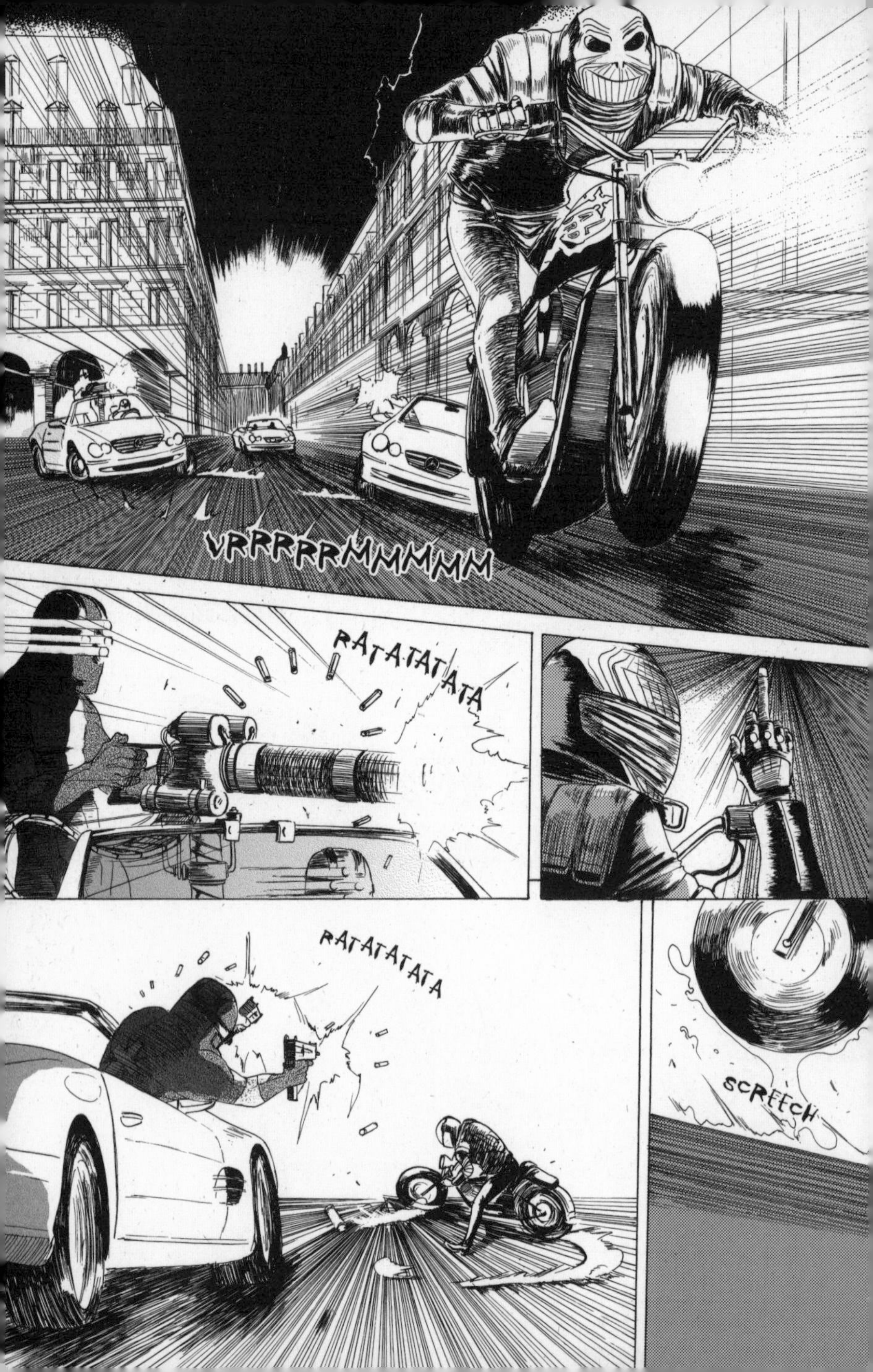
VRRRRRMMMMM
RATATATATA
SCREECH
RATATATATA

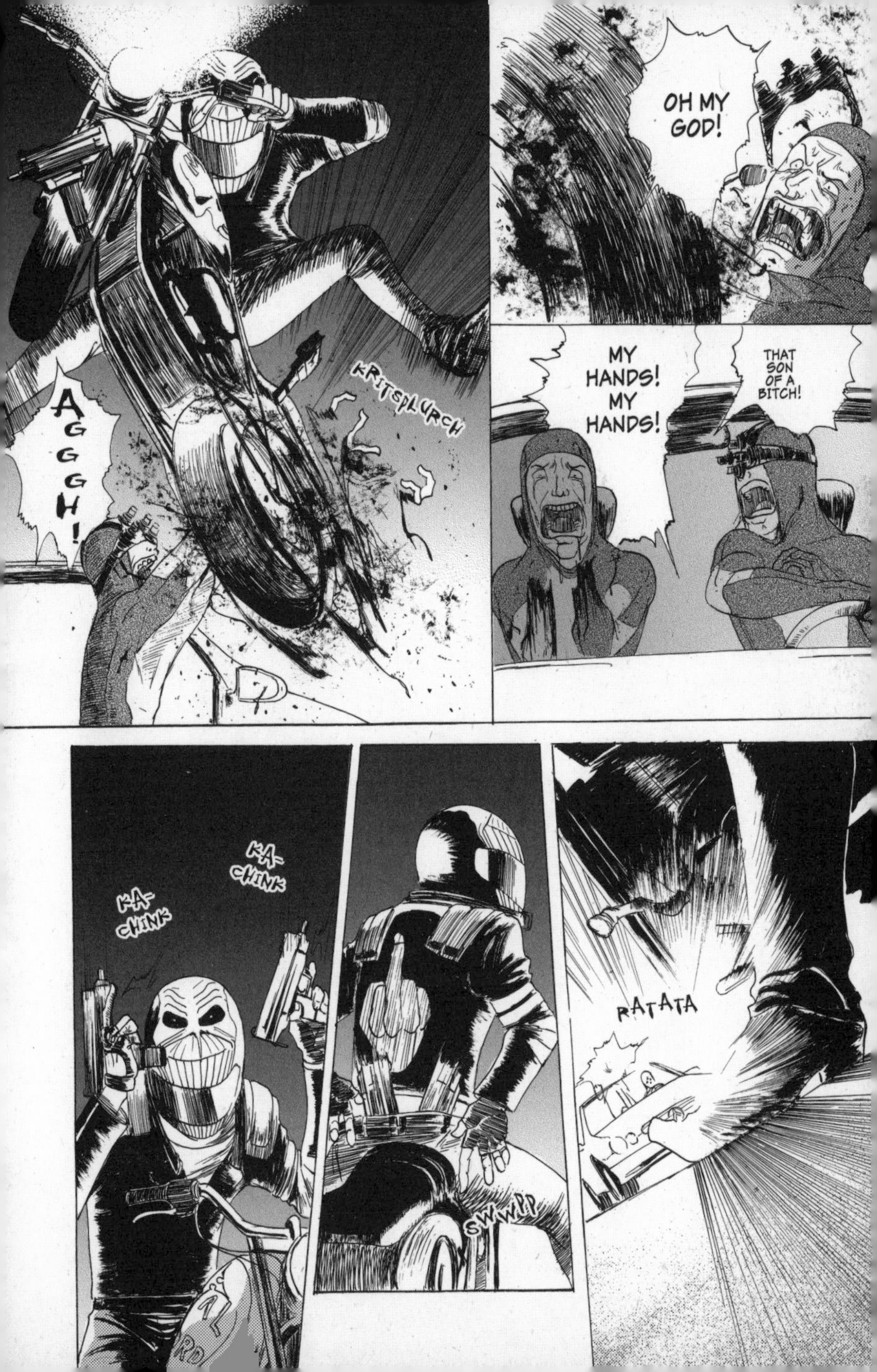
OH MY GOD!
THAT SON OF A BITCH!
MY HANDS! MY HANDS!
KRITSPLURCH
AGGGH!
RATATA
SWWIPP
KA-CHINK
KA-CHINK

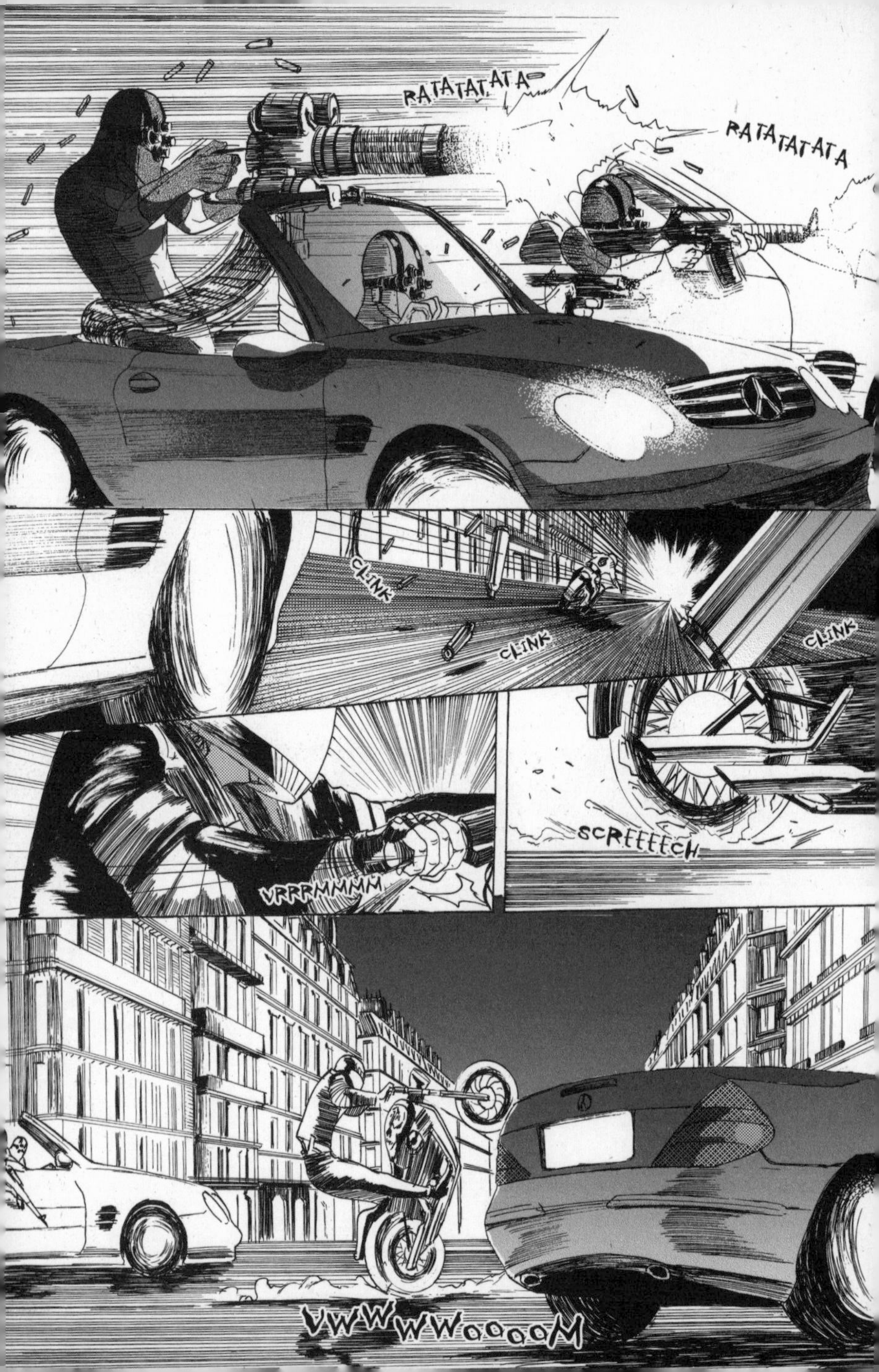
RATATATATA
RATATATATA
CLINK
CLINK
CLINK
SCREEEECH
VRRRMMMM
VWWWWWooooM

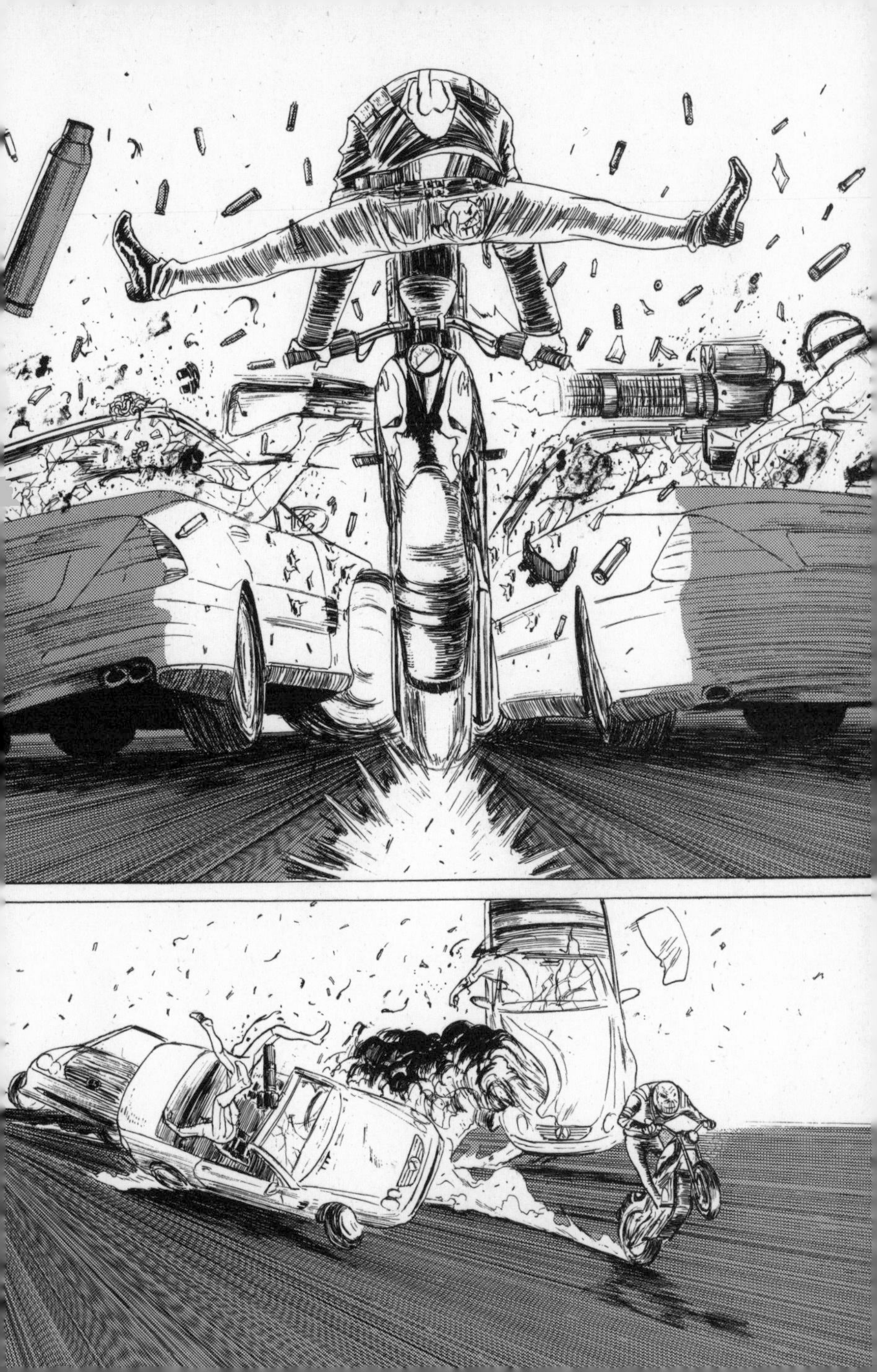

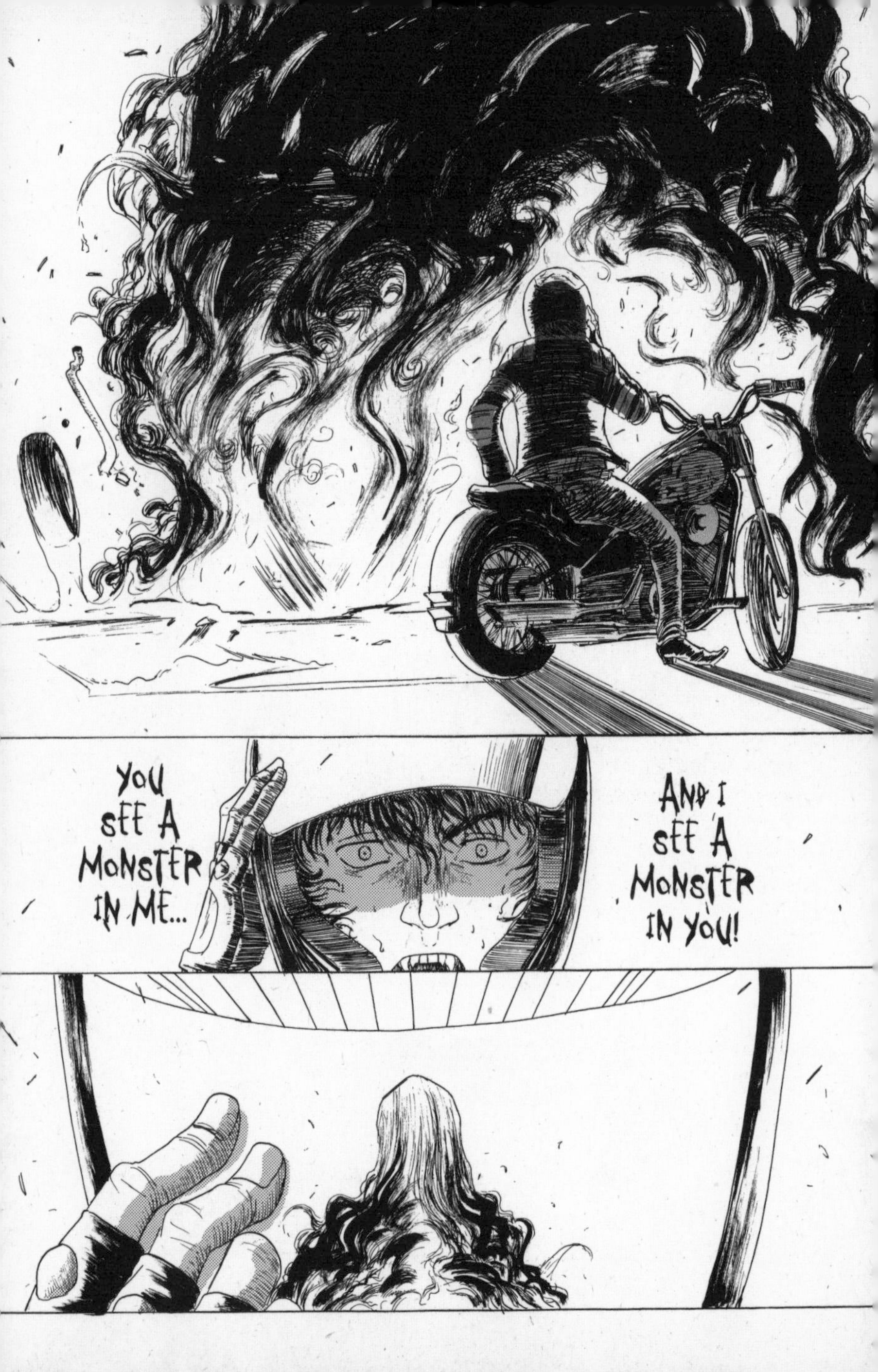
YOU SEE A MONSTER IN ME...
AND I SEE A MONSTER IN YOU!

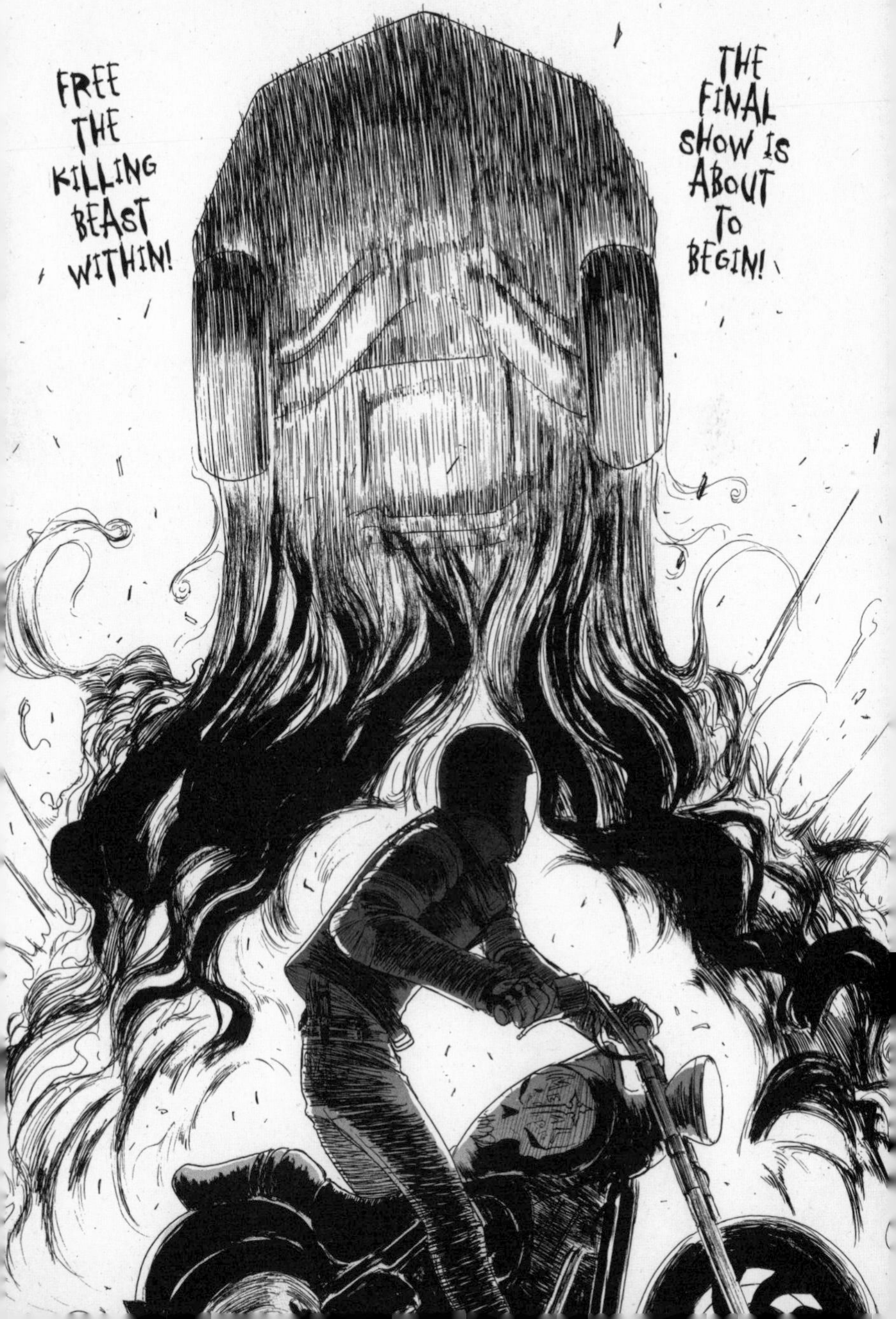
THE FINAL SHOW IS ABOUT TO BEGIN!
FREE THE KILLING BEAST WITHIN!

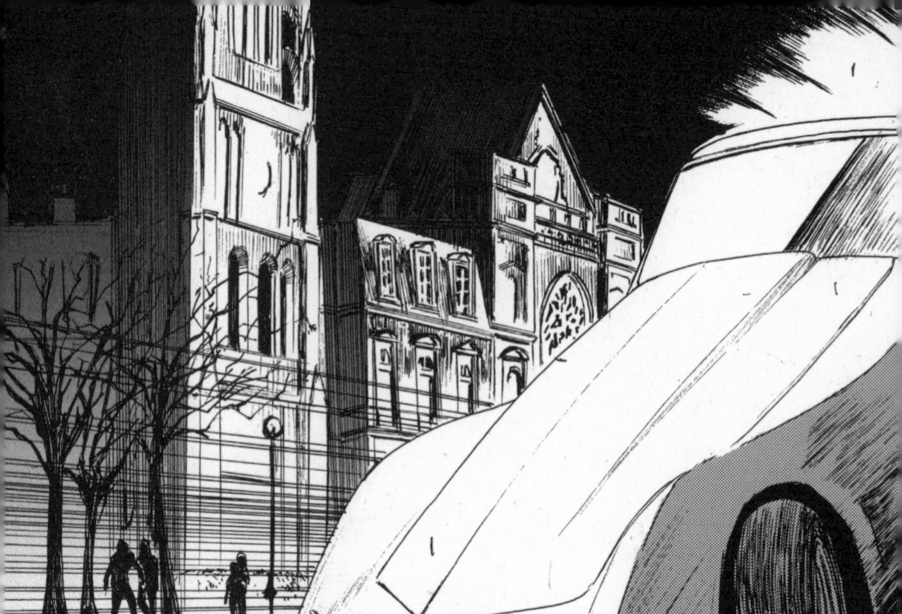
2 HELL

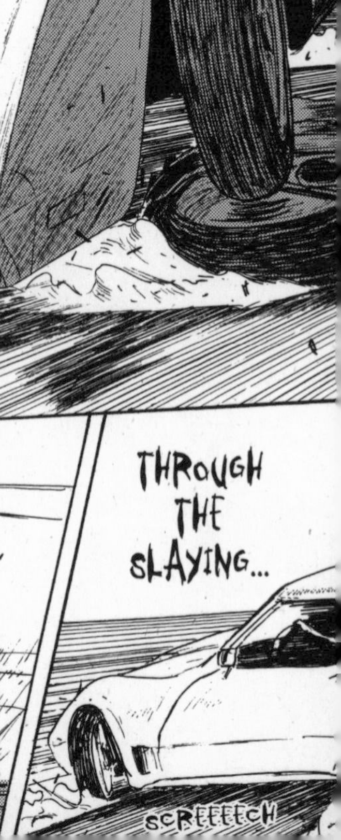
THROUGH THE SLAYING...
SCREEEECH

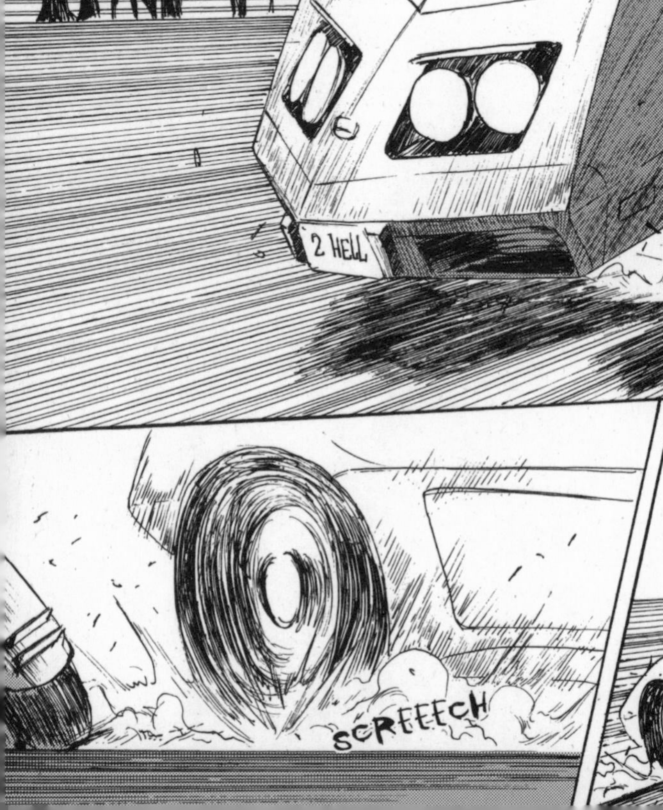
SCREEECH

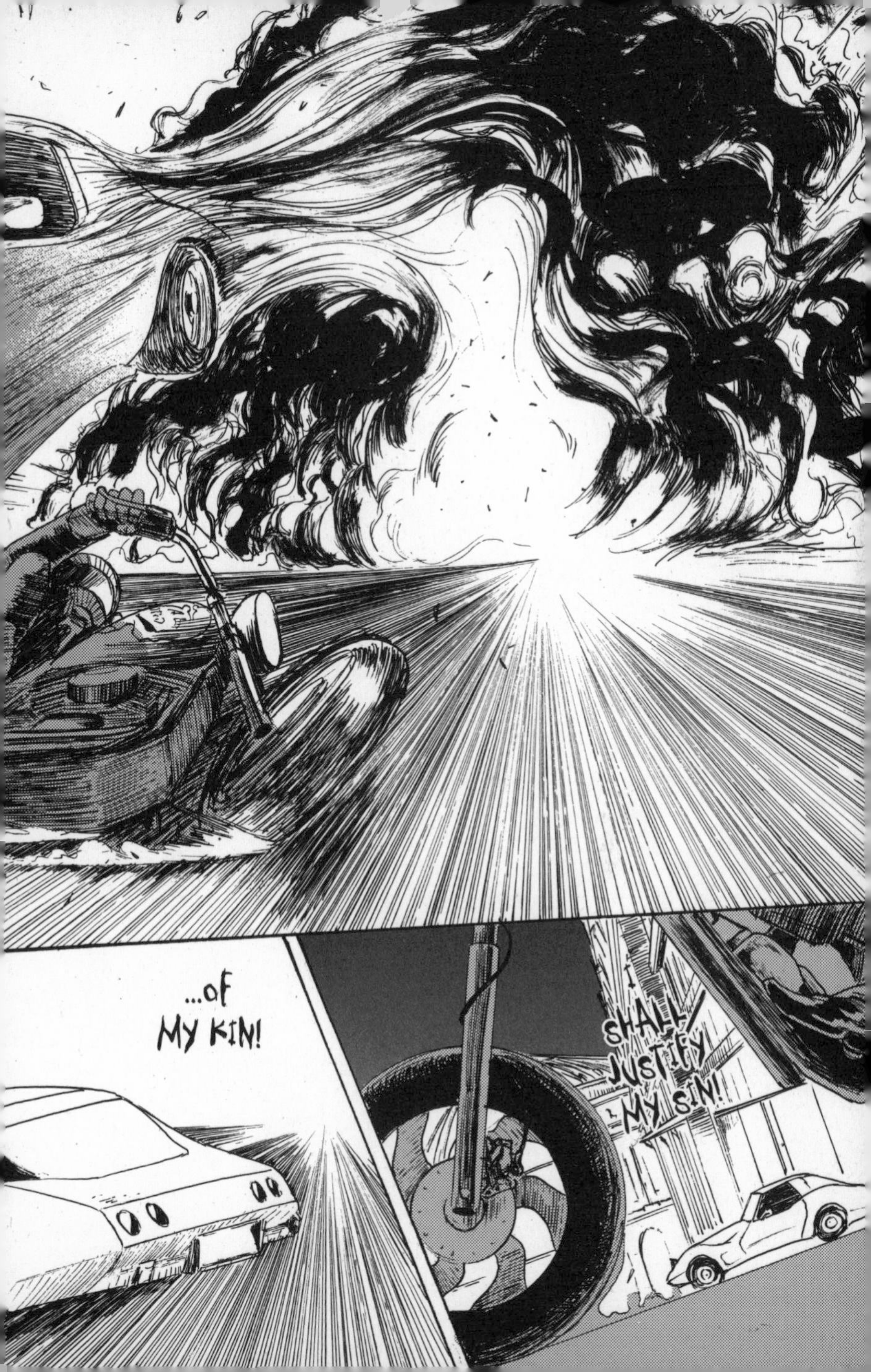
I SHALL JUSTIFY MY SIN!
...of MY KIN!

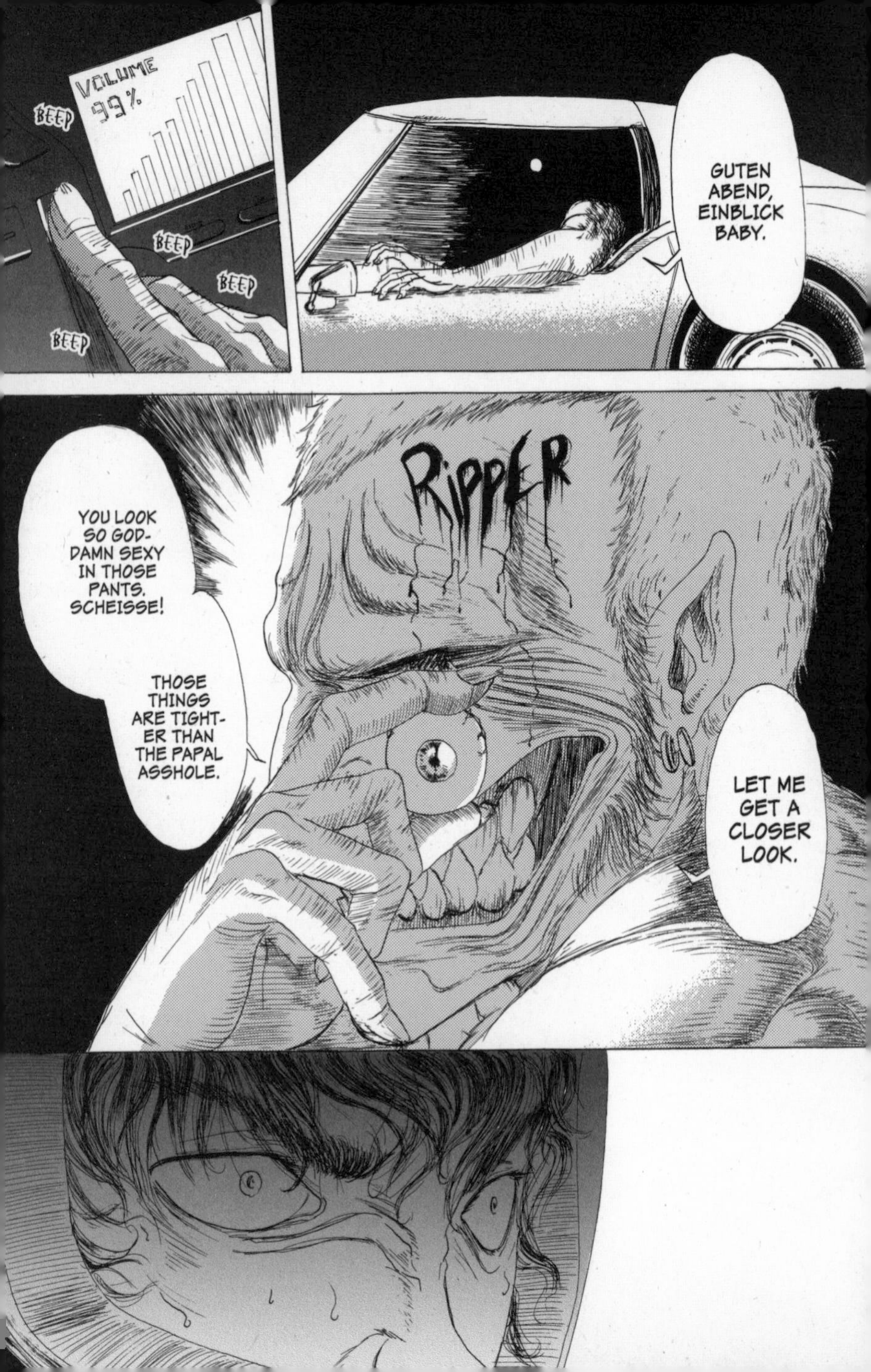
GUTEN ABEND, EINBLICK BABY.
VOLUME 99%
BEEP
BEEP
BEEP
BEEP
RIPPER
YOU LOOK SO GOD-DAMN SEXY IN THOSE PANTS. SCHEISSE!
THOSE THINGS ARE TIGHTER THAN THE PAPAL ASSHOLE.
LET ME GET A CLOSER LOOK.

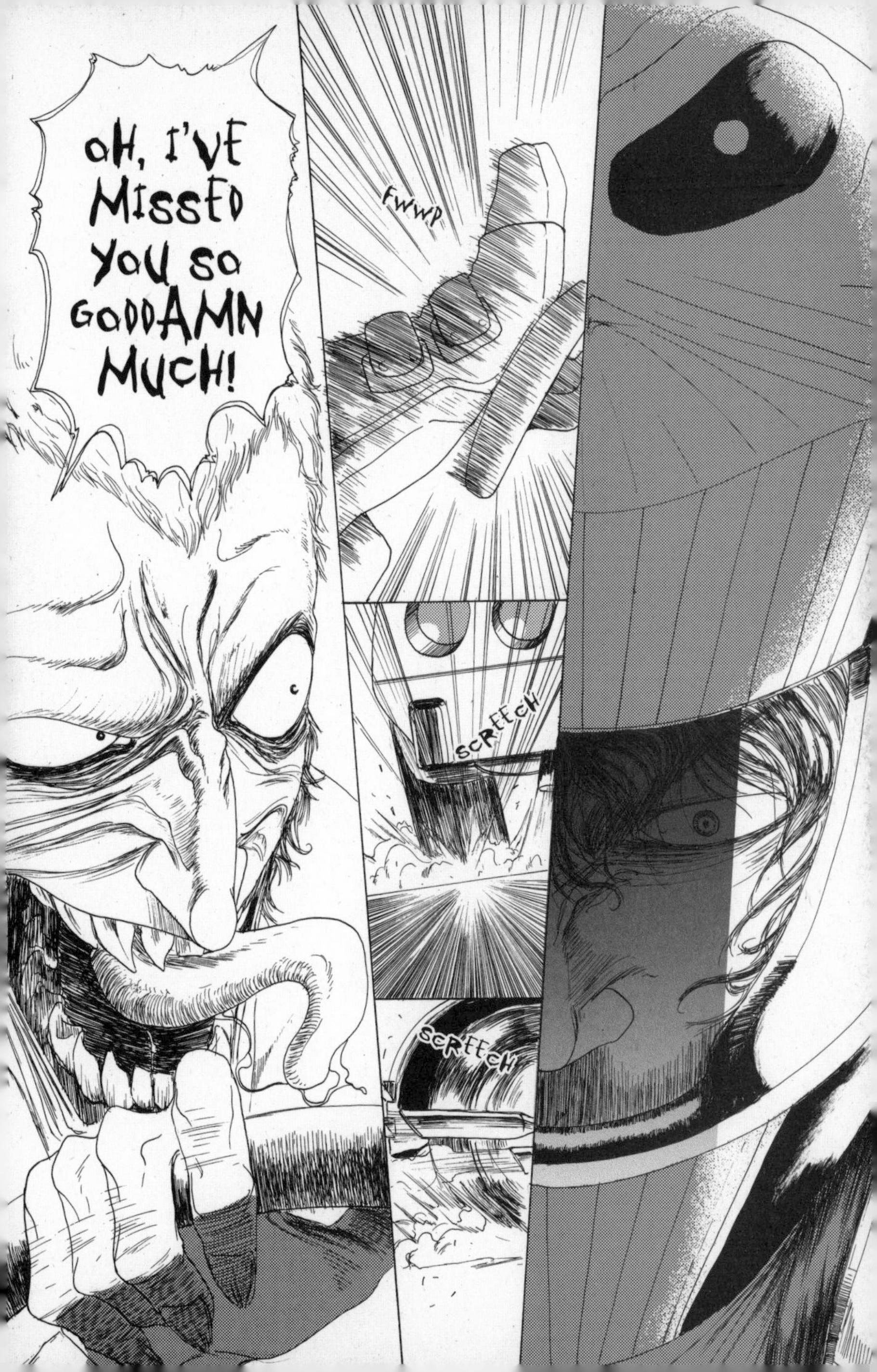
FWWP
SCREECH
SCREECH
OH, I'VE MISSED YOU SO GODDAMN MUCH!

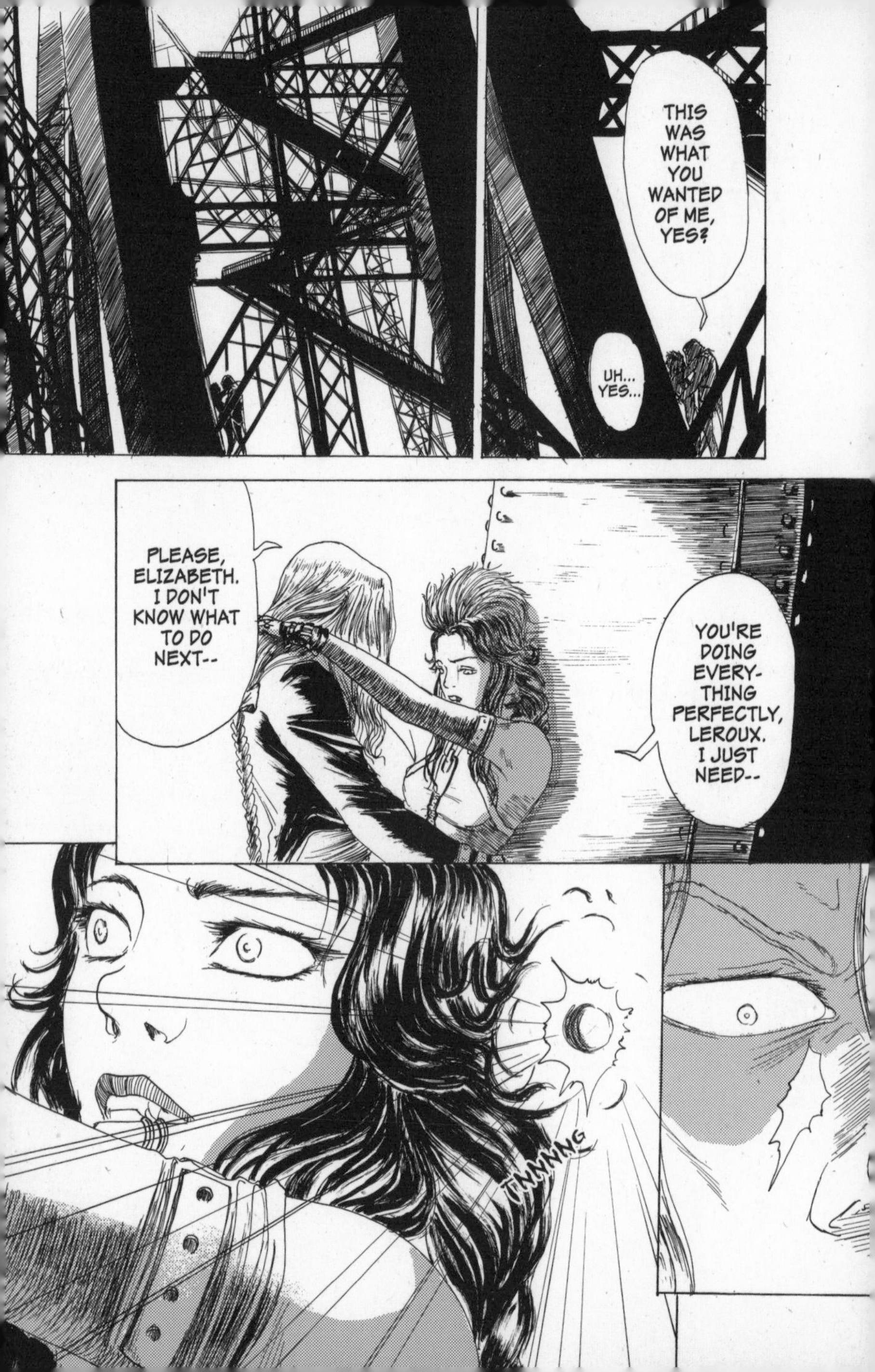
THIS WAS WHAT YOU WANTED OF ME, YES?
UH... YES...
PLEASE, ELIZABETH. I DON'T KNOW WHAT TO DO NEXT--
YOU'RE DOING EVERYTHING PERFECTLY, LEROUX. I JUST NEED--
TNNNG

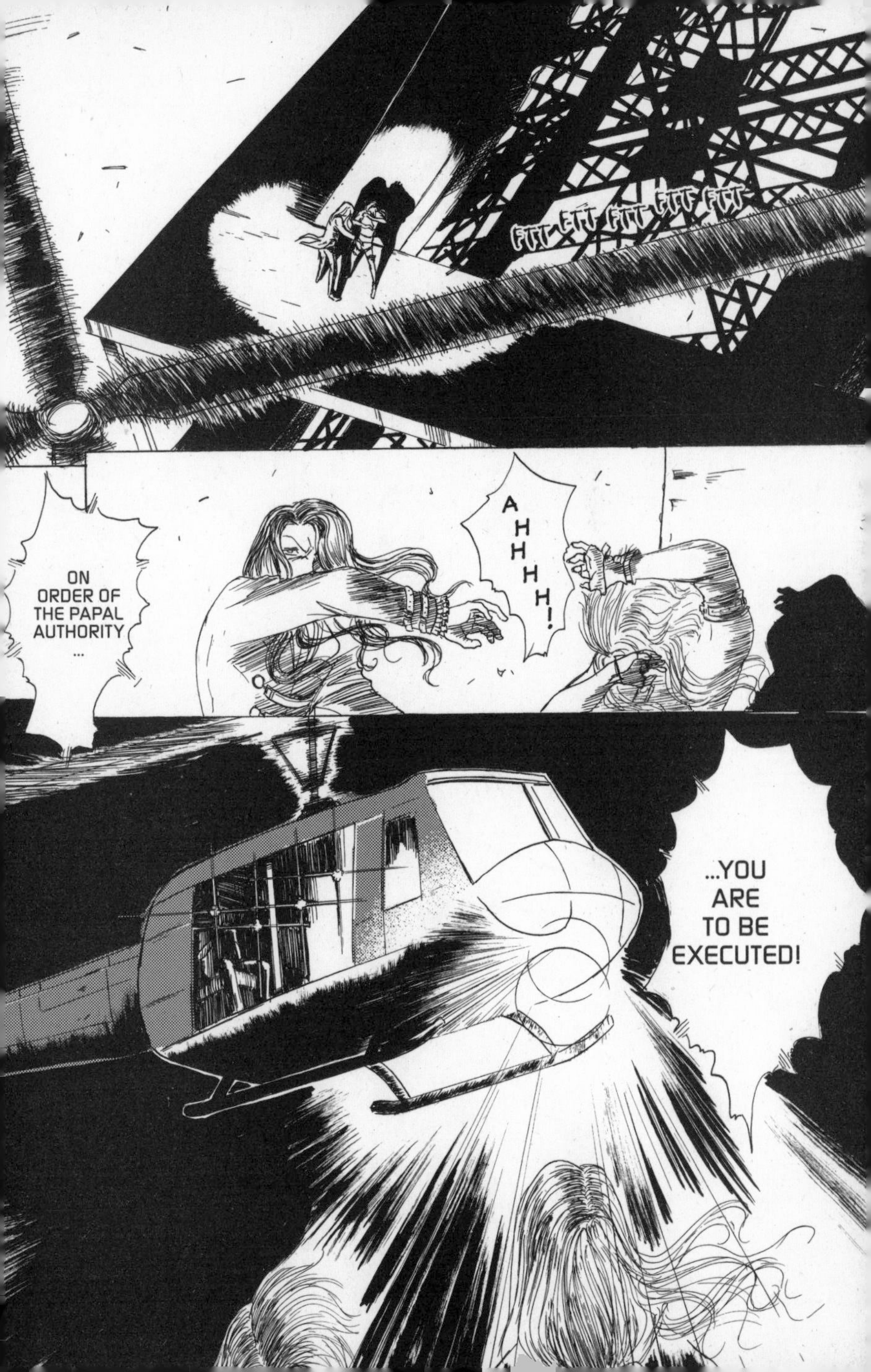
FTT FTT FTT FTT FTT
AHHHH!
ON ORDER OF THE PAPAL AUTHORITY ...
...YOU ARE TO BE EXECUTED!

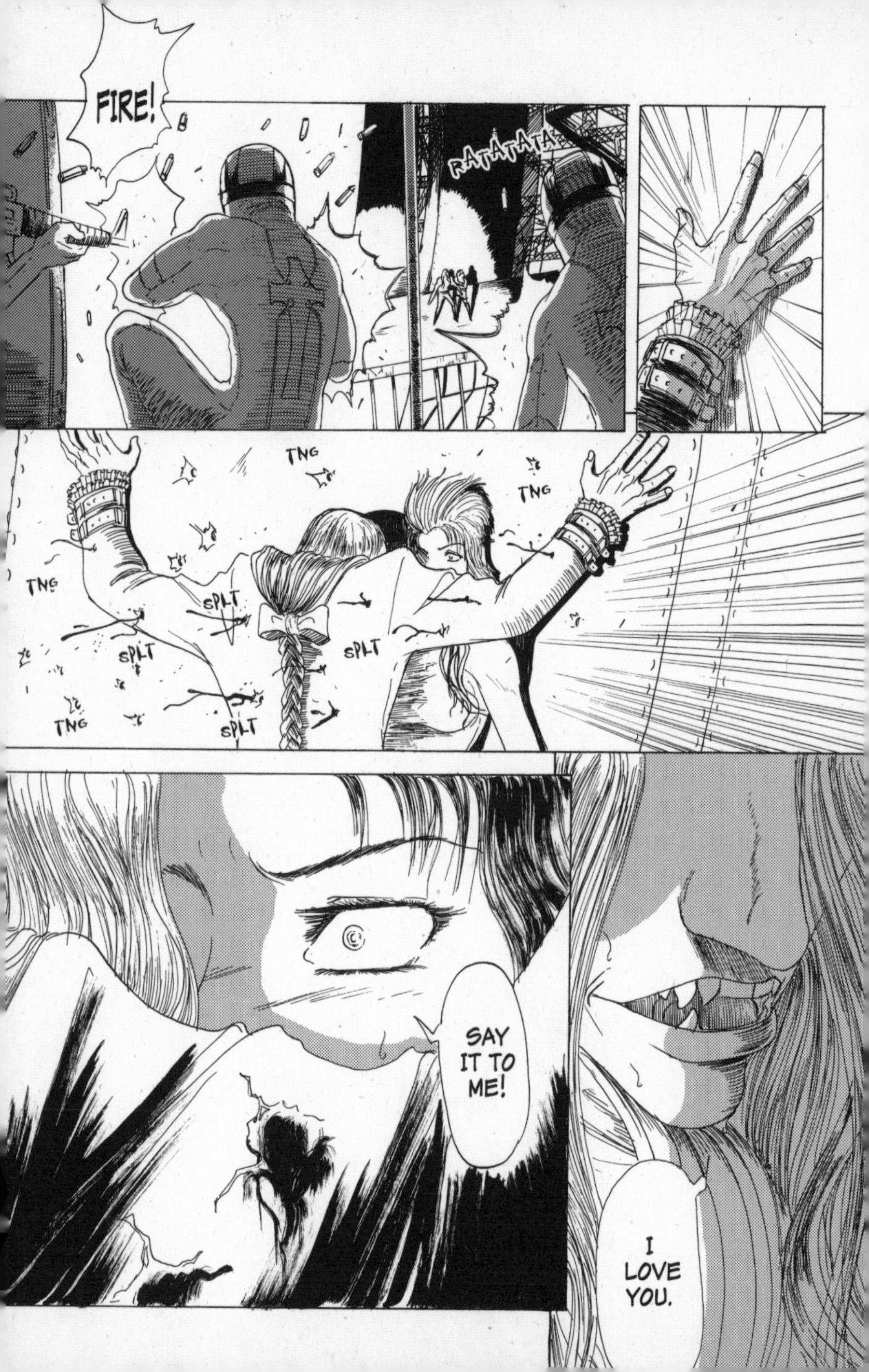
FIRE!
RATATATA
TNG
TNG
TNG
SPLT
SPLT
SPLT
SPLT
TNG
SAY IT TO ME!
I LOVE YOU.

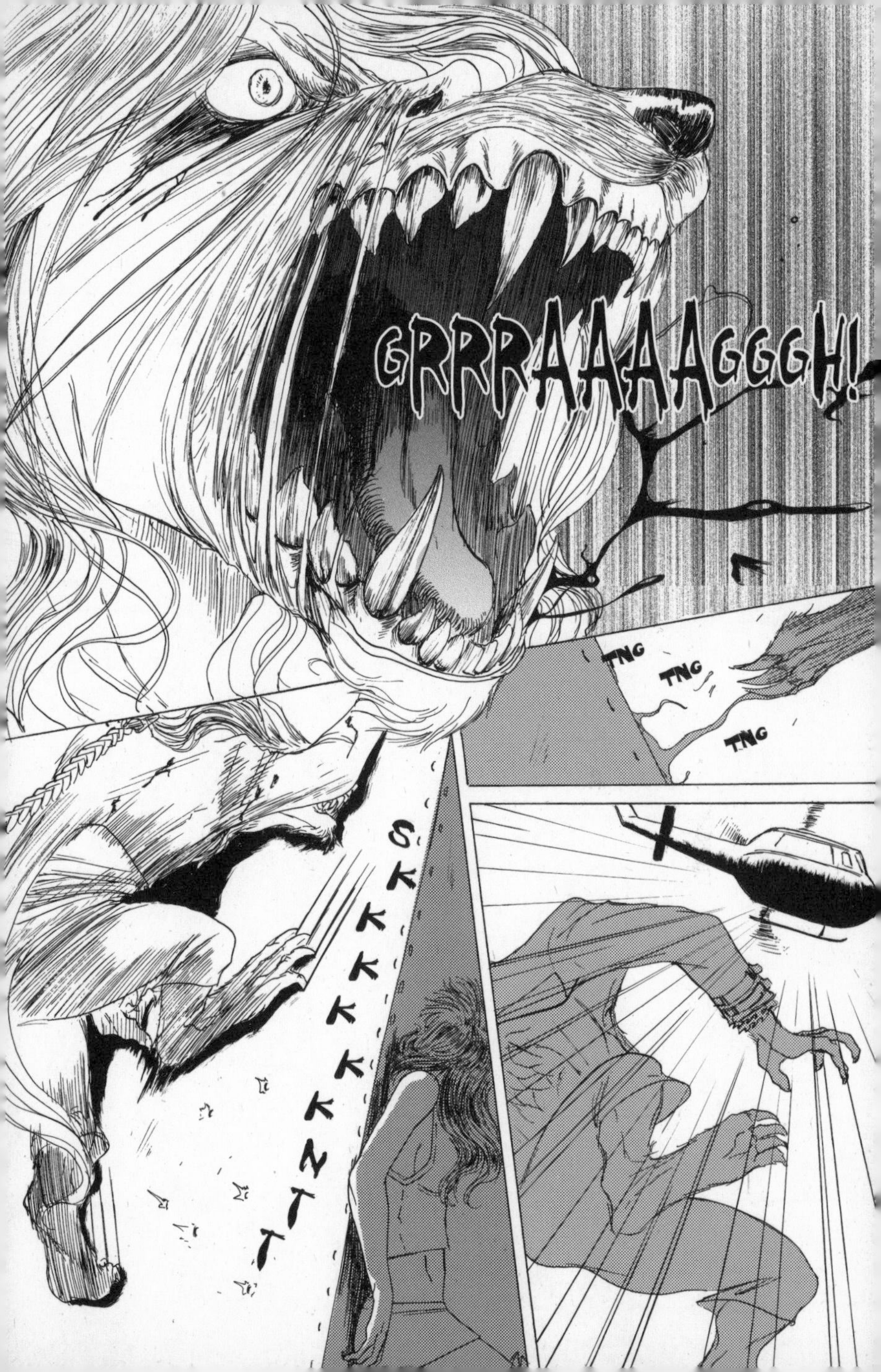
GRRRAAAAGGGH!
TNG
TNG
TNG
SKKKKKKKNTT

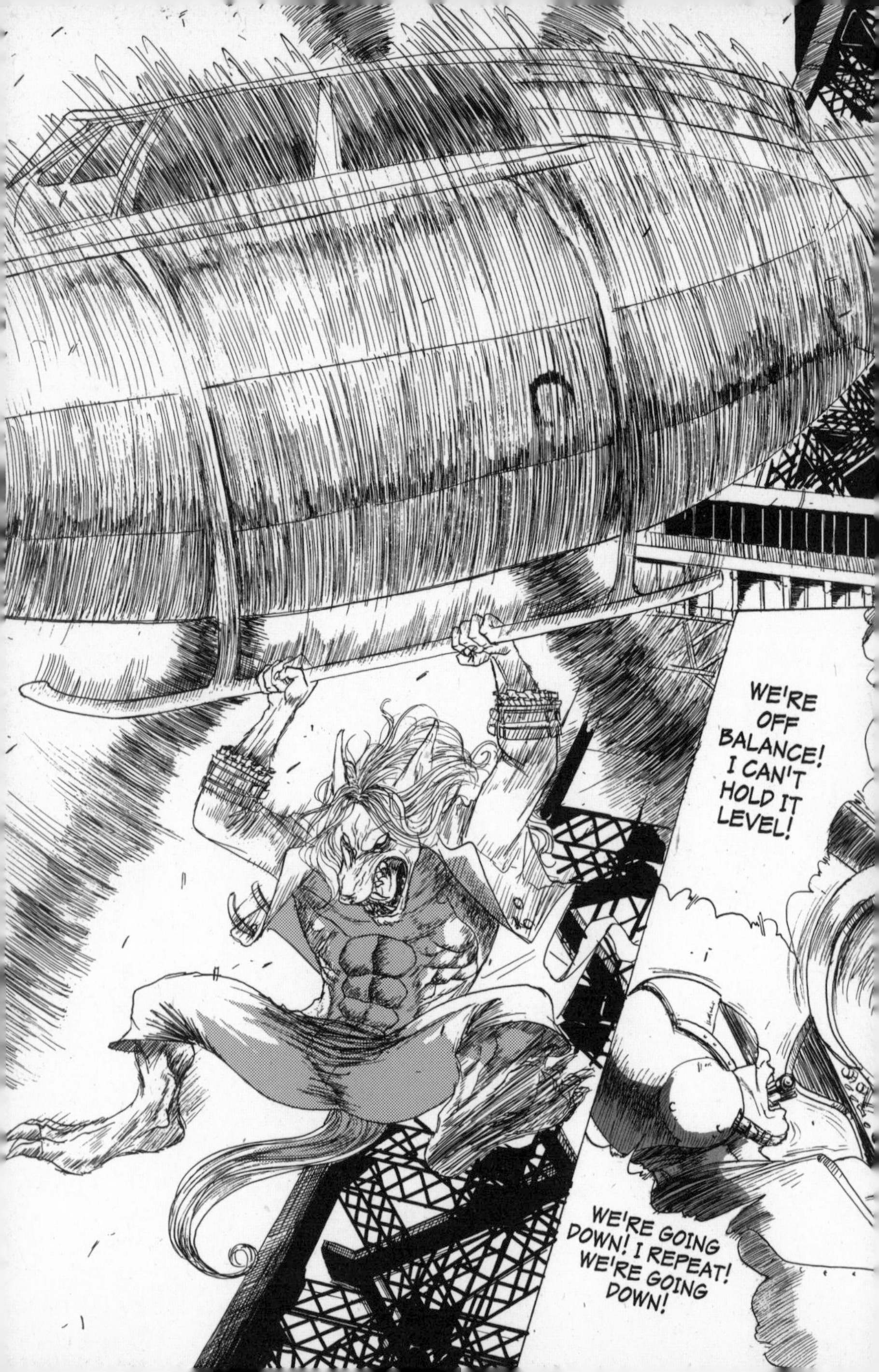
WE'RE OFF BALANCE! I CAN'T HOLD IT LEVEL!
WE'RE GOING DOWN! I REPEAT! WE'RE GOING DOWN!

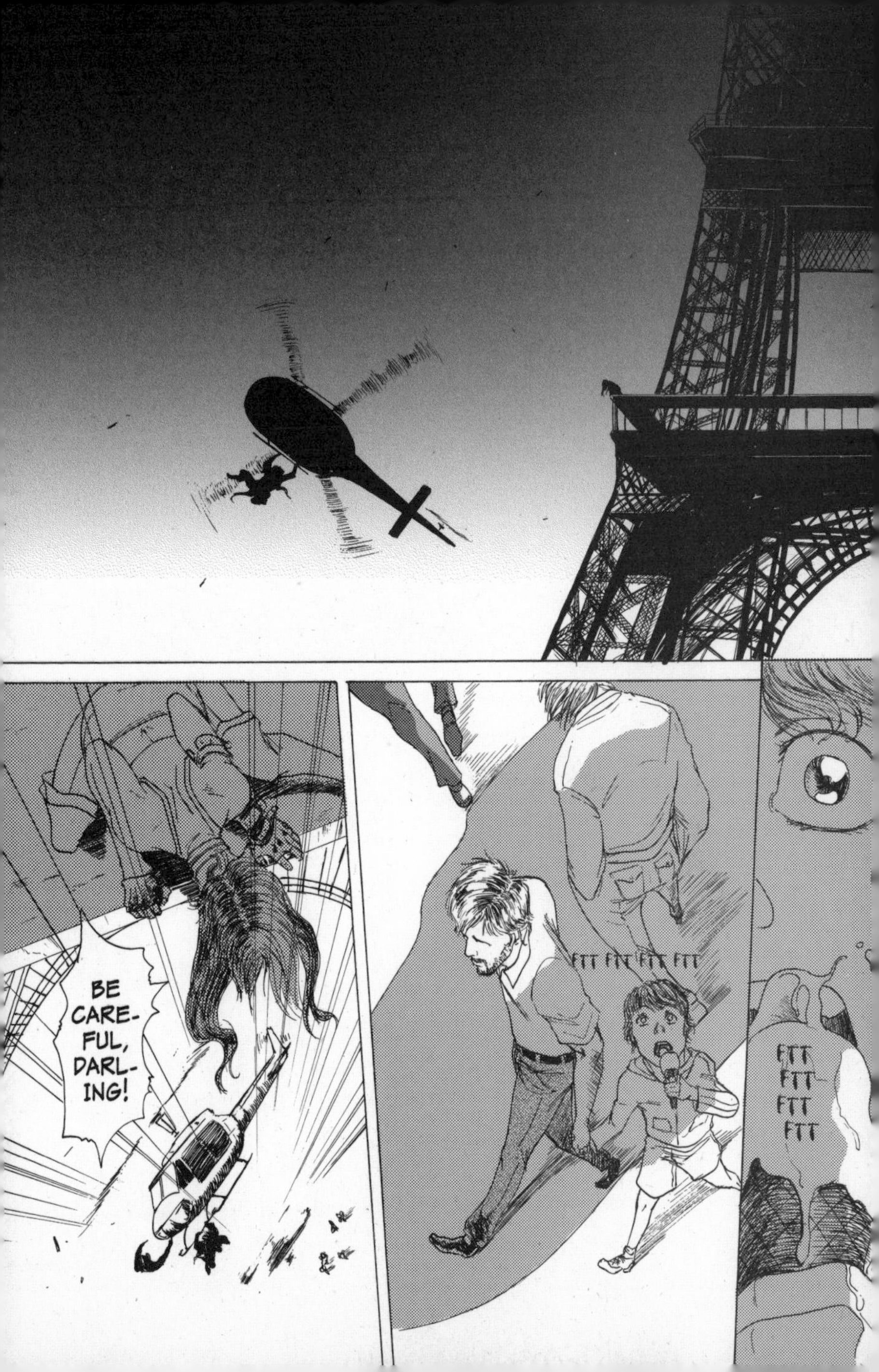
FTT FTT FTT FTT
FTT FTT FTT FTT
BE CARE-FUL, DARL-ING!

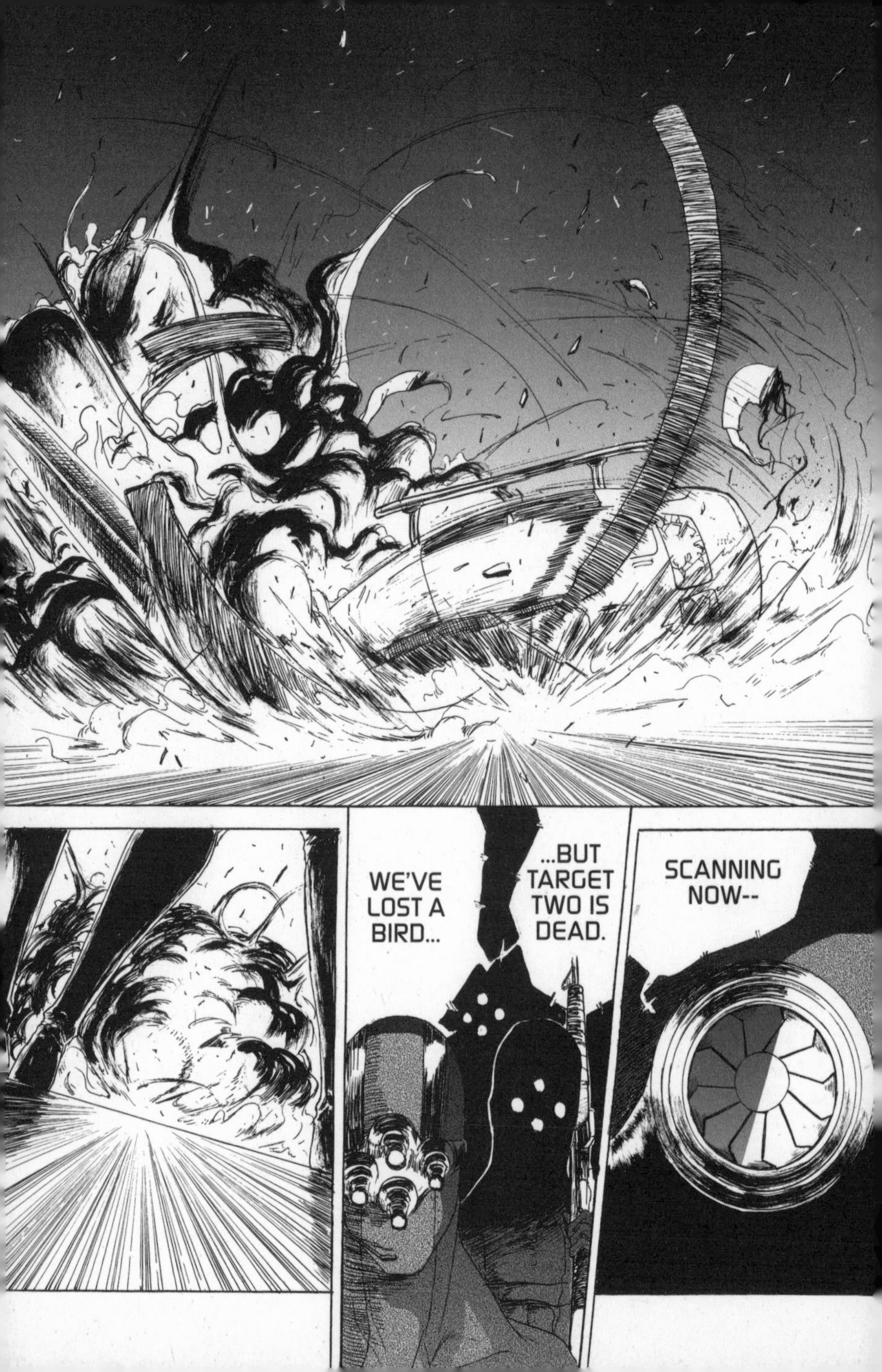
WE'VE LOST A BIRD...
...BUT TARGET TWO IS DEAD.
SCANNING NOW--

ANALYSIS INCOMPLETE
SCANNING...
ZOOM 35%
SCANNING...
ANALYSIS LOCK-ON
ZOOM
MERDE!
READY
ANALYSIS READY

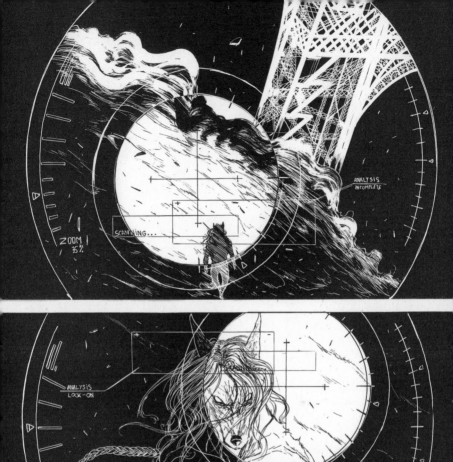

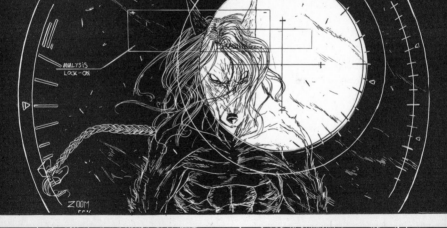

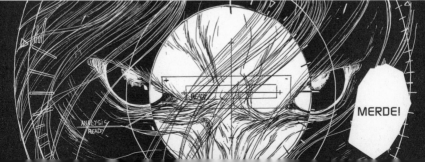

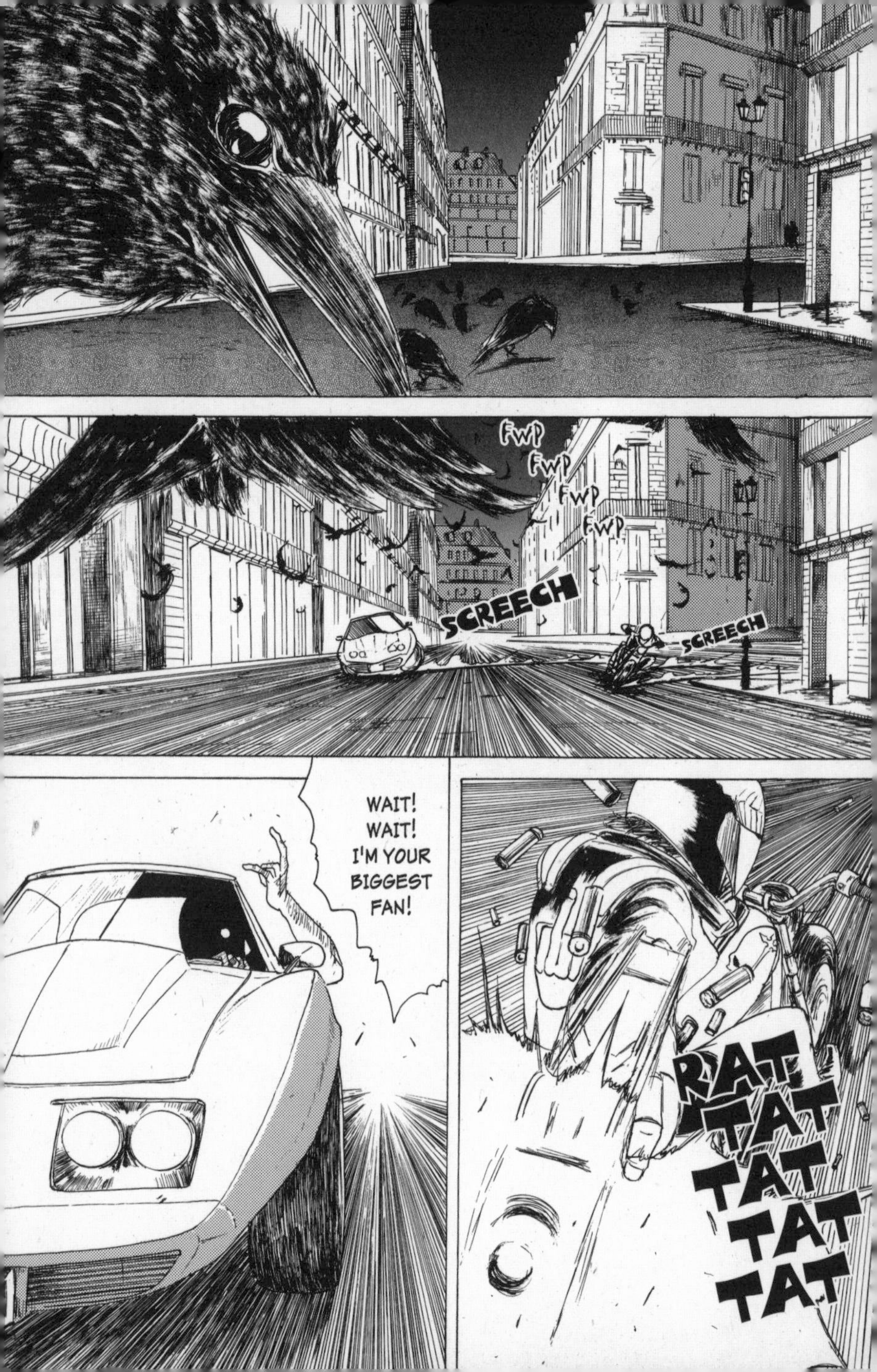
FWP
FWP
FWP
FWP
SCREECH
SCREECH
WAIT! WAIT! I'M YOUR BIGGEST FAN!
RAT TAT TAT TAT TAT

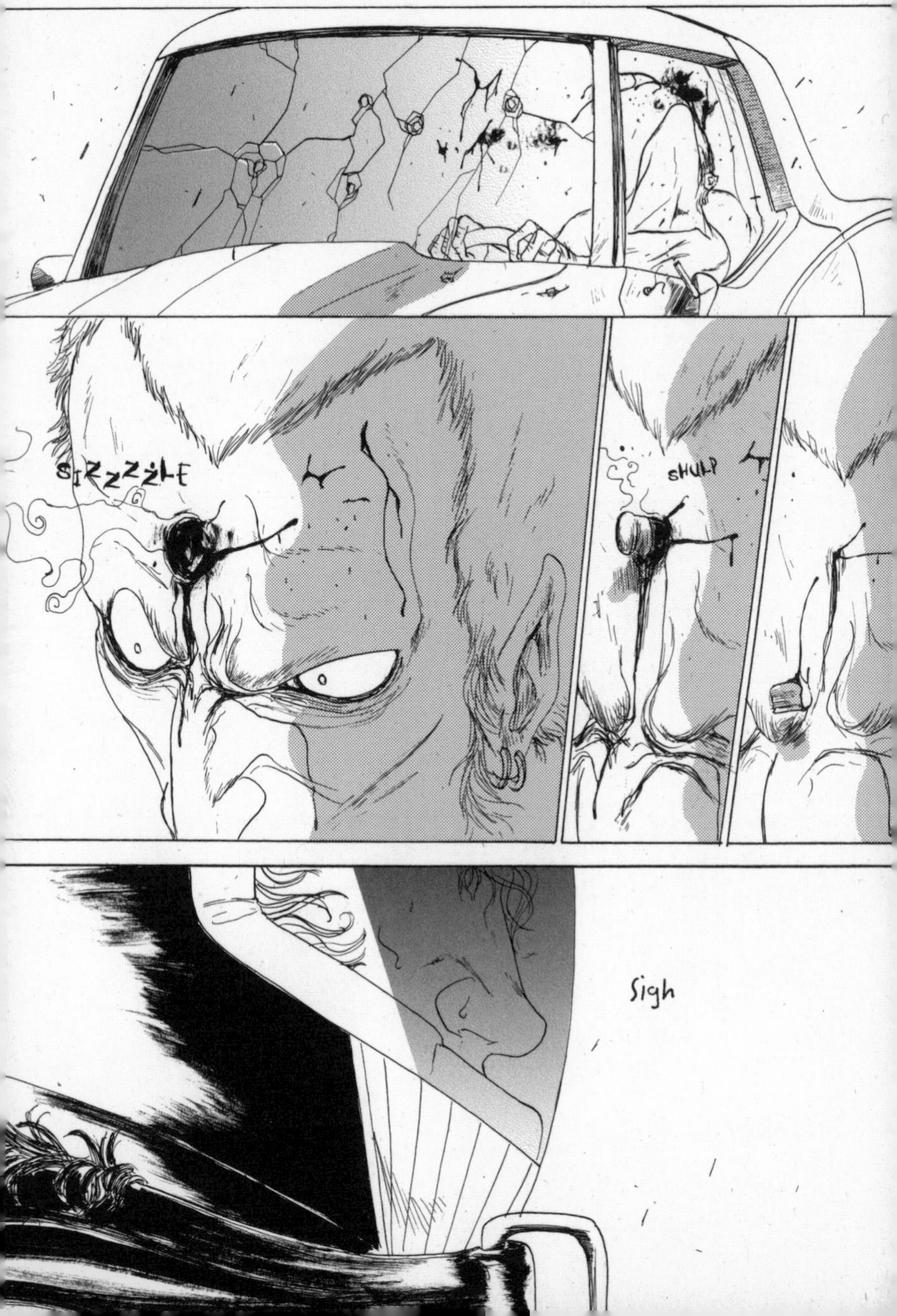
SIZZZZLE
SHULP
Sigh

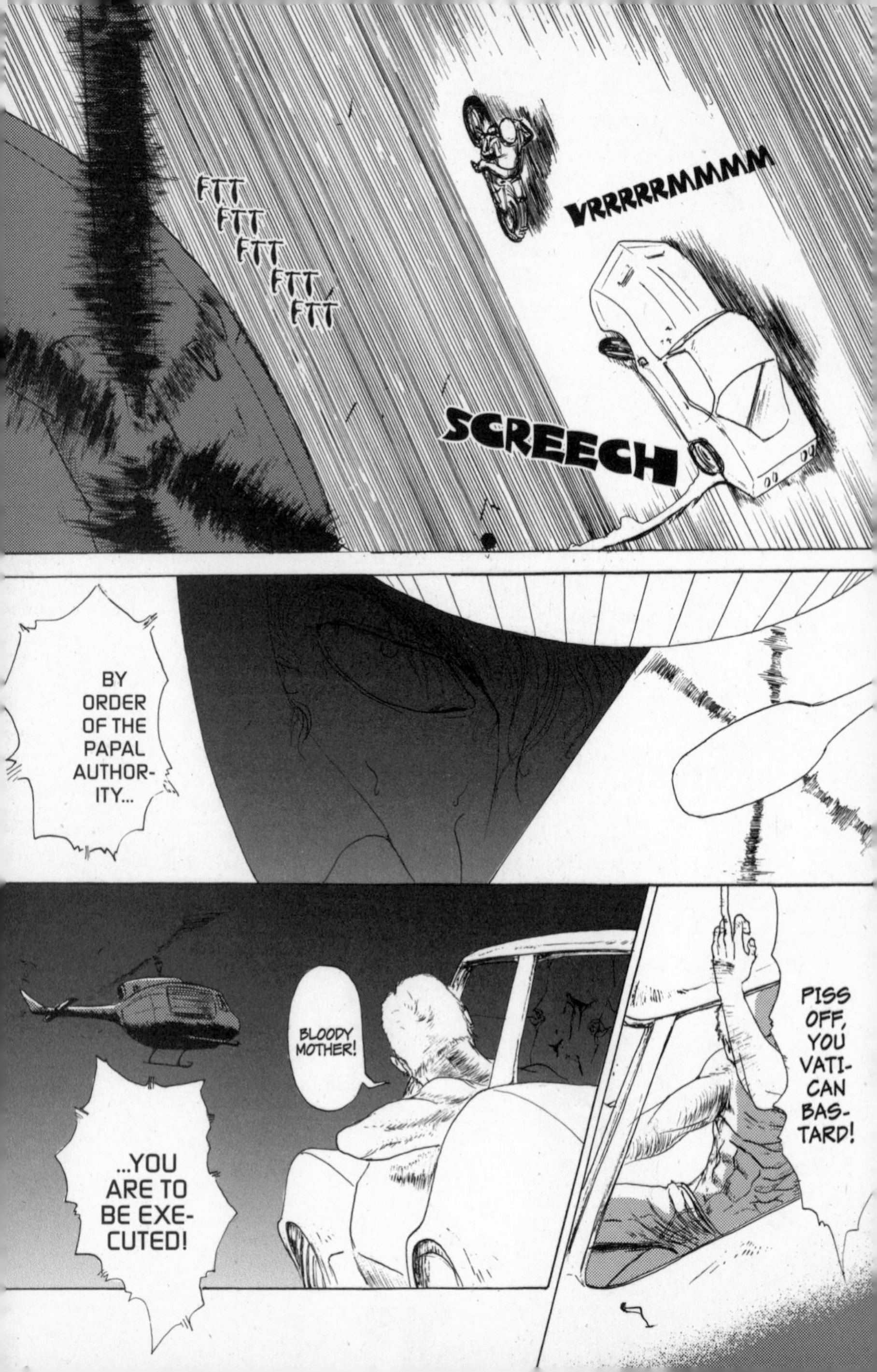
VRRRRRMMMM
SCREECH
FTT FTT FTT FTT FTT
BY ORDER OF THE PAPAL AUTHORITY...
PISS OFF, YOU VATICAN BASTARD!
BLOODY MOTHER!
...YOU ARE TO BE EXECUTED!

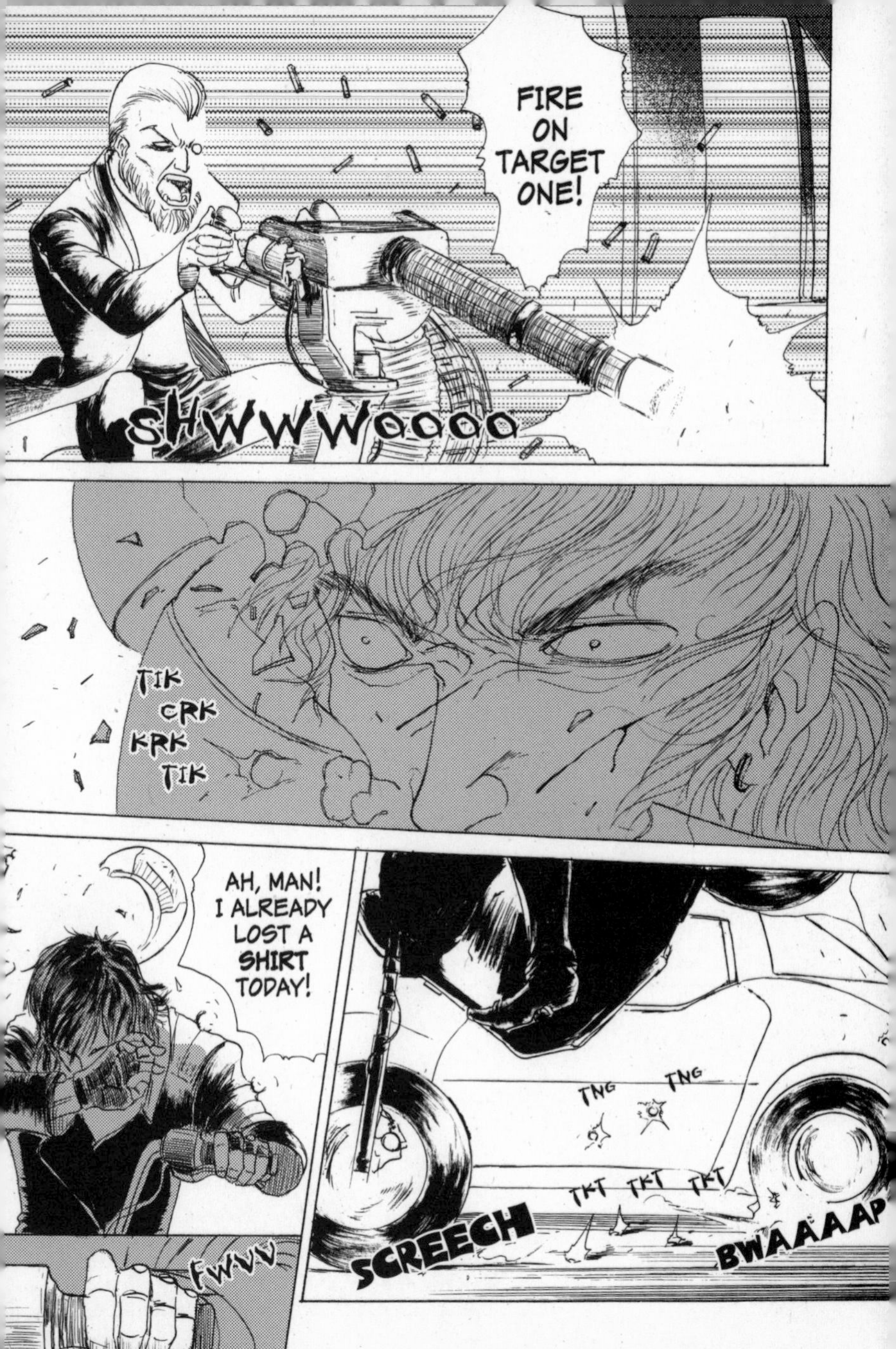
FIRE ON TARGET ONE!
SHWWWOOOO
TIK CRK KRK TIK
TNG TNG
TKT TKT TKT
SCREECH
BWAAAAP
AH, MAN! I ALREADY LOST A SHIRT TODAY!
FWVV

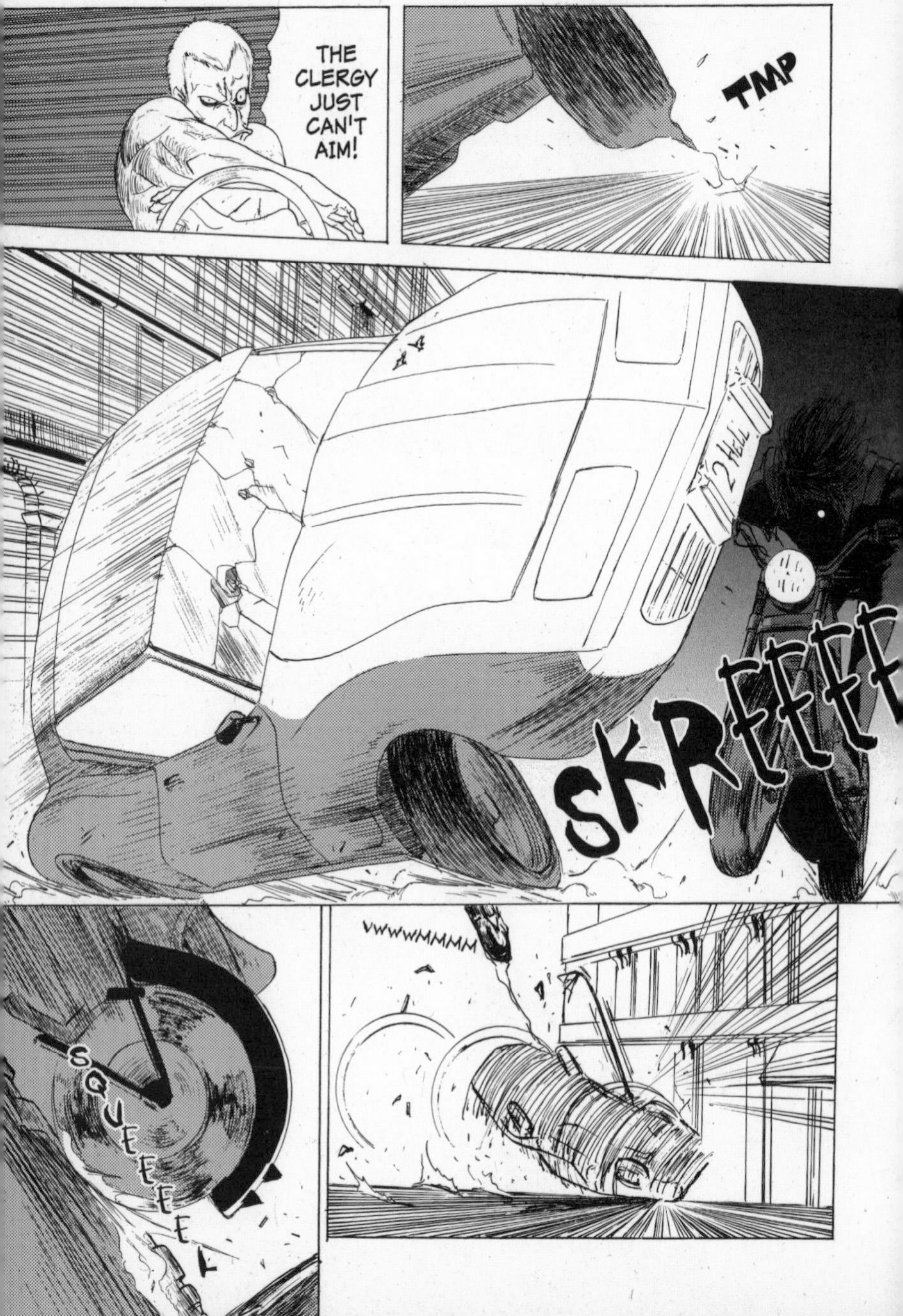
TMP
THE CLERGY JUST CAN'T AIM!
SKREEEE
VWWWMMMM
SQUEEEEL

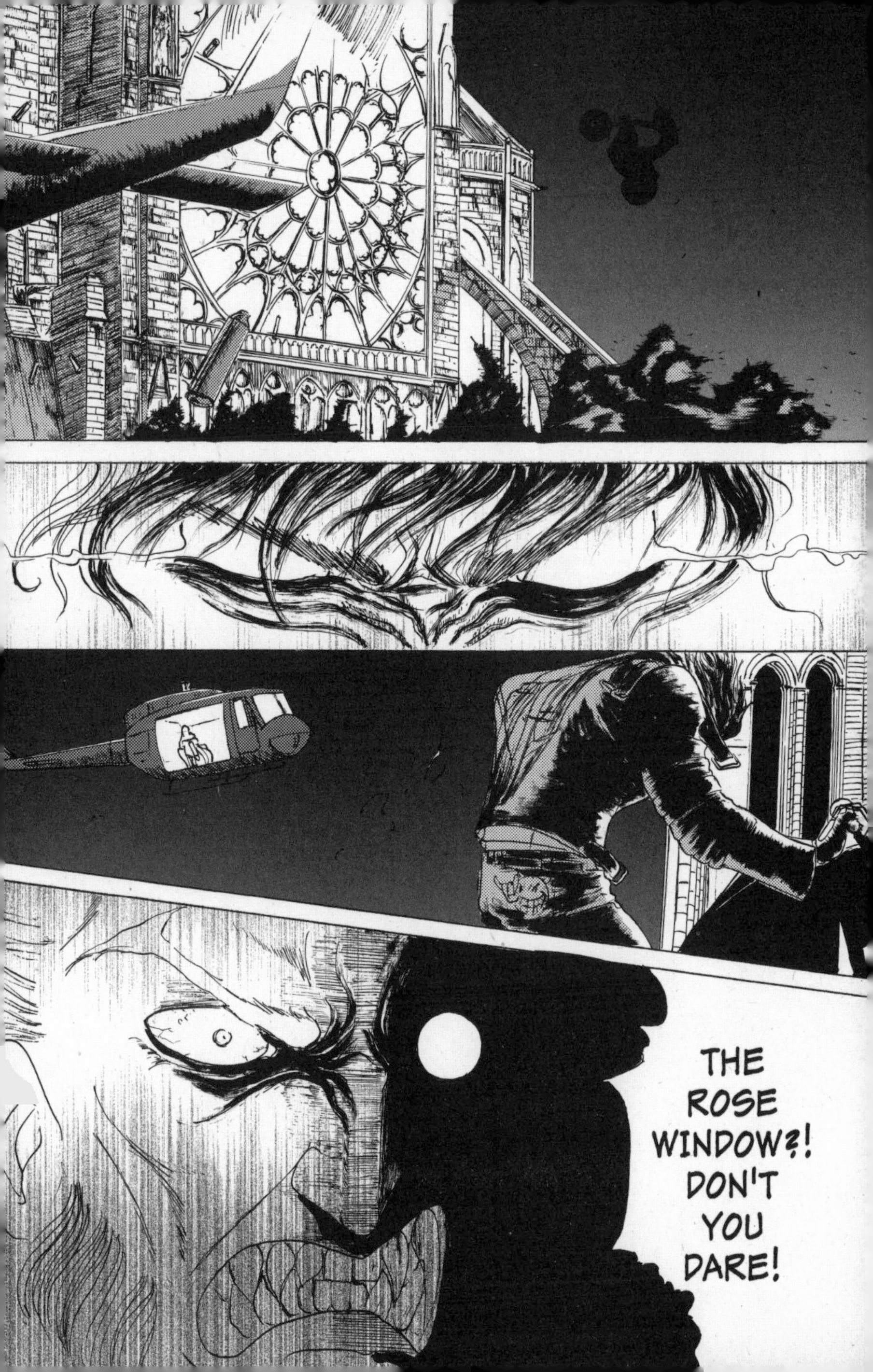
THE ROSE WINDOW?! DON'T YOU DARE!

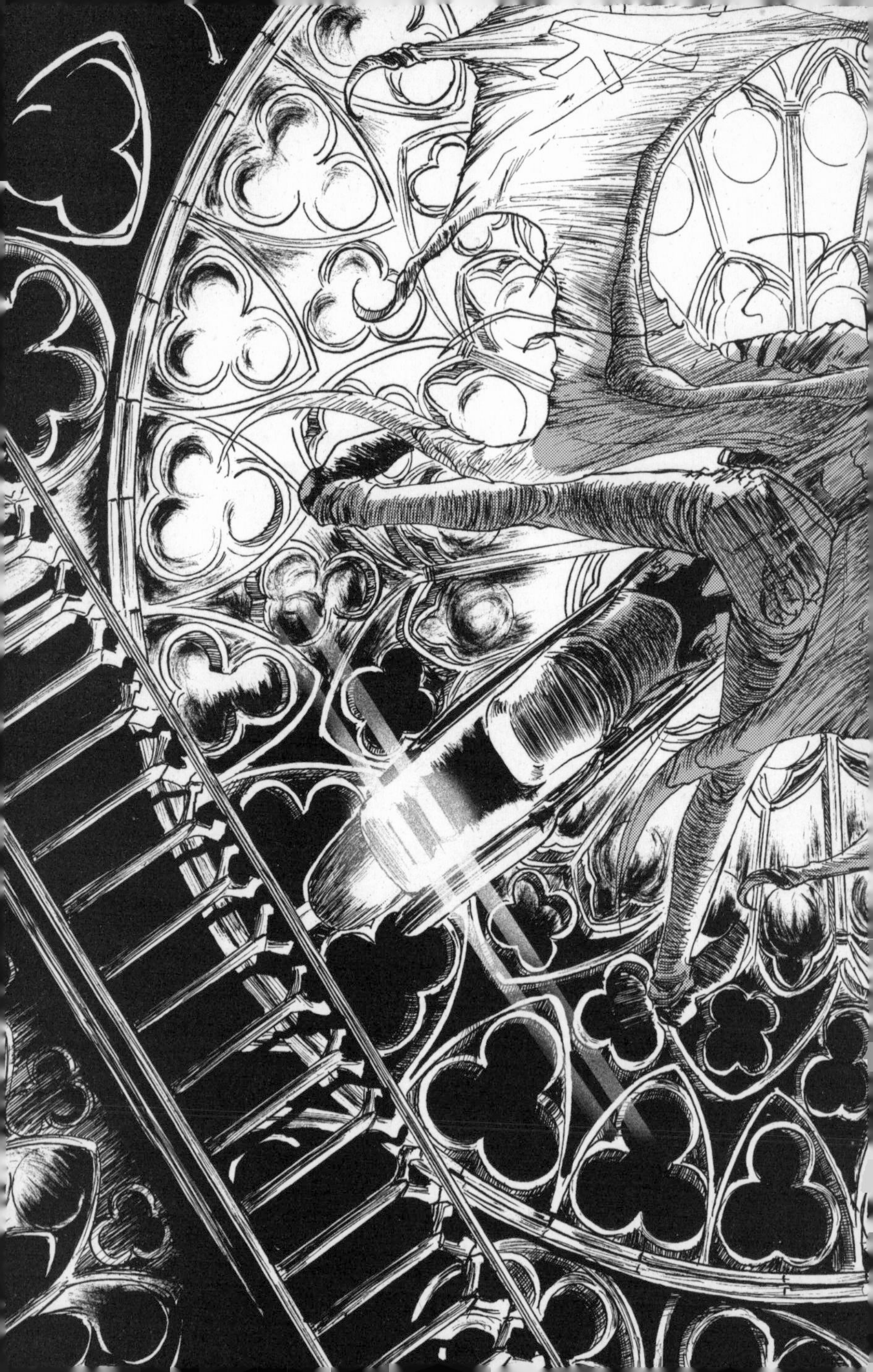

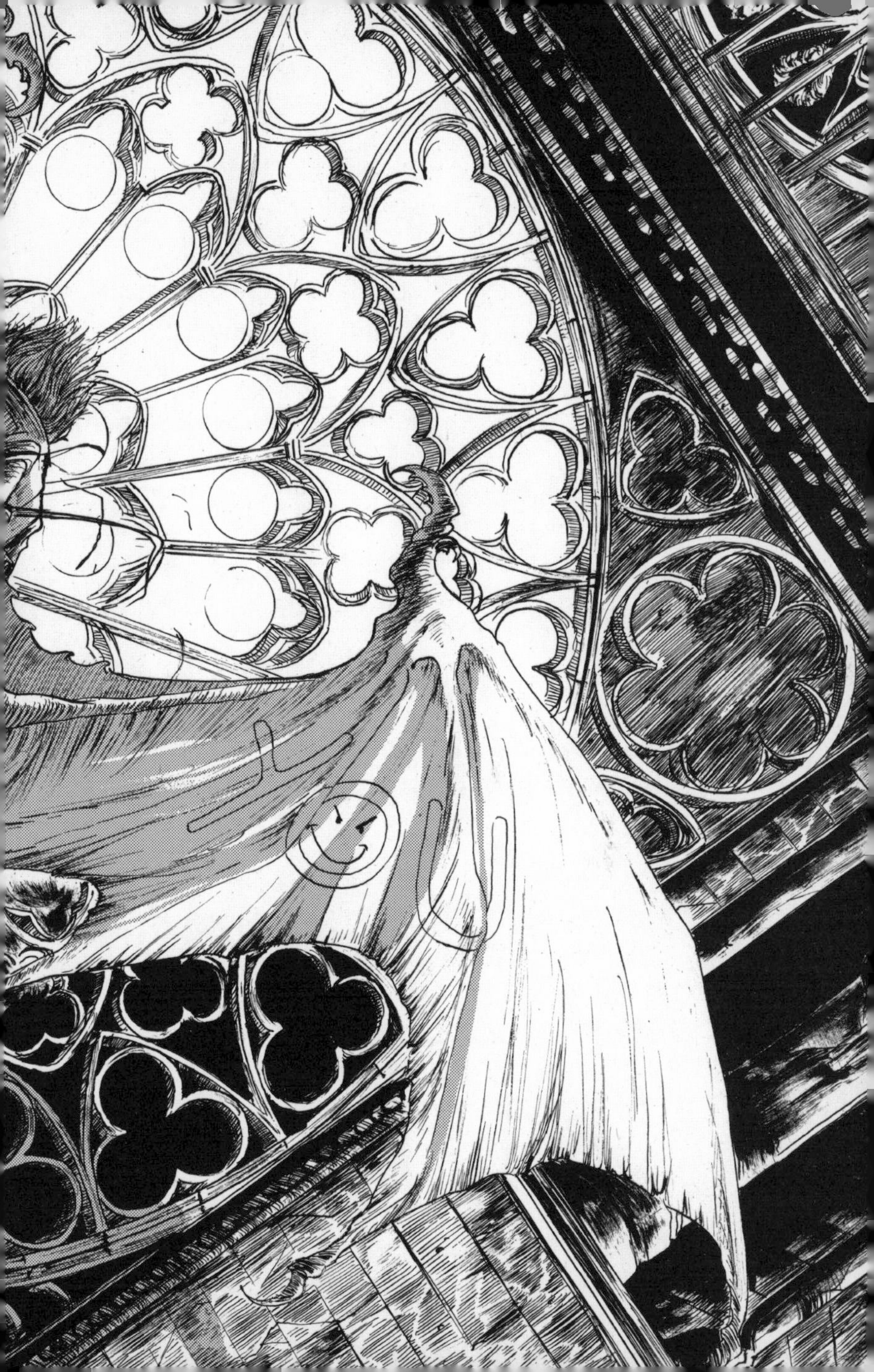

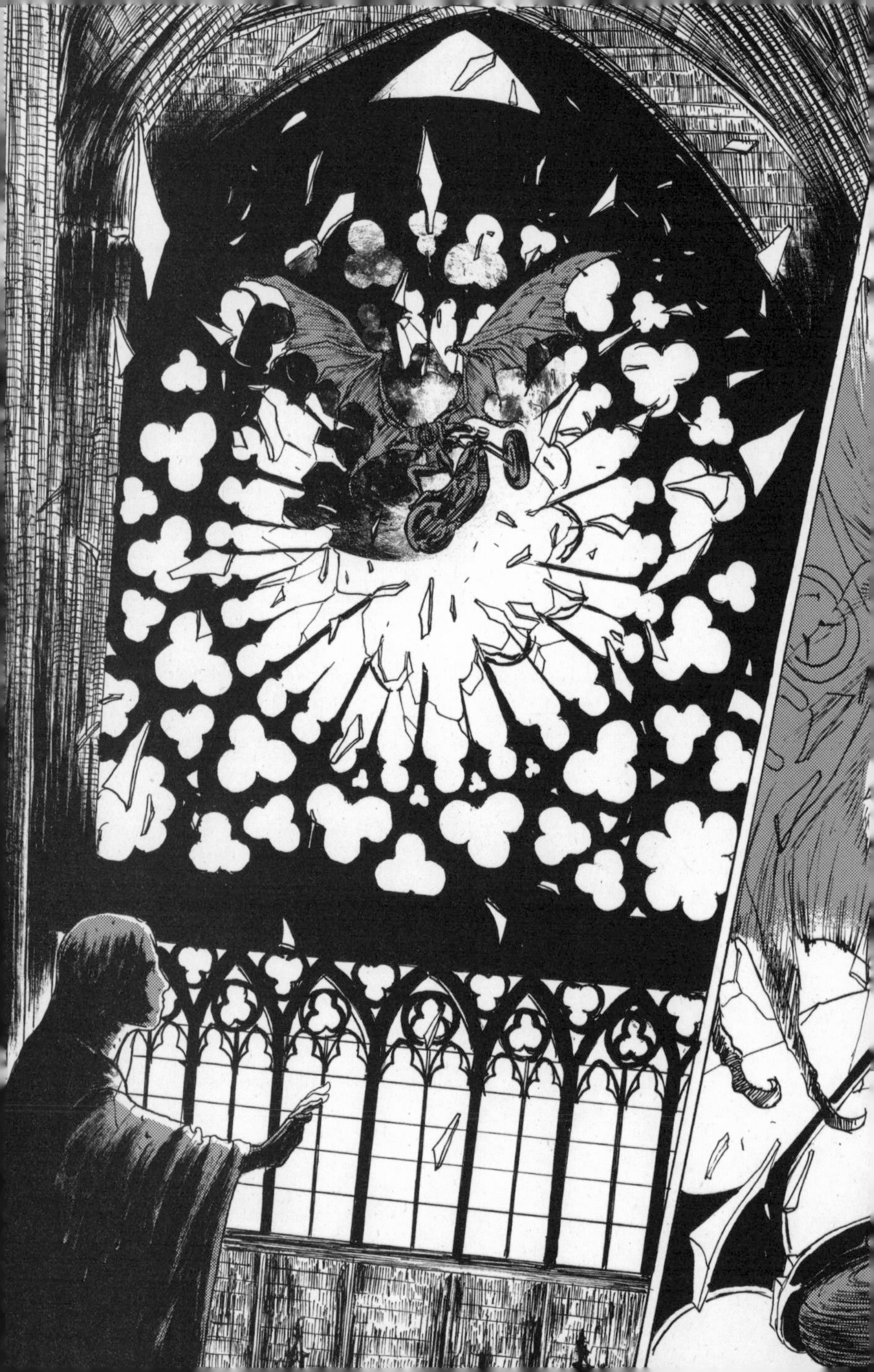

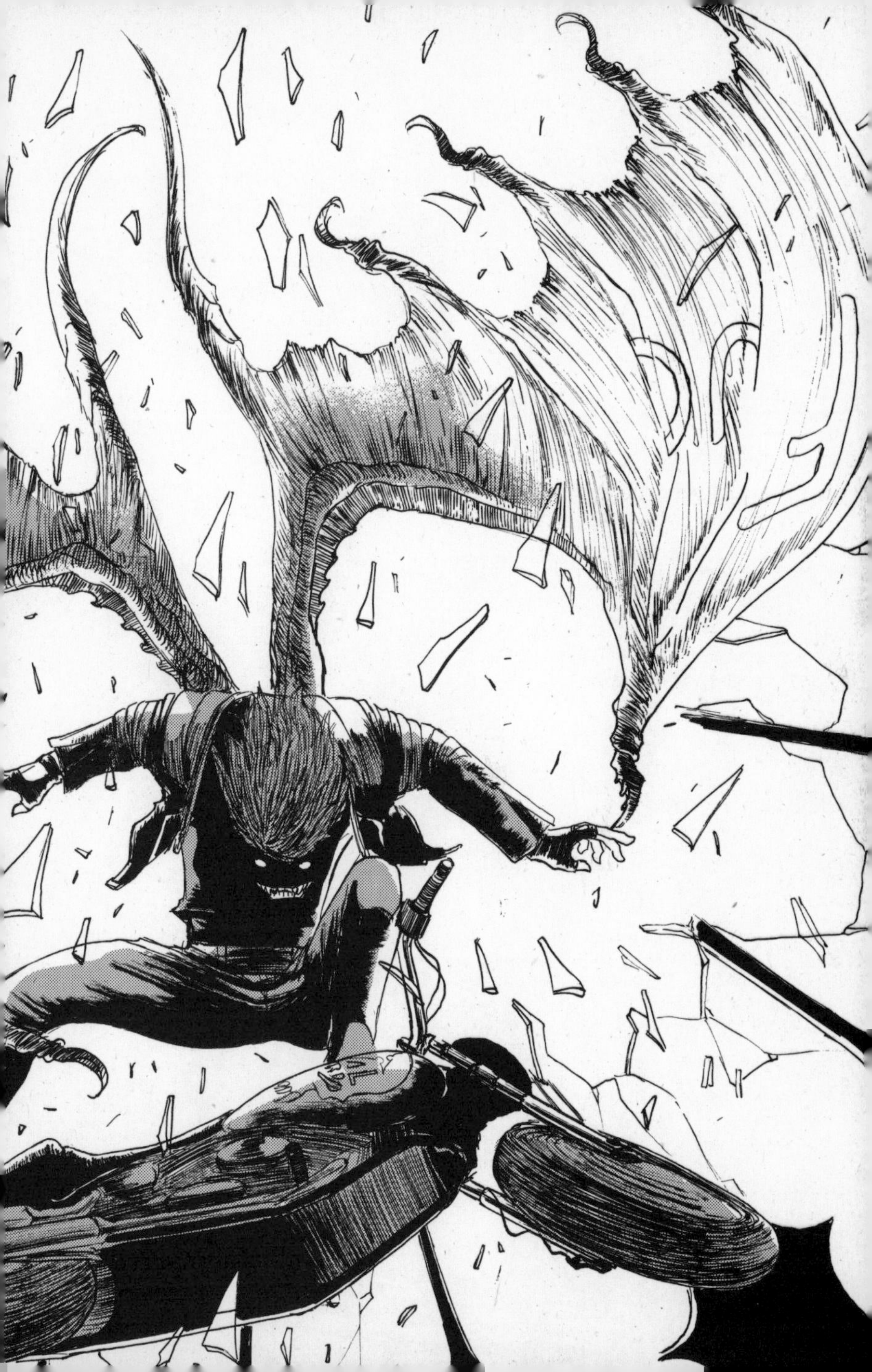

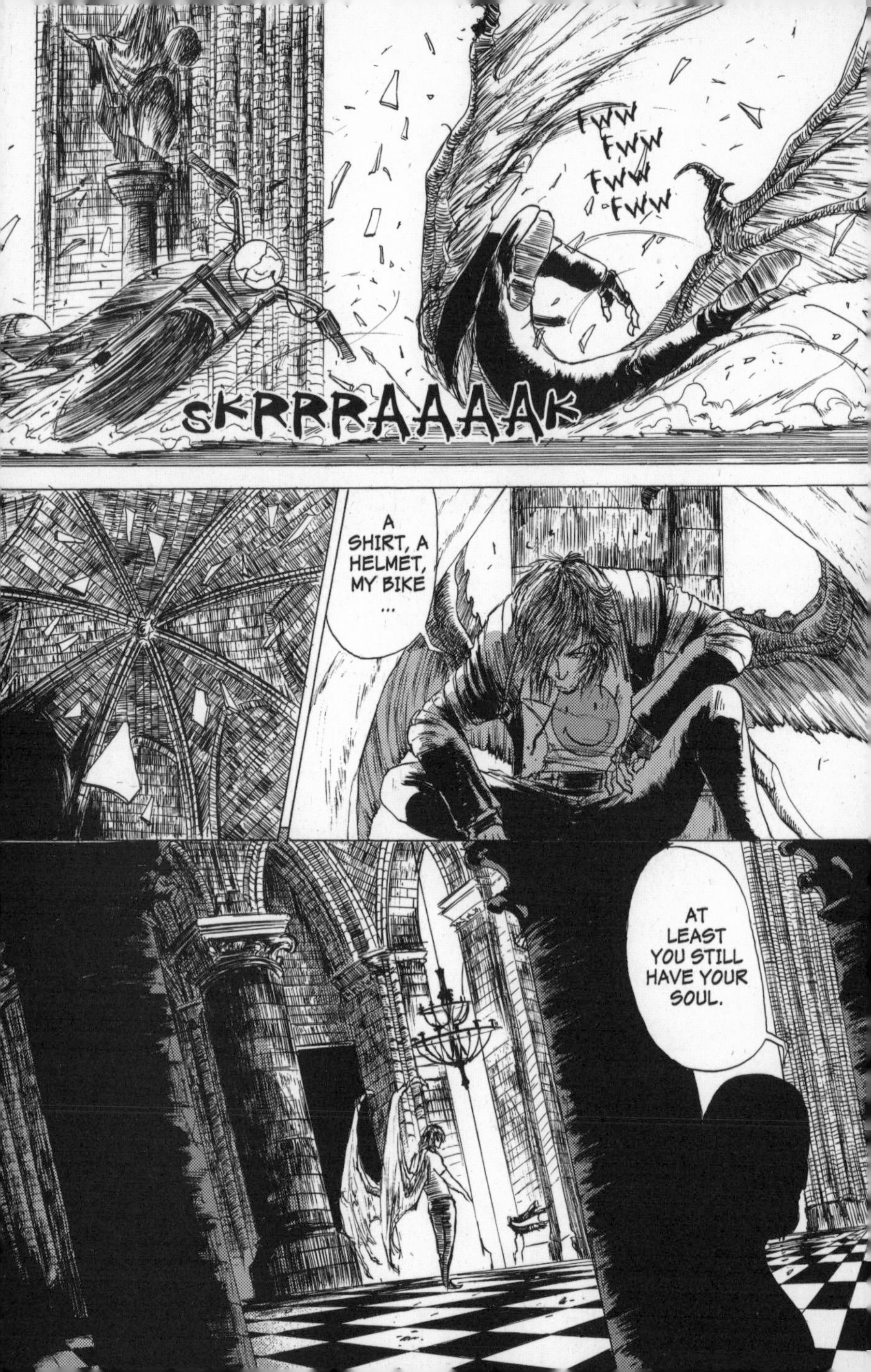
FWW FWW FWW FWW
SKRRRAAAAK
A SHIRT, A HELMET, MY BIKE ...
AT LEAST YOU STILL HAVE YOUR SOUL.

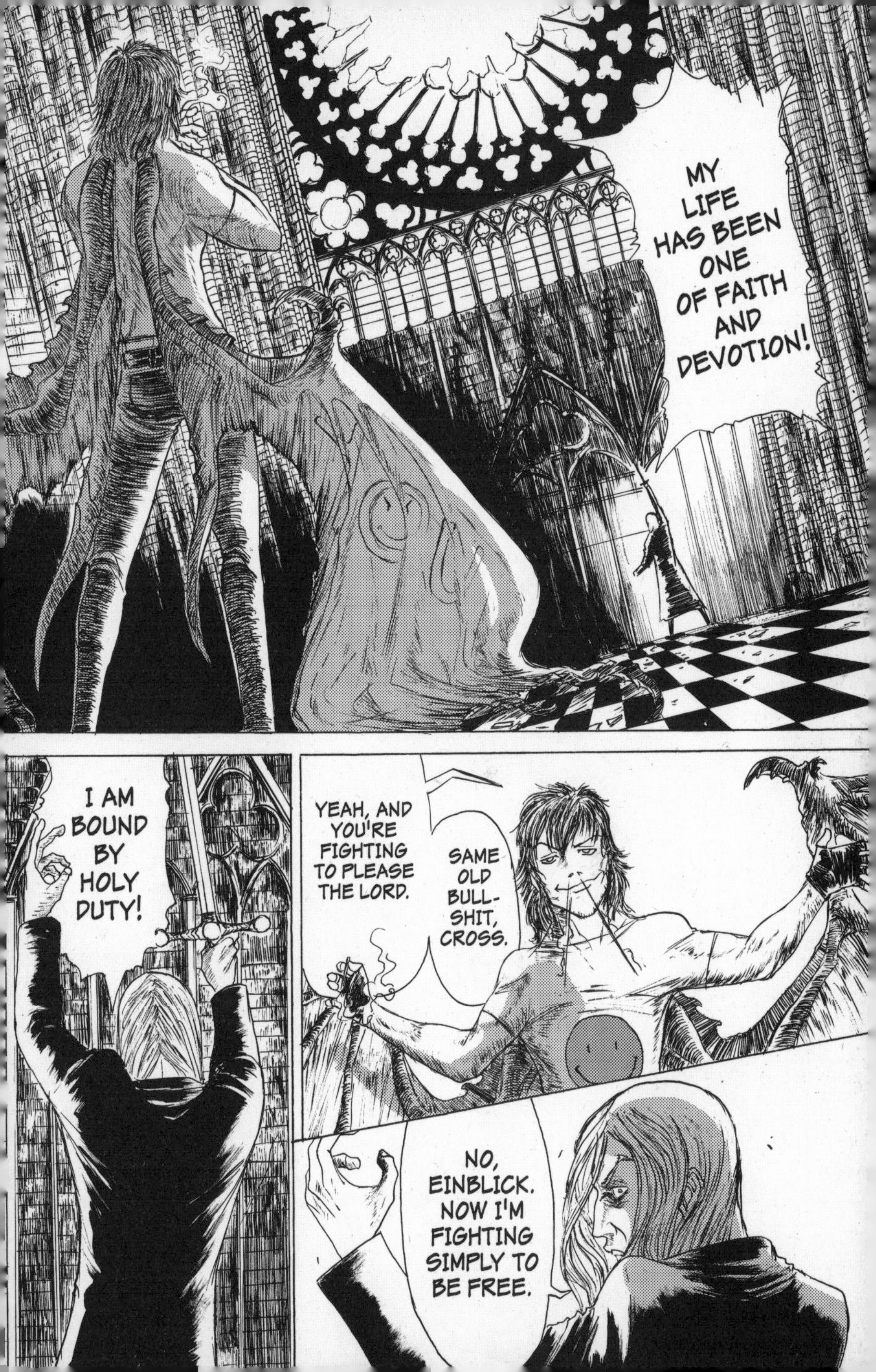
MY LIFE HAS BEEN ONE OF FAITH AND DEVOTION!
I AM BOUND BY HOLY DUTY!
YEAH, AND YOU'RE FIGHTING TO PLEASE THE LORD.
SAME OLD BULL-SHIT, CROSS.
NO, EINBLICK. NOW I'M FIGHTING SIMPLY TO BE FREE.

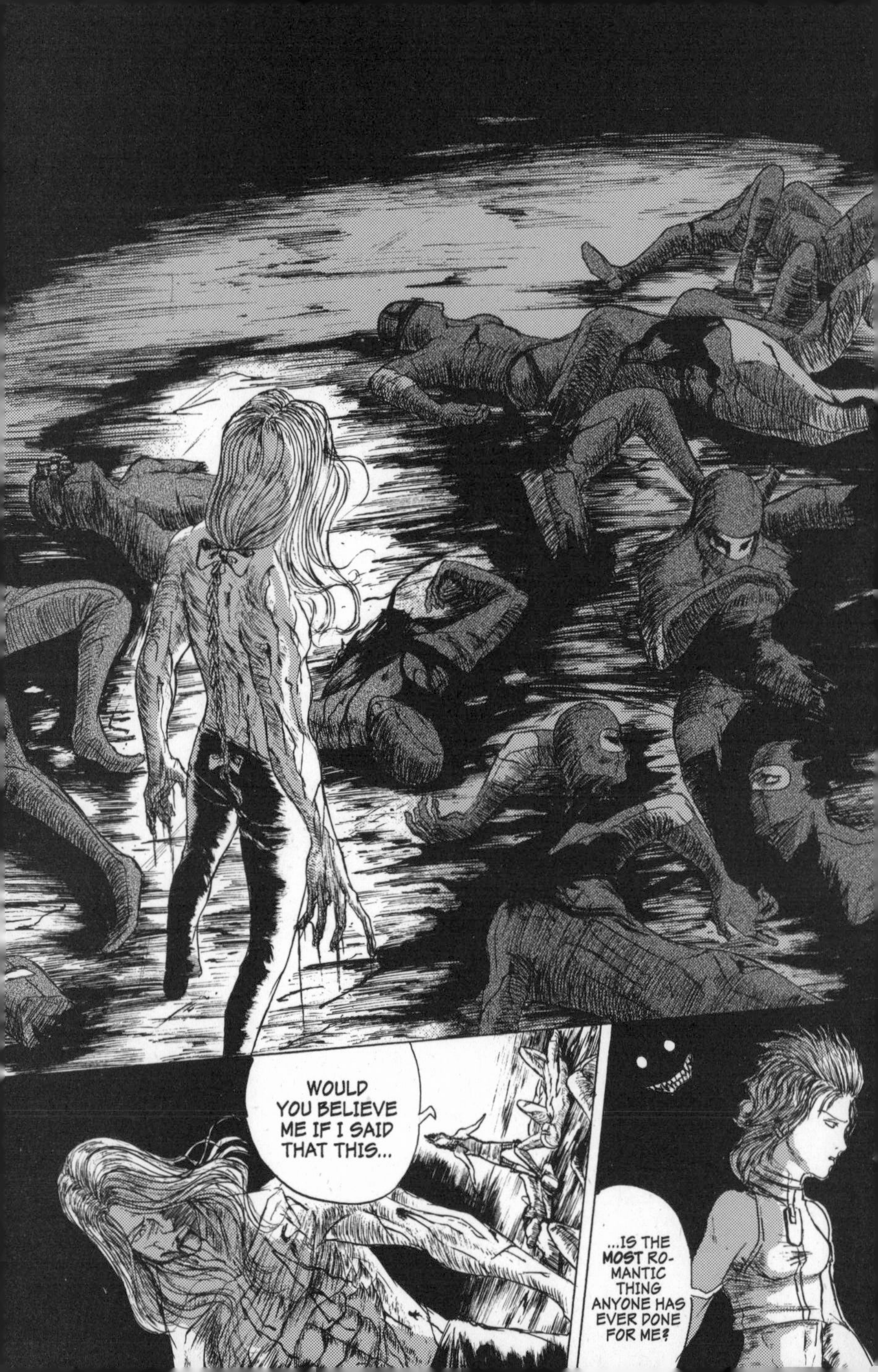
WOULD YOU BELIEVE ME IF I SAID THAT THIS...
...IS THE MOST RO- MANTIC THING ANYONE HAS EVER DONE FOR ME?

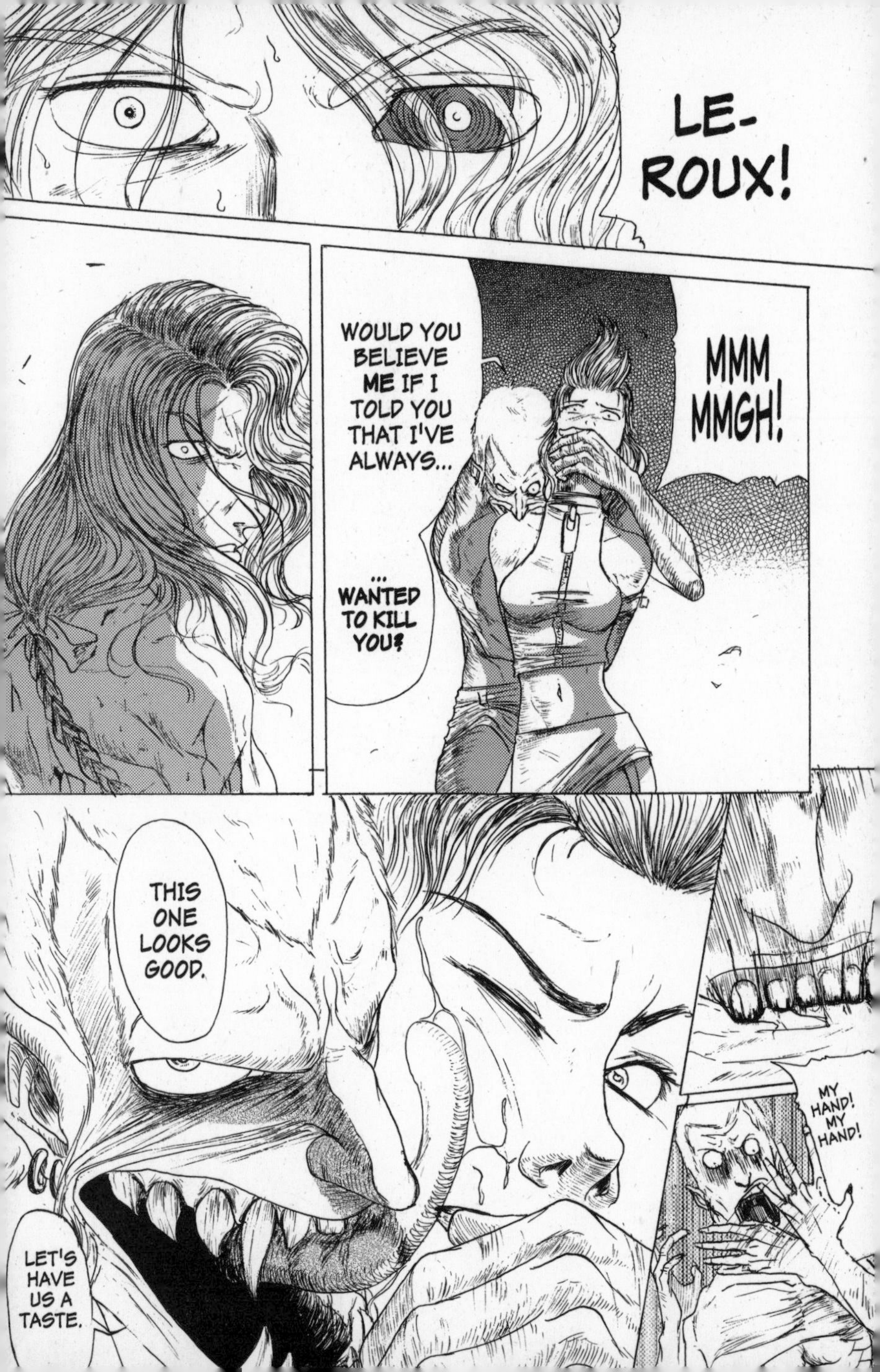
LE-ROUX!
MMM MMGH!
WOULD YOU BELIEVE ME IF I TOLD YOU THAT I'VE ALWAYS...
... WANTED TO KILL YOU?
MY HAND! MY HAND!
THIS ONE LOOKS GOOD.
LET'S HAVE US A TASTE.

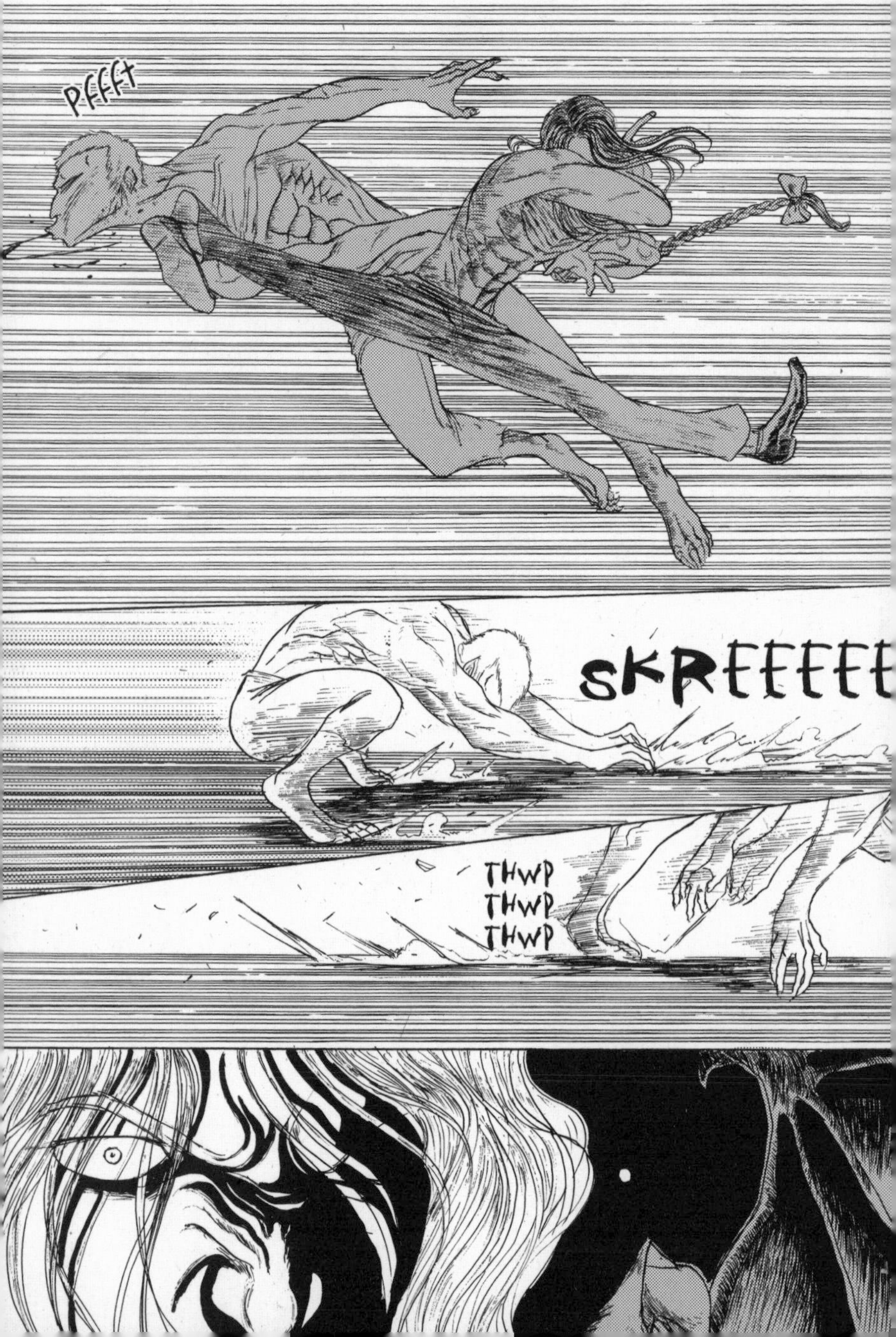
PFFFT
SKREEEEEE
THWP
THWP
THWP

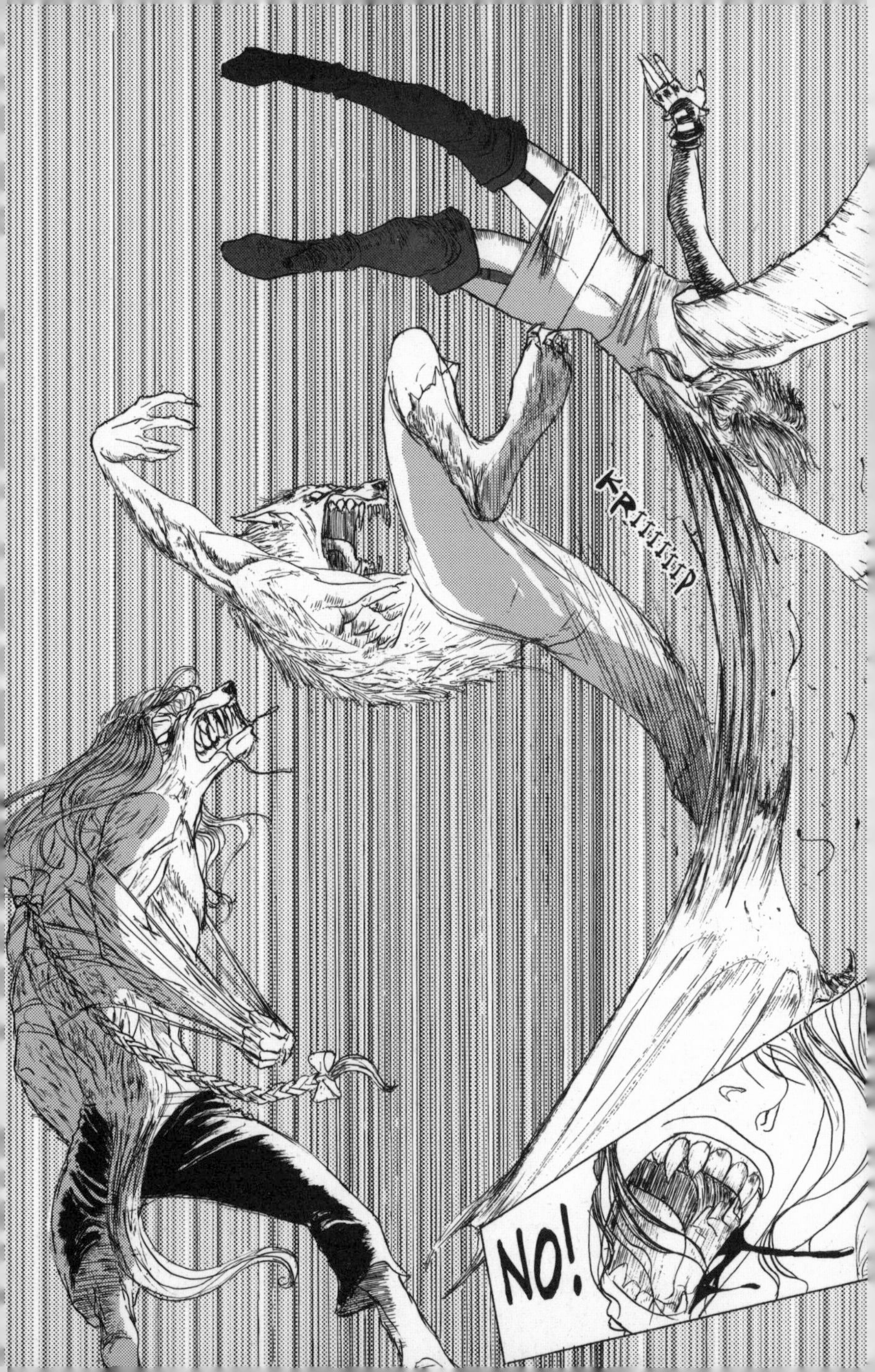
KRIIIIIIP
NO!

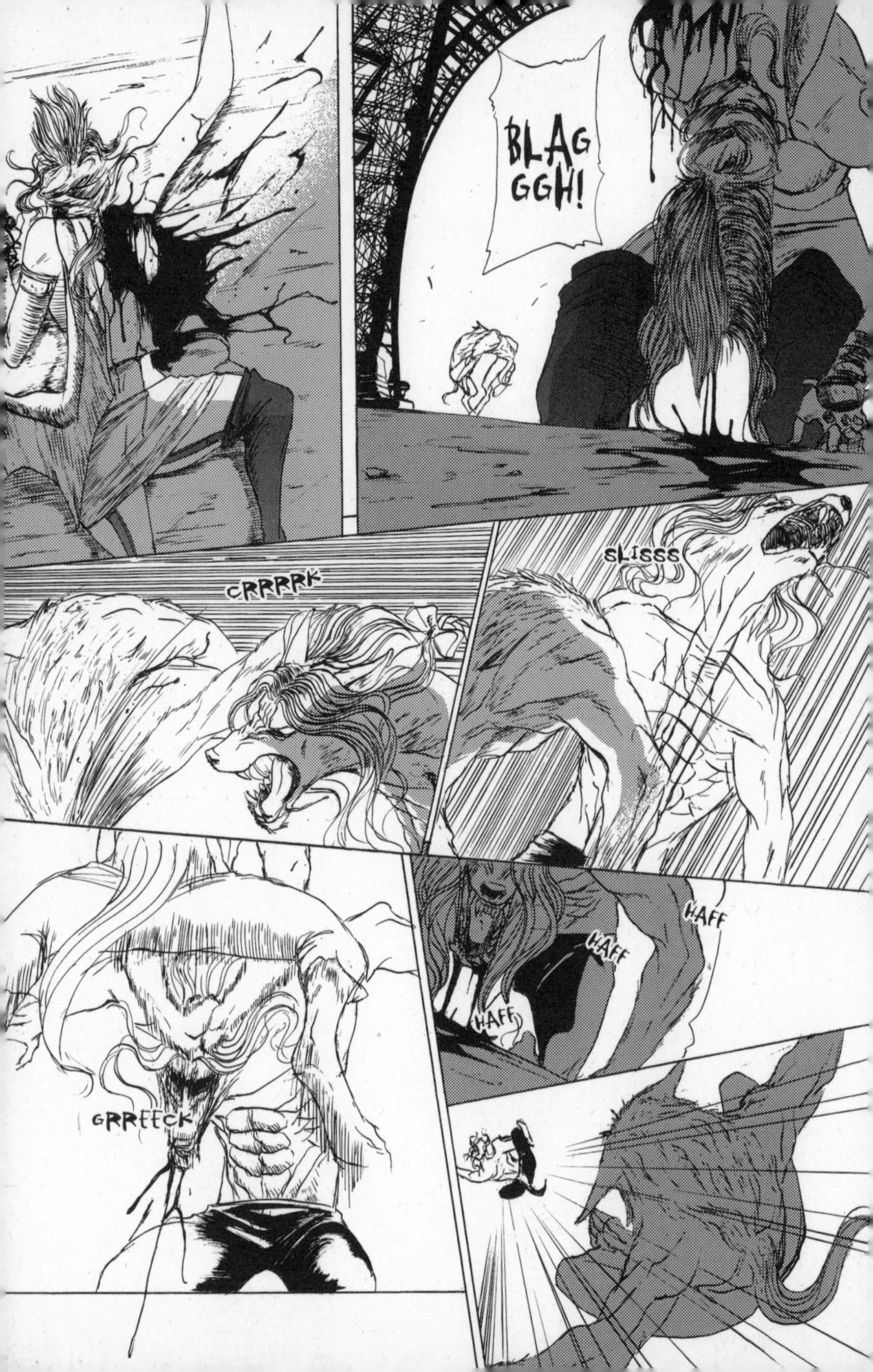
BLAG GGH!
SLISSS
CRRRRK
HAFF
HAFF
HAFF
GRREECK

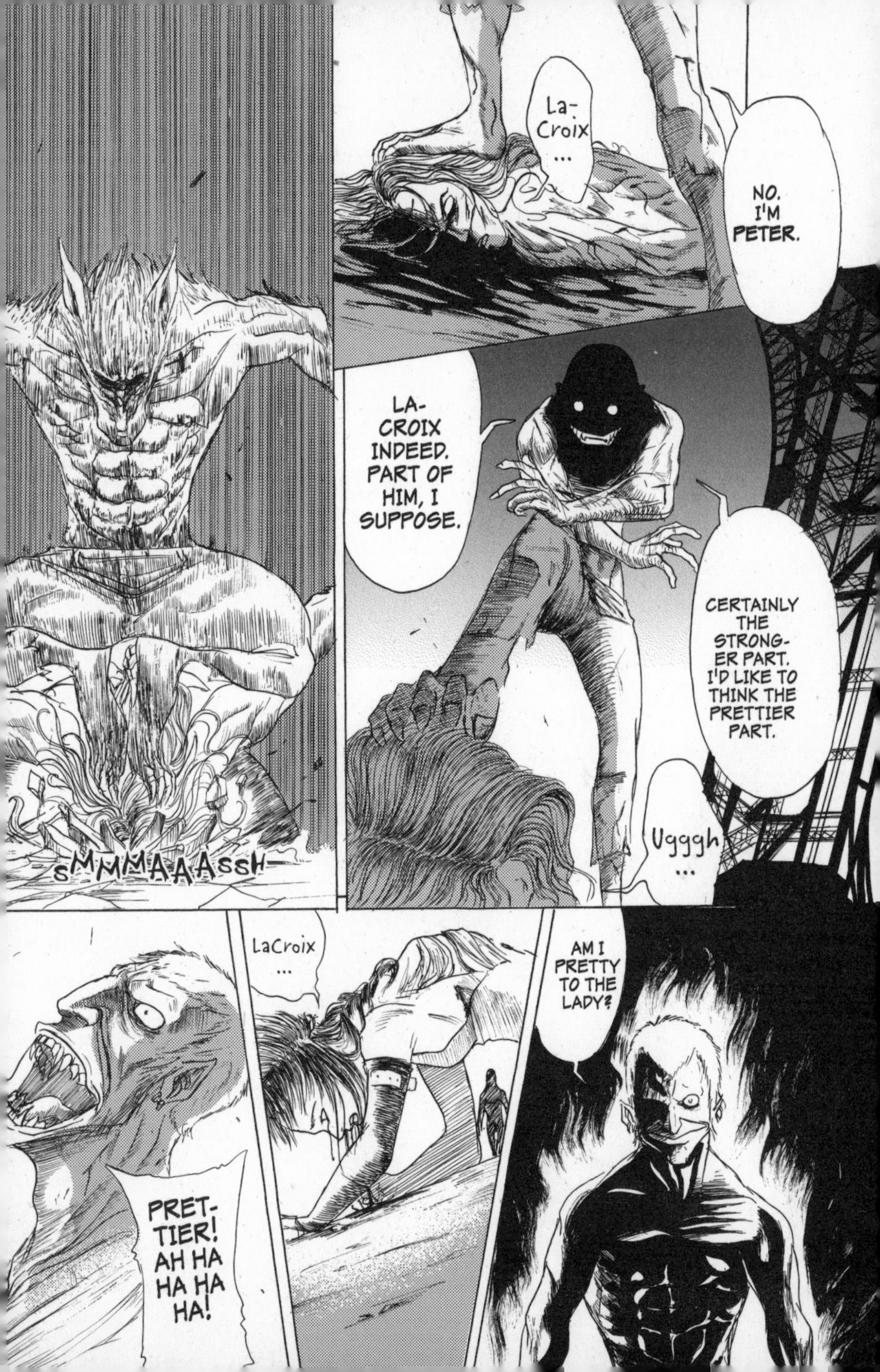
La-Croix ...
No. I'm Peter.
La-Croix indeed. Part of him, I suppose.
Certainly the stronger part. I'd like to think the prettier part.
Ugggh ...
SMMMAAASSH
Am I pretty to the lady?
LaCroix ...
Pret-tier! Ah ha ha ha ha!

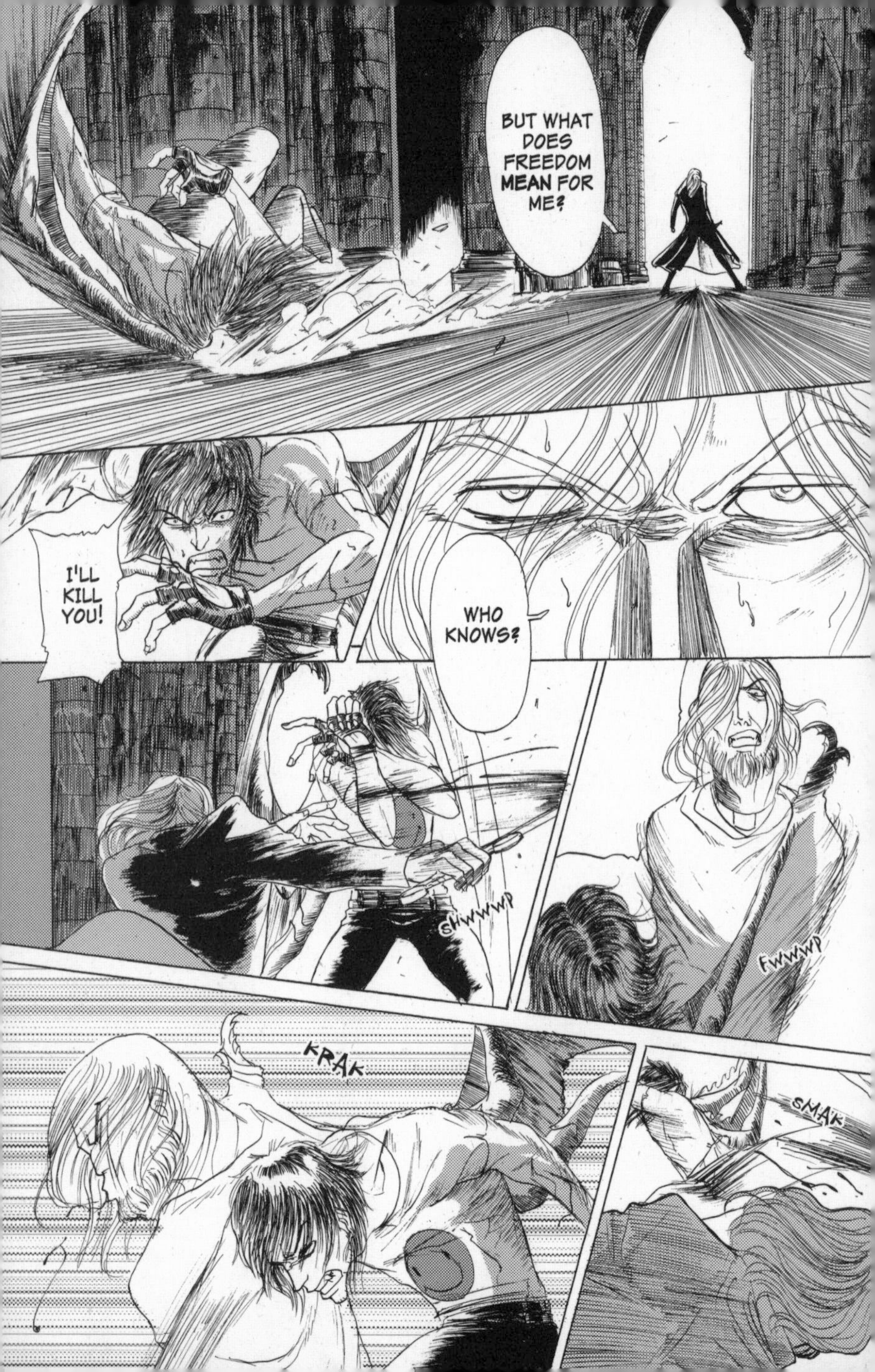
BUT WHAT DOES FREEDOM MEAN FOR ME?
WHO KNOWS?
I'LL KILL YOU!
FWWWP
SHWWWP
SMAK
KRAK

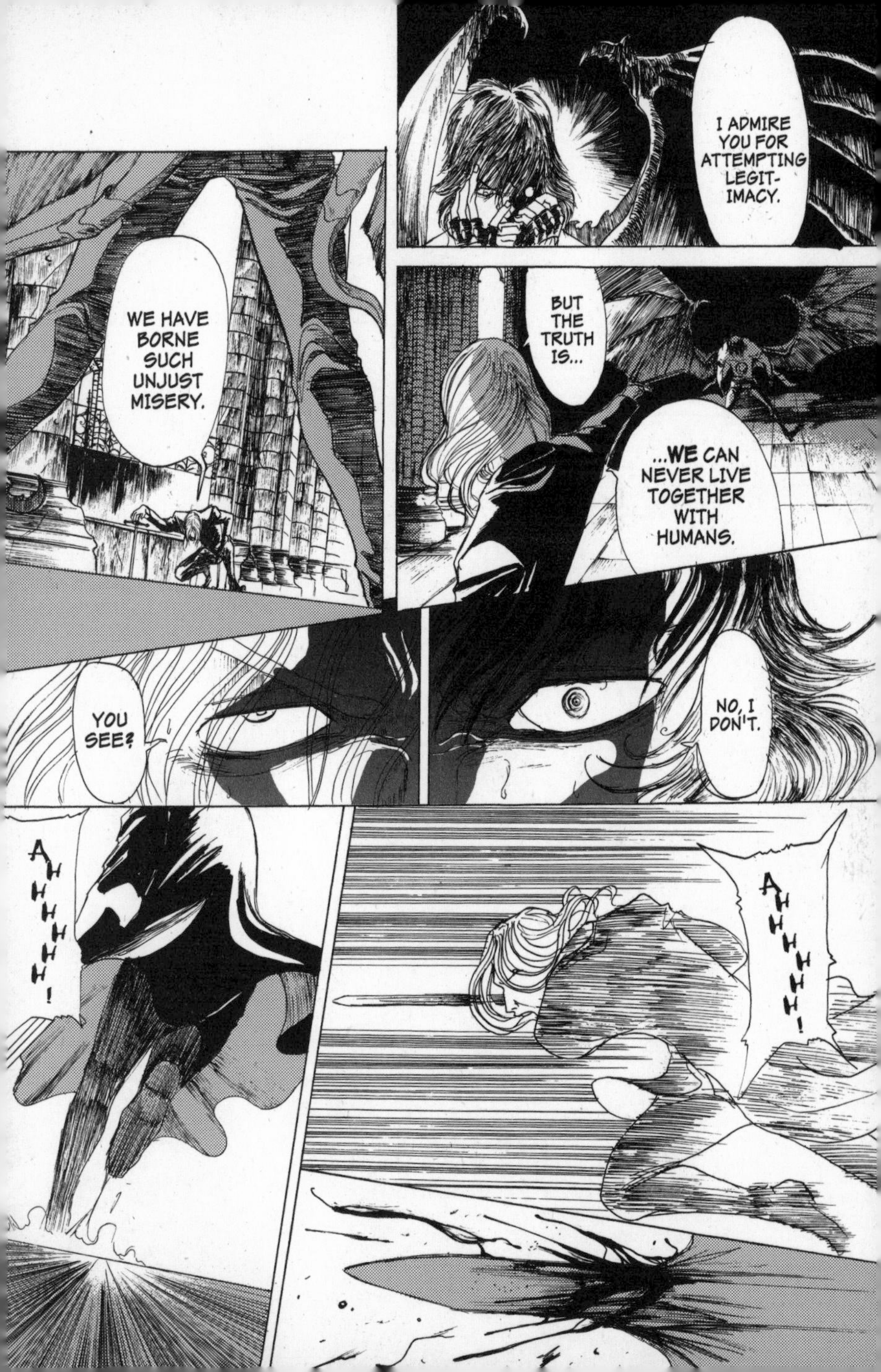
I ADMIRE YOU FOR ATTEMPTING LEGIT-IMACY.
WE HAVE BORNE SUCH UNJUST MISERY.
BUT THE TRUTH IS...
...WE CAN NEVER LIVE TOGETHER WITH HUMANS.
NO, I DON'T.
YOU SEE?
AHHHHHH!
AHHHHHH!

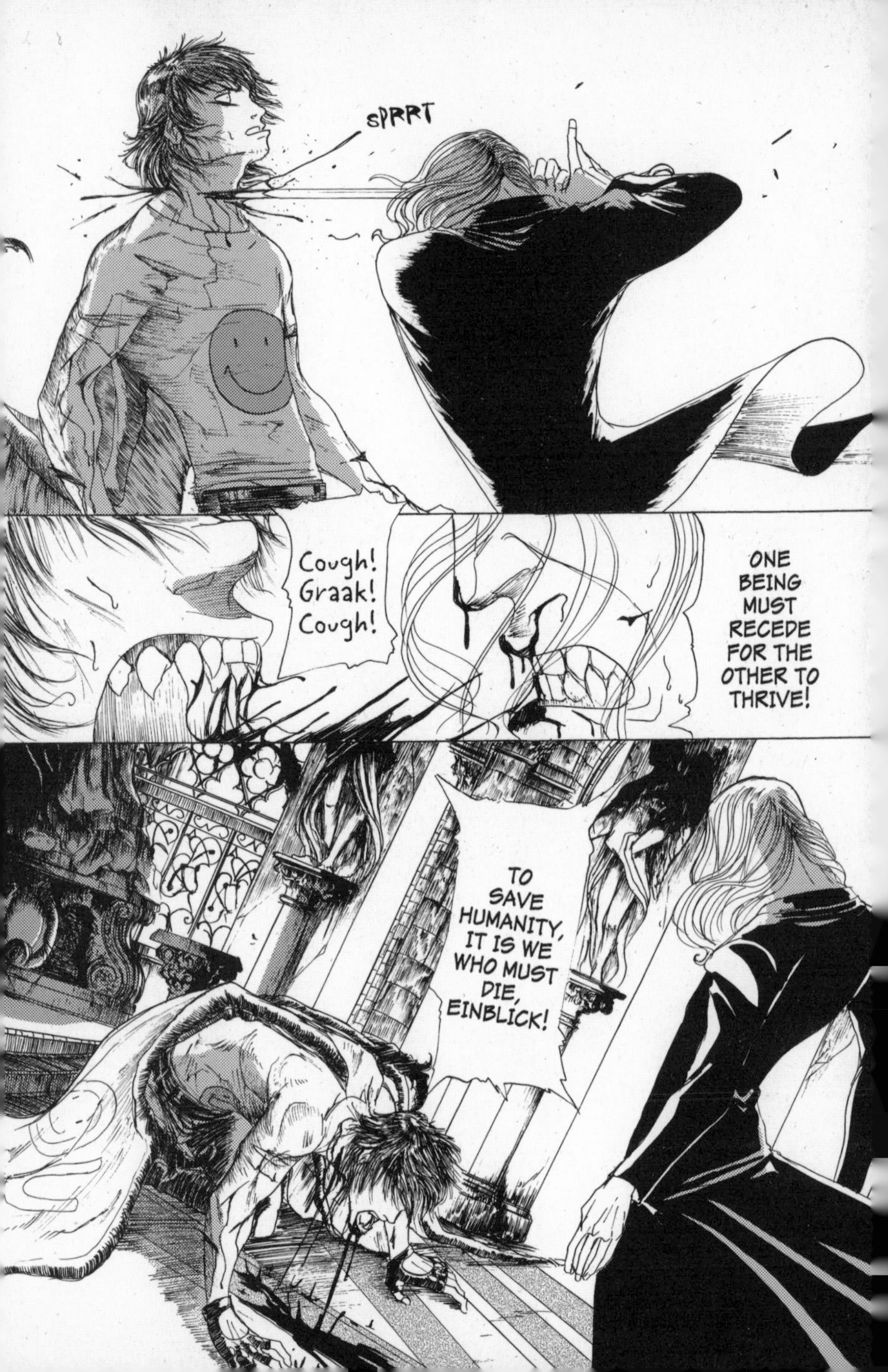
SPRRT
ONE BEING MUST RECEDE FOR THE OTHER TO THRIVE!
Cough! Graak! Cough!
TO SAVE HUMANITY, IT IS WE WHO MUST DIE, EINBLICK!

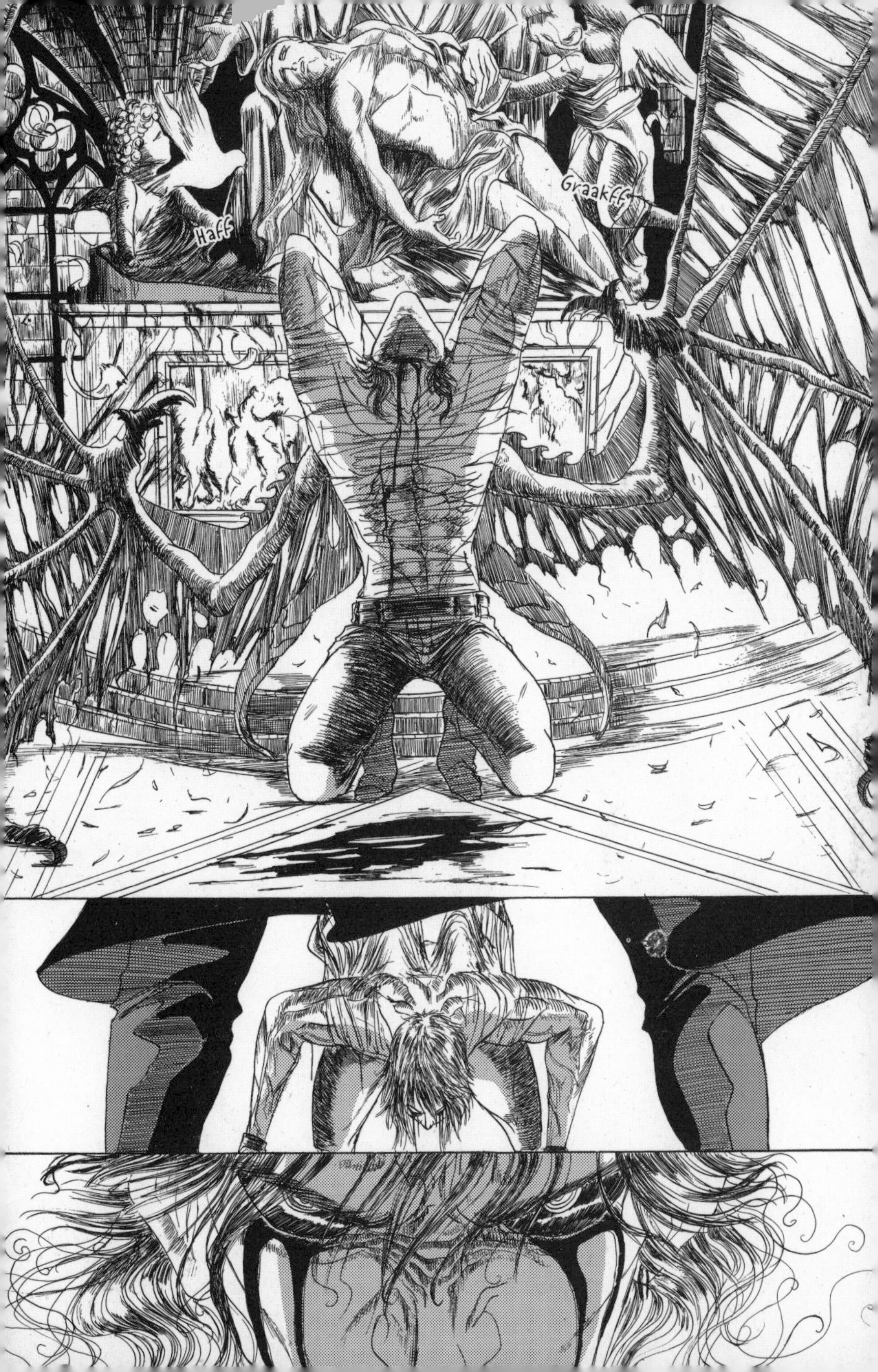
Graakff
Haff

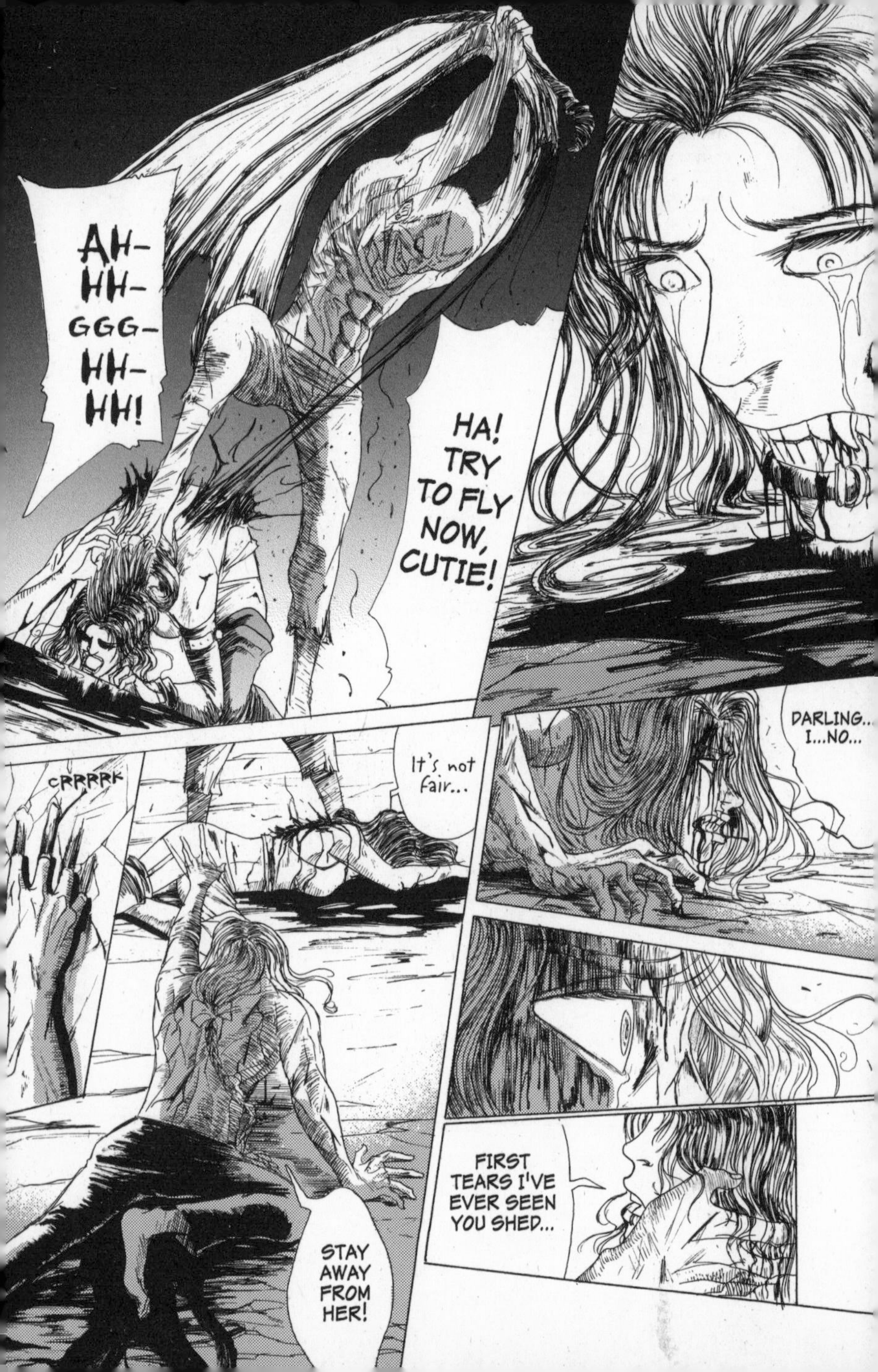
AH-HH-GGG-HH-HH!
HA! TRY TO FLY NOW, CUTIE!
DARLING... I...NO...
FIRST TEARS I'VE EVER SEEN YOU SHED...
It's not fair...
CRRRRK
STAY AWAY FROM HER!

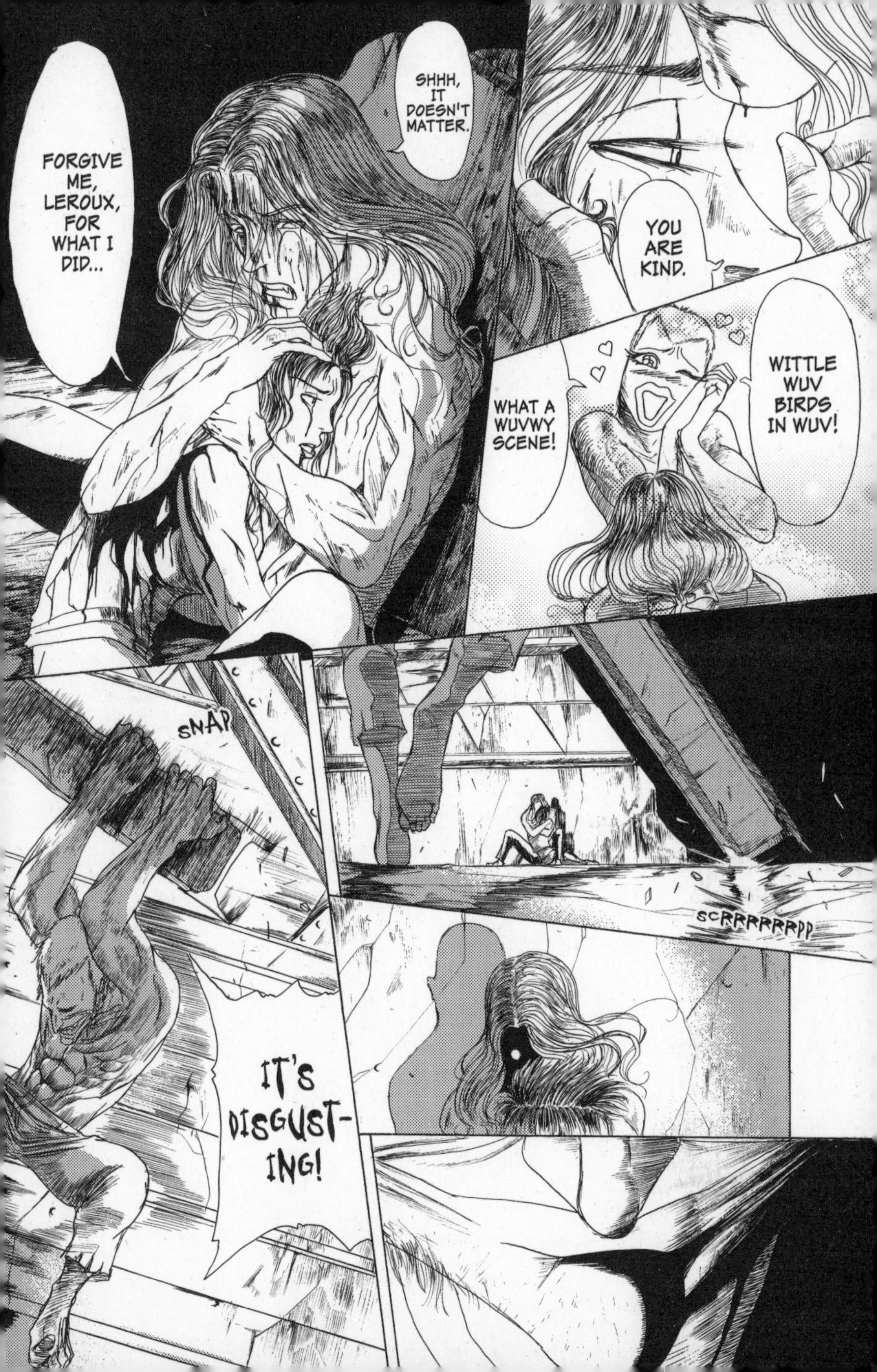
FORGIVE ME, LEROUX, FOR WHAT I DID...
SHHH, IT DOESN'T MATTER.
YOU ARE KIND.
WHAT A WUVWY SCENE!
WITTLE WUV BIRDS IN WUV!
SNAP
SCRRRRRRPP
IT'S DISGUST-ING!

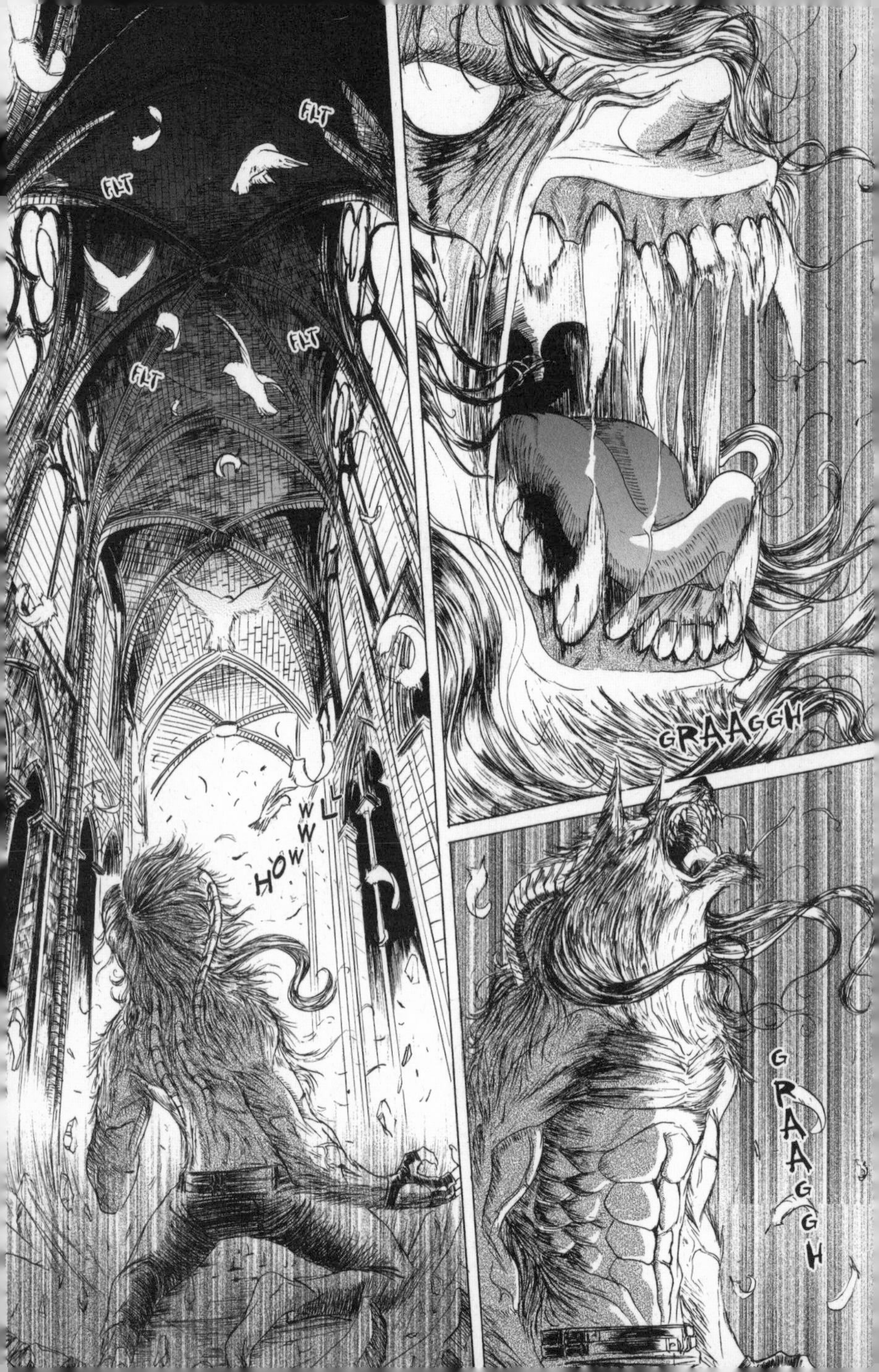
GRAAGGH
GRAAGGH
FLT
FLT
FLT
FLT
HOWWLL

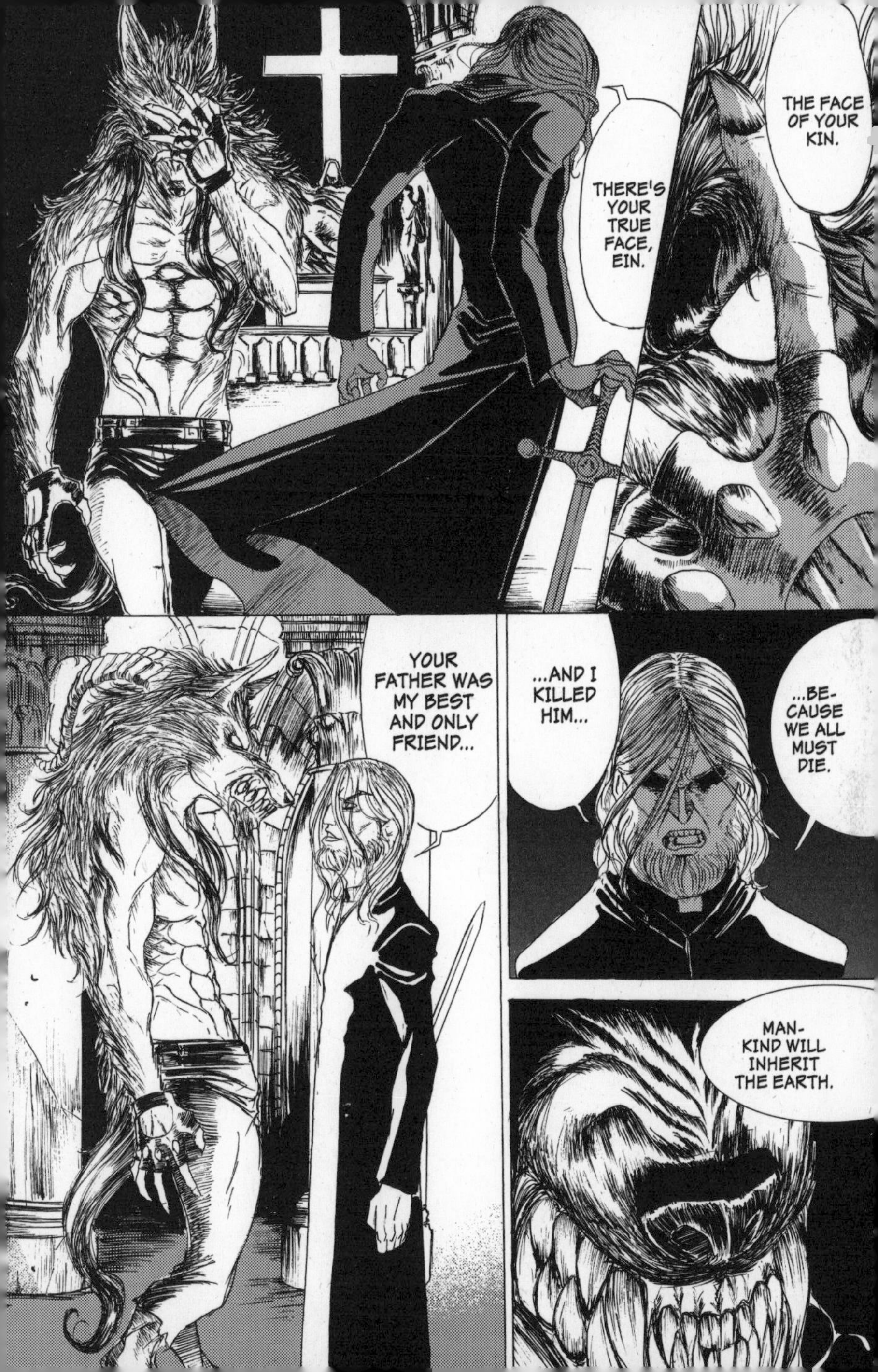
THERE'S YOUR TRUE FACE, EIN.
THE FACE OF YOUR KIN.
YOUR FATHER WAS MY BEST AND ONLY FRIEND...
...AND I KILLED HIM...
...BE-CAUSE WE ALL MUST DIE.
MAN-KIND WILL INHERIT THE EARTH.

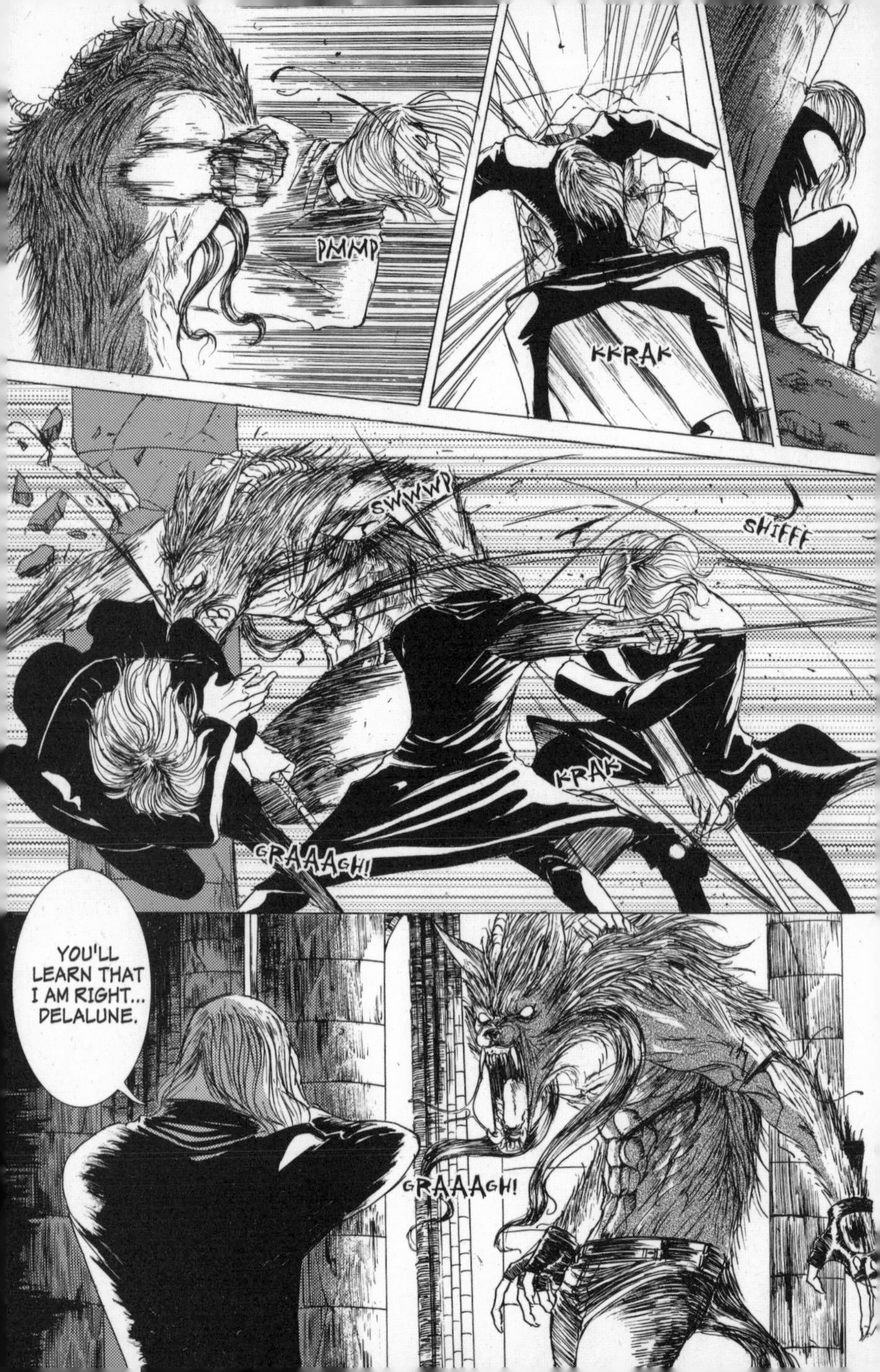
KKRAK
PMMP
SHIFFF
SWWWP
KRAK
GRAAAGH!
YOU'LL LEARN THAT I AM RIGHT... DELALUNE.
GRAAAGH!

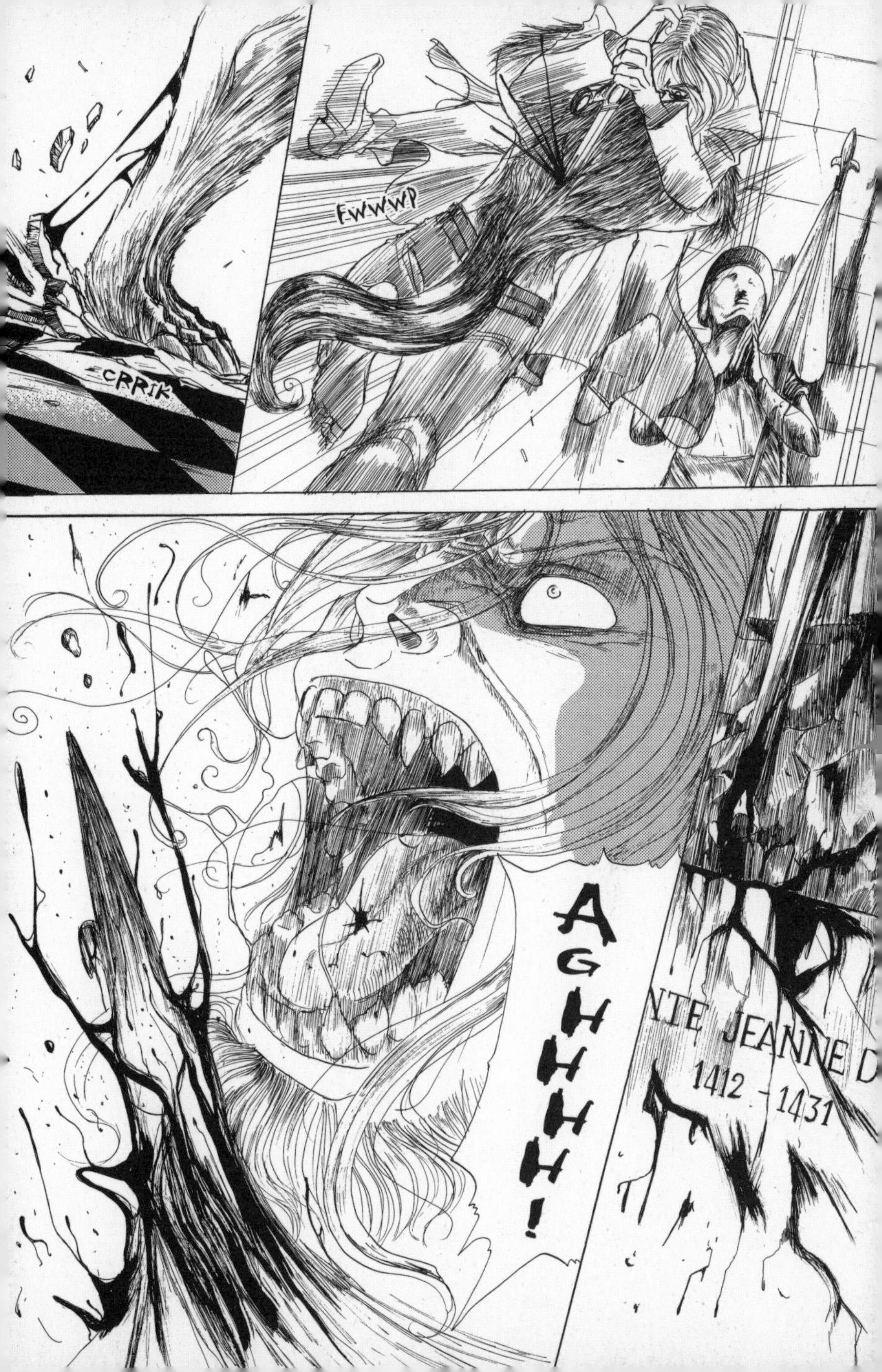
FWWWP
CRRIK
AGHHHHH!
NTE JEANNE D
1412 - 1431

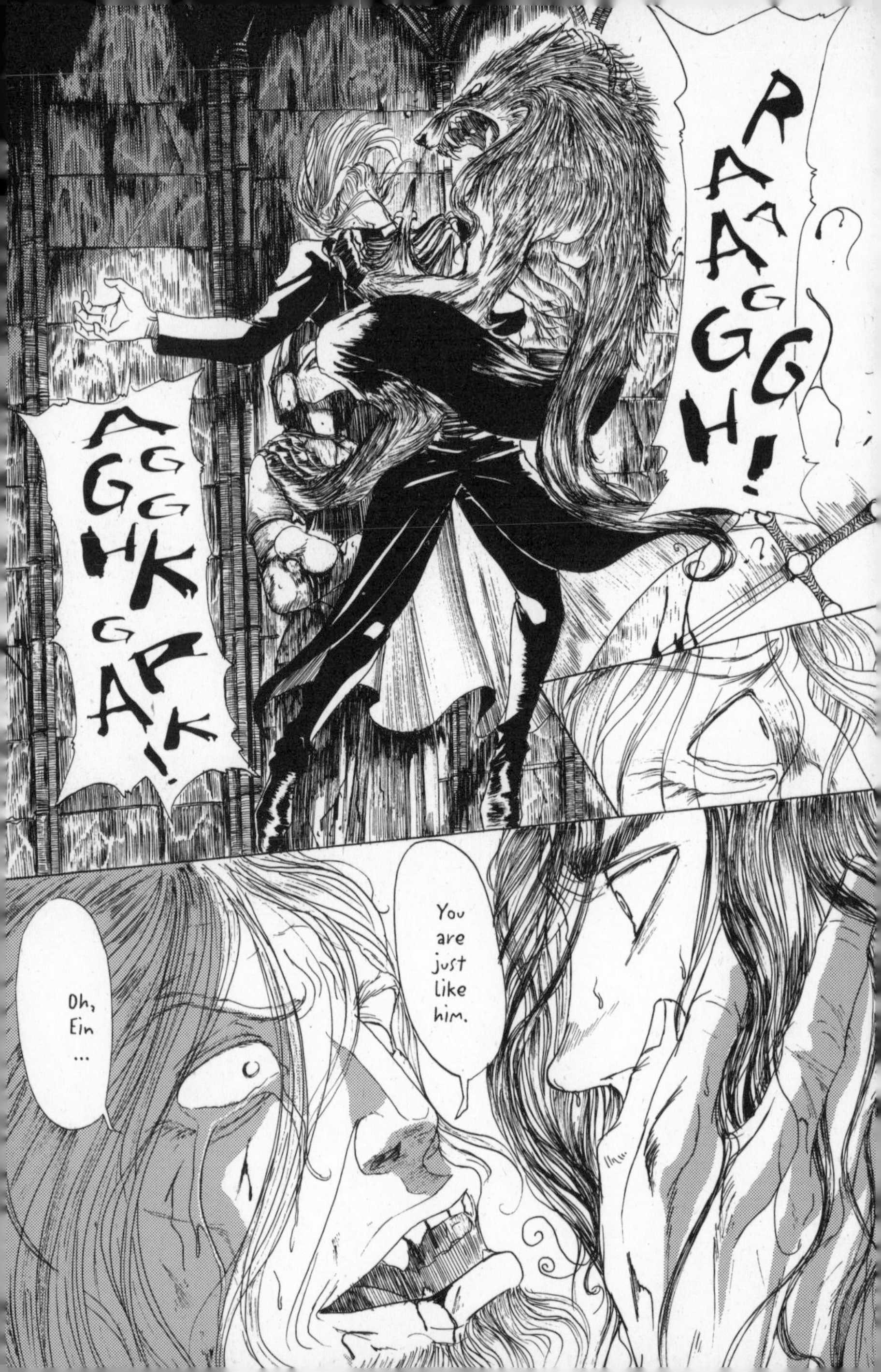
RAAAGGGH!
AGGGGHKGAAK!
You are just like him.
Oh, Ein ...

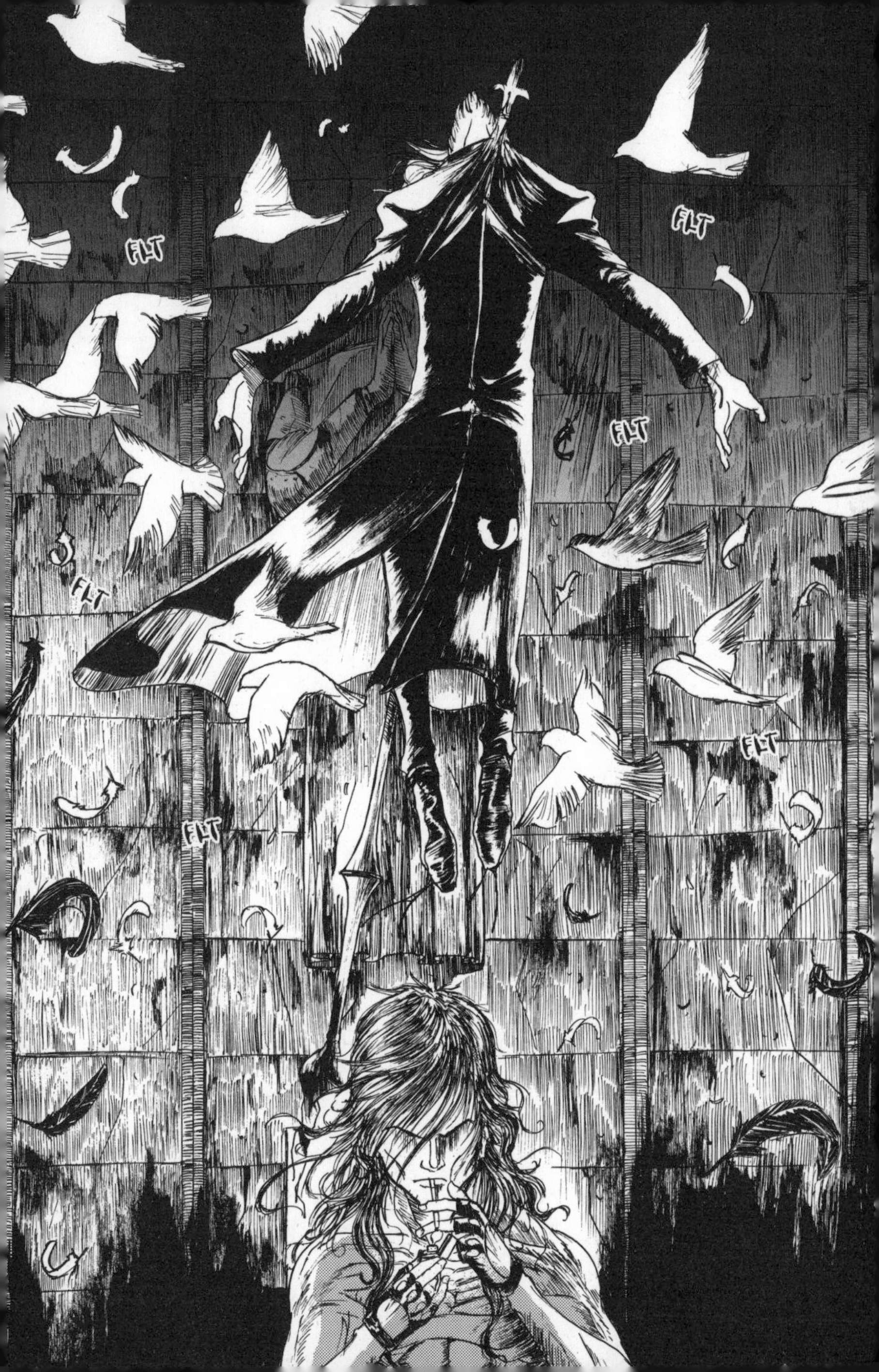
FLT
FLT
FLT
FLT
FLT
FLT

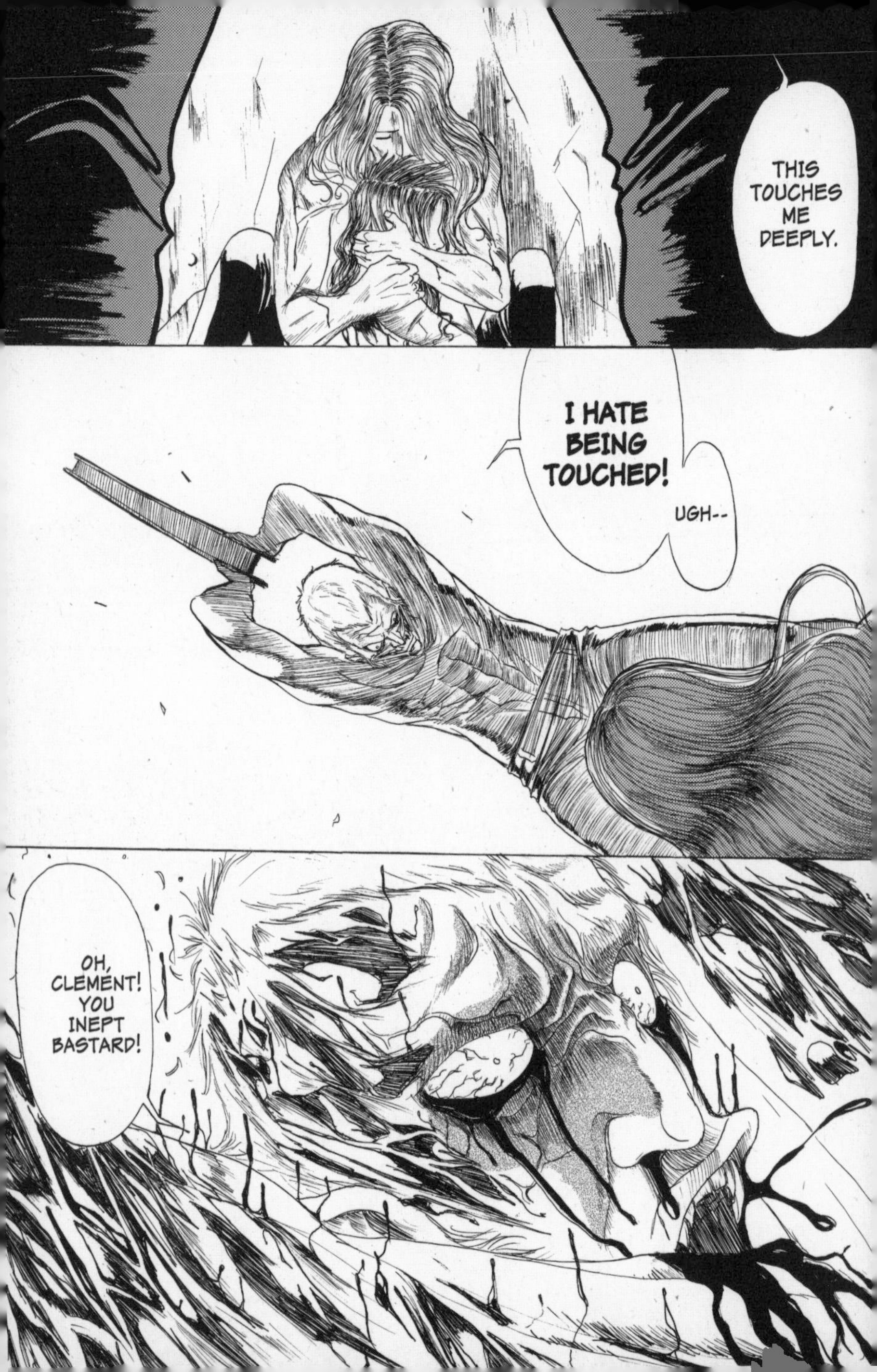
THIS TOUCHES ME DEEPLY.
I HATE BEING TOUCHED!
UGH--
OH, CLEMENT! YOU INEPT BASTARD!

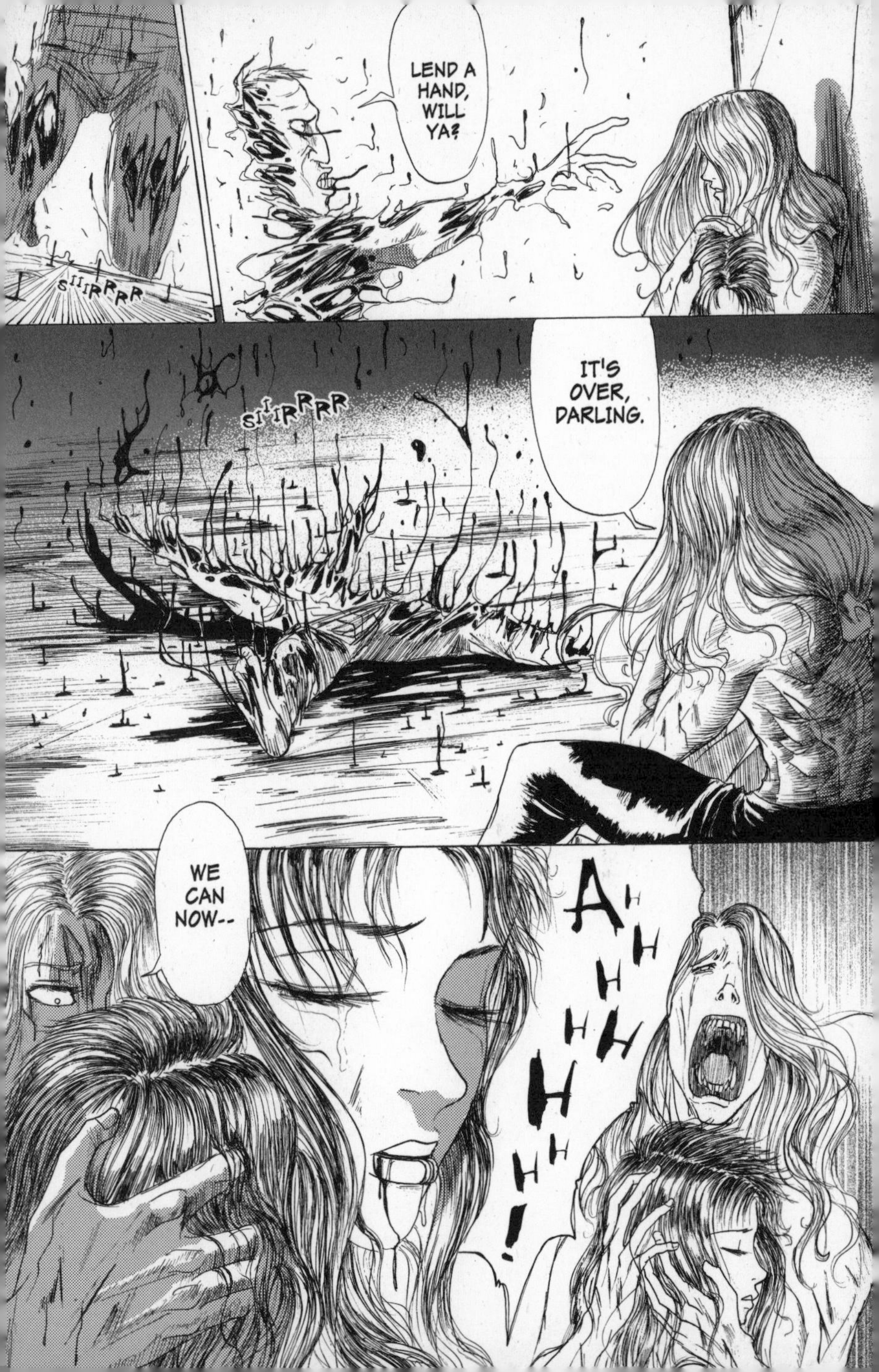
LEND A HAND, WILL YA?
SIIIRRRR
IT'S OVER, DARLING.
SIIRRRR
AHHHHHHHHHH!!
WE CAN NOW--

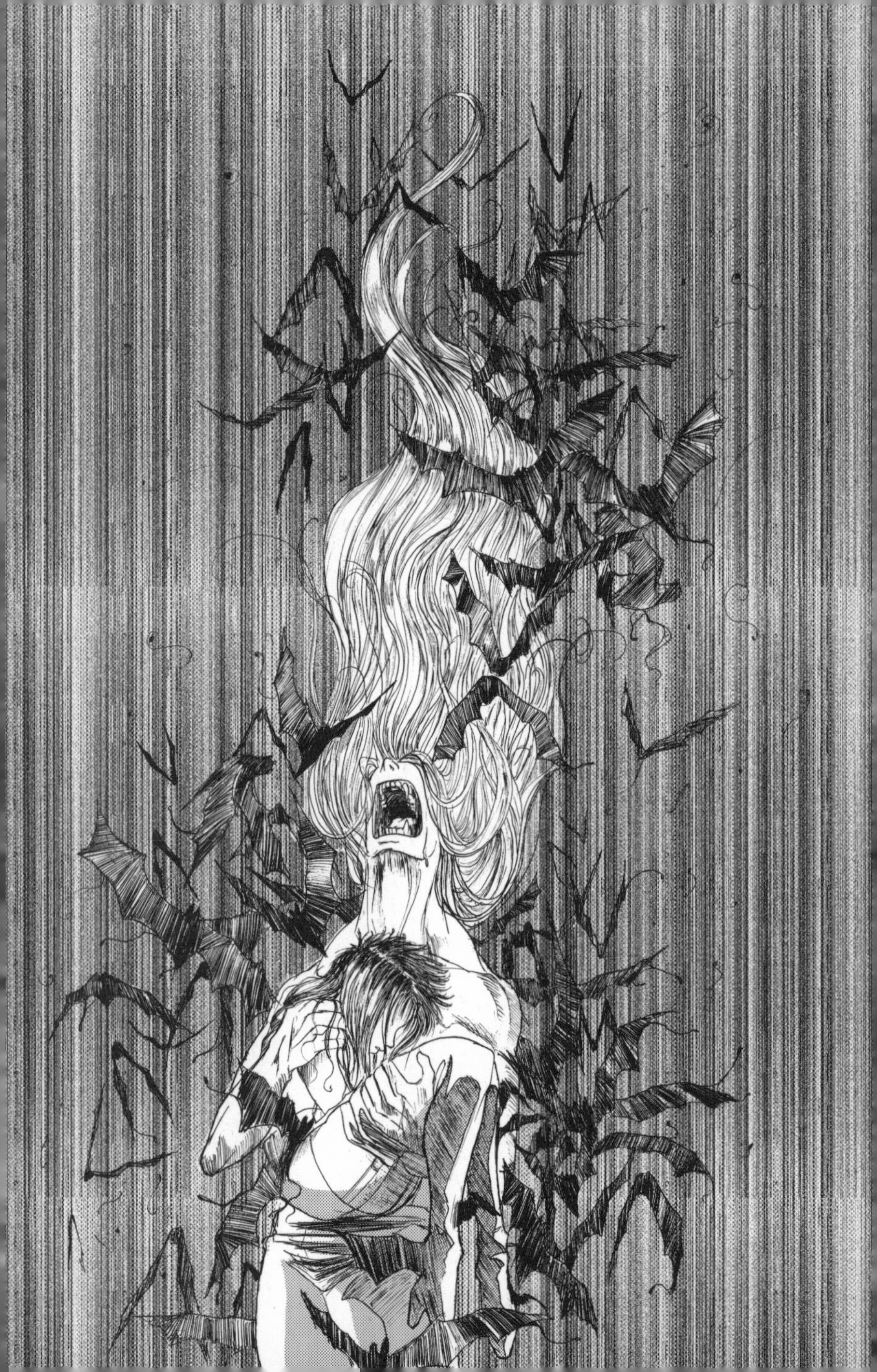

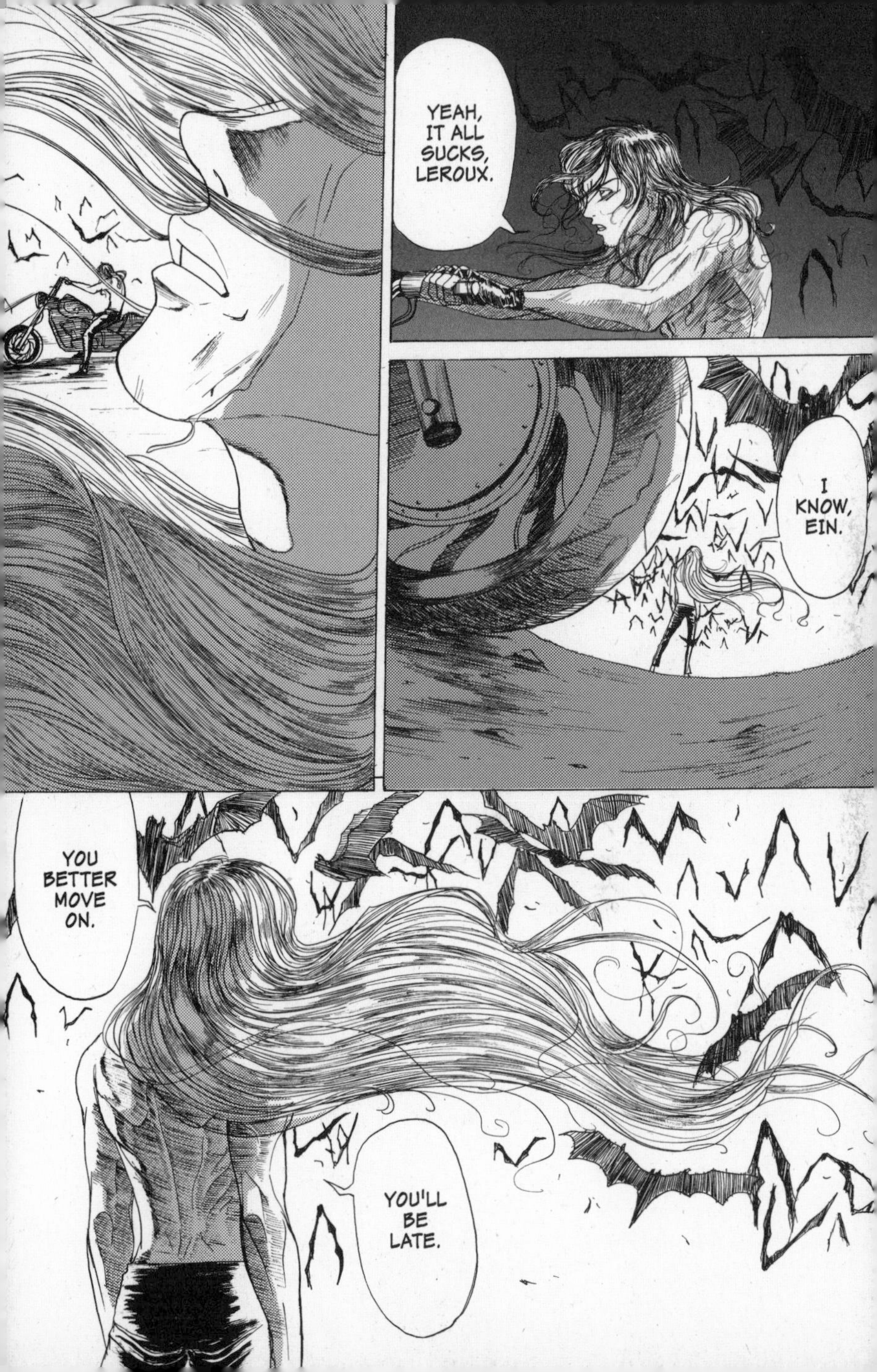
YEAH, IT ALL SUCKS, LEROUX.
I KNOW, EIN.
YOU BETTER MOVE ON.
YOU'LL BE LATE.

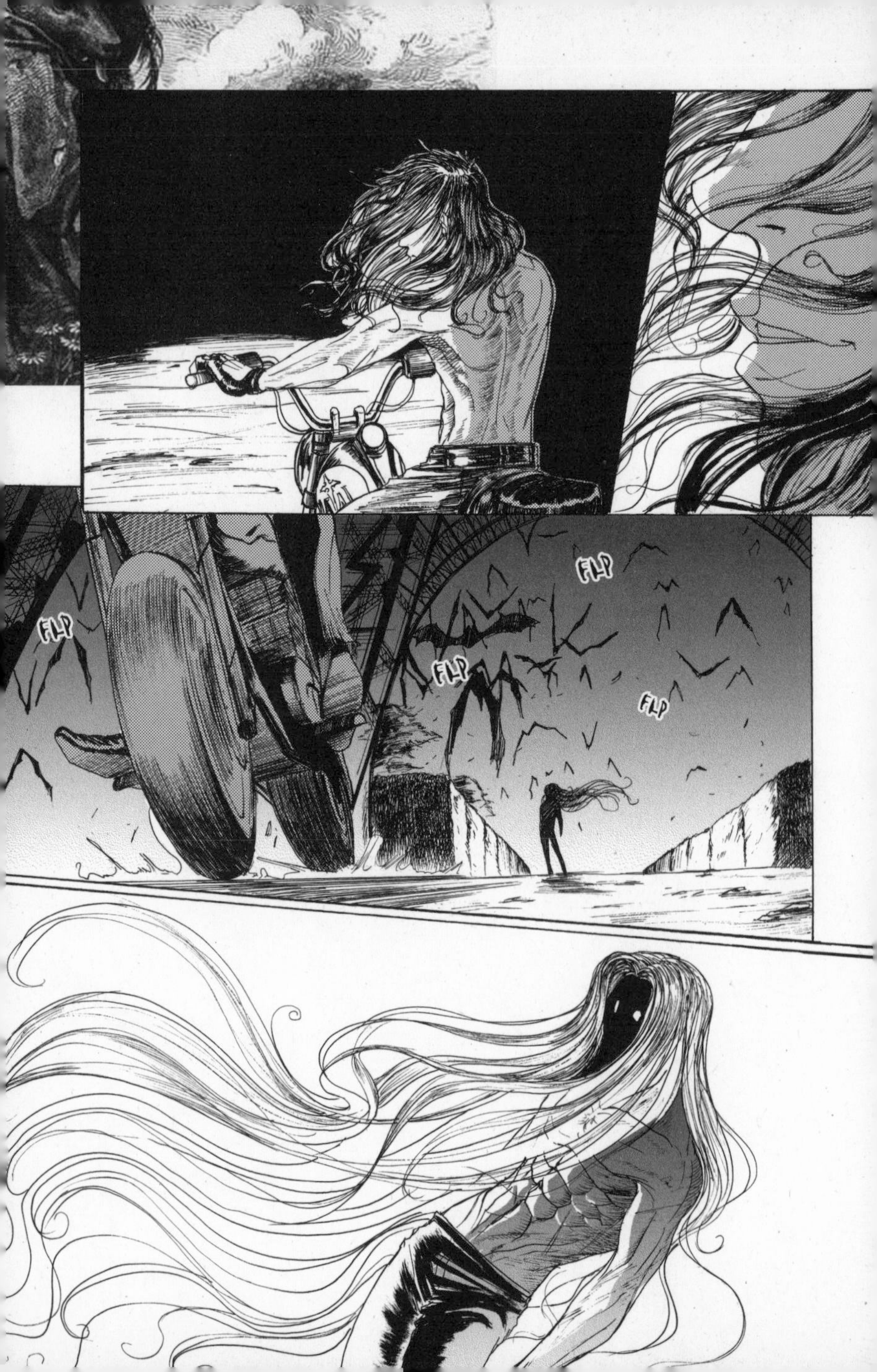
FLP
FLP
FLP
FLP

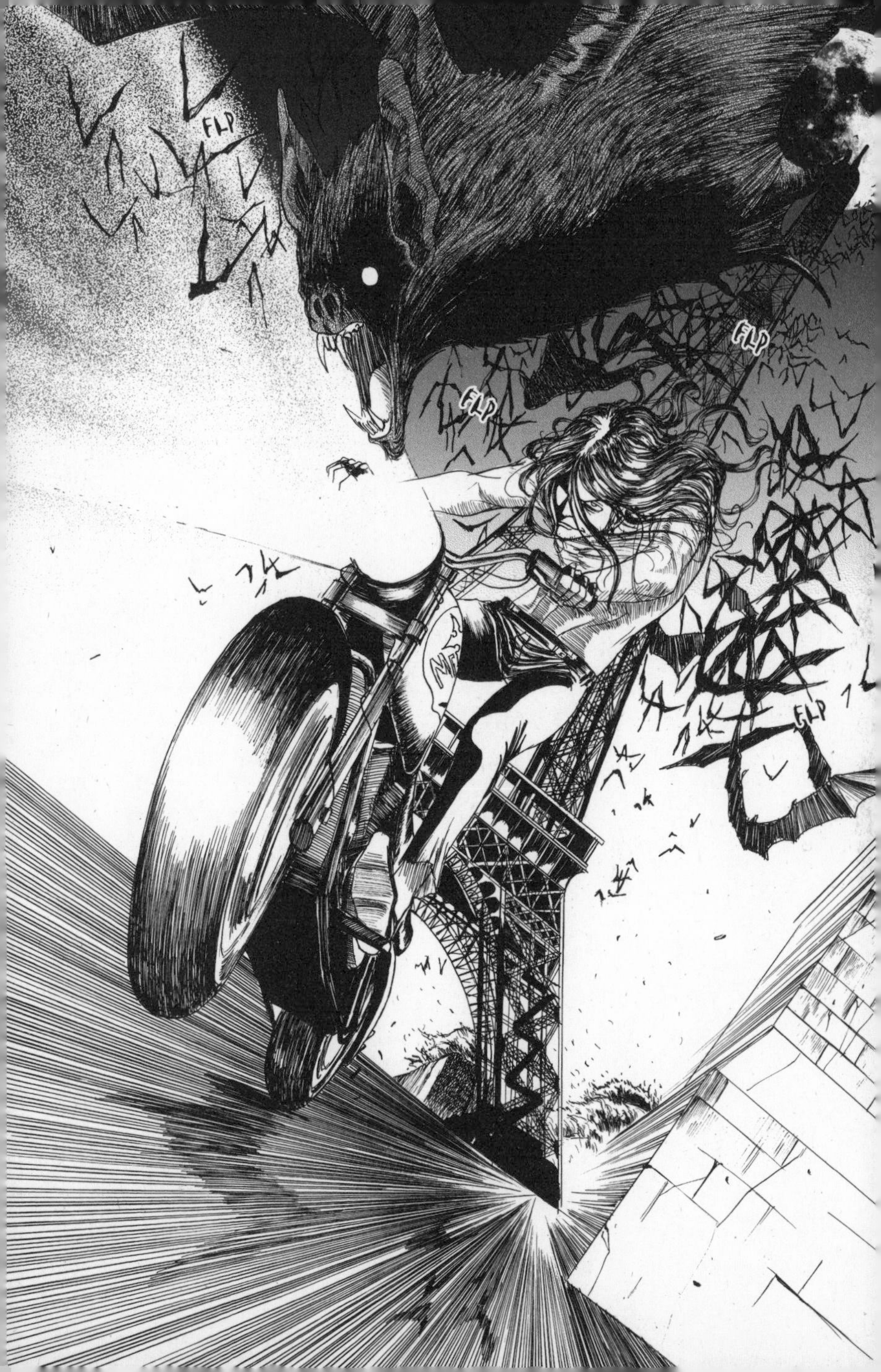
FLP
FLP
FLP
FLP

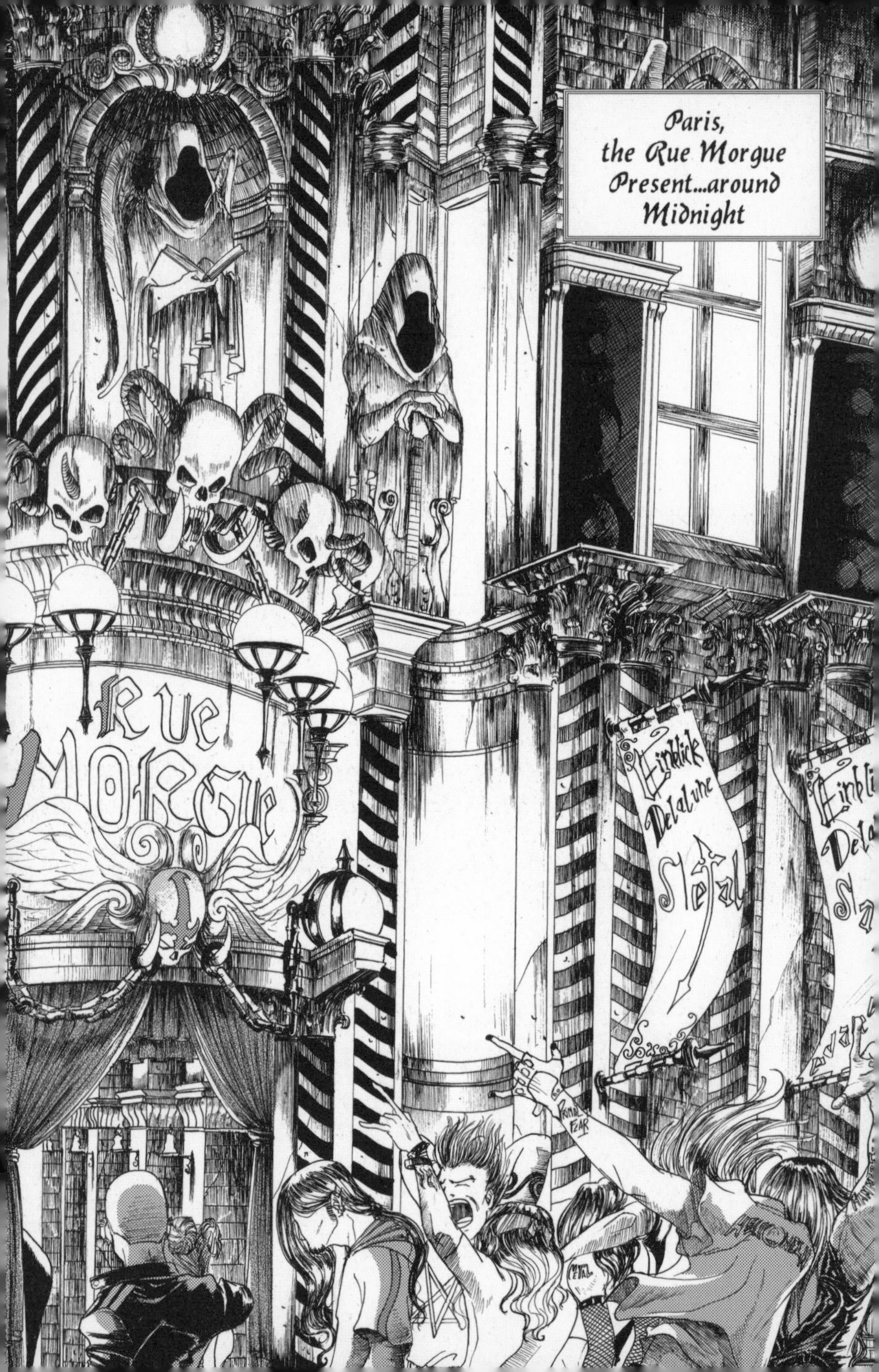
Paris, the Rue Morgue Present...around Midnight
Rue Morgue

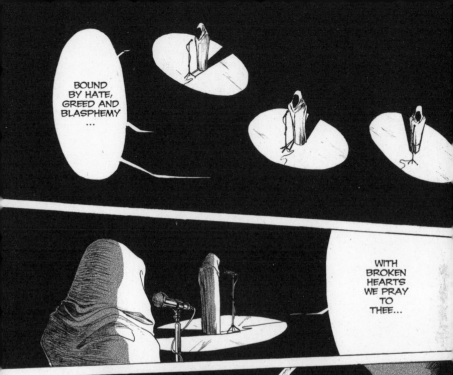

BOUND BY HATE, GREED AND BLASPHEMY ...

WITH BROKEN HEARTS WE PRAY TO THEE...

OH LORD, FORGIVE OUR SHAME ...

HALLOWED BE THY ...

NAME!

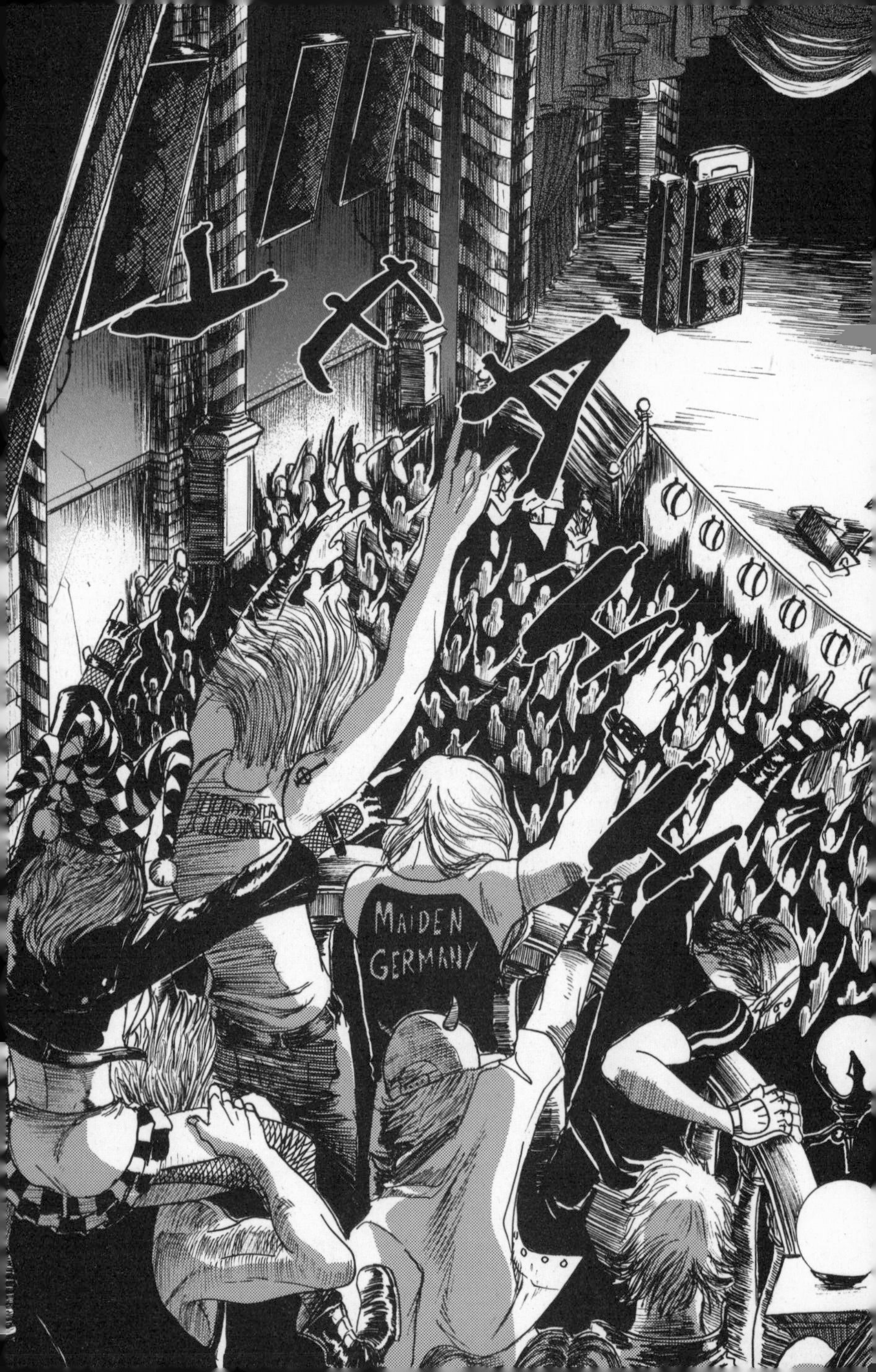
MAIDEN
GERMANY

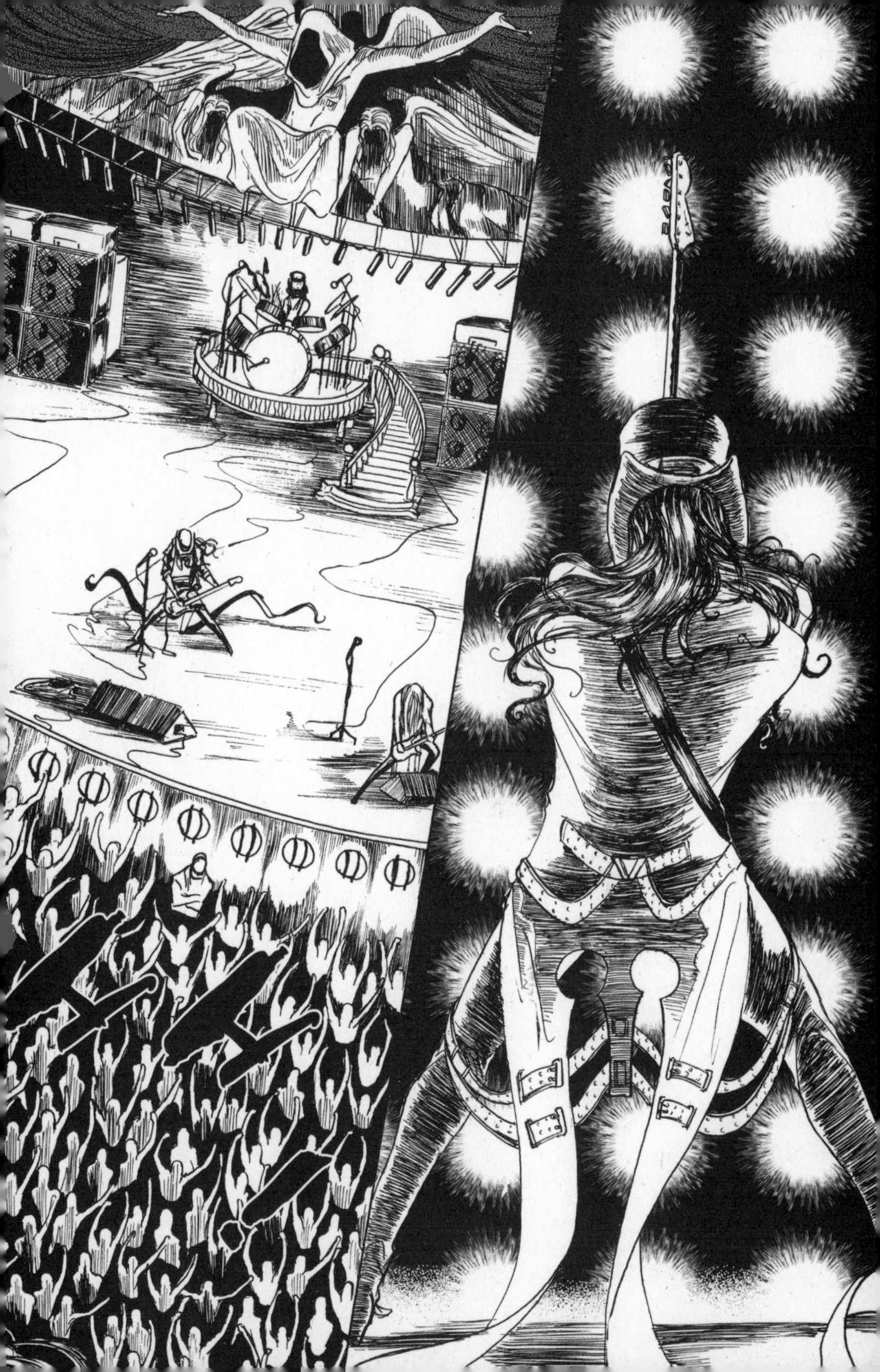

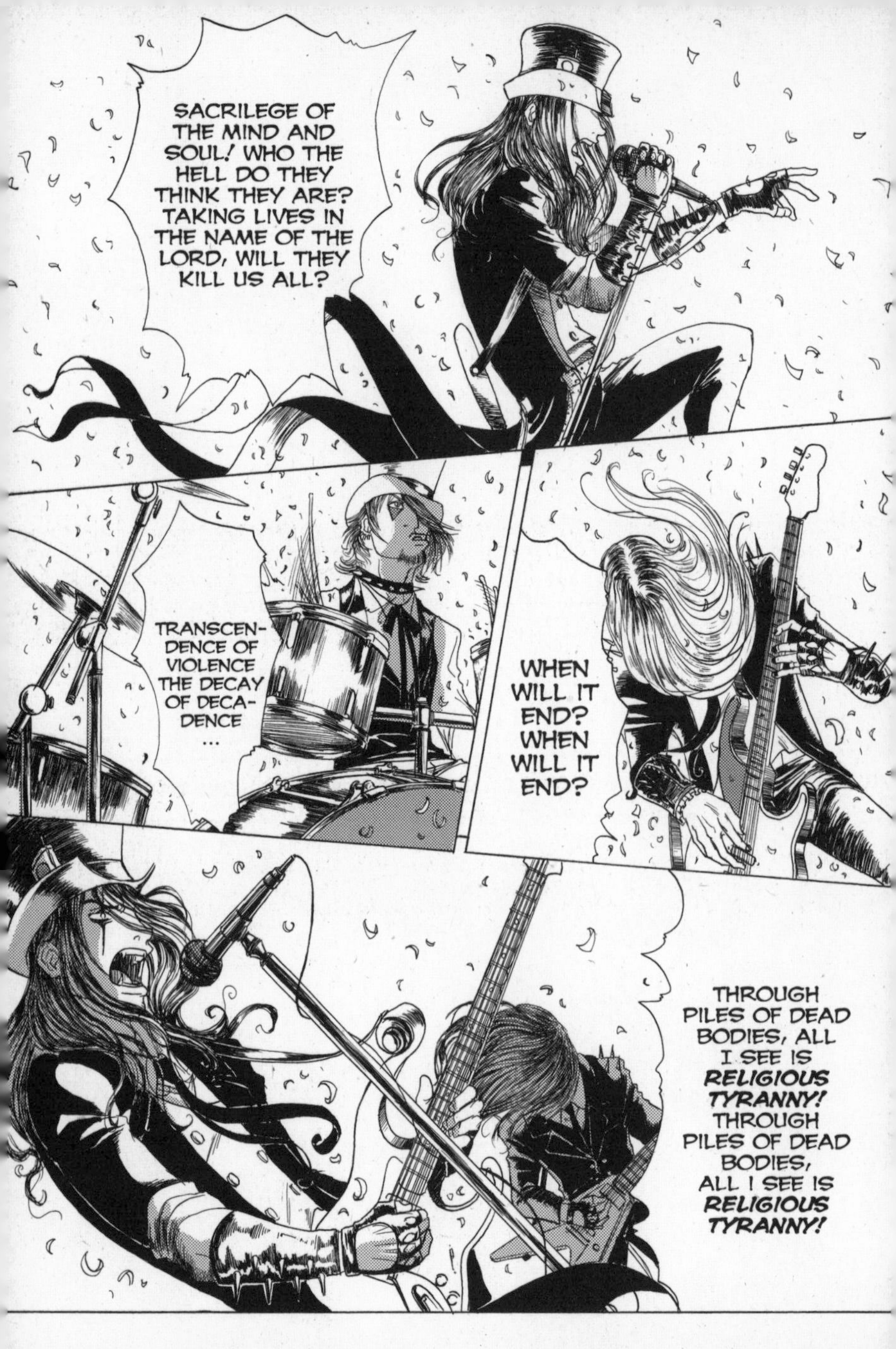
SACRILEGE OF THE MIND AND SOUL! WHO THE HELL DO THEY THINK THEY ARE? TAKING LIVES IN THE NAME OF THE LORD, WILL THEY KILL US ALL?
WHEN WILL IT END? WHEN WILL IT END?
TRANSCEN-DENCE OF VIOLENCE THE DECAY OF DECA-DENCE ...
THROUGH PILES OF DEAD BODIES, ALL I SEE IS *RELIGIOUS TYRANNY!* THROUGH PILES OF DEAD BODIES, ALL I SEE IS *RELIGIOUS TYRANNY!*

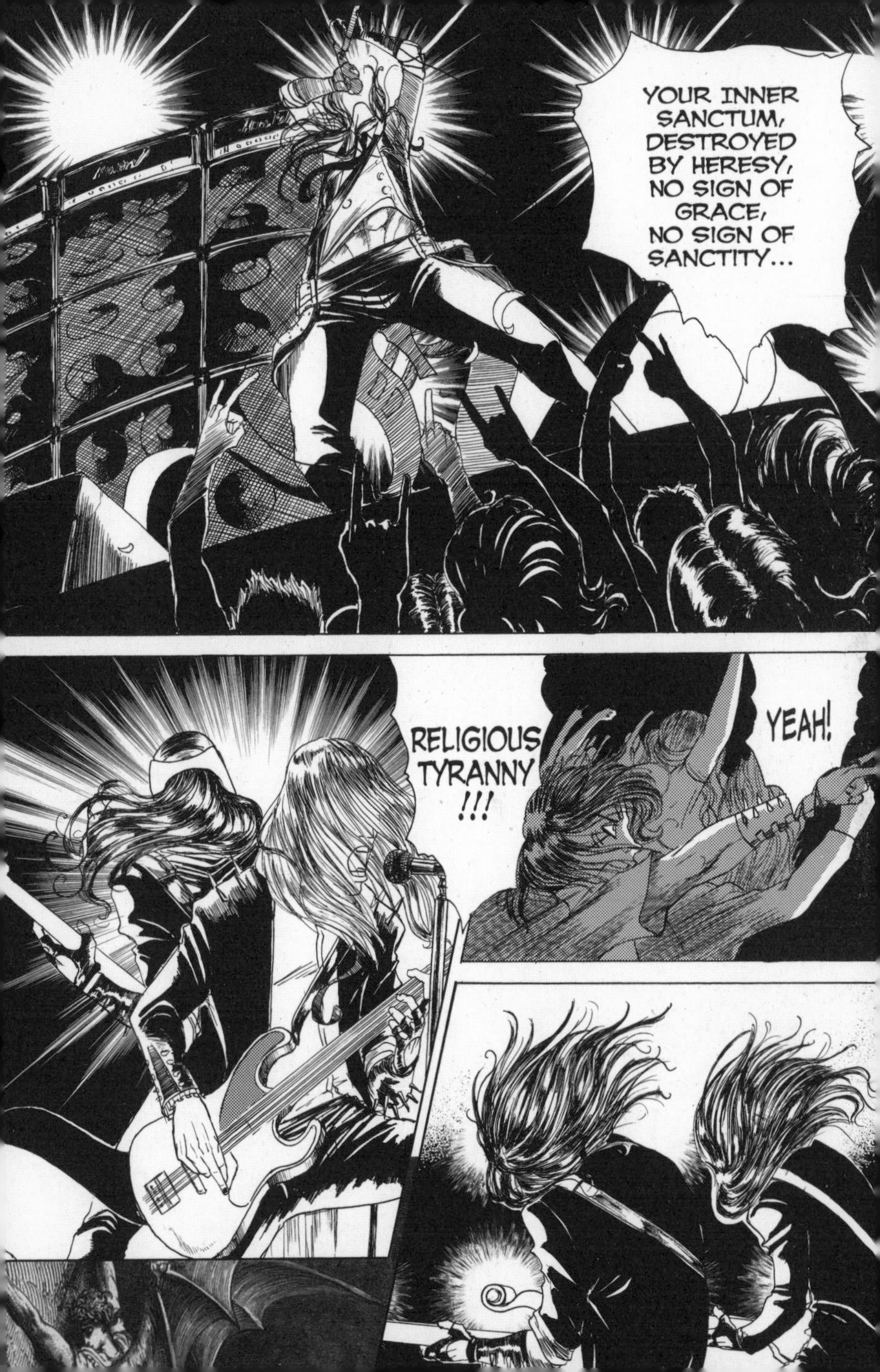
YOUR INNER SANCTUM, DESTROYED BY HERESY, NO SIGN OF GRACE, NO SIGN OF SANCTITY...
YEAH!
RELIGIOUS TYRANNY !!!

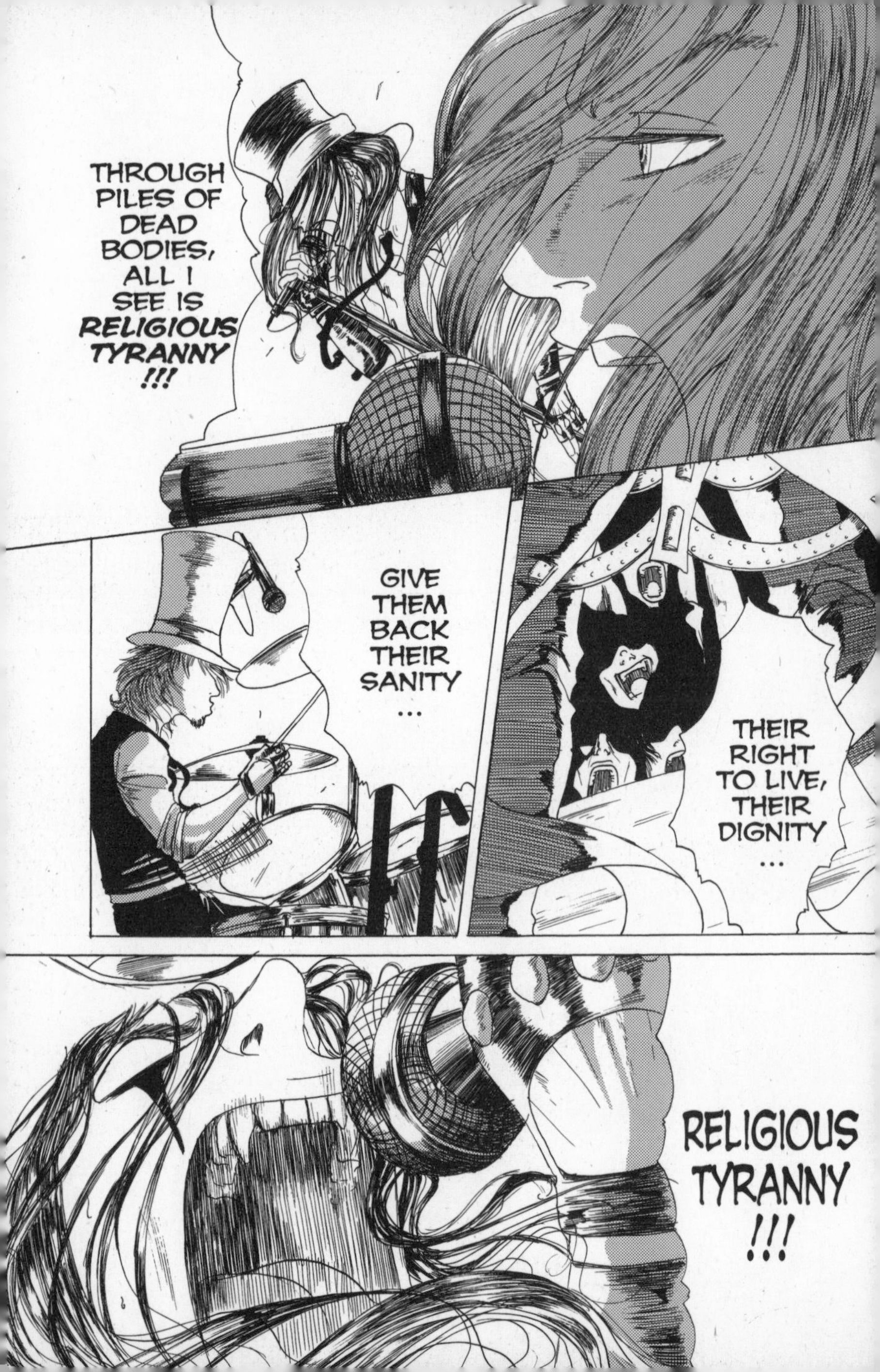
THROUGH PILES OF DEAD BODIES, ALL I SEE IS RELIGIOUS TYRANNY !!!
THEIR RIGHT TO LIVE, THEIR DIGNITY ...
GIVE THEM BACK THEIR SANITY ...
RELIGIOUS TYRANNY !!!

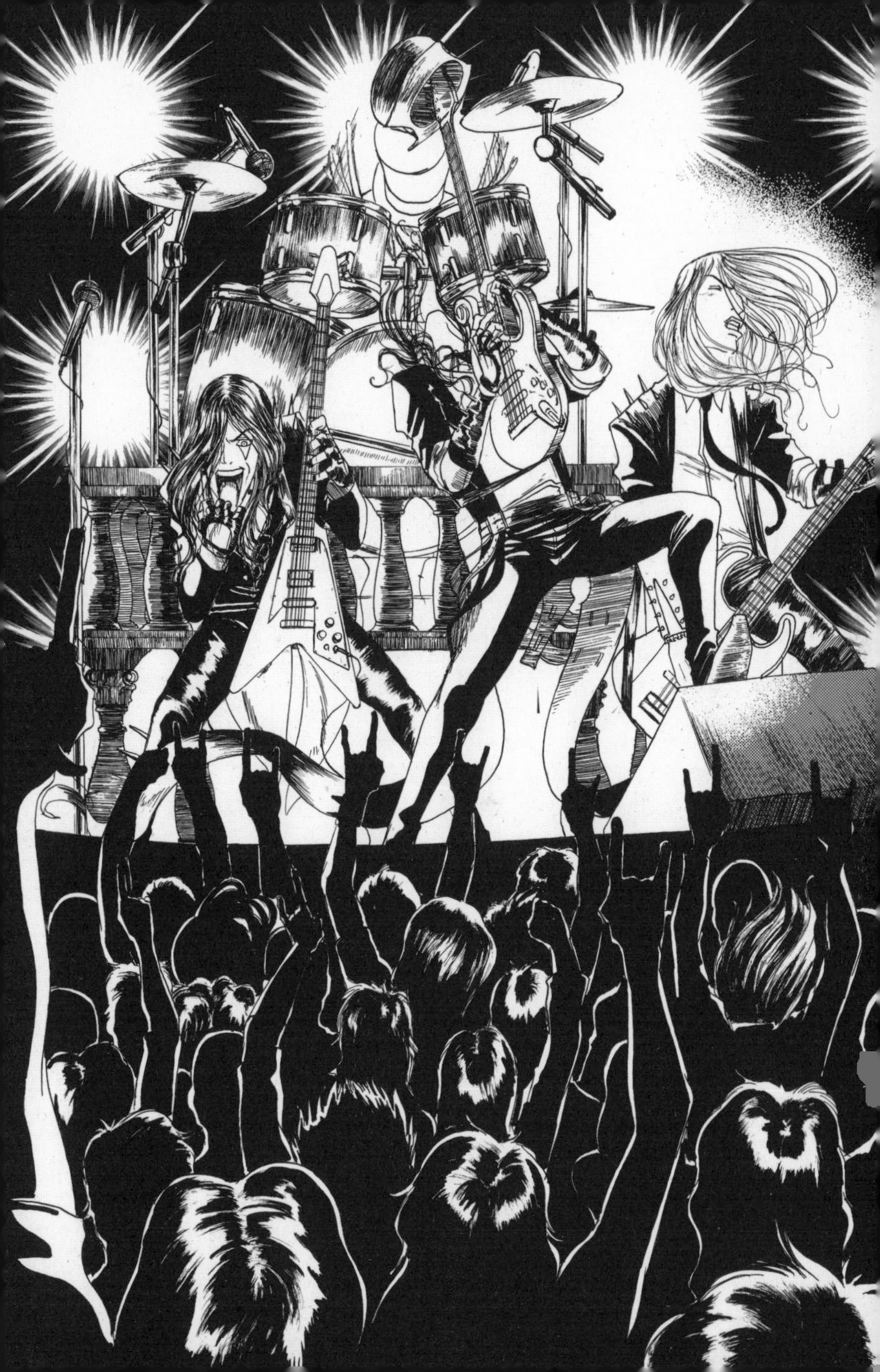

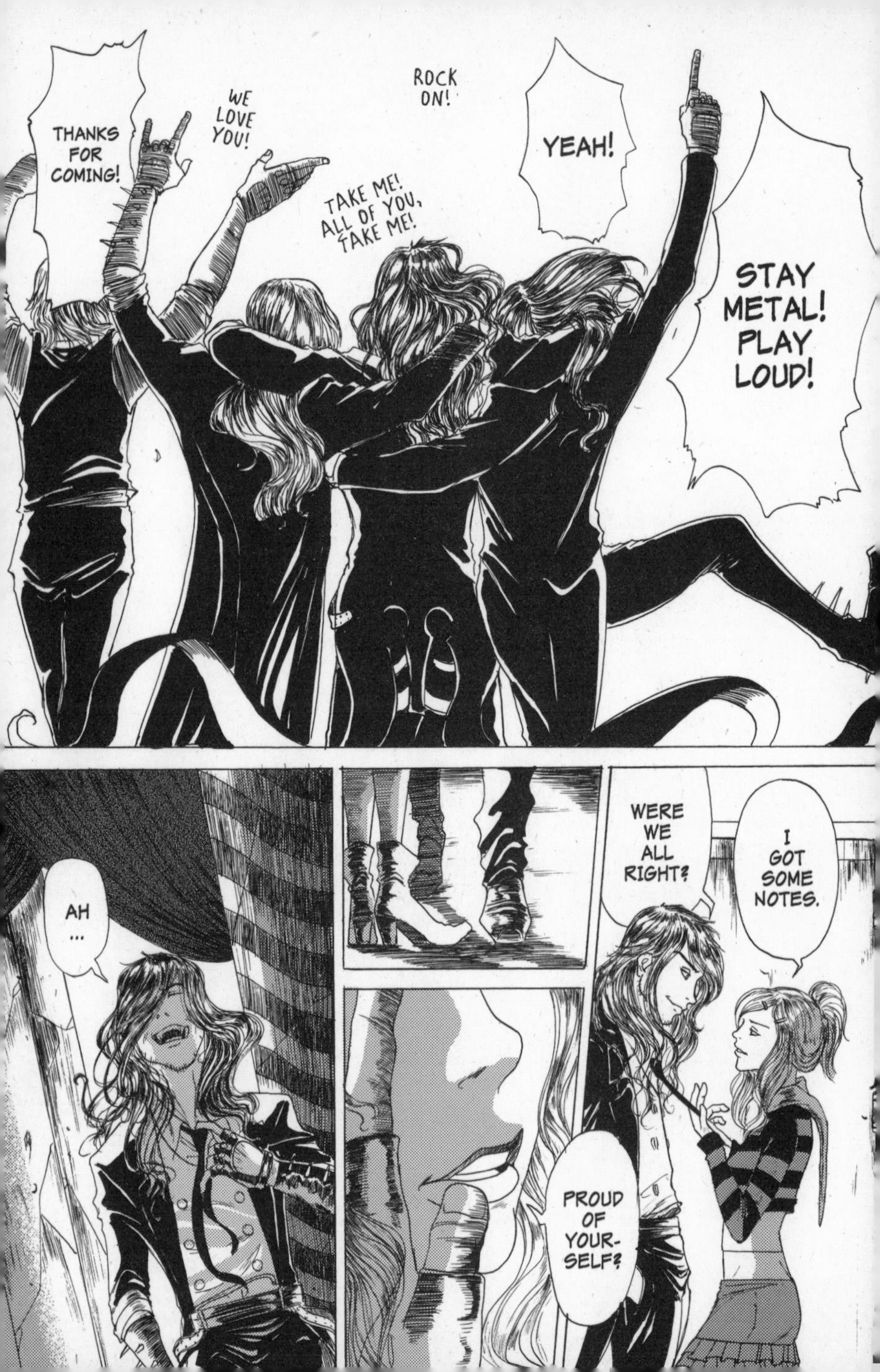

THANKS FOR COMING!
WE LOVE YOU!
ROCK ON!
TAKE ME! ALL OF YOU, TAKE ME!
YEAH!
STAY METAL! PLAY LOUD!
AH ...
PROUD OF YOUR-SELF?
WERE WE ALL RIGHT?
I GOT SOME NOTES.

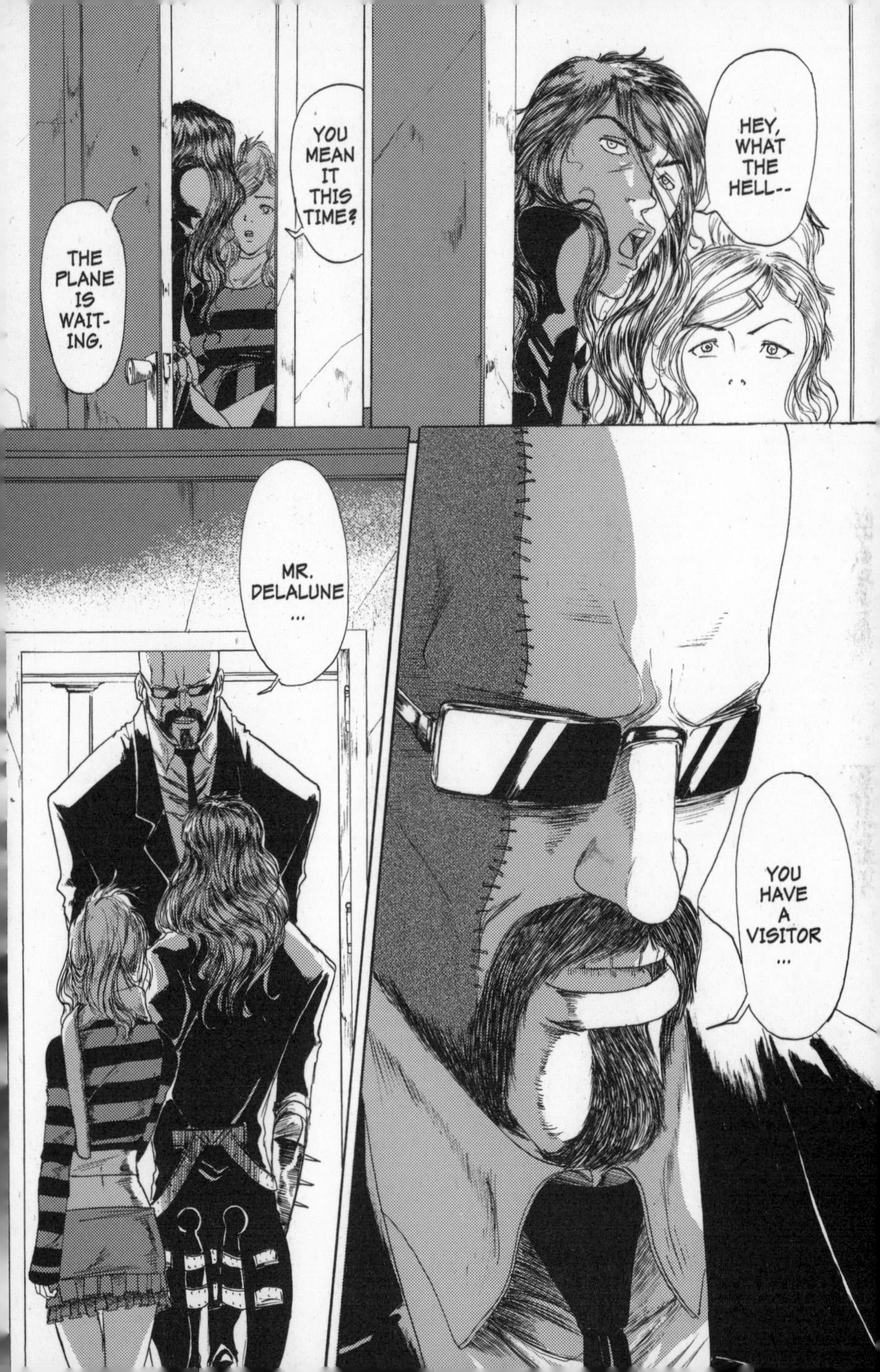
HEY, WHAT THE HELL--
YOU MEAN IT THIS TIME?
THE PLANE IS WAIT-ING.
YOU HAVE A VISITOR ...
MR. DELALUNE ...

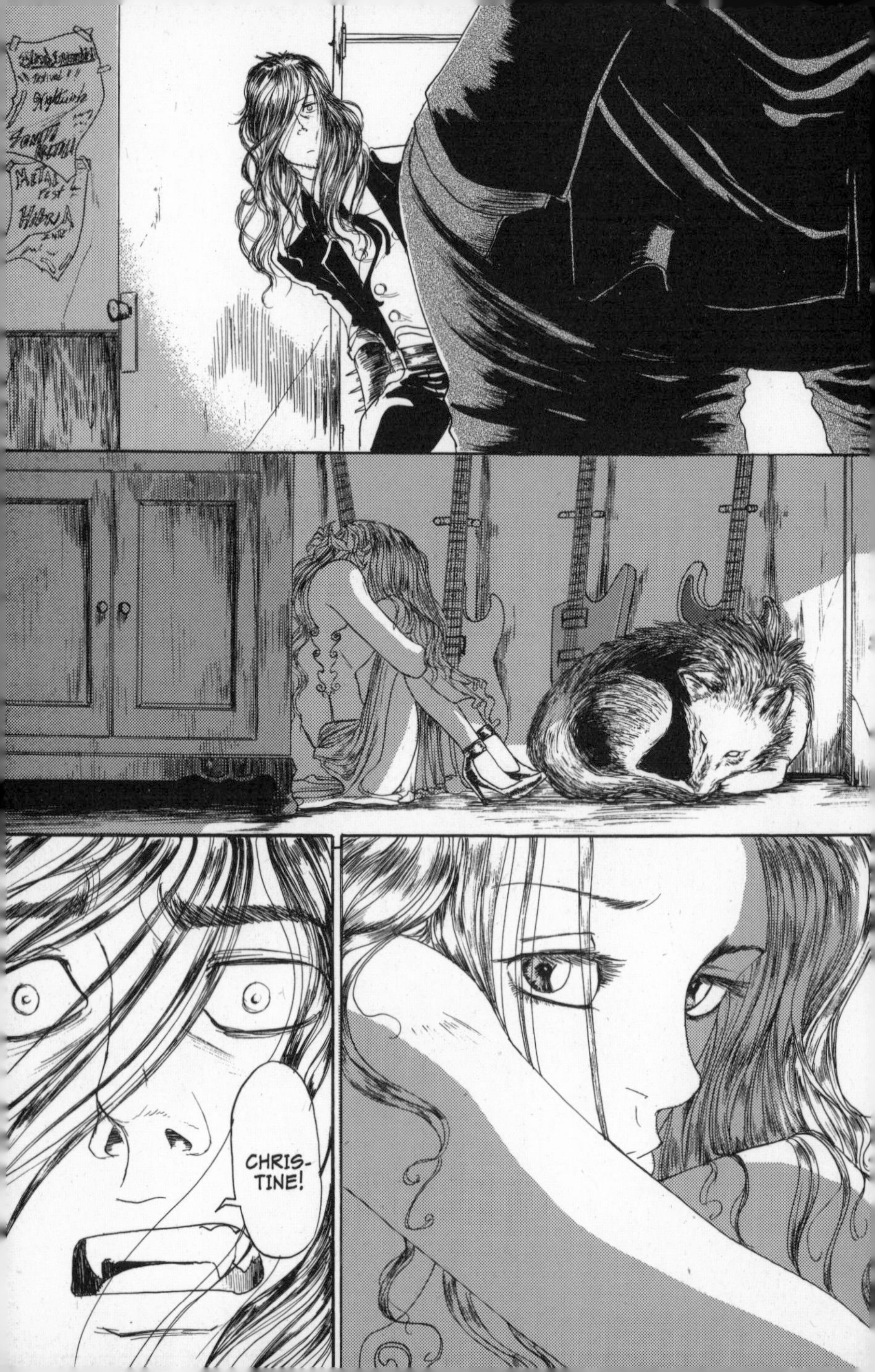
CHRIS-
TINE!

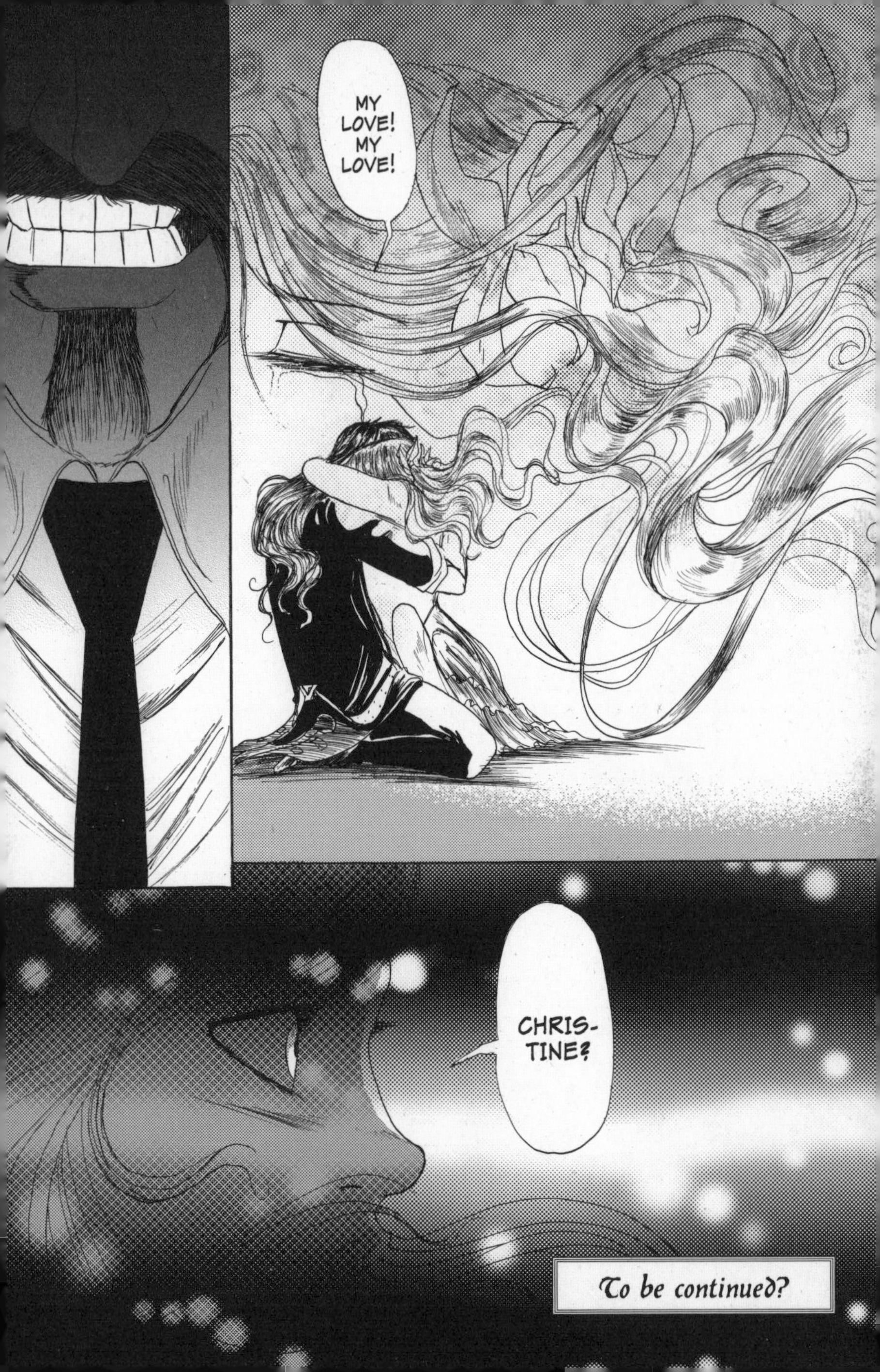
MY LOVE! MY LOVE!
CHRIS- TINE?
To be continued?

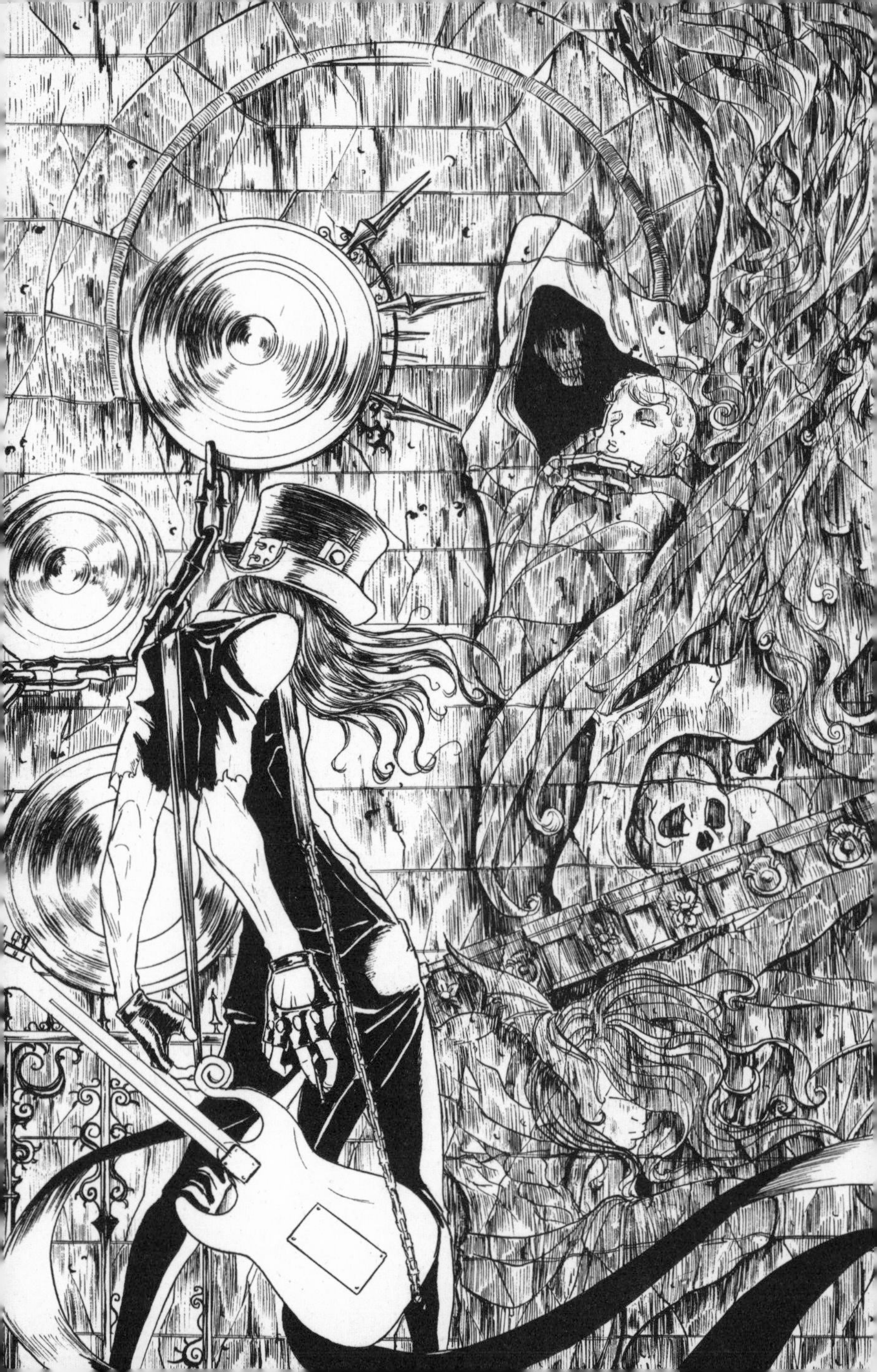

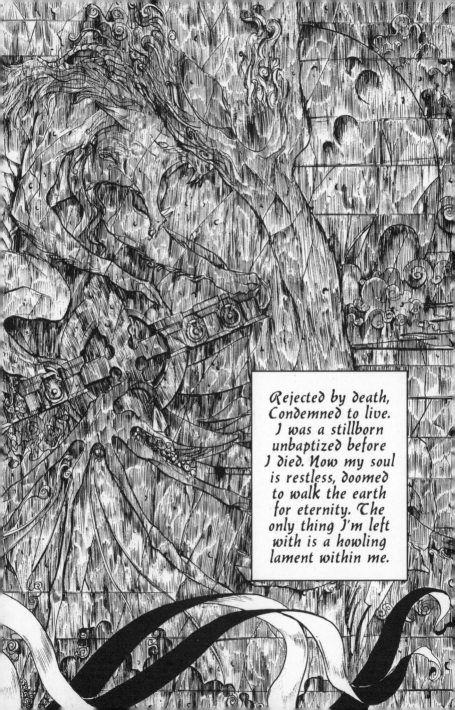

Rejected by death,
Condemned to live.
I was a stillborn
unbaptized before
I died. Now my soul
is restless, doomed
to walk the earth
for eternity. The
only thing I'm left
with is a howling
lament within me.

The Creator Speaks:

When I first started working on *A Midnight Opera*, a personal goal of mine was to somehow combine Manga with Heavy Metal, and since I was pretty much starting my career as a manga artist, the chances of that happening were pretty slim. Having finished volume three, I felt like I had to do something big. So I got in touch with a brazilian metal band called **Hibria**. They had just released their debut album *Defying the Rules*, they were fresh and exciting...they were somewhat like *A Midnight Opera*. It just felt right to have such a young and powerful metal band become a part of *A Midnight Opera*. (Hopefully it won't end there. I'm planning on taking over the Metal industry *evil laugh*) I hung out with Marco--Hibria's AMAZING bass player--for a while and talked about teaming up. He was just as excited about the project as I was. Metal be praised! So please check out Hibria, an In-Your-Face, Kick-To-The-Balls Power Metal band from Brazil taking over where Judas Priest left off.(And I mean that in all kindness*Hail Judas Priest!*) **www.hibria.com**

And thanks to all who have read my books and appreciated the story.
I hope you enjoyed volume three and here's to many more volumes to come.
Stay Metal!!

-- Hans "Hanzo" Steinbach

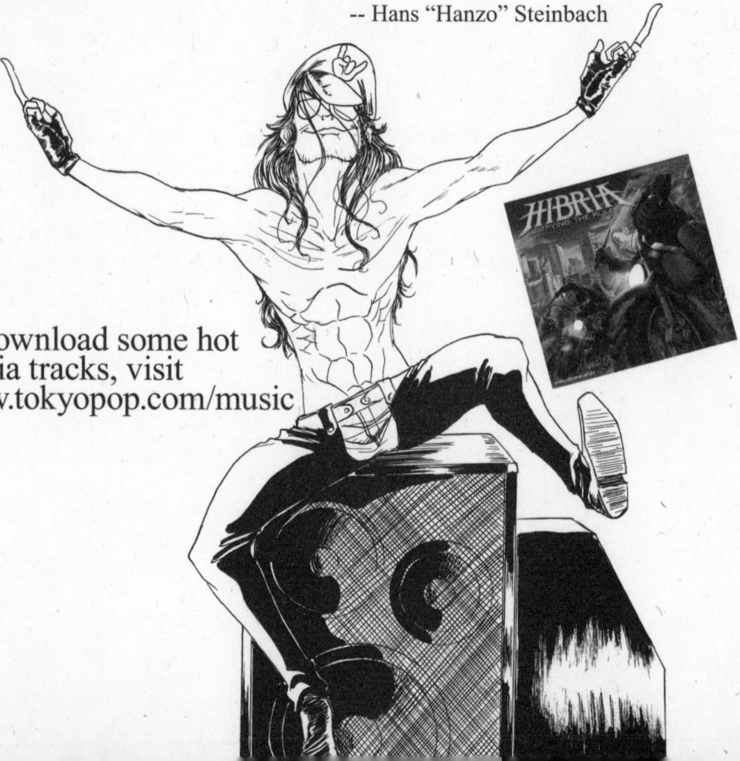
HIBRIA

To download some hot Hibria tracks, visit www.tokyopop.com/music

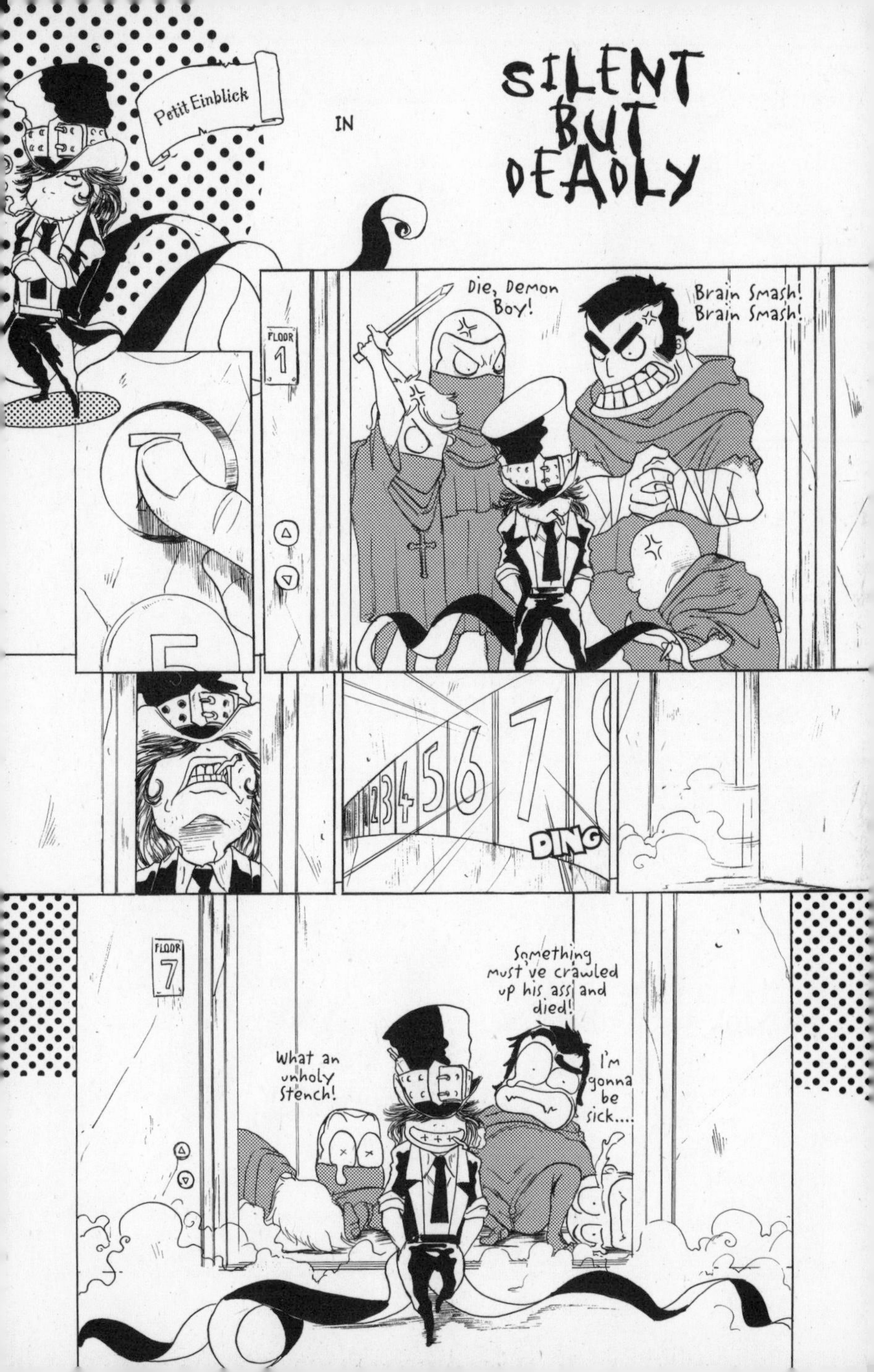
Petit Einblick
IN
SILENT BUT DEADLY
FLOOR 1
Die, Demon Boy!
Brain Smash! Brain Smash!
5
1 2 3 4 5 6 7
DING
FLOOR 7
Something must've crawled up his ass and died!
What an unholy Stench!
I'm gonna be sick....

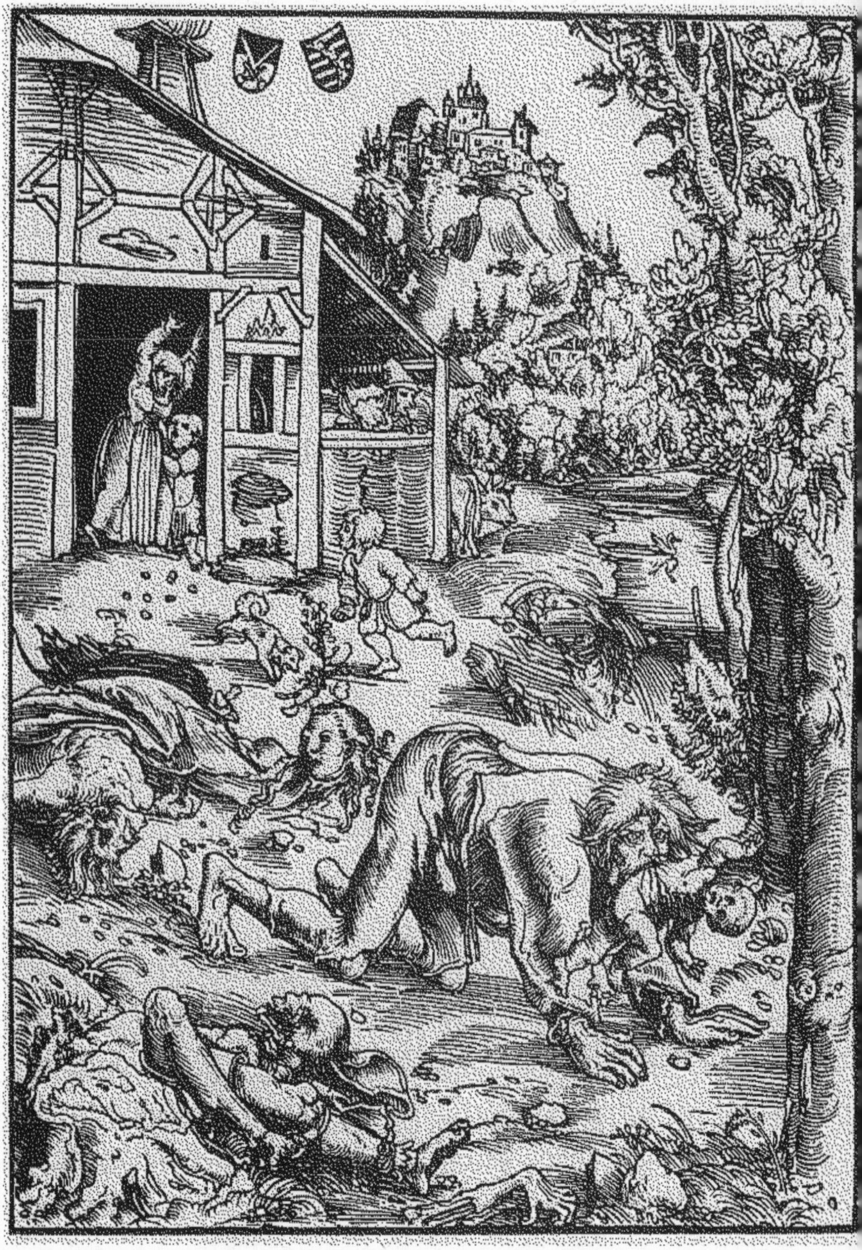

German Werewolf
woodcut, 1722

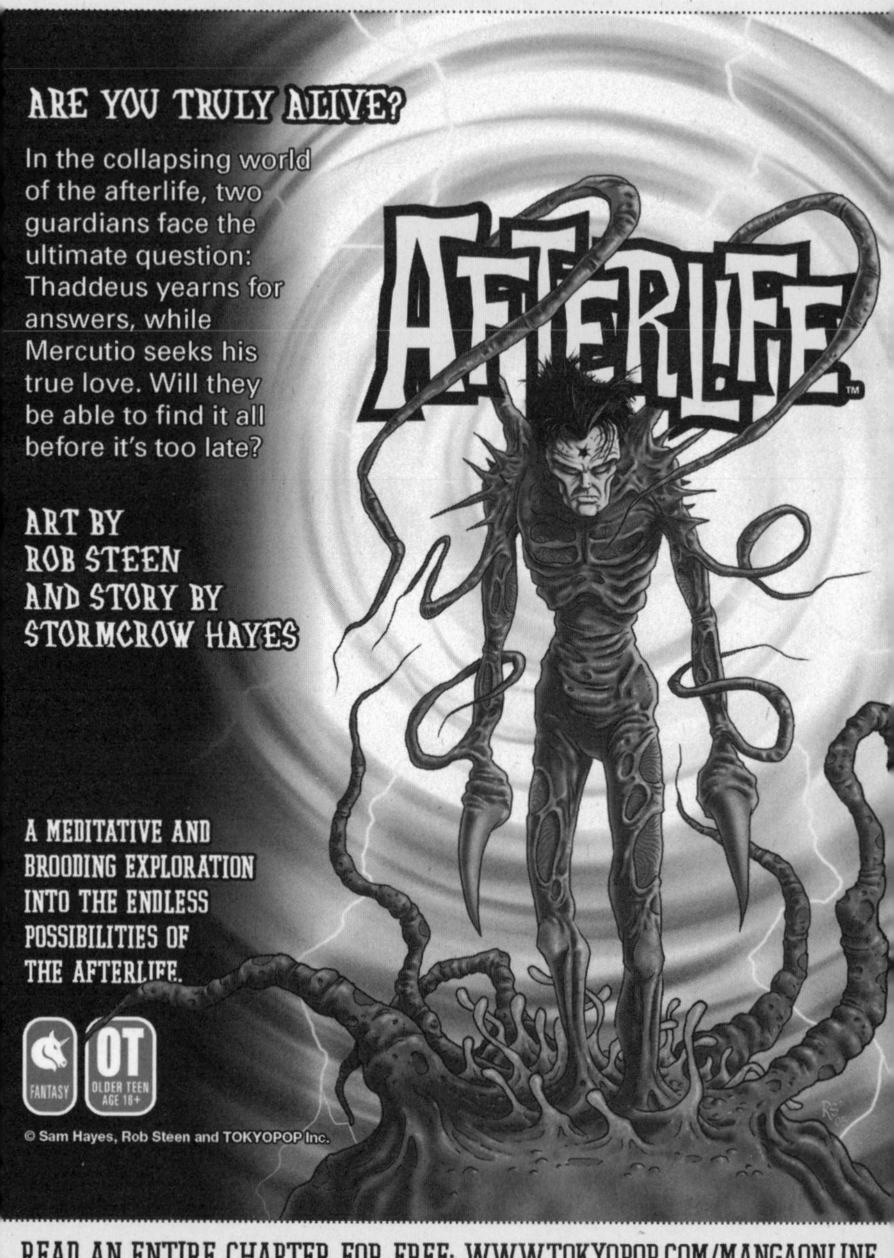
ARE YOU TRULY ALIVE?
In the collapsing world of the afterlife, two guardians face the ultimate question: Thaddeus yearns for answers, while Mercutio seeks his true love. Will they be able to find it all before it's too late?
AFTERLIFE™
ART BY ROB STEEN AND STORY BY STORMCROW HAYES
A MEDITATIVE AND BROODING EXPLORATION INTO THE ENDLESS POSSIBILITIES OF THE AFTERLIFE.
FANTASY
OT
OLDER TEEN AGE 16+
© Sam Hayes, Rob Steen and TOKYOPOP Inc.

BLAME!

BY TSUTOMU NIHEI

WALK SOFTLY AND CARRY A BIG GUN!

CREATOR OF MARVEL'S *WOLVERINE: SNIKT!*

In a future rife with decay and destruction, Killy is a man of few words who packs one very powerful gun. He wanders an endless labyrinth of concrete and steel, fighting off cyborgs and other bizarre creatures. Everyone is searching for the "Net Terminal Genes," but no one is certain of the genes' function. The answer may lie hidden among the scattered human settlements of this vast and desolate world. Can Killy unlock the mystery of this nightmarish future and save the last remnants of humanity?

BLAME!
TOKYOPOP
1
Tsutomu Nihei

OT
OLDER TEEN
AGE 16+

FOR MORE INFORMATION VISIT: WWW.TOKYOPOP.COM

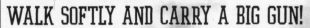

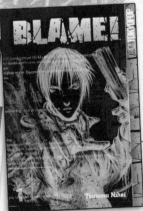

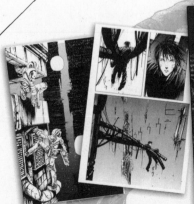

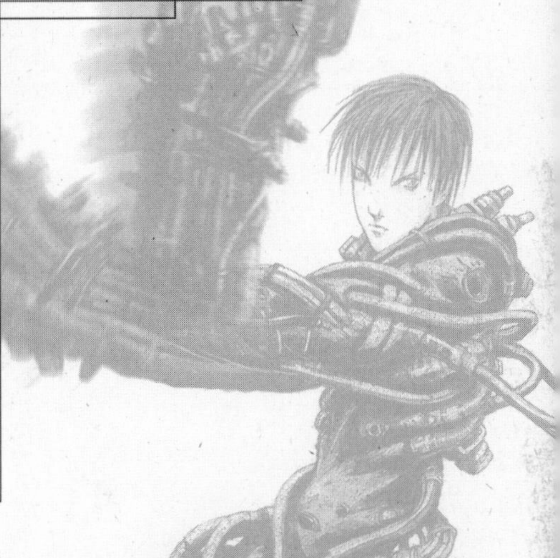

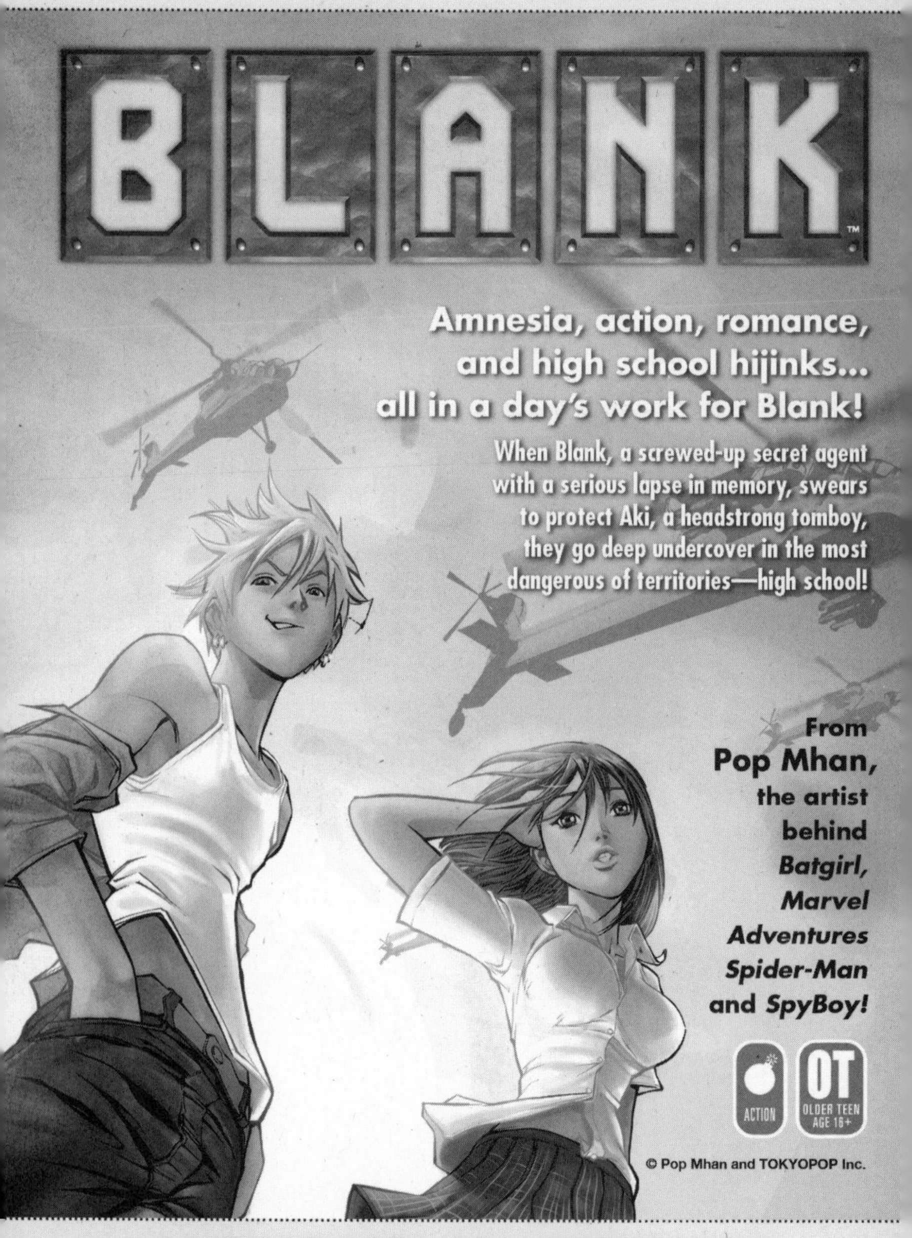
BLANK™
Amnesia, action, romance, and high school hijinks... all in a day's work for Blank!
When Blank, a screwed-up secret agent with a serious lapse in memory, swears to protect Aki, a headstrong tomboy, they go deep undercover in the most dangerous of territories—high school!
From Pop Mhan, the artist behind Batgirl, Marvel Adventures Spider-Man and SpyBoy!
ACTION
OT OLDER TEEN AGE 16+
© Pop Mhan and TOKYOPOP Inc.

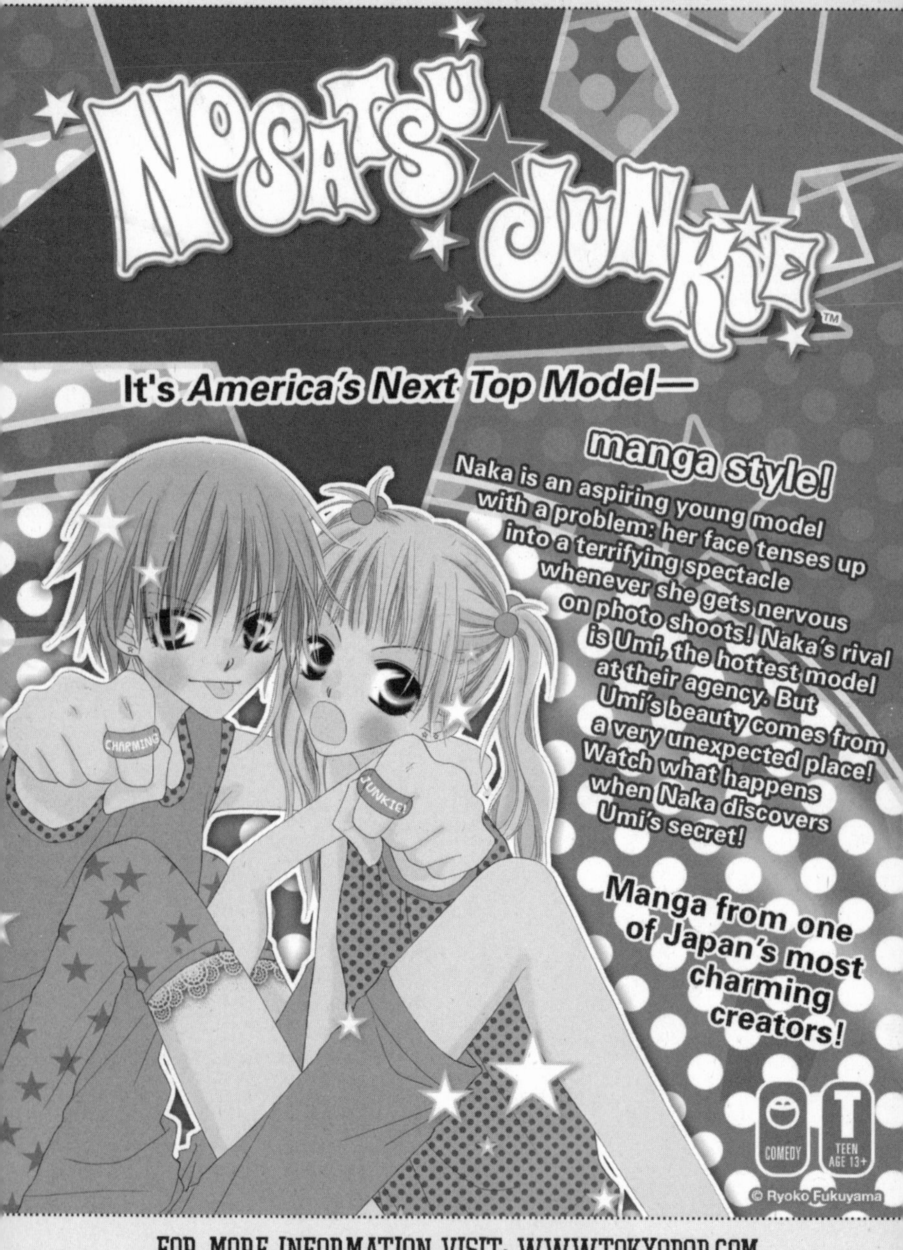
NOSATSU JUNKIE™
It's *America's Next Top Model*—
manga style!
Naka is an aspiring young model with a problem: her face tenses up into a terrifying spectacle whenever she gets nervous on photo shoots! Naka's rival is Umi, the hottest model at their agency. But Umi's beauty comes from a very unexpected place! Watch what happens when Naka discovers Umi's secret!
Manga from one of Japan's most charming creators!
CHARMING
JUNKIE!
COMEDY
T
TEEN AGE 13+
© Ryoko Fukuyama